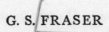

G. S. FRASER

THE MODERN WRITER AND HIS WORLD

ANDRE DEUTSCH

FIRST PUBLISHED BY DEREK VERSCHOYLE 1953

THIS REVISED EDITION FIRST PUBLISHED 1964 BY
ANDRE DEUTSCH LIMITED
105 GREAT RUSSELL STREET
LONDON WCI
COPYRIGHT © 1953, 1964 BY G. S. FRASER
ALL RIGHTS RESERVED
PRINTED IN GREAT BRITAIN BY
HAZELL WATSON AND VINEY LTD
AYLESBURY, BUCKS

(1) 50p.

Contents

Contents

Preface to New Edition

THIS is the third edition of a book originally composed and published in Japan in 1950, and then revised and expanded for an English audience in 1953. The purpose of the first version was to give Japanese students of English literature, cut off not from our language but from our country by the Second World War and its aftermath, a plain and clear though not simplified account of the main new movements and great innovating figures in English literature since about 1880, set against an impression, as vivid as I could make it, of the changing English social scene. Back in England, and doing a lot of lecturing in evening classes, I realized that many English readers are just as grateful for being given a sense of the 'feel' of a writer's world – his social setting and ideas – as are the Japanese. The 1953 version is out of print, but the copies I find in public libraries are well-thumbed and, by the evidence of the date-stamps, very regularly taken out. That version had many faults but, when it appeared, it was, so far as I know, the only book covering its ground – the background of ideas behind 'modernism' in English literature, and the main innovating figures in the novel, drama, poetry, and criticism – with the intelligent non-specialist reader in view.

Since 1958, when I became a lecturer in English literature at the University of Leicester, I have realized that, brought up to date, the book might be useful not only to the general reader but also to teachers and learners, both in universities and in schools. Teaching any subject, one wants not only special monographs but a map of the country, a general prospect of the whole scene, such as this book sets out to provide. The two first versions brought the story up to about 1950; this version brings it up to the end of the 1950s and a little beyond. I dictated the first draft of the first version in a fortnight; it has taken me about two years to prepare this third version. There is, of course, a great deal of new material: all the exciting new developments in English drama since *Waiting for Godot* and *Look Back in Anger*; a new disabused, sometimes glumly cantankerous, sometimes hysterically aggressive tone, summed up by journalists as that of the 'angry young men' or of the 'satire industry'; a shift of interest in plays and novels from the lives of the privileged and the problems of the over-sensitive to the frustrations, and the protests, of the deprived and exploited; a movement in poetry away from the mysterious, the intricate, the implicit, the elliptical and towards the lengthily plainspoken, perhaps also from what Professor C. S. Lewis calls 'the golden' to what he calls 'the drab': an ironical cult, certainly, of the ugly; and, in criticism, a growing stress on content rather than form, the moral rather than the aesthetic, the social rather than the technical qualities of literature; and, with that, a grudging or deflating attitude towards great names. All this was in the foreground of my mind in revising, and it necessitated a rewriting – sentence by sentence – and a rethinking and reproportioning of the whole book; so that I can claim that this third version of *The Modern Writer and His World* is essentially a new work.

My emphases in the first two versions were on novelty and surprise as the essence of 'modernism', and on the great isolated figure. In this version, these emphases are qualified by a greater awareness both of continuity (of the Victorian roots, for instance, of Pound and Eliot) and of the total literary scene as something from which the great isolated figure cannot be disconnected. That awareness has, I hope, been reflected in a more sober style, and more careful, if less dashing, generalizations.

Leicester, May 1963   G. S. **Fraser**

PART ONE

A BACKGROUND OF IDEAS

1

'Modernity' and the Historical Sense

THIS book is an extensive but necessarily summary consideration of the 'modern movement' in English literature: it is a book less concerned with stressing my own personal preferences than with digging out, and putting tidily on the page, a rough working scheme of the development of English literature since about 1880. I have taken novels, plays, and poems as the three main kinds of writing demanding consideration, and I have added a more tentative chapter on literary criticism. I have made no attempt at an exhaustive coverage of each subdivision of my period, but on the other hand I have not confined myself to major writers. I have directed my attention mainly to writers who seemed to me to express vividly a mood of their time; I have left out many interesting writers who seemed to me to lack the crude illustrative value I was looking for.

Illustrative of what? Over the past seventy or eighty years our society has been changing in many drastic and also in many subtle and complicated ways. I have concentrated on writers who display an imaginative awareness of the stress of social change. There are fine writers, though perhaps mainly fine minor writers, who show little awareness of such change; I have little to say, for instance, about Norman Douglas, Maurice Baring, Max Beerbohm. I have much to say about writers like H. G. Wells or Rudyard Kipling, who both represent philosophies of history that are out of fashion but who, whether welcoming it or repelling it, have a vivid imaginative awareness of change. For the topic which gives this book what unity it has is the writer's relation to his age.

I would like to make some reservations here. Literature cannot be 'explained' by setting it against its historical background; nor can the historical background itself be 'explained' by reducing it to some definite set of factors. But an attempt, however informal, to relate literature to its historical background can at least give us the feeling that we are finding our way about better. More broadly, thinking about the life and literature of even the fairly recent past helps us to find our bearings in the present. But the life and literature of the past are also interesting for their own sakes. Disinterested curiosity – to be disinterested is not to be un-interested – is one of the noblest qualities of the human mind.

Modern English literature is not a self-contained subject. What we call modernity in literature has common charac-teristics in all countries. In this first chapter I want to ask what some of these characteristics are. For when we describe a work as 'modern' we do not merely mean that it has been published (according to the stretch of our historical per-spective) in the past five or ten years, in the past fifty or sixty years, or perhaps since the Renaissance. When we describe a work as 'modern' we are ascribing, however vaguely, cer-tain intrinsic qualities to it. We find something 'modern' in Catullus, but not in Virgil; in Villon, but not in Ronsard; in Donne, but not in Spenser; in Clough, but not in Tennyson. There is something in the mood of the first of each of these three pairs of writers – something abrupt, restless, mocking, dissatisfied, possibly – that comes home to us today in a way in which the more serene and elaborate art of their partners, here, does not. What are, then, some of the characteristics which, wherever we come across them, give us this feeling of 'modernity'?

Paradoxically enough one of the main marks of 'modern-ism' in literature is often a lively imaginative interest in the past for its own sake. We can push the beginnings of 'modern' literature indefinitely far back. I am starting here around 1880 but on a book with a larger scale I might have started in 1800, with the English romantic movement. One of the important aspects of that movement was a new rever-ence for the past. Augustan writers like Gibbon are curious about the past, but do not reverence it. They are civilized, and ancient Greece and Rome were civilized, and the centuries between are centuries of barbarism, bigotry, and decay. Yet the eighteenth century was also the century of ballad collecting, of mock-Gothic architecture, mock-Gothic romances, the taste for the picturesque and the sublime, follies, spleen, sensibility, hired hermits, ornamental artificial ruins. The romantic movement has, in fact, very deep roots in the Augustan age. The static civilization of the eighteenth century could not be indefinitely preserved. The French Revolution showed that it is more true that man is controlled by historical forces than that he controls them. If man lost, in this way, the dignity of being the master of events, he could at least enlarge himself by uniting himself with the long perspective of history; and the new interest in outer nature, which begins with Thomson and reaches its climax in Wordsworth, sprang from a similar impulse of enlargement, a wish to belong to something more invigorating and life-inspiring than the polite and intellectual society of towns.

The new romantic interest in history was one of the most important factors shaping the development of English culture in the nineteenth century. In many ways, the Romantic and Victorian ages were without a style of their own. But there is a common Augustan style which can be recognized in the way the poets of the period handle their couplets, although the diverse talents of Pope, Goldsmith, or Dr Johnson are still individually recognizable. The Victorians, who had no common romantic mode, cover their nakedness in fancy-dress. St Pancras station and the Law Courts in the Strand are both medieval fantasies; so are a good many of the poems of Browning and Tennyson. An interest, almost an obsession, with the past prevented many Victorian poets from doing justice to their own age. Tennyson turns to classical legend and the Arthurian romances; Browning to Renaissance Italy; Rossetti and Morris, in tone and mannerism as well as theme, to the medieval world. Matthew Arnold, a prose writer acutely aware of living, contemporary problems, in poetry sometimes (though not always) retreats from these to a vision of Oxford when 'wits ran clear beside the sparkling Thames'. But, on the other hand, the fancy-dress style can mask a contemporary relevance: Tennyson's *The Lady of Shalott* is on the surface a fairy-tale with an Arthurian setting; more deeply, it is a parable about the thwarting and killing effect of just this indirect relationship of the artist to reality. The bad sense of 'romantic' – meaning 'not facing reality' – probably dates from the Victorian age rather than from the great Romantic age itself.

With writers like Rossetti and Morris, however, with the second wind of Victorian poetry, the past is no longer an indirect way of talking about the present. The past is something to be contrasted with the actual world the Industrial Revolution has produced, a world which arouses in them a sense of desecration. Yeats inherited from the pre-Raphaelites this wistful attitude:

> We were the last romantics – chose for theme
> Traditional sanctity and loveliness;
> Whatever's written in what poet's name
> The book of the people; whatever most can bless
> The mind of man or elevate a rhyme;
> But all is changed, that high horse riderless,
> Though mounted in that saddle Homer rode
> Where the swan drifts upon a darkening flood.

Homer *rode* Pegasus. Can we ask or answer the question, Pater demands in the opening pages of his *Plato and Platonism*, whether Plato's theories are 'true' or not? He thinks that we cannot. We can merely try to understand Plato the man, to understand his background, and to see how natural it is that such a man, at such a time, should evolve such theories. Pater fully understands that in due time a similar approach can be applied to his own theories; full-blooded historicism implies the relativity of all values, including one's own.

The seventeenth-century Italian scholar Vico thought that God made nature, but man made history, and history was therefore the more proper human study. He fascinated Yeats and Joyce because of his insistence that the earliest and most primitive force in human history is the imagination; the language of poetry, of myth, is much older than the language of law and reason and debate. He fascinated them also because, like Nietzsche much nearer their own time, he saw history as a cycle. It was in the nature of human society to go through a certain number of definite stages, and then to collapse, and start again at its beginnings in primitive awe; so in Joyce's *Finnegans Wake* the opening page begins in the middle of a sentence and the beginning of the sentence is the last thing in the book. One could turn back from the beginning to the end, and go on for ever, which is what history does.

A cyclical theory of history is, obviously, accepted largely for emotional reasons; because it seems to promise earthly immortality, and because it offers an escape from complete moral relativism. It is a strange illustration of the difference between the European and the Far Eastern temperaments that the Eternal Recurrence which arouses the enthusiasm of Nietzsche, Yeats, Joyce, and Spengler is just the Great Wheel of Existence from which world-denying religions like Buddhism and Hinduism seek for the self's ultimate escape. Marxism has something in common with these cyclical theories: Marxists never explain why a classless society, once achieved, will not sort itself out into classes again, as primitive classless societies have done in the past. Marxism also shares with the theories of Nietzsche and Spengler that *amor fati* or joyful embracing of one's destiny, in which romantic historians evade rather than solve the old puzzles about determinism and free-will. (Evade rather than solve, because, if my destiny is pre-determined, so is the fashion in which I will embrace it; if my attitude is not pre-determined, then neither is my fate, for my attitude is part of my fate.)

I have been attempting here to suggest briefly some of the ways in which a mere curiosity about the past, an often rather superficial costume-drama interest in it, could develop into an elaborate, all-inclusive philosophy and *mystique* of history: the sense of the sacred, deprived of the High God of Christianity, displaces itself upon a hypostatized Historical Process. The historical process, dialectic or cyclical recurrence, becomes a Logos, mankind in history the Incarnation of that Logos; the historian becomes its high-priest. Thus, for Carlyle, earlier than most of the writers I have been mentioning, the history of the Western nations was to become a new Bible of the Peoples, replacing the Jewish Bible. Bernard Shaw, in his belief in the 'Life-force' – a divine spirit living and working through human history – is essentially a disciple of Carlyle.

Perhaps the modern poet who has thought most deeply about history, and yet who has not been contented either with a cyclical theory or a theory of immanentistic optimism – a divine spirit, or reason, working irresistibly forward *in* history – is Mr T. S. Eliot. For Eliot, there is a huge gap between the High God and His world. The world is a fallen world, man is a fallen creature. Most change is of the nature of decay. When he seeks for a commanding abstraction, in his thinking about history, Eliot turns neither to Recurrence nor the Dialectic but to the idea of Tradition, the idea of something unchanging handed down amid all the change, like the *depositum fidei* in Christian belief. Eliot's image for Tradition is spatial, not temporal. The great achievements in art and thought of the past are spread out before us, as on a map. They cannot be altered in themselves, but the creation of new works of art and thought in our own time will alter our appreciation of the relationship of the past to the present, and of parts of the past to each other. At the core, it is always the same landscape, but our view of it is extending, we are colonizing the outer edges of it, and our perspectives upon it are changing. Eliot likes to think of time timelessly; and for him the meaning of history is to be found not *in* history, but outside it, in man's relation to God, and God's relation to man.

Eliot is not, of course, the first man to protest against the nineteenth-century tendency to see everything in history. In the early nineteenth century, the Danish thinker, Kierkegaard, was especially aware of the burden and the mystery, the anxiety and dread, of one's individual existence to oneself – a burden which he thought speculative, systematic philosophers like Hegel tended to ignore. Philosophers talk about the development of tendencies or the movement of ideas, but ours, Kierkegaard insisted, is not a world of tendencies and ideas, but of men, each of whom is a mystery both in and to himself. Hence Kierkegaard is thought of as the first existentialist. For him the most important thing in life was man's relationship to God. Reason could not prove either God's existence or his goodness. Faith was a leap in the dark to which men were driven by awe and dread and anxiety. History is in a sense irrelevant.

The most successful purely artistic development of Kierkegaard's ideas is in the novels and tales of Kafka, which beautifully illustrate Kierkegaard's concepts of awe, dread, and anxiety, but which provide no leap in the dark to save at the last moment the unfortunate heroes. Of his two most famous novels, *The Trial* is about a man who finds himself condemned and punished for a crime which he is not aware of having committed, and of whose very nature he remains oblivious. *The Castle* is about a man who has been appointed to act as an agent, in a village, for the authorities at a castle; he never manages to get in touch with the authorities, to discover what his duties are, or to get definite confirmation that he has duties. The novels are 'about' the nature of sin, or guilt, and the nature of authority that might redeem or absolve us from them. But these books cannot be read as straight religious allegories either in the Christian or in Kafka's own Jewish tradition. Like the effect, on some readers, of *The Book of Job*, Kafka's narratives arouse a profound sympathy with the bewildered victim or the suffering seeker, and raise two fundamental questions: is there really a final authority at all, and, if there is, is it a just one? But Kafka makes his widest appeal to contemporary readers because he conveys with unparalleled purity and intensity the generalized anxiety of our time (perhaps of *all* times, but it is in our own time that we have become most lucidly conscious of it).

Some of Kierkegaard's later successors, for instance the French philosopher, novelist, and playwright Jean-Paul

Sartre, are not men of religious belief like Kafka but atheists; but the dread, awe, and anxiety with which they regard what appears to be the unnecessary and arbitrary intrusion of human consciousness into the world – man, 'a useless passion' – makes them as eager as Kierkegaard was to insist on the unique significance of every individual human life. For them, if there is no God, it is man who must choose; and in each choice I make I stand for mankind. And this is a heavy burden.

Existentialism, whether Christian or atheist, transcends, like Mr Eliot's Christian traditionalism, a merely historical attitude to experience. All three attitudes suit the static tension of our time, the sense of history stuck in ice which, when it begins to break, may well sink the ship. It is a sense which has increasingly been our attitude towards history since the beginning of the Cold War: life, that is, in a time of arrangements and adjustments, when the penalty for the wrong action is total disaster. We no longer live in a time of historical growth. Yet, just because we live in precarious times we ought not to write off our whole historical culture; the great works of the past can still strengthen our spirits, and we owe a debt to our ancestors which we ought to repay.

A modern writer who has made a very strenuous effort to repay this debt is the American poet Ezra Pound. There is no critical agreement about the total merit of his most ambitious poem, *The Cantos*, though there is an agreement that it contains wonderful pieces of exhortatory and evocative language and what Wyndham Lewis called 'the grand granitic landslides of translation'. Pound is not an existentialist, either Christian or atheist, and is not a Christian poet. But he has his own kind of religion, a cult of the high and heroic moments in human history, of the great civilizations and the great codes: his answer to disaster is an attempt to strengthen us by making us remember triumph:

> What thou lovest well remains,
>   the rest is dross
> What thou lov'st well shall not be reft from thee

> What thou lov'st well is thy true heritage
> Whose world, or mine or theirs
> > > or is it of none?
> First came the seen, then thus the palpable
> > Elysium, though it were in the halls of hell,
> What thou lovest well is thy true heritage

He wants us to live according to nature, to see the proportions and models of human achievement in the natural world, and thus to learn humility:

> The ant's a centaur in his dragon world.
> Pull down thy vanity, it is not man
> Made courage, or made order, or made grace,
> > Pull down they vanity, I say pull down
> Learn of the green world what can be thy place
> In scaled invention or true artistry,
> > > > Paquin pull down!
> The green casque has outdone your elegance.

He has no illusions about what a vain and destructive creature man is, perhaps he himself is; but it is at least something to have loved natural beauty and to have loved art and poetry, and after the lines of self-reproach which I am about to quote he rejoices that in his youth he had the courage to go and offer his shy admiration to the fine old aristocratic radical poet, Wilfrid Blunt. That, at least, was not vanity. But perhaps the self-reproach rings stronger:

> 'Master thyself, then others shall thee beare'
> > Pull down thy vanity
> Thou are a beaten dog beneath the hail,
> A swollen magpie in a fitful sun,
> Half black half white
> Nor knowst 'ou wing from tail
> Pull down thy vanity
> > > How mean they hates
> Fostered in falsity,
> > > Pull down thy vanity
> Rathe to destroy, niggard in charity,
> Pull down thy vanity,
> > > I say pull down.

Pound has had a strange, mixed history. But if one wished to communicate a sense of loyalty to what is best in our similarly diverse inheritance, a proper attitude to history, one could hardly find better words than these of Pound's: 'What thou lov'st well is thy true heritage.'

Thus, the sense of history in modern literature has a wide diversity of forms, it has produced both its own *mystique* and a reaction against that *mystique*: but it is a vital element, and can be a source of moral strength.

2

Realism, Psychology, and Experiment in Modern Novels

I AM using 'realism' not in the narrow sense in which the word is sometimes used to describe novels, like Zola's, which are based on an elaborate documentation of fact, deal often with the drabber or more sordid sides of life and for which the proper term is 'naturalism', but rather in the sense in which, in ordinary speech, we contrast a 'realistic' with an 'idealistic' attitude to life. That again differs from the technical way in which these two words are used in philosophy, so perhaps we might describe the 'realistic' writer as one who thinks that truth to observed facts – facts about the outer world, or facts about his own feelings – is important while the 'idealistic' writer wants to create rather a pleasant and edifying picture. Dr Johnson, for instance, could not re-read the last act of Shakespeare's *King Lear* because it struck him as too harrowing and unjust; he preferred the version written by a Restoration hack writer in which Lear lives and Cordelia marries Edgar. It would be no answer to his criticism of *King Lear* to say that virtue often fails to triumph in real life; he would reply that it ought to triumph in dramatic poetry. Though we can respect the tender feelings that lay behind Dr Johnson's criticism, we probably do not agree with it today: we feel about Lear, with Charles Lamb and with Shakespeare himself, that

> he hates him
> That would upon the rack of this tough world
> Stretch him out longer.

We see that a 'happy ending' to *King Lear* would be a tepid and tedious anticlimax. Have we gone through so much, and only for that? ... Yet Johnson's criticism is never foolish. Teaching the play to undergraduates, I have found that some of them find the conclusion – 'Is this the promised end?' – unbearably cruel, others insist that Lear dies happily with the illusion that Cordelia has begun to breathe again, and others again insist that an Elizabethan audience, seeing this Christian play with pagan images, would be consoled by the thought of Lear and Cordelia at last safe in heaven. Thus, even allowing that Johnson's discomfort was not mawkish or pointless, we can see that the 'idealistic' critic, in his urgent desire for edification, may be blind not only to the outward truth of life, but also to the inner truth of poetry. The 'realistic' attitude is one more bravely exposed not only to the outer shocks but also to the inner springs. *King Lear*, of course, is 'real', but not in the sense that a novel is 'realistic': it is an image of what life *is*, not of what life is *like*.

The realistic attitude, in the wider sense, might be contrasted with the Augustan convention of decorum. In a neoclassical poem, like many of Dryden's panegyric odes, it is assumed that for propriety's sake the poet must treat kings as if they were noble and gracious, statesmen as if they were wise and just, soldiers as if they were brave and merciful, great ladies as if they were chaste and fair, whatever actually may be the case: even though, in fact, as at the Restoration Court, everybody knows the opposite to be the truth. The same tone of solemn official praise can be heard in the funeral sermons of Bossuet. One cannot call the tone flattery, for no one was deceived by it; nor was it felt as irony or sarcasm; it was the appropriate ceremonial language to use about a public role, however inadequate the actor of the role might be, or however distinct his private from his official character. The convention still survives in public life as when one M.P. refers to another as the Hon. and Gallant Member or the Hon. and Learned Member without implying any personal belief in his honour, his gallantry, or his learning. A convention of decorum gives life dignity, and people sometimes try to live up to the virtues they are officially assumed to possess. But we can see the other side of the picture in works like Pepys's *Diary* or the *Memoirs* of Grammont or Saint-Simon, where what stirs the writer is a curiosity, often malicious, about real motives and actions; and these works are more 'modern' in tone, and can perhaps be read today with more pleasure, than more formal writing which I have been describing.

Interest in people's real actions and motives lay, of course, behind the rise of the novel. Prose narrative long precedes the novel, but it tends to be either in a convention of decorum, like Malory's *Morte d'Arthur* or Sydney's *The Countess of Pembroke's Arcadia* or to be picaresque, to exploit a superior interest in the seamy side of life, like Defoe's *Moll Flanders*. There are fictions like Bunyan's *Pilgrim's Progress* or his *Life and Death of Mr Badman*, or like Swift's *Gulliver's Travels*, which have a flavour that reminds us of novels, since they are full of everyday detail and natural-sounding conversation, but which are allegories or fables constructed to expound a previously determined scheme of ideas. The true novel rests on no such scheme; it is an exploration, not an exposition, and the true novelist arrives at his sense of life through his story, he does not construct his story to illustrate that sense. The novelist is interested in what life is *like*, in its everyday texture. As a central literary interest, this is comparatively new, and literary historians connect it with the rise, in the eighteenth century, of a middle-class public, not interested in literary conventions, nor eager to read idealized accounts of their superiors or scabrous accounts of their inferiors, but curious about themselves and their own world. The more traditional literary forms, epic, tragedy, comedy, satire, pastoral, romance, allegory, rest less on a curiosity about the detail of life than on a wish to impose certain firm patterns on its bewildering diversity. The novel as such does not impose a pattern in advance and it is not accident that its rise coincides not only with an increase in the middle-class reading public but also with the beginnings of English empirical philosophy. My own definition of the novel as a form would be that it is an exploration of the variety of life, through realistic prose narrative, in the hope of finding a pattern.

On the other hand, Dr Tillyard thought that the novel is not really a new form in itself, but that all novels are epics, tragedies, comedies, satires, pastorals, and so on, with the sharp outlines of the older forms more or less disguised by realistic detail. Certainly, among the earliest English works of fiction that are recognized as being novels proper, *Robinson Crusoe* is partly, like *Sinbad the Sailor*, a tale of voyages and marvels, and partly also an allegory of human solitude; Richardson's *Pamela*, though based on a real life story, reminds one of the fairy tale of 'Beauty and the Beast'; and Richardson's greatest novel, *Clarissa*, is an artificial tragedy, in the sense that we talk of some Restoration plays as artificial comedy. But what is new in Defoe and Richardson is their indifference to literary elegance, their wish to present their fictions as real-life documents, memoirs, or collections of letters made plausible to the reader by their very lack of literary finish.

From the point of view of our argument here, Fielding is more interesting than Richardson or Defoe. Unlike these two, Fielding was not a member of the lower-middle-classes, he was a hard-up aristocrat, with a good classical education, and a respect for, and interest in, traditional literary forms. Though there was not a critical formula for realistic prose fiction, Fielding felt that there ought to be one. In his preface to his first novel, *Joseph Andrews*, he defines the novel as 'the comic prose epic'; he sees it as a form of literature dealing light-heartedly with the ridiculous, but the ridiculous of real life, not of burlesque imagination; he sees himself as an artist of Hogarth's type, viewing life sharply and critically, but not wildly distorting or caricaturing it. The entertainment of a novel should arise, he thinks, from satire upon affectation, whether arising from vanity or hypocrisy; the satire will be directed against types rather than individuals; the novelist will allow himself passages of burlesque writing (mock-heroic similes to make low or gross episodes amusing and palatable), little digressions, short addresses to

24

the reader, small essays on relevant general topics. Fielding is always there in person in his novels, manipulating the puppets, and commenting on his own performance. The live character in *Joseph Andrews* who escapes from Fielding's own formula is the innocent, generous, blundering Parson Adams; but Fielding is always very 'literary' and Adams, in his chivalrous, absent-minded high-mindedness and his escapades, is an English Don Quixote. In his second novel, *Tom Jones*, Fielding created the prototype of most future heroes of English novels; the young man, new to the world, accessible to temptation, but saved from final shipwreck by a candid mind and a generous heart: Tom Jones represents mixed, average human nature, raised rather above itself by an unusual warm-heartedness, and very warmly viewed by Fielding. The burlesque and farcical elements are less important here, and have almost vanished from Fielding's third novel, *Amelia*, where the hero is a kind of Tom Jones, married: Captain Booth suffers agonies brought upon him by a single act of adultery. He is a character of good nature without fixed principles. The darker colours foreshadow the depth and complexity that were to mark the novel in the nineteenth century.

Fielding had not found the final formula for the novel; George Moore observed that in *Tom Jones* there is no psychology and no description in the modern sense, 'no inner or outer world'. Instead there is perhaps a firmer grasp of action and character than in many later novels, like Moore's own, which are full of psychology and description. These were two directions, however, in which the novel was to develop. I am not sure that Jane Austen is a psychologist or that she has an 'inner world' in George Moore's sense, though she understands human character far better than he does; her occasional indications of scene, Lyme Regis, for instance, have a delicate perfunctoriness, like a young lady's water-colour drawings. She is my favourite novelist, and the one English novelist who seems to me to achieve classical perfection, but her very serenity, poise, and balance mean that she is *not* 'modern'. John Thorpe's praise of Fielding in

Northanger Abbey suggests that Jane Austen herself disliked Fielding; but given her greater delicacy and deeper penetration, at least into women's minds, her method is not unlike Fielding's. She uses irony as he does; she is ready to summarize, as he is; like him, she uses dialogue to bring out the comic, or moral, essence of a situation.

Much more 'modern', in Moore's sense, is Dickens, for whom lonely marshland, decrepit house, slum tenement, fog or darkness by the London river, not only project a mood but also define a theme: in the first pages of *Little Dorrit*, for instance, the heat shine, and smells, the garishness, vitality, and danger of Marseilles prepare us by way of contrast for the choking brick-dustiness of London. As a psychologist Dickens has not much advanced on Fielding or Smollett; he presents us with some of the most vivid figures in all literature, but as Henry James observed, in reviewing *Our Mutual Friend*, they are figures, not characters. They are to be observed in action, not to be internally dissected. But Dickens's eye is open. He sees.

But the opening of the novelist's inner eye to the intricate workings of the human soul, with its noble and base motives, can be traced more strikingly in French novels, like those of Stendhal, or like Benjamin Constant's cruel and incisive piece of introspective analysis, *Adolphe*. There is no more description, or real evocation of scene, in *Adolphe* than in *Tom Jones*; but the classically simple form, the restricted and colourless vocabulary, the touch of surviving chilliness from the *ancien régime*, overlying the new romantic malaise of self-doubting and soul-searching, are used to lay bare the human heart in a new and frightening way. Finally, in the massive European novels of the middle nineteenth century, in Tolstoy's *War and Peace*, Dostoyevsky's *The Brothers Karamazov*, or George Eliot's *Middlemarch*, both description and psychology have been firmly grasped as tools, the structure of the novel has become as solid, its texture as supple and various, as that of life itself. I feel this easy capaciousness also, though few except Scotsmen would agree with me, in the best novels of Sir Walter Scott. 'If life could speak,' said Charles du Bos of Tolstoy, 'life would speak thus.' Such novels are more than merely 'modern': they are among the great achievements of the human spirit at any time.

But if the novel, as an art-form, had perhaps reached its peak with George Eliot and the great Russians, the urge to experiment, to make it more elegant, more definitely a form with its own internal rigorous rules, continued. For Henry James the novels of Dostoyevsky and Tolstoy were 'fluid puddings'. His masters are Flaubert and Turgenev. He disliked the way earlier Victorian novelists like Thackeray had perpetually broken down the illusion they were trying to create by addressing the reader direct. He introduced the technique of telling a story from the point of view of an observer who is not necessarily a main participant in the story, but whose curiosity, and success or failure in satisfying it, may become the main theme; and while the observer is judging the other characters, we may find ourselves being manoeuvred into judging the observer. He brought into the novel points of view so subtle, characters so reserved and refined, delicacies of motive so intangible, that probably no previous writer would have thought them solid enough for fiction. His peculiar delicacy and fastidiousness have made some critics compare him with Jane Austen. His 'world', however, is not so tangible as hers; his fine characters have to spin their fineness out of their own bowels. Sometimes they seem to be swimming in a great goldfish bowl, sometimes moving in a world from which the air is being gradually exhausted. He loved the atmosphere of mystery: through labyrinthine sentences we pursue a dangerous precision.

Over-reliance on subtlety and on delicate impressions of mood, scene, situation, and the careful unravelling of the psychological strands that make up these impressions, may make the novelist lose his sense of architecture, of structure. James's central care, however, was for structure, he roughed out what he called the *charpente*, the solid skeleton, of his stories well in advance. But in writers like Dorothy

Richardson, Katherine Mansfield, or Virginia Woolf, who carry the impressionist technique further, who introduce into the novel so much of the stuff of poetry – but diluted, or, as I. A. Richards has observed, 'like gold to airy thinness beat' – there is the danger that the novel as a structure, as an architecture of character and action, will begin to fall apart.

To discuss structure in the novel is to come sooner or later to James Joyce's *Ulysses*. Richards' criticism that *Ulysses* falls apart is unjust: few novels are more solidly constructed, and few characters in fiction more solidly imagined than Stephen Daedalus and Leopold Bloom.

It is true, however, that the first impression of *Ulysses* on a reader may be one of rich confusion, that it takes time and effort before the artistic and moral structure of the story can be firmly grasped; and also that though the theme of *Ulysses* is adequate and complex enough, the plot – one not outwardly very eventful day in two not outwardly very significant Dublin lives – seems at a first reading too frail to support the huge, thick weight of atmosphere of observed detail. But a proper reading of *Ulysses* is more like living the events which the book describes than is the reading of most other novels; the pressure is so thick, so heavy, that a reader has almost to cut his way through. Some critics have described the book as the culmination of the possibilities of the novel as an art-form: as the novel to end all novels. Others have felt that *Ulysses* is not a true novel because our sense of the art that has gone into it takes away from our sense of, or sympathy with, the life it represents. This, I think, is nonsense: Joyce had a great sympathetic comic imagination. His contemporary, D. H. Lawrence, had not that sort of imagination. Lawrence takes sides, angrily, among his characters, and hectors his readers, in a way in which no other major novelist does. But it may be that there is a special sense of life which he conveys, and which Joyce cannot: Gerald Crich, on his mare at the railway crossing, cruelly reining her in, the two girls watching him and hating him, is a page or two of prose of Shakespearian concentration to be set alongside the Christmas dinner and the argument about Parnell in Joyce's *Portrait of the Artist as a Young Man*. But what is notable about Lawrence is the quickness, the impatience, the spurtiness of his way of writing; he scamps or hurries or doodles till he comes to a scene that will come alive for him. If the novel begins in Fielding by adapting a number of established literary conventions, and if in James and in Joyce it is making things difficult and interesting for itself by inventing new conventions of its own, with Lawrence it seems often to want to get away from being literature at all; impatient truth to his own uneven energy at any moment of writing may perhaps have been Lawrence's greatest contribution to literature. Certainly, after Conrad, Lawrence, and Joyce, though one can point to many writers of genuinely original talent, from Virginia Woolf through Ivy Compton-Burnett to Henry Green, they have not altered the overall form of the novel. Most of the good novelists since about 1930 are plain straightforward writers, using old-fashioned story-telling methods: though symbolic overtones or allegorical meanings can often be found in the work of Rex Warner, Graham Greene, and Christopher Isherwood, and since 1950, in the work of William Golding and Iris Murdoch.

One of the great modern thinkers who has had a deep influence on the modern novel, and on all forms of literature and art, is Sigmund Freud. Freud's ideas have become so much a part of the intellectual climate of our time that one tends to take them for granted, and to forget what a startling, indeed shocking impact they had on the literary mind when they first became a matter for public discussion. His concepts of the ego and the id, the censor and the unconscious are too well known to discuss here, except to note that the basic pattern of Freud's thinking has a good deal in common with that of the romantic pessimistic German philosopher Schopenhauer and that both had much influence on the great German novelist Thomas Mann. Freud's concepts can be applied not only to writers who were influenced by him, like Mann, but to writers who had never heard of him, like Shakespeare. Freud is not therefore a thinker whose influence, like that of Kierkegaard, can be tracked down over a narrow range of imaginative works: one can find Freudian patterns wherever one cares to look; but his direct influence no doubt accounts in part for the frankness about family relationships and the sexual realism of much modern fiction.

We can see then that 'realism' is an elusive and ramifying conception. New subtleties of psychological approach, or new delicacies of presentation or description, which at first appear to open out new country for the novelist, may in the end send him chasing so many different hares that he forgets what he was primarily after: a purposeful exploration of life, a quest for a certain kind of moral centre based on a just and varied sampling of typical human experience.

3

Complexity, Allusiveness, Irony, Obscurity in Modern Poetry

It is in poetry that readers have the sharpest sense of what the 'modern' is. Yet it is hard to suggest a single and simple touchstone for the note of modernity in poetry. Again, much poetry even of the remote past strikes us as 'modern' in tone, while some good poetry of our own time, Walter de la Mare, Ruth Pitter, or Andrew Young, does not seem contemporary at all. Perhaps the nearest we can get to it is the presence in a poem of a feeling of harsh, unresolved complexity; Catullus, for instance, is very 'modern' when he says:

> I hate and love.
> You ask how that can be?
> I do not know, but know it tortures me.

Robert Bridges, on the other hand, though he died well within living memory, is not at all 'modern' when he writes on Purcell's bicentenary:

> Love unto Love calleth,
> Love unto Love replieth ...
> From the ends of the earth, drawn by invisible bands,
> Over the dawning and darkening lands
> Love cometh to Love.
> To the heart by courage and might
> Escaped from hell,
> From the torment of raging fire,
> From the sighs of the drowning main,
> From the shipwreck of fear and pain,
> From the terror of night.

Where Catullus is tying a knot and pulling it tight till it hurts, Bridges is beautifully unwinding the same knot. The hell, the fire, the sighs of the drowning main, the shipwreck and terror, the fear and pain in his lines are what Catullus is talking about: the rage, the shame, the jealousy, the humiliation, the dark side of love. But in Bridges a personified love, divine or ideal, transcendent or Platonic, soars happily and musically away from its own dark side, where in Catullus the personal unabstracted 'I love' is painfully tied to the equally personal 'I hate'. Catullus's way of talking about love comes more intimately home to us, here and now, than Bridges's way: but because I think it more 'modern' I do not necessarily think it better. The 'modern' tone is the one which appeals to us in our situation. So long as the age ties itself into tight knots, we are likely to enjoy such hurtful knots in poetry.

But though Bridges was in no sense a 'modernist' poet, he reflects one of the predicaments that have created modern poetry. One of the reasons why it is impossible to agree with Yvor Winters in assigning major status to Bridges is that his voice seems so remote from the urgent and harsh voices of common speech in his time. The high and fine traditional tone seems to impinge nowhere on everyday life. It is thin and distant even where Bridges is lamenting the failure of poets in the 1890s to bring a trumpet-voice to public affairs:

> Lament, fair hearted queen, lament with me ...
> For when thy seer died no song was sung
> Nor for our heroes fal'n by land and sea
>   Hath honour found a tongue.

The lines have a very cool, formal, distant ring; and when Bridges himself became Poet Laureate he steadfastly eschewed the poem on the public occasion, leaving honour to find, for our heroes fallen by land or sea, the more urgent and brassy tongue of Rudyard Kipling. Kipling's special kinds of success and failure showed that, in the late Victorian and Edwardian ages, it was becoming more and more difficult to strike a common note without catching a 'common' tone. As T. S. Eliot has said in a fine essay, Kipling is not setting out to write 'poetry' in the ordinary sense at all.

What is remarkable is that the hymn and ballad metres, the frank intentions of journalistic propaganda or amusement, the drum-thumpings, the Cockney impersonations, so often fail to prevent Kipling from writing poetry. George Orwell has at once praised and condemned him as the poet of the copy-book headings, the memorable platitudes which stick in the mind often because, in a nasty and nagging way, they are uncomfortably true. From an opposite political point of view, both Orwell and Eliot see Kipling as the poet of Imperial responsibility. Kipling first caught the public ear with a poetry of popular impersonation : trying to imitate the talk of Cockneys and tramps, the soldier and the uneducated man. In this sense Kipling is a 'modern' writer in a way in which Bridges is not : his complexity took the form of a too artful imitation of simplicity, but he did manage for a time to bridge the growing gap between poetry and public, although he often paid too high a price.

Nevertheless, Kipling's equivocal success, like the high public status of Browning and Tennyson earlier on, was a sign that the estrangement between poet and public had never become so acute in England as it had become in France. Perhaps the historian of 'modern poetry' – in the sense of difficult, complex, abstruse poetry whose statements or attitudes puzzle the ordinary reader – might date its rise in England somewhere between 1910 and 1920: he would be thinking of the early poems of Pound and Eliot, the realistic war poetry of Owen, Sassoon, Graves, Blunden, Isaac Rosenberg, and Herbert Read; the hardening and maturing of Yeats's style, as seen in such a poem as *Easter, 1916*. He would mention Gerard Manley Hopkins, a poet of the 1870s and 1880s who died young and whose poems were not published as a volume till 1919, as a 'modern poet' before his time. He would say something about the poets of the 1890s, Dowson, Lionel Johnson, John Davidson, Arthur Symons, who had been friends of the young Yeats, and whom the young Eliot, as an undergraduate, had admired; it was Arthur Symons's book on the French symbolist poets which put Eliot, at Harvard, on to the poetry of Jules Laforgue, perhaps the most important influence of his early work; Symons also, in very minor poems, anticipated Eliot in the use of urban imagery and of what might be called impressionism (in the painter's sense) in verse. Earlier poets like Whitman and Swinburne and William Morris were important technical influences, the last two on Yeats, the first two on Pound, the first (unconsciously, and in spite of a conscious reaction against him) on Eliot. Both Eliot and Pound also learned something from Browning's dramatic monologues. The kind of symbolism used by Yeats derives, also, much more profoundly from Blake, and perhaps from the English romantic movement generally, than from Mallarmé. Yet, though the *sources* of modern poetry can be traced very far back, critics are right in seeing a note of absolute novelty in a poem which the young Eliot wrote in 1910 and could not get published, so strange did it seem to editors at that time, till 1915: *The Love-Song of J. Alfred Prufrock*. Fifty years after it was written this poem still delightfully shocks and surprises those finding it for the first time; it topples over their inert notions of what a poem is, or should be. We can today see modern elements in the work of Hardy and in the work of Yeats from the turn of the century onwards, but the young Eliot could not; his originality partly arose from his being thoroughly bored with his contemporaries. Ezra Pound, though admiring both Yeats and Hardy, felt a similar boredom, a boredom which drove him to restless and unceasing experiment. The Imagist movement, in which Pound played a great part, reflected an impatience with conventional diction and metres. Pound affected Yeats, whom he knew well, and critics rightly feel that around 1910, in Pound, Eliot, and Yeats, something new crystallizes. Grierson's great edition of Donne suggested to young poets (or to middle-aged poets like Yeats) that there was a tradition of witty and abstruse writing in verse other than the Victorian and Romantic. But whereas the 'modern' movement in English poetry begins around 1910, with early Eliot, early-middle Pound, and middle Yeats, a historian of the 'modern' movement in French poetry would have to go back at least as far as Baudelaire. One reason for this earlier development of 'modernism' in France was an earlier and more complete estrangement of some important French poets from the tone and attitudes of the public life around them: not of all French poets – Lamartine and Victor Hugo are examples of poets who were deeply involved in that public life. But these have not the kind of complexity that would have interested the young Eliot: they are not, as Baudelaire or Laforgue or Tristan Corbière were, 'modern'.

I shall now turn to a discussion of French poetry to look at the roots and influences of the 'modern' movement, with its symbolism, its complexity, and its irony. In French poetry too can be found the basis of surrealism and here also one will discover the influences which made Eliot and Pound so interested in reconciling culture and tradition: life and art.

It seems at first surprising that the estrangement of the poet from public life should have become noticeable, earlier, in France than in England. For in France literature has been a part of public life, and the man of letters a public figure, in a way that has not usually been the case in England; but in fact the traditional values of much French literature – values of clear, rapid, sometimes superficial reasoning, of incisive generalization, of dignified rhetoric, and pointed wit, while real virtues in themselves, were, as Baudelare noted, anti-poetic virtues. The whole tendency of French thought, after Descartes, was to exalt abstract reason against concrete intuition; the tendency of French poetry after Malherbe was to exalt propriety and decorum of language against an original and personal note; and the eighteenth century, though a very great century in French literary history, has been notable above all for its prose. In spite of the great triumphs of French romanticism, something of that anti-poetic tone lingered on in Baudelaire's time, and lingers on today, in the French literary atmosphere. The poet may not be merely a poet; he must justify himself at the bar of current opinion which, in France, assumes the air of a final court of appeal. It might not be wholly unfair to say that the claims of public life on the

French poet have, since the early seventeenth century, tended to turn his poetry into rhetoric.

If the poet in any country is hemmed in by hostile, probing yet shallow orthodoxies, he will, of course, be driven in self-defence to eccentricity, defiance, the fortress of a private world, or a self-contained circle of activity. Baudelaire put on the mask of the dandy, hoping to outstare the starers, by his own insolence to make the insolent drop their eyes. Gautier (determined that if the world were going to insist on poetry having a vulgar relevance, poets should proclaim the vulgar irrelevance of the world) announced the doctrine of art for art's sake; an inadequate doctrine in itself – art for life's, love's, or delight's sake is nearer the truth – but a useful shield, then and since, for poets who do not feel like becoming tools.

It was about this same period that there was invented, in reference to Vigny, the famous phrase about the poet's 'ivory tower'. It might have been more accurate to talk of the poet as the inhabitant of a besieged city; a city not strong enough to sally forth and destroy her enemies, but well-provisioned, and with strong walls. By the time of Baudelaire's successors, Mallarmé and his school, it might have been truer perhaps to speak of a Philistine city with the poets moving about it as spies, wearing a disguise, and communicating by a code that made their presence unsuspected. Baudelaire still made enough direct impact on his age to have *Les Fleurs du mal,* his masterpiece, condemned for immorality. Yet Baudelaire, as Eliot has pointed out, is essentially a poet of Christian feeling; he shocked his contemporaries just because in the century of gaslight, of the railway, of the Great Exhibition of 1851, of an unheard-of expansion of manufacture, population, and trade, he insisted that the only true progress consisted in diminishing the traces of original sin; and because he knew, all too intimately, what sin is, in what its attraction and horror consist. His life, in which, as Sartre truly observes, he 'did' nothing (apart from creating his masterpieces), was as momentous and as morally significant as that other contemporary, ap-

parently monotonous, empty, and dawdling life that Kierkegaard led. In a bustling, noisy age both were capable of
contemplation, capable of knowing the vanity of the world.

Mallarmé, on the other hand, the spy in disguise in the
enemy city, made no such direct impact, but unobtrusively
gathered round him his small fifth column. Living the life
of a poor schoolmaster, he seemed, to the large world around
him, merely the leader of a set of faddists, the high priest of
a precious cult that would pass. Yet Mallarmé, it might be
said, was more profoundly subversive than Baudelaire, and
would have appeared so if his work had been accessible to
the common reader. He is even, at times, a more vividly and
disturbingly sensual poet than Baudelaire: I quote from
Aldous Huxley's version of *L'Après-midi d'un faune*:

> I love that virginal fury – ah, the wild
> Thrill when a maiden body shrinks, defiled,
> Shuddering like arctic light, from lips that sear
> Its nakedness . . . the flesh in secret fear!

But we are not to take that literally, as we are to take, with
a sad literalness, so much that is sordid or sinister in Baudelaire. Mallarmé is, as Baudelaire is not, consciously a symbolist.

To use Mr Iain Fletcher's distinction between allegorical
and symbolical poetry, if a poem is allegorical, 'it works out
the details of something already given, something which
has received prior justification as theology or political
theory, an organization of intuitions and judgements. Valua-
tion of this will depend on the structure of the poem, its
music, its detail. With the poetry of symbol none of these
things is of the first importance. A symbol has been defined
as the expression of some otherwise inexpressible truth; and
it is not on the verbal music, or on the incidental illustra-
tions of the theme, that judgement will depend, but on the
insight which the poem accords into the life of the soul.'

What insight does Mallarmé accord into the life of the
soul in the lines I have quoted? The faun and the two
nymphs, seen remotely, have a meaning that is themselves

but also other and more than themselves; not, however, that allegorical meaning which can be tightly tied down, but the symbolical meaning that opens out in vague, endless suggestions, conveying something that could not be otherwise conveyed. Perhaps we think, when we read these lines, of the beautiful possible poem, existing as an ideal even before it has been written, yet eluding the poet's urgent grasp. For if it is not an essential limitation of the symbolist method, as Mr Fletcher defines it, it does seem to be a limitation of it as Mallarmé developed it, that it becomes more and more shut in on itself, the subject-matter of the poem being ever more narrowly confined to the nature of the poetic experience itself: poems are about poetry, the individual poem is an attempt to make its own nature transparent to itself. This is certainly true of Wallace Stevens, the last great poet in Mallarmé's tradition.

In this tradition, the nature of poetry is something inexpressible, or something that can be expressed only through the symbols of particular poems. Let me quote my own version of one of Mallarmé's most famous sonnets, which will illustrate, for all its beauty, the terribly 'shut-in' nature of symbolist poetry:

> The virgin, bright, and beautiful today
> Dare it now shatter with a drunken wing
> This hard forgotten lake, this ice where cling
> These flights of mine that never flew away . . .?
> Once was a swan, remembers it is he,
> Magnificent but hopeless in his strife
> For never having sung the realms of life
> When winter shone in bleak sterility.
> His neck in a white agony is shaken,
> Shattering the space that mocks him for his pride
> But not the soil in which his plumes are taken:
> Phantom mere brightness to this scene has drawn,
> Immobile in the cold, where dreams deride,
> Clothed in the useless exile of the swan.

It is of the very nature of symbolist poetry that it cannot be tied down to any single and simple interpretation; however much of the intention one may think one has dredged up to the surface, it retains always a residue of mysterious suggestiveness; so that the interpretation of such poems is as tricky, and full of traps, as the interpretation of dreams. But I think that in this case we are at least not very far wrong in equating

> This hard forgotten lake, this ice where cling
> These flights of mine that never flew away ...

with the beautiful but almost entirely self-enclosed world of the symbolist poem itself; the poet is lamenting that it is his fate to be the poet, that is, to be himself, *only* in the poem, that is, in something other than himself, and other than himself in the most complete and hostile fashion; for one's own life is not and cannot be the 'life' as we call it, the 'order' as we perhaps ought to call it, of words upon a page. The most wonderful flights of the symbolist imagination cannot take it away from its merely symbolic mode of asserting itself: cannot take it into reality, into life itself. The poet suffers, he is trapped like the swan (and the swan, in verse, is one of the permanent emblems of the poet) as a punishment for

> never having sung the realms of life
> When winter shone in bleak sterility.

The sterile bleakness of winter, the icy crystalline order of pure art, of the poem as something utterly self-contained, trapped and held that 'poetic' quality in Mallarmé's nature which should have flowed warmly, and perishably, out into life. The 'space' in which the swan's neck 'in a white agony is shaken' as well as being the perceptual space of the poem's winter landscape is perhaps the physical space of the outer universe, a space empty and meaningless to Mallarmé, who did not share Baudelaire's Christian beliefs. There was no God there, not even Baudelaire's harsh God of Justice. And we may remember the tremendous, frightening sentence of Pascal, battling with his own fears of atheism: 'The eternal silence of these infinite spaces frightens me.' The frosty soil in which bird's wings are caught and trapped is that of the poem itself. It is only within the poem that poetry is now possible, the world outside has become unpoetical; yet that world 'outside' includes, of course, the poet's everyday self, and, drawing no life even from that, the poem acquires a glittering and killing frigidity, which in the end will drive even the poet, or the possible poet, away. As poetry acquires more and more of a self-subsistent crystalline order, it becomes more and more inhospitable to the poet. So we are told in the last three lines that even the swan (that is, the poet as apart from his poem) has become an illusion:

> Phantom mere brightness to this scene has drawn,
> Immobile in the cold, where dreams deride,
> Clothed in the useless exile of the swan.

The 'brightness' of the ideal possible poem has drawn the poet rather as the brightness of a lamp draws a moth; but his death is a different kind of death, in the end the symbolist dream has become something too freezing and inimical to life for the poet to live in, or to live anything but a hallucination of life in. The poet is *elsewhere*, but his only proper place, as a poet, is inside this glittering, sterile poetic world'. His 'exile' is useless,' since it is only in this world, which in purifying so drastically he has now rendered uninhabitable, that he could have had his proper life. Thus the symbolist poet (like Mallarmé's disciple, Valéry, working in a newspaper agency for many years, or like Valéry's admirer, Wallace Stevens, to his death the staid vice-president of a New England insurance company) can cease to be a spy in the Philistine city and become, to all outward appearances, at least, for many years a dutiful citizen; feeling that it is the poetic experience which matters and that the actual writing of a poem is in a sense a death and a profanation, an arbitrary and brutal limitation of the infinite and ideal world of poetic possibility. In the end is any actual poem as beautiful, or as suggestive, as a pure white page?

I have dealt with this one poem at great length because it seems to me a very handy model, indeed, of what I have called not only the complexity, but the allusiveness and irony, of the typical 'modern' poem. The complexity is obvious; but, as for the allusiveness, I have shown, I hope, that a reader can make no deep sense of this poem unless he is on the look-out for a complex set of allusions to the whole place of Mallarmé and his school in French literary history. And perhaps one must be a poet oneself, and also deeply interested in the history of poetry, to grasp immediately and intuitively that this, to put it crudely, is what the poem is *about*. I cannot see what clues and hints Mallarmé has given to the ordinary reader, other than the use of that facile and common symbol (so unlike the run of his symbols) of the swan for the poet. The irony of the poem lies in the contrast between what it is and what it says. It is a strikingly beautiful poem (the reader will have to take my word for that, about the original, whatever he thinks of my version); in its harmony, its brilliance, its condensation, it seems to embody an ideal of poetic beauty; and yet what it says is that it is impossible for the poet to go on writing the sort of poem it is. The winter images stand at once for an incredible bright beauty and for an atmosphere in which no life can exist. Heaven is hell. The price of the poem's beauty is the poet's death. With Mallarmé, indeed, one can think of symbolism as reaching one of its culminations, and making it necessary for immediately subsequent poets to free their wings from the ice and to find their way back, at whatever cost, to the 'realms of life'. Yet Mallarmé was to have at least two important, fairly direct disciples: Paul Valéry who had known him personally; and Wallace Stevens who adapted the symbolist method to the American temperament and the American version of the English language.

Strangely enough, one of the first results of an attempt by post-symbolist poets to bring art and life together again was not a new simplicity and clarity but a new confusion. Mallarmé is a difficult poet but it is doubtful whether he can properly be called an obscure one; the difficulty of working out the meaning of such a poem as that which we have just examined is like that of solving a complicated set of equations; the symbols of symbolist poetry, like those of mathematics, offer us a severe coherence of pattern held at some distance from life.

With Rimbaud, on the other hand, who may be taken as one of the main precursors of post-symbolist poetry, obscurity is intrinsic. For Rimbaud, unlike Mallarmé, does not know, or want to know, quite what he is doing. He speaks in a trance like an inspired drunkard:

Ladies strolling on terraces by the sea; little girls and giant-esses, superb negresses in the verdigris moss, jewels standing on the rich soil of the groves and the little thawed gardens – young mothers and older sisters with their eyes full of pilgrimages, Sultanas, princesses with tyrannical costumes and carriage, little foreign girls and gently unhappy people.

What a bore, the moment of the 'beloved body' and 'dear heart'! *

Or:

I became a fabulous opera: I saw that all beings are fated to happiness: action is not life, but a way of wasting some force, an enervation. Morality is the weakness of the brain.

To every being, several *other* lives seem to me to be due. This gentleman does not know what he is doing: he is an angel. This family is a pack of dogs. In front of several men, I conversed aloud with a moment out of one of their other lives – Thus, I have loved a pig.†

Rimbaud plunges poetry into life, and life into poetry once more, but at the cost of introducing into both a new element of bewildering disorder. Mallarmé led a life of sedate respectability. Rimbaud's life, during his short, dazzling period of creative activity, was one of drunkenness and vice, accompanied, moreover, by a savage and brutal violence of manner, a coarseness of language, which estranged from him all the older men of letters, except the infatuated Verlaine, who might otherwise have wanted to help him. Yet it would be wrong to think of Rimbaud as simply a genius who happened to be a moral imbecile. He was, rather, a

* *Rimbaud* (Penguin Poets), p. 236. † ibid, p. 334.

young man of sturdy peasant physique, of excellent intelligence (the best classical scholar in his country school), and of strong will who deliberately set out to dislocate the normal patterns of life, as Mallarmé had dislocated the normal patterns of language. The 'magical' world of poetry was, for Mallarmé, something that offered an escape from the drab emptiness of actual existence; but why, Rimbaud asked himself, should not the 'magic' be projected back on to existence, why should only poems, and not life, be 'poetical'? Why should one compromise ever with the prose world?

Rimbaud's excesses, then, were pursued not so much for their own sake, or for the sake of some delusive abstraction like 'pleasure', as for the sake of an attempt at transformation and possession – an attempt to transform the matter of life into something magical, and to possess at every moment the feeling of tense, bewildering exaltation which belongs to a poet who has completed a successful poem. Rimbaud would make no compromise with the outer world at all; in his writing, he did not start off from perceptions, but from self-induced hallucinations, from a state of delirium in which everything heard or seen is systematically misinterpreted according to a momentary obsession. Through wallowing in excess and flirting with madness, he hoped to make himself a visionary, to reach a certain primal innocence of poetic awareness; even at the cost of moral suicide. If we try to make life more intense by steadily increasing the dose of some stimulant, we either kill ourselves or, if we are too strong for that, end in apathy. Rimbaud was too strong and he ended in apathy. Unable to transform the real world permanently and successfully into the world of poetry, he deserted poetry, became a merchant and explorer in the Sudan and Ethiopia, made many friends there by his kindness, courage, and honesty, wore himself out with his exertions, and died, finally, back in France, in great pain, reconciled perhaps on his death-bed to the Roman Catholic Church. Behind some of his rebelliousness there lay the social resentment of the peasant boy of genius, the fury of adolescent sexuality revolting against Catholic morality, and a bitter mixture of love and hate for his stern mother. But the achievement and the personality are much more interesting than reductive explanations of them.

Rimbaud, at least, whatever the reasons, is the poet as rebel; not only against political or religious order and social conditions but also against the very nature of human life. He helped to inspire the atheistic French Surrealist movement which, as its name suggests, seeks to transcend and destroy everyday reality; on the other hand, he very much influenced the notable Catholic poet, Paul Claudel, who called him 'a mystic in the wild state'. Claudel said that Surrealism (see page 324 for a fuller account of Surrealism) was a mere mask for pederasty; and the Surrealists, who hated Claudel for being a Catholic and an Ambassador, would have been insulted by the suggestion that they had anything in common with him, but perhaps they had this, that they both sought to use words not merely to *record* existence but to key it up, for themselves and their readers, to a new pitch; they sought not merely to engage the reader's attention but to alter his life. By the power and richness of their language they hoped to overpower the reader, to drag him into their nets; it is a doctrine and a way of life and a means of persuasion that mattered with them, not, as with Mallarmé and Valéry and Wallace Stevens, the poem. Thus it is almost hopeless to ask, as we have been asking with Mallarmé, what Rimbaud *means* by his poems: the answer might be something like Hamlet's to Ophelia: 'Marry, this is miching mallecho, it means mischief.' If to understand Mallarmé, we have to know the literary theories of his school, to understand Rimbaud we have to know every detail of his personal history; and the whole bulk of his poems can be taken as a single design, a fantasticated autobiography, except that it is the fantasy, not the autobiography, that matters. Facts, what we call facts, are for this kind of poet nothing in themselves, they are merely a point of departure for imaginative transformations. Similarly, critics sometimes discuss whether Surrealist texts of automatic writing, for instance, are 'meaningless'; and it can be pointed out that they have at least a clinical meaning, that they would give an analyst many clues to the writer's obsessions, convictions, and general state of mind; but this clinical meaning is not what interests the Surrealists themselves – what interests them is the delirium, richness, confusion, and terror of experience which the writing and reading of such texts (if one does not find them merely tedious) can evoke.

Such 'mad' poets might claim that their 'madness' is a state which gives them deeper insight into reality than what is generally called 'sanity' does. In England and in the United States, poets are less likely to go all the way with a theory than in France: but an American poet like Hart Crane, with his dizzying use of language, in which the strict meaning of the sentences is irrelevant and everything depends upon the emotional associations of words and phrases, is in Rimbaud's tradition. And so are the Welshman, Dylan Thomas, with his puzzling dream-like 'literalness', and the Scottish poet, W. S. Graham, whose thorny personal syntax supports his recurrent obsession with the sea,

> Very end then of land. What vast is here?
> The drowning saving while, the threshold sea
> Always is here. You may not move away,

The image of the sea tends to play an important part, in fact, in all poems in this tradition. The land is the surface on which we walk, as we think, safely – it is the waking conscious mind; the sea with its greater depth, in which we can drown under huge pressures and suffer unimaginable terrors, is the mind of sleep, as full of disturbing apparitions as the sea is full of strange fish. We may not 'move away' from the sea, in the sense that we must go to sleep every night and descend into the primitive part of ourselves. The preconscious and unconscious part is the larger part of the psyche, just as the real sea covers so much a greater part of the globe's surface than the emergent patches of dry land. It is a part of which we feel a terror (the idea of losing consciousness, of being lost in the world of sleep and dreams for ever, is like the fear of hell); it is also a part for which we feel a certain wistfulness, a homing desire, for it was from the sea after all that life first came – and it is from the submerged parts of the psyche that there come all the desires and impulses that move us, and that we strive to prove rational, in the waking world. Poets like Rimbaud should be thought of as the first explorers of this fatal ocean, at least in terms of poetic art.

One most notable cause of obscurity in modern poetry is, thus, this submergence of the poet in a sea in which he can no more account for his presence, his actions, or his sufferings than any dreaming or drowning man. Yet poetry at the conscious level – at the level of what T. S. Eliot, in his essay on Dante, has called the 'high dream' as opposed to the 'low dream' – has its own obscurities, too. The poems of Eliot and Pound avoid that split between art and life which led the Symbolists on the one hand, and Rimbaud's followers on the other, into so many blind alleys. The idea of the work of pure art in abstraction from life is, as we have seen, and as Mallarmé saw, a finally sterile one; so is the idea of the utmost possible impurity, of vitality at all costs, for if many Surrealist texts are 'vital documents' in some sense – vital witnesses to the agony and incoherence of our time – few are or would even claim to be 'poems'. Once the idea of a continued transformation of life into art, and of art into life, has been accepted from Rimbaud (as the Surrealists on the whole accepted it) as a mechanical formula, the quality of both art and life suffers; art turns to cheap tricks of surprise, life to silly poses; and the final home of Surrealistic juxtaposition of image is in smart shop-windows and advertisements in the *New Yorker*.

Faced with the distance from each other of art and life in their time, Eliot and Pound, like many Americans, were interested in the larger reconciling idea of 'culture' or of 'the tradition'; for it is, after all, within the framework of the 'culture' of a human society that both life and art impact on each other. Unless the 'culture' is of a fairly high quality, both life and art will be at a low ebb; conversely, we think

of periods of 'high culture' as producing noble lives as well
as noble art. But what exactly do we mean by this difficult
word? In its modern sense, it dates from the late eighteenth
century, but its modern sense is metaphorical. Dr Johnson,
thinking of its literal sense, objected to the phrase 'the cul-
tured fields' where the more correct phrase, formed from a
verb instead of a noun, would be the 'cultivated fields'.
When we talk of the cultivation of the fields, we mean that
there is a good soil, we plough it, we sow it with what seeds
we choose, we keep it free of weeds, we reap the harvest; we
keep the ground in good condition, and plant again, perhaps
with a different crop. As applied to the human mind, culture
carries metaphorically the idea of our mental capacities as
the soil, the rudiments of various kinds of knowledge as the
seed, our wills and our powers of self-discipline as the farm-
ers. Culture is thus something cared for, and a product of
the mind's spontaneous powers of growth. The word tends,
often, however, to be used with particular reference to the
cultivation of knowledge and taste in literature and the fine
arts; wrongly perhaps we do not think of science or politics
or technology as being a part of culture, in the central sense.
The idea of culture can also imply the possession of fine
manners, just as a number of romance languages, French,
Italian, Spanish, for instance, use the words (or their equivalents) 'educated' and 'uneducated' to imply the possession, or
lack, of gentlemanly manners. But the word culture is also
used in a wider sense, by social anthropologists and sociolo-
gists, to mean all the customs, manners, habits of a nation,
a tribe, or a social class, whether or not these customs, manners, and habits issue in anything that we could call literary
form; and, of course, in any society literary and artistic work
is a product of culture in this wider sociological sense. For
cultivated Americans, Europe as a whole is the ancestor of
their own culture, in the wide as well as the narrow sense;
and they are therefore sometimes able to see the European
scene, the European 'tradition', in a broader perspective than
the European himself can, with his sharp and often bitter
sense of national differences. The obscurity, at any rate, of

Pound and Eliot comes not from any use of the unconscious dream material I have been talking about, but from the bewildering range of their literary-cultural allusions. This range assumes in the ordinary reader a knowledge of languages and literatures which he often does not possess.

In Eliot's later poems, the embedding of fragments from other writers whole into his work has become less obtrusive, but in Pound's later *Cantos* it has become more so: Chinese characters alternate with passages from Greek, Latin, and the romance languages. This display of learning is sometimes irritating (more so in Pound than in Eliot) but it should not be dismissed as mere ostentation: it enables the poet to achieve certain effects of irony. Thus, when Eliot writes in *The Waste Land*,

> But at my back from time to time I hear
> The sound of horns and motors, which shall bring
> Sweeney to Mrs Porter in the spring.
> O the moon shone bright on Mrs Porter
> And on her daughter
> They wash their feet in soda water,

we are to think both of Marvell's famous

> But at my back I always hear
> Time's wingèd chariot hurrying near;
> And yonder all before us lie
> Deserts of vast eternity,

and of the less known poem which Eliot cites in his notes, Day's *Parliament of Bees*:

> When of the sudden, listening, you shall hear,
> A noise of horns and hunting, which shall bring
> Actaeon to Diana in the spring,
> Where all shall see her naked skin. . . .

and therefore we are to contrast Marvell's grave seducer, for whom the thought of death and judgement gives a finer edge to passion with the simple hunter Actaeon who will be torn to pieces by the hounds for his presumption. And we are to set against both these passages the slack immunity

with which Sweeney (we have to know about Sweeney from
other poems by Mr Eliot himself), the modern unheroic
equivalent of Marvell and Actaeon, the lustful and drunken
haunter of low oblivious dives, pursues *his* sordid 'love-life':
Sweeney lacks both Marvell's sense of sin and Actaeon's
sense of nemesis, and therefore he has no bright awareness
of beauty ... the lines from a probably bawdy modern
Australian folk-song,

> O the moon shone bright on Mrs Porter
> And on her daughter
> They wash their feet in soda water,

mock his banal idea of 'glamour' (more complicatedly, with
their mocking gusto, they mock *back* at Marvell's and Day's
idea of the goddess-woman, also). So there is not a line in
this passage which has not been either borrowed by Mr
Eliot or suggested to him by another poet's line and adapted;
and yet the passage is very distinctively his own. And this
use of allusion and concealed quotation enables him to set
the present and past in perspective; and to exhibit ironically
a decay of past standards, of courtliness and seriousness and
awe, in some of our coarser modern attitudes to sex. We
have now seen that poetry of any age which strikes us as
having a specifically 'modern' ring about it possesses certain
qualities, and when we know something about the poet's
relation to his age and the special problems that preoccupied
him, we find 'difficult' poetry less difficult. I think much
modern poetry *is* very difficult, and that it does not always
repay the labour of working it out. There are times when we
turn with relief to poetry that is *not* modern. Simplicity
and clarity are perennially refreshing. Difficulty, however,
has its proper place in literature; our world, and our place
in it, are increasingly hard to understand and the sense of
that difficulty has been increasing for more than a hundred
years. A false, or affected, simplicity is a detestable thing.

4

'Modernity' in the Drama

THIS chapter will be longer than the preceding chapters, even though I am leaving the revival of verse drama to be considered later in the book. I will consider the influence of European and American writers on recent English drama. Yet perhaps this chapter ought to be a short one. Any play is 'modern' if it can still hold the stage. Old poems and old novels can still be kept savoury for a scholarly palate in pickle jars. But a play is either fresh or rotten. It has no in-between state. It either retains the potential stage life it started with or it is dead. Great poets, like Shakespeare and Racine, polished and witty writers of prose and verse like Molière, Congreve, Shaw, have been notable dramatists. But a play can be a great play and yet not, in the ordinary sense of the word, literature. In William Archer's stilted translations, Ibsen's plays, for instance, make very tedious reading; the stiff language makes us too much aware of the machinery of construction and the planting of key speeches or episodes; yet they come alive on the stage. A good modern dramatist makes use of pauses, silences, stage grouping, sudden transitions from one mood to another, which, to a reader unfamiliar with the theatre, convey nothing on the page. Samuel Beckett is a notable man of letters, a master of language; yet it is necessary to have *seen* a performance of *Waiting for Godot* in order to enjoy the text, with all its repetitions, and its apparent lack of development. The development of drama, therefore, is not strictly a *literary* development. It is also true, in spite of occasional experimentalists like Brecht or Ionesco, Beckett or Pinter, that dramatists, compared to novelists and poets, tend to be conservative about form. There is nothing, for instance, in John Osborne's most famous play, *Look Back in Anger*, which would have seemed technically impossible to Bernard Shaw in the 1890s. And Chehov's best plays of fifty to sixty years ago, like Ibsen's best plays of seventy to eighty years ago, do not seem to us, when we see them well performed, the least old-fashioned.

It is true that neither Ibsen nor Chehov any longer appear to us, as they may have done to their contemporaries, strictly 'naturalistic'. I have seen a performance of *The Cherry Orchard* by undergraduates, in which an excessive emphasis on some of the technical mannerisms of Chehov, combined with an immature response to his deeper emotions, turned that melancholy and profound tragi-comedy into near farce. Chehov's technical invention of not letting his characters directly answer each other but making them, instead, carry on vague soliloquies which they allow others to interrupt is just as much an 'artificial' convention as the unremitting exchange of repartee in Congreve or Wycherley; it is intended to underline the isolation of individuals, just as the opposite convention asserts the cohesion of a society or the common tone of a clique. Chehov's convention is very true to the way in which self-absorbed and absent-minded people talk; but Chehov's characters can become, in the hands of all but the most skilful actors, mere 'humours'. Ibsen's middle-class Scandinavian backgrounds have for us – and had even for his non-Scandinavian contemporaries – an irrelevant appeal of grotesque local colour; and his use of almost Thurberish physical properties, like the wild duck in the attic, as symbolic centres for his plays is disturbing just because our sense of the poetic abrades grittily our sense of the absurd. Both Chehov and Ibsen sometimes seem, but only seem, to be leading us into fantasy worlds. There is a thin naturalistic surface; fantasy lies close underneath; but the profoundest human grasp is to be sought deeper still. In this, Ibsen and Chehov might be compared to Dostoyevsky. That novelist likes to give his narrations and conversations a surface air of the humdrum and the matter-of-fact; just under that surface there is wild farce and melodrama; deeper still there is tragic wisdom. It might be said that one great achievement of 'naturalism' (as a convention rather than a programme) both in plays and in novels of the nineteenth century was to make the tragic impact, the deep perception, possible once more, by rescuing them from the languid embraces of an outwardly lofty style. But the 'non-literary' approach can today itself be recognized as just another, though more cunning and inclusive, literary convention.

A play in a non-literary convention can include bits of 'literature', thus making perceptive members of the audience aware of its own art. A good example is the fragment of Trepilov's experimental play in the first act of *The Seagull* – Trepilov says, 'We don't have to depict life as it is, or as it ought to be, but as we see it in our dreams' – counterpointed by Trigorin's bitter account of the life of a real writer in the second act: 'I look over there and see a cloud shaped like a grand piano. ... At once I think I must put into some story or other – the fact that a cloud shaped like a grand piano floated by.' Hamlet's address to the players and the archaic language of the First Player's speech about Hecuba similarly had the purpose of making the conventions of Jacobean acting, and Hamlet's own language in his blank verse speeches, seem relatively 'natural'.

Chehov and Ibsen, then, were brilliant innovators; but, until quite recently, it could be said that their successors – though these included men of great gifts, like Shaw – had simply taken over their inventions, without adding to them and without even making the fullest possible use of them. Shaw certainly differed from Chehov and Ibsen in the wide use he made of the drama to air his view on current topics; so much so that Robert Graves considers him not as a dramatist in the proper sense, but rather a writer of satirical dialogues like Lucian, a 'philosopher turned demagogue'; for the fine scene, for instance, between Don Juan and the Devil in *Man and Superman* is rarely performed, though for the reader it is the most exciting part. It is not acted, because it contributes nothing to the action; and, after all, it is the action of a play that is properly dramatic.

On the other hand, if what Shaw adds to Ibsen or Chehov

is not properly dramatic, something that he fails to take over from them is. He took over from Ibsen the idea that real, serious, and uncomfortable problems of contemporary life could be handled on the stage; and, in *Heartbreak House*, he took advantage of Chehov's trick of making characters sometimes fail to answer each other properly but instead use what they say to project their own continuing preoccupations. (And this, after all, was not wholly new: there is something like it in Ben Jonson's comedy of humours.) What Shaw failed, however, to take over from Ibsen and Chehov was their ability to use symbols – the shot sea-gull, the primeval forest, the cherry orchard that has to be sold, the wild duck in the attic – to give their plays, under the prose surface, the third dimension of poetry. Such symbols stand for an aspect of a situation that cannot be explicit, that the characters themselves are not *consciously* aware of, but Shaw always feels that every situation can be made explicit, that at least those characters who are his spokesmen can be aware of everything, and therefore poetry escapes him. The history of English prose drama till about 1955, when there was a kind of problematic renaissance, is mainly one of the exhaustion of Shaw's original inspiration. It was exhaustible because of that lack of poetic depth, though there were attempts to tap the roots of poetry elsewhere – Synge sought them in Irish peasant life, Sean O'Casey in the Dublin slums. But English life, though it lends itself to verse drama like Mr T. S. Eliot's, does not seem to lend itself to poetry in that deeply human sense.

Shaw's successors in his own or a broadly similar vein have a closer feeling for everyday atmospheres, and a warmer feeling for human nature, but they are lesser men, and they too lack poetic vision. Galsworthy and J. B. Priestley are Shaw without his wit, James Bridie is Shaw without his power of coherent thought. Sean O'Casey, in his early plays of Dublin life, was perhaps the only twentieth-century dramatist writing in English, who turned afresh to Ibsen and Chehov to learn their lesson of 'poetic realism'; but since, after *The Silver Tassie*, he jettisoned realism for a kind of German expressionism and a conscious heightening of his language into an inflated 'prose poetry', his great talent has become crippled. A fierce propagandist intention paradoxically makes his later plays less effective in making one think seriously about politics than *The Plough and the Stars*, which infuriated Dublin audiences by its objectivity. The Irishman who settles abroad often finds himself exaggerating and finally unconsciously guying his own national characteristics. He becomes a stage Irishman. This may have happened to O'Casey. Or he may have been crippled, after a certain stage in his development, by being dubbed not a 'straight' but an 'experimental' dramatist.

The novelist and the poet can experiment as they please. If they have any talent, they are sure to find some small publisher who may not gain money from them, but will not lose much either, and they may add to the reputation of his firm. But the dramatist requires a theatre, and somebody willing to risk paying the rent of that theatre and the salaries of the actors and the general cost of the production. So the dramatist cannot, as the novelist and the poet can, give the public twenty or thirty years to catch up with him: he must, however original his views, be ready to compromise with the conservative tastes of the 'big theatre' audience and the even more conservative standards of 'big theatre actors' and producers. That is one reason why the history of drama is so different, not only in England but I think in most European countries, from the history of any other kind of literature. Periods of excellence in drama tend to be short and to peter out: and, after such a lapse, it is hard to get the drama on its feet again. Once a dramatic tradition is firmly established, new dramatists imitate the work of established elder dramatists. The plays of Beaumont and Fletcher, for instance, are full of imitations of Shakespeare, which is why T. S. Eliot has compared them to cut flowers stuck in a glass. They mark the decadence of the Jacobean drama.

What seems natural and 'realistic' dialogue to actors is *not* dialogue which catches the tones of contemporary speech (as Harold Pinter's does) but dialogue that reminds them of what they are used to speaking and hearing on the boards. This applies not only to dialogue but also to atmosphere and properties. There flourished in the 1920s and the 1930s, and there still survives today, a mild sentimental comedy set in a spacious living-room with french windows, with the curtain rising on a comic servant dusting. The cast of characters includes a fluttery matron, a young man in tennis flannels, and so on, none of whom seems to have to work for a living. In fact the middle-class English audiences that enjoyed these plays immediately after the Second World War were suffering from a housing shortage, rationing, and lack of servants. The scene which is accepted bears no relation to the scene lived in. The same audience today has been taught, by writers like John Osborne, Arnold Wesker, and Harold Pinter, to enjoy a stage setting and atmosphere equally foreign to its own way of life: untidy cluttered rooms, Cockney or rustic accents, protests, quarrels, tramps, oratory, rage, despair. The kitchen sink, like the french window, becomes a glamour-symbol of a possibly authentic mode of life from which the audience feel themselves shut out. We should beware of assuming that audiences ever really want a reflection of their own lives.

Because actors and dramatists are such imitators and audiences such creatures of habit, drama in England is constantly coming to a dead halt. Then there is usually a long interval before drama begins to flourish again. Once the Restoration impulse had petered out around 1700, there were no English plays with literary and theatrical value (apart from Goldsmith's and Sheridan's comedies) till the 1890s. The Victorian age, a great period in English life and literature, contributed nothing at all to the theatre until the last decade. And in this century we have been living on a double impulse, a brisk push, given by Wilde and Shaw – the one to the comedy of pure entertainment, the other to the comedy of ideas – until the theatrical revolution of 1955. The verse plays of Yeats, T. S. Eliot, and Christopher Fry have aroused critical interest, and those of the latter two have had considerable public success, but they have not changed our general picture of the theatre. In spite of Shaw and Wilde and Synge and O'Casey, four Irishmen of genius, the history of the drama since about 1890 in the British Isles makes a thin show compared to the history of poetry or the novel.

If we look abroad, we find another picture. Although both novels and poems by young English writers in the 1950s had a certain insularity of mood, the breakthrough in the theatre would not have been possible without foreign influence. Particularly the influence of such European plays and dramatic ideas as Bertold Brecht's concept of the epic theatre and his much-discussed device of audience-alienation; and of the theatre of the absurd, centred in France, whose most distinguished representatives are an Irishman, Samuel Beckett, and a Rumanian, Eugène Ionesco. What post-1955 English dramatists have contributed on their own is a special and local note of social protest and sometimes, for instance in the plays of Harold Pinter, Shelagh Delaney, or Brendan Behan, a non-literary concept of stage dialogue. It is in the theatre, more than in any other branch of literature, that recent English writers have been breaking through to new concepts of purpose and form, and to a new audience.

In the English provinces there has always been a distrust of the theatre, distrust which reflects the English puritan tradition, the closing down of the theatres during the Commonwealth, and perhaps a vague folk memory of the licentiousness of Restoration drama. London audiences, on the other hand, consist of the keen Shakespeare enthusiasts who used to support the Old Vic; a small core of those who like to see Congreve, Wycherley, Farquhar, or Sheridan revived with good settings and actors; and what might be called an Esther McCracken-Dodie Smith-Terence Rattigan audience. But since 1956, the Royal Court Theatre in Sloane Square, Chelsea, has staged plays that would previously have been turned down by West End managements as box-office poison, and has made its financial successes out of some of the most controversial of these plays, such as John Osborne's *Look Back in Anger*. At the Theatre Royal, Stratford, East London, in a working-class district with no solid theatre-going tradition, Miss Joan Littlewood founded, and kept going with tremendous drive and energy, a group called Theatre Workshop. She took risks, which again proved to be financially justified, with unknown working-class dramatists like Shelagh Delaney. All this has brought about a change of fashion: the West End audience that can welcome *Waiting for Godot, The Caretaker, The Rhinoceros, Luther* is not quite the middlebrow audience it once was. At the same time, in the English provinces, dedicated groups like Theatre in the Round, the Century Theatre (four great caravans opening out in a small theatre on wheels), or the Living Theatre, acting in a disused church hall in Leicester, have been making a valiant assault on puritan dislike and philistine indifference. Coventry and Nottingham have their own theatres, Coventry has seen the first performance of some of Arnold Wesker's plays and Nottingham of John Osborne's *Luther*.

There are some obvious reasons for the crusading zeal which one finds today in young dramatists and actors, but not in young novelists and poets. It is not ridiculous – in fact, it touches the roots of drama – to say that going to the theatre is in some ways like going to church. It affords an experience of communal participation and corporate membership which is becoming rare. In England today, church membership is declining and people no longer excitedly attend political meetings; at elections, candidates and their helpers spend more energy in door-to-door canvassing than in making speeches. The public-house is not the social centre that it used to be. In an increasingly prosperous community the men tend to stay at home and find hobbies about the house and garden rather than go out to meet each other. There are good things on television, but it does tend to encourage passive or indiscriminate receptivity. The theatre, on the other hand, can awaken in us a sense of belonging, of emotional involvement. To be part of a really receptive audience is to escape from the narrow prison of the self. And the theatre, as Brecht (with Shaw, of course, behind him) has shown, can force us to think as well as feel. The emotional disease of England in the 1950s was apathy; the theatre used a variety of shock tactics, very courageously, to combat that disease.

Having said this one must add (though my detailed estimates of recent English plays will come later, in the general chapter on drama) that it is much more difficult to arrive at provisional estimates of the permanent value of recent plays than it is to arrive at such an estimate of any other kind of literature. It might be helpful, however, as a very general remark in this introductory chapter, to say that very few notable plays of the 1950s fall into the traditional categories of either comedy or tragedy.

Aristotle said that the roots of tragedy are the same as the roots of panegyric, the roots of comedy the same as those of flyting.* Classical tragedy concerns those often nobler than ourselves who make some error, usually an intellectual rather than a moral blunder – though they are not perfect people – which draws upon them a seemingly excessive retribution. We feel pity for the hero in his growing isolation and helplessness, fear for a fate that might be our own; there is always a certain tension or unbalance of latent pity and fear in the human psyche and Aristotle thought that we come out of the theatre, after seeing a tragedy, with our pity and fear in a more relaxed and balanced state. (When he talked of tragedy as purging us, he was not thinking of pity and fear as unwholesome waste matter, or of tragedy as castor oil; the metaphor was more from adjusting medicines or procedures, like tonics, sedatives, and blood-letting.) Classical comedy, on the other hand, presents characters to whom we feel rather superior; they are sillier or naughtier than we are, and the comic writer's sharp treatment of them should enable us to correct our own follies and minor vices. There is also romantic and sympathetic comedy, like Shakespeare's, which is partly concerned with painting an ideal picture of

* *Flyting*: a word used by late medieval Scottish poets for a personally directed, comically insulting poem. There is no equivalent word in Standard English. An equivalent phrase might be 'Comic Invective'.

a happy life and partly with assuring our indulgence for the more harmless kinds of naughtiness and folly. And there is again, in Shakespeare, the mixture or alternation of the comic and tragic modes, which is not classical but is, as Dr Johnson said, like life. Much traditional 'naturalistic' or 'realistic' drama, the plays of Ibsen and Chehov, for instance, has been traditional tragedy or tragi-comedy in disguise, but with a growingly uneasy questioning of just how valid are conventional standards of morality (whose validity all the traditional modes, or nearly all of them, imply).

But there is another important mode of drama: the mode, for instance, of medieval mystery and morality plays. In such plays, if they deal with Biblical history, there is no suspense, for the story is known already; and if they deal, like the morality plays, with personified virtues and vices, there is no special sense of personal involvement on both sides, for of course we approve of virtue and disapprove of vice. It might be said that where the primary purpose of both classical and Shakespearian tragedy and comedy is to delight and move us, the primary purpose of mystery and morality plays is to instruct and edify. The great German dramatist, Bertold Brecht, was a kind of neo-medievalist. His plays are either, like *Mother Courage* and *Galileo*, chronicles or, like *The Good Woman of Setzuan*, quite straightforward moralities. Brecht's theories about what a play should be altered during his working life, but one central idea was that of the alienation-effect; the idea of destroying stage illusion, rejecting the audience's impulse to identify itself with some of the characters on the stage, in order to make the audience think.

In Brecht, there are no heroes; nobody transcends his social condition; or if an individual does display unusual virtue, that virtue, often, in a bad society, has bad effects. For as a Communist, no 'I' could be hero, the only possible hero is the collective 'we'. In Brecht's plays, bad men often make penetrating moral remarks; sympathetic characters are often forced by circumstances to behave badly; purely private beliefs have little or no effect on public action, and a

Pope who is interested in science and an admirer of Galileo is forced, in his social role, to threaten Galileo with torture. Italian businessmen, on the other hand, back Galileo not because they have a disinterested love of science but because they glimpse, in his thinking, the seeds of the industrial revolution. Galileo himself is a man who has a special gift and who has some ordinary human courage; he takes a risk in smuggling out scientific papers, even when he is in the Inquisition's house-custody. Yet Galileo is more like a coward than a hero, even if he is a sensible coward. He knows that, once set on its way, science does not need martyrdoms to advance it; once men have learned the art of mathematical thinking, science becomes an impersonal and inevitable process. What one scientist is prevented from finding out, another scientist will discover. At the same time, Brecht's Galileo is either a prudent hypocrite, writing pious and flattering letters to churchmen, or he combines great scientific gifts with a remnant, as Brecht himself would see it, of muddled superstition. And as a person, at the end of the play, Galileo is selfish and unpleasant: he callously exploits the devotion of a daughter whose simple faith he despises though he dare not mock it, and finds his main surviving pleasure in life in solitary gluttony. Brecht forces us to ask ourselves whether we should even idealize the scientific era of which this very imperfect man was one of the main founders. It will bring a great deal of misery in its train. Might not the churchmen who feared it have had some social insight?

Brecht's *Galileo*, then, is neither a tragedy nor a comedy. We do not feel that Galileo is a character grander than ourselves, who makes one fatal intellectual or moral blunder; we do not feel, either, that he is a figure of comedy, whom we are in a position to despise. We are left reflecting that the individual man can, in some degree, protect himself against social forces that are out to crush him, but only if he is willing up to a point to appease these forces; and also only if there are other social forces (the Italian merchants, in Brecht's play) which are, secretly or openly, supporting

him. We are left reflecting also, perhaps, that the sort of
man Galileo was hardly mattered at all. What he and his
work meant for others mattered enormously: the public
image may be more lastingly important, and even in a historical sense more 'true', than the private character. Among
recent dramatists, John Osborne owes a lot to Brecht in his
play *Luther*. There are Brechtian touches also in *The Entertainer*.

But though Brecht has been much talked about, his actual
influence on the contemporary English theatre has been exaggerated. Brecht's theatre is essentially rationalist. It assumes that men have solid motives for their acts, even if
these motives are usually grounded in individual selfishness
or class interests. (Love or charity where it occurs in a
Brecht play, as in the character of Galileo's daughter, is
usually treated as a kind of amiable idiocy.) It assumes that
morality is empty talk at least till empty bellies have been
filled, and that excessively idealistic moral behaviour may
often be socially inexpedient; but it does also assume that
there are certain moral qualities which all men admire or
find sympathetic, even if they exploit the persons who display these qualities. Brecht's theatre is also, like Shaw's,
extremely intellectual. Brecht's basic theatrical postulate is
that rational communication, however dangerous, is possible.

There is, however, also an important non-intellectual contemporary theatre; this has sometimes been described as the
theatre of the absurd, or the theatre of non-communication.
The most famous and influential play of this school, performed in England in the last decade, is Samuel Beckett's
Waiting for Godot. An Irishman, a friend, and in some degree a disciple of James Joyce, Beckett writes his novels and
plays more often in French than in English. His plays embody very personal memories and obsessions but also preach
or symbolize Christian nihilism, which is the pattern left in
the mind when Christian beliefs that were very important
in childhood have been bitterly rejected and blasphemed
against. *Waiting for Godot*, though it puzzled critics very
much on its first showing at the Arts Theatre in London in

1955, is now so well known, and has been so widely discussed, that one need not deal with it in quite the same detail as *Galileo*.

The heroes of *Waiting for Godot* are two tramps, Didi and Gogo, or Vladimir and Estragon, who compare themselves to the two thieves who were crucified beside Christ, and who are uneasily and unhappily attached to each other. Gogo, who is unintellectual, is always being beaten up, never remembers things, and worries about eating, may stand for the body, and Didi, an intellectual worrier, for the soul. They are waiting for help at an indefinite place from a local landlord (who never appears) called Godot. There is perhaps an allusion in the title, in English, to Clifford Odets' one-act play of the 1930s, *Waiting for Lefty*. Lefty in that play is a trade-union organizer who does not turn up at a meeting because he has been murdered. Odets' name might have suggested Godot's name which is also obviously a half-comic adaptation of the English word 'ho' and the name 'God' ('God ho'! like 'Right ho'!). Godot sends the same little boy as a messenger or angel at the end of each of the two acts of the play, but at the end of one act he is the angel who guards the sheep (the saved souls) and is beaten (God chastises those whom he loves), and at the end of the other he is the angel who guards the goats (the lost souls, or perhaps the scape-goats) and is not beaten. Didi and Gogo are left at the end still waiting; they want to move away, but since the stage represents the world there is nowhere else to go. There are two other characters, Pozzo, a Master, and Lucky, his Slave. The Master becomes growingly dependent on the Slave and the Slave makes a terrifying speech of which the gist, though it at first sounds like gibberish, is a serious one: not all the discoveries of science or improvements in social comfort can alter the basic fact that man, as an individual animal, pines and wastes and dies. The Master, who has become blind in the second act, is more hopelessly tied than ever to the Slave, who has become dumb. Perhaps Pozzo and Lucky together are a symbol for social man as Didi and Gogo are a symbol for individual identity; or the two pairs may stand for the life of action (Pozzo, though naughty, is in desperate need both of conversation and an audience) and the life of contemplation. The Christian symbolism, of which there is a great deal in the play, indicates, as I have suggested, that for Beckett Christianity is a system that once made sense of the world. Beckett's other plays, though nearly all little masterpieces in their way, have not *Godot*'s universality of interest; they are about loneliness, solitary drinking, sexual guilt towards a Father Figure. The one other play which is in a similar mode to *Godot* is called in English *End-Game*, and contains a famous line about God which perhaps sums up the paradox about Godot: *'Salaud, il n'existe pas!'* ('The dirty dog, he doesn't even exist!') If Beckett is an atheist, his atheism springs from the scar left by a Christian belief once deeply felt, in which one has a grudge against God even for *not* existing. I remember when I saw this play at the Royal Court I was the only person in the audience to laugh at this line; but of course it *is* a funny line, and I am sure Beckett intended it to be, in its childish petulance and logical absurdity. I would call Beckett's plays, in a peculiarly desolating way, religious drama. Perhaps this desolation of the sense of God's absence or of one's wilful childish rejection of him is the only way that religious drama can now exist. Beckett's novels (I have never been able to read more than a few pages of any of them) pile up desolation at more length and to greater heights, in endless images of mud, filth, and tedium.

The other European dramatist who has the closest affinity with Beckett, not in mood but in method, is a Rumanian, who writes in French, Eugène Ionesco. I have been told by an old friend of his, Mrs Carole Grindea, that one of the things that started him writing was the absurdity of the conversations in an old-fashioned English-Rumanian traveller's phrase-book. Ionesco is a much more cheerful writer than Beckett, even if the farcical gaiety of his plays often has strongly sinister overtones. If Beckett's subject is the atheism of a man for whom God could have been a passion, Ionesco's is the willed irrationalism of a man who has never been able to conquer his fatal passion for logic. And if Beckett could be described as anti-humanist, Ionesco is a humanist of the absurd. His most successful play, *The Rhinoceros*, could be taken as a humanistic protest against movements like Fascism and Nazism. The hero (he also appears in another play of Ionesco's) is a good-natured, commonplace clerk, fond of a drink, called Berenger. He has a friend who is always telling him he should be more serious. Gradually, all the characters in the play begin to turn into rhinoceroses. The reaction of another friend of Berenger's to this is one of reasonable compromise. There must be *some* point in it; shouldn't we turn, at least temporarily, into rhinoceroses ourselves, in order to get the rhinoceros's point of view? Berenger's closest friend turns into a rhinoceros before our eyes. His girl friend finally deserts him to join the rhinoceroses; their life obviously is an attractively simple one, of rushing to and fro, roaring, and eating grass. (If Ionesco distrusts logic, he also distrusts the cry of 'back to nature'.) Berenger is left alone and frightened, with no rational reason for clinging to his humanity, but, with desperation and with relief, managing to cling to it all the same. Other plays of Ionesco's have a gloomier or more sadistic note. In *The Lesson* a private tutor asks an adolescent girl pupil increasingly wild and absurd questions, works himself into a rage and her into a panic, and then murders her in a way that represents rape. In *The Chairs*, a couple, elderly caretakers of a dilapidated mansion, arrange chairs for an imaginary lecture which is to reveal the old man's great message to the world, greet imaginary guests, and, their task performed, fling themselves from high windows. On the empty stage the announcer who is to give out the great message starts to read, but what he says is meaningless sound, and the announcer is apparently a deaf-mute; curtain falls. Other Ionesco plays are satires on platitudes and convention, on the ineptness of *bourgeois* life. He has influenced at least two recent English dramatists, N. F. Simpson in his nonsense plays, and Harold Pinter (who also gets something from Beckett) in his drama of imperfect communication.

'Modernity' in the Drama

The influence on recent English plays of the American dramatists Tennessee Williams, Arthur Miller, and Eugene O'Neill is harder to assess. Tennessee Williams is essentially a poetic dramatist in naturalistic disguise, with a taste for extreme and morbid situations, for contrasting, as in Blanche Dubois and her brother-in-law, decadent refinement with brutal virility. John Osborne has expressed, in a review, great admiration for Williams, particularly for his attitude to women, but there is a special 'Southern Gothic', Edgar-Allen-Poe-plus-sex, American local colour in Williams's plays, which is perhaps outside the English temperament. It is a very far cry from the nursery naughtiness of John Osborne's 'bears and squirrels' to the very peculiar goings on, indeed, in Williams's *Suddenly Last Summer.* I myself prefer those plays of Tennessee Williams like *The Glass Menagerie* and *Summer and Smoke* where pity for a trapped refinement – even if it is a slightly false, hysterical, shabby-genteel refinement – is a stronger part of the play than the stress on sub-tropical sexuality.

Arthur Miller's bleaker and more puritanical temperament is closer to some English emotional climates, and John Osborne and Arnold Wesker are also in some of their plays didactic dramatists under a naturalistic mask. However, Miller's protest is primarily political and is concerned with power and freedom, with the basic political decisions which should be made; whereas the didactic content of both Osborne's and Wesker's plays discusses the everyday social attitudes and antagonisms of those with differing social backgrounds, the problems of group and class.

I do not know any English drama which resembles Eugene O'Neill's masterpiece, based on his own unhappy family background, *Long Day's Journey into Night*. This is a drama with no didactic content at all, and no poetic symbolism. It is a study of a family in which the father, a successful actor, who has given up classical drama for the sake of commercial success in repertory, is a miser; the mother, of a higher social class than the father, charming, gentle, and refined, but cut off by her husband's meanness from people of her own kind, has become a drug-addict; one son, an inferior actor in his father's company, is a womanizer and a drunkard; the other son, based on O'Neill himself, is a consumptive and an admirer of decadent poets whom his father, a bigotedly superstitious Irish Catholic of peasant stock, hates. The members of this family are compelled to watch each other, always to say the hurtful thing, and then to apologize, and sooner or later say the hurtful thing again; they are bound to each other by habit, by remorse, by real affection, by mutually inflicted pain. The strength of the play is the compulsively detailed working through of one average day in the life of this family. It seems to me that family life in this sense is not a compulsively gripping theme for English dramatists (Wesker is an exception, but he is dealing with Jewish family life), and also that love and antagonism between sons and a father, and an inadequate father's desperate need of recognition, which are strong cards played again and again in American drama (a good example is Miller's *Death of a Salesman*), take fewer tricks in England. I cannot think of a first-rate English play (except perhaps Peter Shaffer's *Five Finger Exercise*) which is an exploration of the tensions of family life for their own sake.

Eugene O'Neill invented a device by which you not only hear what his characters say, but you also hear what they think; this absolved him from packing a proper amount of implicit meaning into the *heard* dialogue, and was essentially a return to worn-out devices like the 'aside' and the soliloquy. When we criticize dramatists of this century for their failure to experiment, we should notice how disastrous some of their experiments have been.

What the experiments have often done is to make one aware of the real merits of convention, even of ideas which we all learned to jeer at when we were schoolboys, like the unities of time, place, and action. Shaw's *Back to Methuselah*, which takes several nights to see, covers a span of time from the Garden of Eden to the remotest imaginable future, and contains much more talk than action, makes one begin to see the point that a play ideally should present, without digressions or irrelevant episodes, a unified action within a moderate space of time. Whatever pleasure *Back to Methuselah* gives us, it is not a *dramatic* one. Similarly, in Arthur Miller's very moving play, *Death of a Salesman*, we get an application to the drama of the loose, flexible construction of the novel or film scenario: flashbacks, dramatized hallucinations, narrative commentaries, changes of scene made possible by having several sets ready on the stage and lighting up one or the other as it is needed. One can, to be sure, think of illustrious precedents: *Hamlet* proceeds in a dawdling, haphazard way, and in structure is more like a novel than a play. But is properly dramatic pleasure not nearer to the model of Shakespeare's *Othello*, the rich implications that can be drawn out of a tight and strict construction?

To sum up, then, let us repeat that all *great* drama strikes us as essentially modern; but that our own period – leaving aside the 'breakthrough' since 1955, which is too near to us to judge coolly – has not been so notable for plays as for poetry and fiction. In nearly all the plays written in England since about 1890 we are too obtrusively aware of the rapidly dating 'period' quality of the play; aware of its diction, sentiment, and characters as belonging to a particular time and place, and unreal from the point of view of our own environment. When we have this 'period' feeling about a play, we may be sure it is not a great play, or not among the very greatest. We have this feeling, for instance, about Congreve's *Way of the World* if we compare that with Molière's *Le Misanthrope*: Congreve's play is his masterpiece, but it is not a universal masterpiece like *Le Misanthrope*, it is a play of a particular time and place. When we read Beaumont and Fletcher, however much we have enjoyed a facile grace of style and a fertility in the invention of episode, we are never for a moment in doubt that this is something very skilfully and perhaps rather cold-bloodedly confected to hit the taste of a particular audience. We do not have that feeling about Shakespeare, even though in his 'golden comedies' Shakespeare is as unashamedly a mere entertainer as Mr Noël Coward or Mr Terence Rattigan.

When we read Shakespeare, or some of the few genuinely great plays by his contemporaries – to take some of T. S. Eliot's choices, *Volpone*, *The Revenger's Tragedy*, *The Changeling* – we forget about the element of local colour, about how much the moral attitudes, the manners, the ways of speech of the Elizabethans and Jacobeans differed from ours. We are caught up in an intense illusion of reality. This illusion can be more intense even in the mere reading of a great play (let alone seeing it adequately performed) than in the reading of a great novel. It may take a busy man eighteen months to get through *War and Peace*; the book is repeatedly put aside, and taken up again. We read *Macbeth* or *The Wild Duck* or *Three Sisters* at a sitting. Again, when we read a novel we are passive: the novelist, with his descriptions and analysis and moral commentaries, does a great deal of our work for us; he seeks on the whole to distract our attention from the machinery, the moral skeleton, the mere predictable plot of his tale. We do not have to cooperate with him, merely to watch and listen. But a play is all plot, all action, it exposes its machinery nakedly. We cooperate with the dramatist even in reading silently to ourselves. We imagine the scene; we become the characters; we recite the speeches; we are possessed by the passions. We weep for Hecuba, though Hecuba is no relation of ours. Thus the drama at its heights does seem to me the great achievement, in literature, of the human race. In epic or heroic narrative poetry, in the *Iliad* or *The Divine Comedy*, there are always flat passages, and the moments that we remember most vividly, Hector's parting with Andromache, Dante's meeting with Brunetto Latini, Satan's speeches in Hell in *Paradise Lost*, are themselves dramatic. And if one compares, similarly, the greatest plays with even the greatest novels, there is a sense in which the latter often look like loose and extended scenarios for a possible drama (Henry James, who both turned plays into novels, and novels into plays, felt this very strongly). Even in a book that seems at the farthest possible remove from drama, Boswell's *Life of Johnson*, the parts that everybody remembers are the dramatized conversations. Many lyrical or meditative poems seem to have their place ideally in some drama of the poet's life of which only these eloquent fragments have been written. Or many short poems, as Elder Olson has pointed out, are essentially small dramas in themselves, involving only one speaker (though not necessarily only one actor, for God or the poet's mistress may play a silent part). And the drama is our model for all writing when we want to delete those passages, perhaps vividly and charmingly written in themselves, which contribute nothing to the total effect. It gives us our idea of *economy of construction* in literature. Henry James's advice to young novelists is good advice also to young poets or even to young writers of essays on general themes: 'Dramatize, dramatize!' The drama, as a form, has an importance for criticism that stretches far beyond the boundaries of the drama itself.

PART TWO

THE NOVEL

5

Two Ancestors

WE can trace the immediate ancestry of the modern English novel back as far as the 1890s, to the work of two novelists who were at opposite poles in their conception of the novel, its form and function, but who felt a half-reluctant admiration for each other. These two friends were Henry James, then in the full maturity of his powers, and H. G. Wells, then making a brilliant beginning. I have said something already about James's high idea of the novel as an art-form; Wells at his best was a natural artist, but when he tried to think seriously about the novel, he thought of it mainly as a vehicle for popularizing his ideas. In his perky, cock-sparrow *Experiment in Autobiography*, Wells describes a conversation in which James reproached him for his lack of artistic conscience in a novel of his called *Marriage*. In this 'novel of ideas', which was more important to Wells for the ideas discussed in it than for the story or the characters, the hero and heroine at one point disappear into a country lane and emerge three hours later, engaged. Wells gives no hint of what they were saying or doing during these three hours, and this, for James, with his strict view of the rules of the game of novel-writing, was cheating. Wells could not see what James's fuss was about: 'The Novel,' he writes, 'was not necessarily ... this real through and through absolutely true treatment of people more living than life. *It might be more and less than that and still be a novel.*'

The novel could be 'more than that', for Wells, in that it could include long discussions of, and digressions about, current social topics that struck Wells as urgently important; it could be 'less than that' in that these discussions need not be 'through and through absolutely true' nor the 'people more living than' (nor, indeed, as living as) 'life'. Wells, writing a novel of ideas, simply hurried over patches of narrative that did not excite him. Yet all that Wells writes has a certain vitality, that came, as James noted, from the odd way in which, through what may be an ill-constructed and implausible story, Wells conveys his own genuine excitement. 'The ground of the drama,' James wrote to him, 'is somehow most of all the adventure for *you*. . . .'

All life was an adventure for Wells, and even today he conveys the excitement that shapes his personality; a personality bubbling over with hope, eagerness, and impatience; warm and irritable; given to the grandiose gesture but also to humorously puncturing self-mockery. In scientific fantasies from *The Time Machine* to *The Island of Dr Moreau* (Dr Moreau could teach Ian Fleming's Dr No a few nasty tricks), in humorously realistic studies of the frustrations and aspirations of the small man, like *Love and Mr Lewisham* and *Kipps*, in a more broadly farcical treatment of the same sort of material, like *The Adventures of Mr Polly*, Wells was a true artist. He was also, in the field of ideas, a genuinely liberating influence for his own class. For a new reading public, literate rather than educated, but aware of a changing world, and interested in change, was coming to the surface in the 1890s. It was a public which read popular magazines and the brighter and lighter newspapers, and in these, like Conan Doyle and Chesterton, Wells found a platform. His humour also has something in common with the new popular humour of the 1890s, best exemplified in Jerome K. Jerome's *Three Men in a Boat*. But he had ambitions to be a serious social thinker, had an uneasy alliance with the early Fabians, knew Graham Wallas, and was interested in the idea of a science of society. Wells was typical of the young men to whom Oxford and Cambridge meant Latin and Greek, obscurantism and reaction, where London meant science, a cheap education, and no class barriers. Young men like Wells looked to science to transform the world – Wells's youth was the time of the first telephones, gramophones, and automobiles – even the homely bicycle had a certain romance for Wells. Men were dreaming of the possibility of heavier-than-air flying machines; science was going to transform the world; and the art of literature, in comparison to science, was a matter of minor importance. That explains Wells's affectionate but also humorously patronizing air in his autobiography towards men like Stephen Crane, Joseph Conrad, Ford Madox Ford, Henry James, and George Gissing, who took the art of the novel seriously. The novel for Wells was nothing much in itself, it was a vehicle for more important matter; a sugaring of the pill of scientific and social instruction for a large, new, eager audience who could not be expected to read a serious book unless there was 'a story in it'. Wells felt, though he felt this without any real social envy or rancour, that he was speaking for those who had been kept in their 'places' by their 'betters' long enough, and who must now have their own say. Thus he was instinctively hostile to convention, formality, restraint, of any kind, which had helped to keep little men in their 'places'. That explains the odd indifference of this sometimes very fine artist to the notion of art as such: art is based on restraint, formality, convention. Wells's god was science; his wish as a writer was not to produce masterpieces but to be an increasingly effective popularizer of scientific ideas, especially in their relation to social change.

And Wells did achieve his ambition. From the point of view of pure literary criticism, he might be thought to have squandered his gifts. An early fantasy of his like *The Time Machine* is unforgettable; a later 'thoughtful' and 'serious' novel like *The World of William Clissold* is so much dead bulk. But he was, what he wanted to be, a liberator. It is easy to say now that one of the effects of the various emancipations for which he worked all his life has merely been to release untidy emotions from a traditional discipline; to make many people discontented with a necessary subordination in society and a necessary routine; and, in relaxing old codes, to destroy a sense of style. But what we do with our new liberties is never a liberator's fault, and we should always honour liberators. Wells was an artist who often scamped his work, a thinker who often let his emotions lead

75

him astray. What is important is that he sought truth to the best of his abilities and that he loved his fellow-men; and in his hopes and fears, his enthusiasms and errors, he was more genuinely one of them than any other writer of his time. He might have said with one of his heroes, President Theodore Roosevelt: 'I am only an average man, but, by George, I work harder *at* it than the average man!'

The intellectual nourishment which Wells wished the novel to carry in panniers on its flanks, James wished fully digested into its supple body. James writes novels on momentous themes. Though he did not admire Tolstoy, he would have agreed with the earlier Tolstoy's repudiation of the novel of mere social purpose as quoted in Cynthia Asquith's *Married to Tolstoy*:

> The aims of art are not to resolve a question irrefutably, but to compel one to love life in all its manifestations. If I were told that I could write a novel in which I could indisputably establish as true my point of view on all social questions, I would not dedicate two hours to such a work; but if I were told that what I wrote would be read twenty years from now by those who are children today, and that they would weep and laugh over it and fall in love with the life in it, then I would dedicate all my powers to it.

At least, he would have agreed up to a point. James arouses intense intellectual amusement and fine pathos, but he does not make us laugh or weep; he seeks to compel us to love, not the infinite variety of life, but life as fine consciousness and conscience; he is the novelist of privileged beings, the extremely rich, the nobly innocent, the splendidly self-sacrificing, the fine ruthless takers, and the gallant sufferers. His sense of life is a special one; the characters who attract him are artists (he has some very good short stories about writers, and some novels about sculptors and actresses), or artists in living, or young people or children with something of the exposed sensibility of the artist. His characters are often impelled by near fanatical curiosity. He has a special interest in the power that goes with wealth, and the good or evil uses to which it can be put; he seems to have no moral objection to it. There is a wonderful and painful short story about a lower-middle-class bookseller in a seaside town who has jilted a plain young woman to marry a pretty one. He is sued for breach of promise by the plain woman, has to give up his small shop, endures poverty, and becomes a petty clerk. His wife and her child, partly because of his poverty, die. He remains alone, nursing his bitterness. The plain woman has been working in London and has saved several hundred pounds. She comes back to stay in the best hotel in the seaside town, to offer the clerk her love and her money, or, if he will not take her love, her money at least. She judges, rightly, that his bitterness will never be able to stand out against the money, and against the idea that the money has been saved up from the moment she heard of the wife's death and felt remorse for him.

James is one of the most 'intellectual' of novelists, but not, in Wells's sense, a novelist of 'ideas'. 'Ideas' in abstraction mean nothing to him; what interests him is how, out of the proper handling and grasping of a 'story' there rises, in both writer and reader, an awareness of the grand theme, 'the pattern in the carpet'. Unlike Wells, James prefers extreme to typical situations.

In *What Maisie Knew* James takes the basically improbable situation of a young child whose parents are divorced, whose mother and stepfather then part, and whose stepfather falls in love with the girl's governess in the father's ménage. The stepfather is everything the girl adores, but obscurely she realizes that she cannot live with him and his mistress, because the mistress's affection for her is largely assumed for the stepfather's sake. In the end, Maisie chooses to remain in the care and the custody of the plain, snuffly, uneducated, but strictly moral Mrs Wix, her other governess. She has made nothing properly articulate to herself, but she comes down on the side of plain, simple morality (not of affection, for the stepfather is devoted to her, and will give up anything for her but his mistress, to whom he is now bound more by obligation and gentlemanly feelings than by love). The conflict of glamour and morality is a favourite theme of James's, Europe standing for a rather corrupt or slightly vulgar glamour, America for an integrity and innocence that is impervious to 'life'. It is a mistake to read him as a wholly realistic novelist. High comedy, of which he is a great master, is always artificial comedy; he devises plots at once neater and more intricate than life ever devises; his romantic nature often makes him see his heroines as fairy-tale princesses, or his taste for the grand and opulent causes him to turn them into real princesses; his great scenes are very consciously staged; he loves melodrama, and he even loves mystery. He admired Robert Louis Stevenson and has influenced Graham Greene. But though it is such a very 'special' world, James's world is still socially relevant to the tensions and predicaments of privileged lives in a high civilization.

The task of the novelist of our century has been to recognize that a high civilization, whose stability James took for granted, though he knew that it was built on oppression and exhibited inevitable moral flaws, is not stable. The novelist must recognize that the foundations of the world he walks are dangerously shifting, that we are living in a time of rapid and disturbing change, so that we can neither say with precision *when* some new pattern of relative stability will emerge, nor *what* sort of pattern it will be. Yet the task of the novelist also, since the human heart hungers after permanence, is to project some image of permanence and to give the novel a coherence that life at large does not obviously possess. To attempt merely to 'keep up with things', with every passing fashion in manners, is fatal to the novelist: 'he that runs against Time,' as Dr Johnson said, 'has an antagonist not subject to casualties.' Nearly all great novels are set at a period somewhat earlier than the time of writing (*War and Peace* in the period of Napoleon's wars with Russia, *Vanity Fair* before and after the period of the battle of Waterloo, *Middlemarch* around the time of the first Reform Bill, for instance). Strictly topical novels, bringing in the latest slang and the most up-to-date problems, are often ephemeral.

War and Peace, Vanity Fair, and *Middlemarch* do not

read like historical novels, in the way that *Henry Esmond* does, though this is largely a disguised account of Thackeray's relationship with Mrs Brookfield. In the nineteenth century, changes in costume and manners were not sufficiently striking to make a period forty or fifty years before the time of writing seem quaint, romantic, or picturesque. The world of possible memory was not felt to be discontinuous with the present as it is today, in our period of very rapid change. Behind the great novels of the past lay the writer's awareness of an established order, which he might judge to be in the main good or evil, but which was in either case reliably *there*; today there is no constant order for the novelist either to accept or to rebel against. All social and political arrangements – indeed, the continued existence of civilized human society and of the human race – have today a provisional air; the marks of our time are uncertainty and anxiety, but also a certain fatalism and apathy, coming from the powerlessness of the individual. In Western countries the individual today is less exposed than Wells's early hero, Kipps, was to petty snubs, humiliations, and frustrations. But he feels himself more open than Kipps to total disaster; if he escapes, he may find a wider range of social opportunities opening before him than Kipps did. But Kipps did, at least, feel that within limits he controlled his own life, and that is becoming harder for anyone to feel today. Unless a man of average goodwill and intelligence has the luck to have strong faith or unusual determination, he is likely to drift through life, moderately contented, doing some routine job quite well, but without any large or passionate sense of purpose.

One of the greatest modern novels in English, James Joyce's *Ulysses*, is concerned, as we shall see later, with this sense of drift. Other novelists refuse to accept aimlessness as something given, and desperately seek to find some belief or purpose, some kind of human relationship, by which a few men at least can give meaning to their lives; that perhaps was the task, as he saw it, of D. H. Lawrence. The novelist like Joyce who appears merely to give a detached portrayal of drift is in the tradition of Henry James: he has a moral theme, but he allows the theme to emerge naturally from the story, he does not seek to abstract it, nor to draw the reader's attention to it as a separate entity.

Artists of the type of Joyce, James, and Eliot who can build their thinking *into* their work are, however, at all times rare. Critics would disagree about whether D. H. Lawrence is one: *Lady Chatterley's Lover* is certainly a didactic novel, and Lawrence's most illustrious commentator, Dr F. R. Leavis, thinks that the didacticism spoils the art; he would probably agree that it is not the only novel or story of Lawrence in which we have a strong sense of the author taking sides and preaching, either out of his own mouth, or out of the mouth of some character who is more or less his spokesman. One novel of Lawrence's at least, *The Lost Girl*, has a great deal of the conversational perkiness and humour of Wells in it. The novelist like Lawrence or like his friend, Aldous Huxley, who uses the novel to propound, to advocate, or even to figure forth experimentally some 'philosophy of life' is (much as he might dislike the idea) in the tradition of H. G. Wells. He may not be so pure an artist as James or Joyce; but he shows a commendably urgent concern for the immediate problems of his fellow-men. If he never succeeds in arriving at complete aesthetic coherence – the warmest admirers of Lawrence would admit, I hope, that he is a singularly *uneven* writer – the moral coherence of his work may, for a long time, resist the dissolvents of social change.

6

Indian Summer

In the years following the death of Queen Victoria, the sense of effortless moral and practical superiority which had been one of the marks of English history in her reign was replaced by a new uneasiness and doubt; there was doubt about the rights and wrongs of the Boer War, about the validity of free trade as an immutable economic commandment. There was a perceptible shrinking in national grandeur and vitality, and that invigorating Victorian atmosphere of perpetual debate about high matters lost its grand style. Writers like Shaw, Belloc, and Chesterton had too much of the performer about them to be taken with the same moral seriousness as Matthew Arnold, Newman, Ruskin, or Carlyle. They expressed, to a popular audience, minority viewpoints in a highly personal way, whereas the Victorian sages had tried to make articulate the uneasiness widely felt by a representative range of educated people.

But a fading splendour and dying warmth still gilded the late afternoon. The Edwardian decade and the reign of King George V up to 1914 were the middle classes' last glimpse of 'normality'. Life above a certain income was good. Even social barriers were gradually being lowered. The country houses, which in the latter part of the Victorian age had been gradually opened to new wealth, began to open themselves to new talent. H. G. Wells, the son of a lady's maid and a professional cricketer, found himself chatting at dinner to Balfour or Haldane (he would put them both into a novel), or exchanging ideas at a dining club – and finding he had a great deal in common – with a progressive imperialist like Lord Milner. And though it is of the working man we should think when tempted to idealize the Edwardian Age, yet for him there were the compensations of cheap

beer and in the music halls cheap and lively entertainment.
In politics, the Fabians were busy, and a new small Labour
Party, which had little connexion with the Fabians, but
which represented rather Trade Unionism and Nonconformist radicalism, was finding its feet in the House of Commons.
The working man had his new popular newspapers and
Kipling paid him the compliment of writing some of his
poems in Kipling's version of the working man's spoken
tongue. If it was not to him, it was to somebody just a little
higher in the social scale, the clerk, the shop assistant, the
elementary school teacher, the man interested in machinery
and gadgets, that Wells's novels of ideas made their great
appeal. The common people were being 'kept in the picture'.

We shall not go far wrong if we think of the years from
1901 to 1914 as the great age, in English cultural and political history, of the middle classes. The working classes were
not yet a major force in British life; the old aristocracy of
birth was ceasing to be so. Thus, the most typical novelists
of the Edwardian age were John Galsworthy and Arnold
Bennett, and their novels epitomize the middle-class ethos.
They give us, in fact, a narrower picture of life than the
great Victorians do; for it is a mark of the middle classes in
all societies that they 'know their place' in regard both to
their inferiors and superiors, and tend to 'keep themselves
to themselves'. What Galsworthy and Bennett give us, therefore, is not a complex picture of the Edwardian world as a
whole, but rather a close view of an important section of
society.

Galsworthy's world was that of the commercial upper
middle classes, of large, overfurnished houses in the suburbs,
offices in the City of London, ramifications of family affection and financial interest, solemn dinner parties, the patient
accumulation of wealth, the damping down of passion, and
the steady honouring of a code. There is a clue to *The
Forsyte Saga* in a sentence of Ezra Pound's: 'So far as I can
make out, there is no morality in England which is not in
one way or another a manifestation of the sense of property.
A thing is right if it tends to conserve an estate, or to main-

tain a succession, no matter what servitude or oppression this inflicts.' Religion – except as a convention or a sentiment – philosophy, art, scholarship, even politics in any expert sense (a basically conservative attitude will be taken for granted), lie outside the boundaries of this world. It is 're-spectable', that is enough: it does not want to be 'smart' or 'clever'. Galsworthy's most famous series of novels, *The For-syte Saga*, is a study, at first with harsh satirical undertones, but later more warm and tolerant, and finally distinctly sentimental, of this world. In the first novel of the series, *The Man of Property*, Galsworthy's chief male character, Soames Forsyte, has a sense of property which extends to his wife as well as to his house so that he breaks into her bed-room when she locks her door against him. Irene, who for Galsworthy epitomizes the disruptive effect of beauty on the ordinary routines of life, then runs away with another man and, once Soames is deserted by her, Galsworthy's attitude towards him, which had been very harsh at first, gradually softens. Starting off as something like the villain, he ends almost the hero of the long tale. He is a dry, rigid, limited person, but he is consistent, he has his own code; in the general dissolving of standards after the Great War, Gals-worthy came to feel that any code, even a stupid and limited one, was better than none. So Soames comes to stand for a sturdy and inarticulate narrow virtue, with its own dignity and pathos – it being part of the pathos, no doubt, that Beauty as symbolized by Irene instinctively flees from it. Ironically, Soames, having lost Irene, develops a fine taste in pictures (which cannot run away) and dies in the end while attempting to save his pictures from a fire.

The Forsyte Saga and its successor, *A Modern Comedy*, therefore reflect a real change over the years in the temper of Galsworthy's mind. He begins by attacking those who cling too hard to tangible things but becomes in the end relieved that so many virtues can grow out of that tenacity. The virtues he admired particularly were loyalty and self-restraint. The defect of his mind was a lack of curiosity and really deep anxiety. Even when he appears to be a satirist he is not questioning a gentleman's code, but asking himself how honestly it is being applied. The figures who stand for Beauty and Art in *The Forsyte Saga* are blurred; the figures who stand for Convention are sharp yet sympathetic, for Galsworthy was at heart a conventional man. His humour is sometimes excellent, but verges too often on the cosy, for his attempts at pathetic intensity result in a kind of muffled sentimentality. Thus, in spite of his social questionings, his early leanings towards sentimental Socialism, it was inevitable that he should become the favourite reading of middle-class ladies taking books out of suburban or provincial circulating libraries. His attitude to life was fundamentally theirs, convention mitigated by humanity.

Arnold Bennett had nothing of the high moral tone, the vague but real distress about the injustice and unkindness of the world, that make Galsworthy such an attractive and dignified figure in spite of his limitations. But Bennett was a writer of far more genuine natural talent. He was born an artist, but he crippled himself by accepting the standards of vulgar success. His best novel, *The Old Wives' Tale*, is in the tradition of Flaubertian realism, and handles, with extraordinary skill, the ageing of the two heroines and the passing of time. He delighted in the commonplace, described with exactness. The life that he understood most intimately was the life of the English provincial lower middle classes in the pottery towns of the Midlands, where he had grown up. This is the background of his best novels and of collections of humorous short stories, such as *The Card*. Unfortunately, though this was the world he both knew and wrote about best, the world that attracted him most was one of vulgar metropolitan luxury; and he found that he could make as much money, which freed him from the provincial world, by popular farcical or romantic novels as by serious work. As a book-reviewer in the popular press, he could make or break reputations, and he lowered the standards of criticism. He became famous and wealthy, and enjoyed the trappings of success, his yacht, his cigars, the deference of head waiters. But the cost of becoming a lion in London society – and writers so different as Osbert Sitwell and H. G. Wells have borne witness to Bennett's social charm – was loss of touch with his roots and squandering of his gifts. Sadly, in his inner life he never appeared very happy. Friendly and charming though he was, he seems to have lacked the gift of intimacy, and his very ebullience as a social personage was that of a provincial not quite able to take his success or position for granted, never wholly at his ease. He was a natural artist making his first great successes in a period when few were discussing literature from a purely aesthetic point of view; the literary journalism of Wells and Shaw and Chesterton was all about 'ideas'. Bennett had no 'ideas' in that sense, and therefore never got any very intelligent criticism from his contemporaries. Mrs Woolf, alone, pointed out something lacking in him in a pamphlet called *Mr Bennett and Mrs Brown*, in which she went tooth and nail for his dogged interest in externals, his lack of feeling for mood or soul or inwardness. Yet it is that feeling for externals, exact and solid, which gives his best books their weight and truth.

Of the other novelists of the Edwardian decade who have a moral or artistic interest, the most important, a much greater writer than either Galsworthy or Bennett, is Joseph Conrad, a Pole, who, after an exciting career as a sea captain in the English Merchant Marine, settled down in England and wrote novels in the English language. Dr Leavis, in his famous book on the novel, *The Great Tradition*, numbers Conrad among the four or five major English novelists. This is a very interesting judgement, and Dr Leavis brings out admirably certain qualities which Conrad has in common with Dickens and also with Elizabethan drama. But it could be questioned whether Conrad is really ever quite a novelist in the strict sense, and not rather a writer of romances.

The other novelists whom Dr Leavis admires, Jane Austen, the Dickens of *Hard Times*, George Eliot, Henry James, and D. H. Lawrence, have this in common for Dr Leavis, that they are 'distinguished by a vital capacity for experience, a kind of reverent openness before life, and a marked moral intensity' and in that they are 'all very original technically'.

At a more humdrum level, however, Jane Austen, George Eliot, and Henry James are obviously novelists of manners, that is they assume a settled social background and its standards, though the standards of the characters they sympathize with most may be finer than the average standards of the world around them. *Hard Times* could still be called a novel of manners in that it is about a sub-civilized world, the raw Victorian industrial world, in which fine standards have not yet been acquired. What worries many readers of Lawrence's novels, and yet what may perhaps be his central subject, is the lack in his books of a 'world' in Jane Austen's or George Eliot's or Henry James's sense.

Now Conrad writes not about any settled 'worlds' but about the dangerous edges of the earth. He is concerned not with manners but with codes of honour, not with complicated moral success or failure but with heroism and disgrace. He was not only a Pole by birth, but also a Pole in all his fundamental habits and loyalties; extravagant, brave, suspicious, chivalrous, irascible. There is a story, for instance, that he once felt himself insulted by Shaw and wanted to challenge him to a duel. As a young man he had been a gun-runner for the Carlists in Spain. As a merchant skipper, he knew best the type of man he had met in distant ports, in outposts of the Empire, or in still uncolonized trading posts, the man with a lingering touch of the Elizabethan adventurer about him. He took the violence and treachery of man, of nature, of one's own inner nature for granted. The qualities he loved in the English nature were courage, a capacity for self-sacrifice and staunch silent endurance, and a high, noble vision; the last expressed, often, by Conrad with an un-English articulateness. Conrad's prose, in its frank and bold rhetoric, its reliance on capitalized abstractions like 'Youth' or 'Romance', is more like French prose than English – it even uses words like 'Poesy'. But the grandiose rhetoric is saved from inflation by an underlying irony; the cult of the heroic also is saved from inflation by Conrad's knowledge that, given adequate pressures upon him, any hero will crack; his knowledge also that an excessively fine and lively self-consciousness, like that of Decoud in *Nostromo* or Axel Heyst in *Victory*, can be disastrous to its possessor, and that stupid stolidity, like that of 'Fussy Joe' Mitchell in *Nostromo* again, is often a fortunate quality, since, precluding imagination, it also precludes terror. Yet, with all that knowledge, Conrad was still for the heroic whenever possible; he was one of the true 'last romantics', because he had lived romanticism as well as dreamed about it.

Conrad is certainly, in Dr Leavis's phrase, 'very original technically'. The most natural way to tell a story of adventure is straightforwardly, from one episode to another. Conrad likes to begin in the middle, or at a climax, like the scene of Jim's disgrace in *Lord Jim*, and then work back to what led up to this climax. The interest is thus shifted from what happens next to satisfying an acute observer's or narrator's curiosity about what lay behind the happening. Yet, at the same time, Conrad is not in the modern sense a psychologist. He presents characters from the outside, as an observer sees them, and the characters seem simple men, even symbolic types. There is, however, always an ultimate mystery about them, which gives many of his novels and short stories a poetic quality; an American critic, Leonard Unger, has worked out some very interesting parallels between Conrad's evocative prose and the early poems of T. S. Eliot – Conrad's long paragraphs with their heavy rhythms, cunning repetitions, vivid images, break down very easily into extremely effective free verse – and Eliot, in fact, prefaces *The Hollow Men* with an epigraph from Conrad's *Heart of Darkness*: 'Mistah Kurtz – he dead'. This story, which concentrates many of Conrad's qualities in a short space, is remarkable for its evocation of the African jungle as, in Mr Eliot's sense, the 'objective correlative' of the possible rankness of the human heart. The narrator is tracking down, on behalf of a woman who loves and idealizes him, a Mr Kurtz, the daring pioneer agent of an African outpost. He travels up-river in the company of disgusting traders who pot the natives on the bank, with rifles, for sport. When he finds Mr Kurtz, he finds him indeed wonderfully eloquent, but also a man who, carried away by loneliness, by drink, by a growing megalomania, has made himself a tyrant, more bloodthirsty and awful than the savage native chiefs whom he oppresses. He is regarded with awe. In the story, we see Kurtz dying of fever and oppressed by hallucinations; his own diseased mind is taking revenge on him, not his victims. He stands for a certain hollowness at the heart of darkness, the heart of hell; and yet he has been in touch with reality, in a way that the callous and vulgar traders on the boat have not: his sick cry, 'The horror! The horror!' means something. The narrator's pity and disgust are tempered by an ironic respect. Thus, Conrad works like a poet in grand symbols and fluent supple shifts of perspective and tone. He is not always, however, at his best. Sometimes the floridity of style is untempered by irony. Sometimes, as in *The Secret Agent*, the irony, for some readers at least, can seem coarsely, monotonously, and self-righteously, heavy. He has a stagey side. *Victory*, which seems to Dr Leavis one of his great novels, seems to me, with its splendid villain 'plain Mr Jones', not much more than a first-rate melodrama; I find Axel Heyst's philosophy of disillusion convincing only in a Stevensonian way.

One might mention, along with Conrad, Rudyard Kipling, whose view of life and whose range of subjects offer certain parallels but also some very striking contrasts. Like Conrad, Kipling admired men of action, but his admiration has the sentimentality of the intellectual who has never become a man of action himself. If Conrad sometimes writes stories for schoolboys, it could be complained of Kipling that he never has a fully adult audience in mind. Kipling gives away his own essential character in *Stalky and Co.* where the bookish boy who is short-sighted, dirty, and awkward very much admires the dash and courage of his companions, the Stalkies and M'Turks, even if, and perhaps especially if, the courage is accompanied by ruthlessness. As a small boy, separated from his parents in India, boarded out in England, Kipling had been cruelly and heartlessly bullied. When his parents came home, and his mother bent over to kiss him, she was horrified to see the little boy shrink his head away, as if to avoid a blow. But the bullying was perhaps less bad for him than the nightmare sense of loneliness. People who have been bullied very young tend, unfortunately, to wish to make friends with bullies, to become bullies themselves, and people who have known nightmarish loneliness will gratefully chum in with any sort of gang. These childhood experiences help to explain Kipling's sympathy for ruthlessness, his fascination with horror (which made Andrew Lang say that the author of *The Mark of the Beast* would die mad before he was thirty). He could give himself up to herd hatred, and in the First World War wrote a story, *Mary Postgate*, about a humane governess who, having lost her little charge in a German bombing raid, lets a German airman who has crash-landed die in pain without trying to help him: the same vile mood went into such lines as

> When time shall count from the date
> When the English began to hate.

But there is another side. Besides the cruelty and the ruthlessness, there is a deep concern with love, loyalty, compunction, and healing. The later short stories tend, I think, to be more humane than the earlier ones. Two remain vividly in my mind. One is the story of a scholar who, out of hatred for another scholar, concocts a wonderful forgery of a Chaucer manuscript; the man he hates is tricked into discovering it, warranting its authenticity, publishing it, and commenting on it. The forger intends to confess the truth, expose his enemy to ridicule, and break his heart. But things go wrong. The enemy falls ill. The enemy's wife, who does not love him, turns out to be in love with his doctor; perhaps they are conspiring to poison the sick man. The wife seems half to have guessed about the forgery and to want to see her husband humiliated before he dies. The dying man turns to his enemy as the only person he can trust and rely on; and his enemy does not betray him. Another tale of Kipling's which I cannot forget (he is strangely convincing whenever he deals with the supernatural) is about life after death. A distinguished man, but a man under a cloud, has just died in loneliness, poverty, and pain. He has made a vow that, after death, he will rejoin the woman he has loved. He finds himself, ill and confused, on the platform of a great railway station where uniformed nurses insist that he must have an injection and be taken away in an ambulance. No, he insists, he is waiting for somebody. But as he *is* ill, he can only insist feebly and unconvincingly. It looks as if they will overbear him, but he resists, and at length she comes. They are not in heaven but in some grim limbo or purgatory, but at least they have each other. Both these stories could be called morbid and sentimental, but for years they have haunted my imagination. One might have to admit that Kipling is never fully adult; one would still have to recognize his disturbing power. And there are books, like the wonderful *Kim*, like *Puck of Pook's Hill* and *Rewards and Fairies*, where the tormenting demon is absent and the power is wholly serene.

But Edwardian readers who were looking for an adult view of their world would turn, probably, neither to Kipling nor to Conrad. The most intelligent and sensitive, though not the most forceful or imaginative, novelist writing in these years was E. M. Forster. Mr Forster is still alive, still writing (though since *A Passage to India* he has written no more novels), and still a living influence on much younger writers, like L. P. Hartley or Christopher Isherwood. Perhaps the central fact about Forster is that he is a Cambridge man, who was at Cambridge in the days of Lowes Dickinson and G. E. Moore, and who is today, in his old age, an Honorary Fellow of King's College, Cambridge. Of the two great English universities, Oxford is at once the romantic and worldly one; it is the home at once of lost causes and of future Prime Ministers. Cambridge is firmly unworldly, and unromantic; it has been the home of Puritanism rather than High Churchmanship, of Latitudinarianism rather than Rigour, of Whigs rather than Tories, of Evangelicalism instead of the Oxford Movement, of Mathematics rather than Classics, of analytic rather than speculative Philosophy. It encourages strict attitudes, and a dry exactness of mind; nevertheless, a greater number of notable English poets, Milton, Dryden, Gray, Wordsworth, Tennyson, among them, have been educated at Cambridge than at Oxford. Lowes Dickinson helped to give the young Forster an interest in the classical background of Western culture and to strengthen his belief in the virtue of a pagan spontaneity. Moore may have helped to instil into him a dislike of rhetoric and abstraction, a taste for a plain and stringent honesty of mind. In Forster's most personal novel, *The Longest Journey*, Cambridge stands for the moral virtues of the honest intellect. Wiltshire, the west of England, still unspoiled when Forster wrote, stands for nature and spontaneity. An imaginary suburb called Sawston stands for all the stiffness, pretence, and humbug which Forster most dislikes in English life.

Forster is the novelist not as speculative but as practical philosopher, interested in human behaviour in so far as it presents us with moral problems; not problems which can be solved in an obvious and heroic way, by embracing a cause or joining an army or going to some distant country as a missionary, but such everyday problems as whether we are doing what we really want, and ought to do; whether we are being kind and understanding enough to our neighbours, judging them as we judge ourselves; or whether, on the other hand, we are sacrificing our own glimpses of truth to our neighbours', or our relations', false standards. Forster has written very few novels – five in all. The first, *Where Angels Fear to Tread*, appeared in 1905, the last, *A Passage to India*, in 1924. This was a remarkably sparse and cautious rate of production, an average of one novel in every four years; though, in fact, there was a very long gap between the fourth novel, *Howards End*, which came out in 1911, and *A Passage to India*. Some of these novels, moreover, are short; none of them, except possibly the last, has the air of aiming at being a 'great' novel. They deal with superficially pleasant, ordinary middle-class English people, just, but no more than just, on the 'upper' side of the great division between 'upper' and 'lower' English middle class. They are written in a smooth, tidy, faintly precious style, with a touch of Cambridge preciseness about it and just a touch, also, of maiden-lady refinement. Writing about 'nice' people, in a 'nice' manner, Forster is important because of his insight into what it is in English life that makes 'nice' people so often behave with quiet nastiness. He is a critic of that English passion for correctness at all costs which makes English people afraid of violent emotion but afraid, even more, of the sudden critical disloyalties of thought. The fear of violence does not prevent violence; in nearly all Forster's novels there are strange, and to some readers jarring, moments of melodrama. Forster is aware of the ruthless lengths to which the unaware can go to protect their unawareness.

The question at issue in these novels can be an apparently trivial one. In his novel which is nearest to pure light comedy, *A Room with a View*, the question is whether a pretty, good-natured, rather ordinary girl, already engaged to a worthy but priggish and tiresome young man, should allow herself to admit that she has fallen in love with, and would like to marry, a very pleasant young man who is truly in love with her, but who has not been introduced in the correct formal way and who is 'not quite of her class'. It is not a matter of class-warfare, as we understand it today – or of any real perceptible gulf to be bridged; it is a matter of invisible distinctions of manner and behaviour between two of the almost innumerable segments of the English middle class. Even so, only the chances of an Italian holiday make the bridging of the invisible, and unreal, gulf possible. The heroine is caught in a comic, but for her exceedingly important and serious, struggle between propriety and sincerity. English people have, or had in Forster's day and in the world he writes about, a very strong sense of the exact social group they belong to, of its shibboleths, its taboos. This is not an articulate sense: one might rather say, like Trotter in *The Instincts of the Herd in Peace and War*, that when two English strangers meet one another they sniff at each other like dogs, to see if the smell is a safely familiar one. If these imperceptible barriers are absurd, they are none the less real, and to break them down even on a small front, in the name of individual responsibility and initiative, has something mildly heroic about it.

This theme of the individual, the individual's own response, his own sense of trust in a stranger, to which he must sacrifice 'tradition' or 'propriety', is Mr Forster's central theme. In *A Room with a View* it is treated in a vein of genteel, almost ladylike comedy, but in his last novel, *A Passage to India*, it has become tragic. Now it is no longer a matter of gaps, barriers, misunderstandings, between different sections of the English middle classes; it is a matter of gaps, barriers, misunderstandings between the British in India and the native educated Indians. The story is that of the strain stood by the friendship between a native Indian doctor and Fielding, a sensible Englishman. The friendship is tested by a false accusation made by an English girl against the doctor, that when they were together on a sight-seeing expedition the Indian tried, indecently, to touch her. The girl is not consciously insincere; she has been in a nervous state, has been going through an awkward and difficult time with the inadequate young man, Ronnie, she came out to marry; the climate has been telling on her; and so on. She is a perfectly decent though plain and ordinary girl, and she has had some kind of tactual hallucination. Her accusation, however, is like a spark in a powder-magazine. It brings out everything that is nasty in the English community, and a good deal that is nasty in the Indian one. One side has a victim, the other a martyr; Dr Aziz's case allows spite, malice, and prejudice on both sides a splendid field-day. Then, at the trial, Miss Quested, having had time to think things over, confesses that she has been suffering from a hysterical delusion. The British community drop her; the young man breaks off the engagement; the Indian community show no gratitude towards her for her magnanimity, but indulge in a mean and vindictive demonstration of triumph. Fielding has to be invited to rejoin the local English club (which, in any case, he detests), having been proved right against the fanatics. The Indian doctor, of course, is let out of gaol. But now that the crisis is over, he and Fielding begin to drift apart. The mere habits of their lives, different circles, different routines, separate them. Much later they meet again. Fielding has gone home and married, and is therefore now increasingly tied to his own community, and Aziz is now much more bitterly nationalist than he used to be. They have a frank, friendly conversation together, on a last ride, but the way their horses race side by side, gallop outwards and away from each other, meet again, part finally, is a symbol of the different ways their lives will now go. This will be their last meeting.

Though Forster is a great master of social comedy, there is in all his novels the sadness that comes from realizing how much every individual, even the most brave, cheerful, and sensitive, is at the mercy of the stupidities of his group. Forster is a liberal who believes that it is up to each man to choose his friends, his work, his convictions. Our profoundest moral duty is to know, sincerely, what and whom we like, never to deceive ourselves about this, always to act on this knowledge. Though he is very much an intellectual, he is not sure that the intellect is the best guide. In each of his novels there is a character, old Mr Emerson, Stephen Wonham, Gino, Mrs Wilcox, Mrs Moore, who is not intellectual or particularly intelligent, who may be primitive or conventional, but who stands for some intuitive sense of reality, some goodness, or, in Stephen's and Gino's cases, some natural force deeper than goodness, which the more intellectual, or articulate, characters in the book need, if they are to make contact with life. These code figures stand broadly either for vitality or for saintliness, for a balance between these two qualities, and always for simplicity; they balance Forster's chilly sense that life is environed by darkness, by meaninglessness, that death is the end.

For all his hatred of that element of sheer stuffiness in the English middle-class character symbolized by Sawston, Forster has a strong sense of how many of these virtues of the liberal tradition are inherent in the British character at its best. These virtues belong especially to those who have had what is traditionally called a 'liberal education'. A 'liberal' education as opposed to a 'mechanical' one will enlarge and humanize the mind, and not merely prepare a man to earn his living at some particular trade. On the other hand, for Forster, education in itself is never enough: the young brother of the Schlegels in *Howards End* is condemned for having 'a little cold-culture' instead of creative warmth. Forster also knows how the code of manners of these classes who are the custodians of the liberal traditions tends to fence them off from other classes in the community. Foreigners, if they often find Englishmen shy and awkward, might learn from Forster's novels both what silly assumptions of superiority sometimes lie behind that lack of grace and how it often masks an honest shyness, a struggle to be fair. British democracy, in so far as it exists, is much more the effect of the sense of fairness of the British upper and mandarin classes than of really efficient pressures from below. Forster understands, as indeed he exemplifies, that sense of fairness. He is a novelist of the liberal tradition, not in the sense of the cult of the individual in isolation, but in the sense of the belief that moral independence in privileged individuals may help to secure, for a changing community, some measure of social justice and peace. But that justice and peace, for Forster, are of the order of means; the ends, or purposes, of human life are friendship, love, the enjoyment of beauty, the achievement of moral courage, and intellectual honesty.

7

The Time of Transition (1910–20)

THE decade of the Great War coincided with a very important period of creative experiment in English literature. The war was not the cause of the new movements, which had begun well before it. Some of the most notable innovators, like T. S. Eliot and James Joyce, did not serve in the war (one was an American citizen domiciled in Great Britain, the other an Irishman teaching in Trieste); nor did another American who had been in England since 1908, Ezra Pound, important both as an organizer of new movements and a publicizer of them. Joyce had been working on *Ulysses* and on the earlier *Portrait of the Artist as a Young Man* and *Dubliners* for years before the war; so, in France, had Marcel Proust been working for some time on his *À la recherche du temps perdu*, and the appearance of the first volume coincided with the outbreak of hostilities merely by accident. These new experimenters were in revolt against the complacencies of Victorian Liberalism: Eliot, Pound, Joyce, and later Yeats were not making literary gestures, nor were they solely inspired by the war, but they were prophesying the advent of a harsher time. The reading public did not take to them at once; but in ten or twenty years' time they were to seem tremendously topical, and now, in the 1960s, they have the status of modern classics.

The Great War unsettled society in many ways. It had a great liberating effect: it hastened the emancipation of women; it promoted a temporary merging of the social classes. Young men from humble backgrounds received commissions; young officers like Graves and Sassoon gained a new questioning attitude towards their inherited code. But above all the First World War shattered Great Britain's national self-confidence and produced doubt, uncertainty, and confusion. Instead of the thoughtless complaisant hopefulness of the Edwardian decade, there was a 'new realism', a tendency to think of man as a strictly limited creature. Man was no longer a giant figure striding to perfection, though he might achieve a certain decency through harsh self-discipline.

James Joyce's *Ulysses*, though in no sense directly influenced by the Great War, is symptomatic both of the new experimentalism and the new sad, realistic attitudes towards human society. It may be, as Mr Anthony Powell and Mr Jocelyn Brooke have suggested, that *Ulysses*, though a great work of literature, is not a great novel. Joyce lacked, perhaps, two gifts which most great novelists have possessed: an interest in a very wide range of characters; and an ability to tell a story so that one reads it, at least for the first time, not to savour the quality of the writing but to see what happens next. *Ulysses* deals with the events of a single day in the life of its two heroes, Leopold Bloom, a Jewish advertising agent, who stands for Ulysses in the Homeric epic, and Stephen Daedalus, who stands for Telemachus. Many of the incidents of Homer's poem are elaborately paralleled and parodied. But the ordinary reader's enjoyment is not greatly enhanced by having these parallels pointed out to him. They were useful rather to Joyce himself, in forcing him to impose a complex outer structure on what might otherwise have been a flood of inner monologue. It is, likewise, to solidify the outer framework that he works out the itinerary of the story so elaborately: mentioning so many Dublin shops, offices, restaurants, public-houses, back streets, low quarters, that his novel is at moments like a guide-book to the city, though not to its Georgian elegance. Much of the action goes on inside the minds of Bloom and of Stephen. There are glimpses of the 'inner workings' of minor characters, too; and at the very end of the book there is a torrential monologue by Mrs Bloom, who stands for an eternal feminine principle – in one sense low, base, sly, dirty, treacherous, dishonest, but in another sense tenacious – a principle of eternal renewal and acceptance. In the character of Mrs

Bloom appetite just triumphs over disgust. Her monologue, though it succeeds, shows to what a shapeless fluidity *pure* 'stream-of-consciousness' technique might have led, if Joyce had not perpetually deflected Bloom's inner monologues or Stephen's with impingements from the outer world. And there is one section (that in which he parodies in succession all the most notable styles in the history of English narrative and reflective prose) in which he steps outside the characters altogether.

Thus Joyce's great achievement in *Ulysses* is not simply the use of a subjective method but the building up of this into an objective framework. We get inside the minds of Stephen and Bloom but we do not simply *identify* ourselves with them. Joyce enables us to put them in a wider perspective than they put themselves.

Indeed, though perhaps more elaborately particularized than any other two characters in fiction, they have a general significance, almost a symbolic value. Bloom, a vulgarian in his attitude to the arts, blankly indifferent to religion, a timid but persistent sensualist, obsessed by comic and sordid anxiety about his wife's faithfulness, cowardly, sly, is nevertheless generous, warm-hearted, full of inquisitive alertness about science and politics; hoping that the world will be transformed by technical improvements and by the substitution of a new internationalism for the old, narrow-minded nationalism. Bloom is almost like a typical Wells hero (or almost like Wells himself) seen from the angle of sympathetic comedy. To Stephen Daedalus, who stands for the despair of the poet in a world of fools, oafs, and bigots, a cultureless, commercial world, also, all Bloom's ideas are nonsense. But Bloom is not contemptible in himself to Stephen, or, indeed, to Joyce. Again and again (as in the episode, modelled on that of the Cyclops' Cave in Homer, where Bloom just escapes from being beaten up by a bigoted Irish nationalist) we see that Bloom stands in Joyce's mind for a civilized and rational cosmopolitan attitude in contrast to native Irish barbarism. For Joyce, if he was not a naïve liberal progressive himself, was far from being an Irish nationalist either.

Bloom is the well-meaning, warm-hearted, tactlessly frank Jew who, because of his liberal attitudes and his imperfect assimilation to a local culture, is the predestined victim of Fascism. He is a pathetic and comic figure in many ways, a compendium not of any major vices but of very many common and ridiculous human weaknesses; with a touch, as Wyndham Lewis noted, of the comic Jew of the music-hall. He is also, as Wyndham Lewis again noted in *Time and Western Man*, a distinctly amiable figure, and even perhaps in many ways his middle-aged creator in disguise (as Stephen Daedalus, a frank piece of autobiography, is the young Joyce *without* disguise). Bloom with all his faults, is the largest and most sympathetic *human* figure in *Ulysses*: Joyce himself said emphatically that he intended Bloom to be 'a good man'.

Bloom, then, stands partly for that social optimism, based on a firm belief in science and in rationality, which was so influential a creed in Joyce's own youth. There are touches of this attitude, after all, in one of Joyce's early masters, Ibsen. Stephen Daedalus, on the other hand, represents the cult of art not exactly for its own sake, but as 'the eternal affirmation of the spirit of man'. The acceptance of that cult is a common result of losing one's childhood religion and of not finding any substitute for it in any merely practical social creed. It is not so much that Stephen despairs of society, though he views his fellow-men with a jaundiced and sardonic eye, as that he cannot make a religion of society. Like T. E. Hulme, he sees the imperfection, and imperfectibility, of men in all their practical relations; yet he knows, too, that man hungers for perfection, and can at once express that hunger and on rare occasions satisfy it, through music and poetry and art. There are more intimate reasons for Stephen's cult of art (I am thinking now of *Portrait of the Artist as a Young Man* as well as *Ulysses*): he is in his early twenties, the great period of male frustration, torn by what he would call kinetic impulses, lust springing from frustration, envy and resentment springing from pride and poverty, remorse springing from his rejection of religion and his refusal to pray by his dying mother's bed-side. That refusal may have been either his greatest act of heroic virtue, or it may have been his greatest crime. Stephen's kinetic impulses rend him and tug him and will not let him rest; art offers stillness, peace, balance, the emotions (if only for a moment in time) at harmonious rest.

Stephen also, like Bloom, combines absurdity with pathos; his dream of beauty hampered by hunger and bad teeth. He is a young man in search of a father to help him and guide him (his own father, like Joyce's, is a charming blarneying ne'er-do-well, a drunken wastrel going steadily downhill); and Bloom is a middle-aged man with no son (his son died in infancy) who needs a son to give him, poor shabby cuckold that he is, confidence in his own manhood. Bloom, too, however gregarious, is lonely; a failure even at his own dim job, living on vulgar daydreams that he knows will not come true; knowing that his handsome, randy, musical wife, Marion, is repeatedly betraying him.

Though the theme of *Ulysses* is momentous, the construction intricate, the atmosphere dense, there is nevertheless, in the working out of the plot, in the old-fashioned sense very little 'story'. Bloom, going about Dublin on his day's work, pausing to attend a funeral, to indulge in scoptophilia, to eat a meal, worrying about his wife, his money, his daughter, his digestion, pursuing persistently his own ruminations but with an alert ear cocked for what is going on around him, runs into Stephen (wandering aimlessly and later drunkenly around) once or twice, observes him with fatherly care, and late in the evening is able to rescue Stephen from a drunken brawl outside a brothel which both have been visiting. He sobers Stephen up, and persuades him to come home with him. For both Stephen and Bloom, the encounter is momentous, though both would find it hard to explain why. Each perhaps has a sense of having achieved human recognition through a chance meeting and of having enhanced his dignity. What is sad and ironical is that these two people, with so much need of each other's trust and affection, have no common language. But if Stephen and

Bloom cannot communicate, they can at least convey good-will; Stephen is strengthened in his sense of vocation, Bloom draws courage to assert himself mildly with his wife. What about her own final soliloquy? It stands, as I have already suggested, for a total, uncritical acceptance of life which lies beyond the scope of the male human animal. Both Stephen and Bloom are idealists; Stephen lives for perfection, Bloom for improvement. Molly Bloom stands for an impulse which has more to do with keeping the race going than any ideal – for the blind and greedy, but eternally creative, principle of life itself. At one level her monologue is the sordid record of a vulgar woman's erotic fantasies; at another, it is the speech of an earth-goddess. Men discriminate and complain, because they are always after something better; it is because women discriminate less, complain less, will always in the end be satisfied with what they can get, that life goes on.

To many people, when it first appeared, *Ulysses* seemed almost unbearably sordid and depressing. Today we are more likely to be struck by Joyce's humorous compassion and by his respect for the bedrock of spiritual reality that underlies, in the end, Bloom's vulgarity, Stephen's weak and peevish self-conceit, and Marion Bloom's trivial grossness. In one sense, the book is, if not tragedy, tragi-comedy, for it depicts a society in which the 'best men' – and at Joyce's special level of lyrical comedy, both Bloom and Stephen represent the 'best men' – have lost the faiths and habits that make life in a society real and noble. It is the comic short-comings of Dublin that have turned Bloom and Stephen into such uncompromising, though such vulnerable, idealists. And, of course, Joyce himself accepts Dublin far more completely than they do; he is like Mrs Bloom in that. Shabbiness and failure and genteel pretence and newspaper head-lines and remembered oratory and medical students' dirty jokes and smells and smoke and clanging trams and the crowded bars of the great city all have their own poetry for him. He conveys that poetry through the ear rather than the eye. He was a very short-sighted man, who saw the world around him through a blur; he was also a singer, with almost a good enough ear and voice to have become a concert-platform tenor; and before he turned to prose had written some slight, and mannered, but at their best very musical poems. He uses his sentences, with their elaborate cadences, to call up impressions that are often all the more emotionally concrete for not being hard and precise. We are immersed *in* his world; we do not see it in perspective. He had a wonderful 'ear' in another sense; just as he could mimic or parody any style in English prose literature, so he could dramatically catch in writing the pitch, rhythm, and idiom of a wide variety of speaking voices. If I were asked for the most notable examples of this last gift, I would choose nothing from *Ulysses*, but the argument about Parnell from *Portrait of the Artist as a Young Man* and the discussion between the political canvassers in what for me is the best short story in *Dubliners*, 'Ivy Day in the Committee Room'. *Dubliners* (like the early version of *Portrait of the Artist as a Young Man*, *Stephen Hero*) shows an early mastery of exact objective description. *Portrait of the Artist* by way of deliberate contrast is almost completely subjective (the Christmas dinner passage is one of the few brilliant exceptions to this generalization) and, wonderful little book though it is, both the prose and the atmosphere remind one too much of Walter Pater. I find that in fact I re-read both of these early books more often than *Ulysses*, which is so much more original, so much grander in scope; it may be that in the earlier books there is some naïve truth to life, to a young man's raw experience, and that this simple truth has in *Ulysses* been embroidered into 'literature'. In *Finnegans Wake*, Joyce's last book, the element of verbal obsession takes over completely: it is pure musical soup. I have attempted to read it through but never, whether with the aid of 'keys' or drink, succeeded; like everybody else, I find Joyce's own recorded reading of the Anna Livia Plurabelle passage very moving and beautiful.

A friend and contemporary of James Joyce was Percy Wyndham Lewis. If Joyce above all was a musical writer, a writer whose appeal is to the 'auditory imagination', Lewis, his primary genius that of a draughtsman, with a thorny, wiry, biting line, is a writer whose first appeal is to the eye. Towards the end of the decade we are considering, Lewis published a striking first novel, *Tarr*. The important characters in *Ulysses* are seen from the inside (though, as I have suggested, by his care for grand structure Joyce also establishes an objective view of them, at least as symbols). In *Tarr*, and in Lewis's subsequent fiction, everything is seen from the outside. Lewis has no interest, except a rather mocking and hostile one, in the feelings and sensibilities of his characters, in how they look or feel to themselves; he is mercilessly interested in how absurd they look and feel to an outside observer, possessed with a humorously destructive animus. For Lewis, the human animal in his behaviour is usually a pretentious and mechanical creature; we laugh at him, Lewis agrees with Bergson, because man after all is a free and vital creature, he is an intelligence, and it is absurd to see a free and vital intelligence behaving like an automaton. Lewis's apparent contempt for most human beings has caused some critics to rank him with T. E. Hulme; but, unlike Hulme, he was a Renaissance man. He adored the great man, the true artist or philosopher, but hated imitation great men; hated even real great men's shortcomings, and their pettier 'human, all too human' manifestations. The scene of *Tarr* is Paris, and the characters are a set of down-at-heel Bohemians, would-be writers, would-be artists, social pretenders. None of the characters is very likeable, but where Joyce would have found the side of them that was human and touching, for Lewis they are inept or violent clowns. The main character is a neurotic German called Kreisler, who rapes the hero's mistress, kills an enemy with whom he is having a duel after the duel is officially over, and finally kills himself. Kreisler is in essence a Dostoyevsky character, 'wild' and 'tortured', but for Lewis it is not his tragedy, though he is represented as being a forceful being in his hysterical way, that matters, but his sheer self-destructive silliness. Lewis's view of satire was a novel one; satire has never been ranked by critics among the noblest of literary forms, and there is perhaps a general feeling that the character of the satirist, like his presentations of his victims, has something deformed or distorted about it. Lewis tried to give satire a new dignity by asserting that it is properly directed not against some moral failing (the greatest satire, he insisted, is non-moral), or the faults and follies of some particular social class, some body of opinion or belief, but against man's general disgustingness and ineptness. D. H. Lawrence, not unfairly, said that Lewis's verdict on his fellow human beings could be summed up in two words: 'they stink'. But Lewis did not allow for the probability that he himself must share the general odour – though there is a new awareness of this possibility in some late novels, the self-inquisiting *Self-Condemned* and the often very moving *The Revenge for Love*. The latter novel, very powerful and, except by Mr John Holloway, almost totally neglected by critics, shows that, even if Lewis disapproved of that natural sympathy with our fellow creatures which most of us feel, he was never able quite to freeze that sympathy at its source. It is interesting that his favourite novelists were the least satirical, though often the most genially humorous, of the great novelists of the world: the Russians. He admired them for an old-fashioned reason, the nobility and simplicity of their heroes, and it was Stephen Daedalus's ignoble pettiness that made him class, in *Time and Western Man,* Joyce with novelists of the second rank, like Robert Louis Stevenson or Laurence Sterne. Lewis's more purely satirical books, however much admired, could never be widely popular. A satire on literary London, *The Apes of God*, made him personally more unpopular still. Perhaps his greatest imaginative work, *The Childermass*, published in the late 1920s, and in the 1950s revised and completed as *The Human Age*, is too confusing in its intention – partly supernatural science-fiction, partly allegorical satire, partly intellectual debate – to rank as a coherent work; the later additions, particularly, include some very sadistic passages (there was a streak of sheer nastiness in Lewis), but it also contains some of Lewis's most vivid and powerful prose.

With fewer obsessions and a firmer moral centre, he might have become a modern Swift. He had the gift, both in fiction and in his abundant critical writing, of uttering uncomfortable truths.

It was in books later than *Tarr* that Lewis was to perfect his peculiar prose style. Just as every sentence of Joyce's has a certain musical cadence, so every sentence of Lewis's calls up some harsh, definite, frightening, or absurd picture to the eye. His prose is not *displeasing* to the ear; for it has an explosive emphasis, and a jogging mechanical force. Nevertheless, Lewis in his works of fiction (the best of his critical writings are another matter) is often hard to read. The reader feels like a punch-ball, receiving thud after thud, rocking upon his foundations; he is never allowed to rest. The most damaging general criticism that can be made of Lewis is that he is too exclusively the virtuoso of negative emotions. The reader begins to wish that Lewis would offer him something to love or admire. Something is offered occasionally: the notion of the lonely and persecuted great artist, or great thinker, among a crowd of gibbering submen. It is difficult for the most sympathetic reader to equal the high, ironical, injured pathos of Lewis's self-regard. He had greatness, he was lonely; and persecution-mania always creates self-justification. But, like Shakespeare's Malvolio, Lewis is 'sick with self-love': Joyce was a greater, not a smaller, writer than Lewis for managing to love his fellowmen, without ever having had any rosier illusions about them than Lewis had.

I have postponed the consideration of Aldous Huxley, Virginia Woolf, and D. H. Lawrence to the next section; but another writer, not English, who should be mentioned in this section, for his importance as an innovator and for his technical and spiritual influence, is Marcel Proust. Proust's great theme is what the French call *recueillement*, which means more than the English 'recollection': rather, the re-plucking in memory of the flowers that time has plucked already; the re-gathering, re-patterning, re-embroidering, of all the loose and ravelled threads of one's life. Life is never still, yet it is easy enough, at any calm time, for a man to number over in his mind some of the main incidents of his life; it is much more difficult to relive them contemplatively, to recapture the sense of what past time was, what in essence it still *is*. It is more difficult still to get that recaptured and revived awareness of the past into perspective with the present. Yet these are Proust's achievements. He is neither a novelist of the ear, of the musical cadence and the living echo, like Joyce, nor a novelist of the eye, of the bitter and incisive visual cartoon, like Wyndham Lewis. His sometimes monstrously long sentences certainly call up image after image and move generally with a graceful and undulating – if sometimes with a cumbrous and confused – motion, but what they are after is neither picture nor music for its own sake but the transmutation of experience into thought. Proust had at once the temperament of a woman and the mind of a philosopher. As we read him, we sink into land-scape, in which the morning sun bleeding through the shutters of a hotel bedroom, the faces of pretty girls passing like figures on a frieze along a beach, the powdered hair of a flunkey on the stairway of a great mansion, the monocled mask and booming voice of some grotesque and inane dandy at an evening-party, the possibility of being smiled at, at the theatre, by a duchess, a small boy's hopeless need for his mother before he can sleep, a young man's half romantic and half perverse craving for the nearness of a cold-hearted flirt, these, and darker and more sinister images, make up a con-fused and flowing tapestry. We are not so sure that we want to be so completely submerged into the warm and viscous depths of somebody else's life; we become oppressed at hav-ing to surrender, again and again, to all the temptations and vices that beset a young man of weak and yielding sensi-bility, but then we find the sensibility controlled, at least at the level of art and recollection, by a persistent organizing will and a powerful analysing intellect. The material, how-ever questionable in itself, is being shaped towards some generalization about love, about selfishness and insincerity, about man's experience of time, which will at least *seem* to have the validity of mathematics. So, out of the material of erotic elegy, material which by its very nature tempts the writer to sentiment, to falsification, to a flattery both of himself and of those whom he loves, Proust gradually and patiently erects a structure of pitiless objective truth.

Thus Proust, like so many great French writers of the past, like Rochefoucauld, La Bruyère, or Vauvenargues, was essentially a 'moralist': a 'moralist' in the French sense of one who seeks out the laws of human conduct, rather than in the English sense of one who lays down the rules. It was just because he was a moralist in this sense that he dealt so often with what are, to English tastes, 'doubtful' subjects; for men's secret vices and follies do, in fact, afford us more subtle clues to the springs of their conduct than the respectable fronts which they put up to the world. A writer to whose family Proust seems to me to belong is Jean-Jacques Rousseau in his *Confessions*. Rousseau is similarly bathed perpetually in an excitement which is partly sexual, but not narrowly or exclusively sexual, and analysing his excitement even at the moment of feeling it:

I am acquainted with another sentiment less impetuous but a thousand times more delightful; sometimes joined with love, but frequently separated from it. This feeling is not simply friendship, it is more voluptuous, more tender; nor do I imagine it can exist between persons of the same sex – at least I have been truly a friend, if ever man was, and yet never experienced it in that kind. This distinction is not sufficiently clear, but will become so hereafter: sentiments are only describable by their effects.

Proust was also the victim, at least in his imagination, of Rousseau's favourite secret vice. Rousseau's frank sentences about this give us, more clearly than Proust ever does himself, our sense of what is essentially morbid in his whole theory of love, in Swann's relation to Odette, the narrator's to Gilberte and Albertine. Even if there is physical contact, love, for all Proust's characters, is in the end something that one does and suffers for oneself, its place of dwelling is the solitary imagination: it is obsession with an image, into which the person, from whom the image took its origin, may even strangely and tactlessly intrude. Rousseau has it in a nutshell:

> This vice, which shame and timidity find so convenient, has besides great enticements for lively imaginations; that is, to dispose in a manner at will of the whole sex, and to make the beauties which tempt [lively imaginations] serve their pleasures without the necessity of obtaining [the beauties'] consent.

There is, indeed, much that is perverse in the feelings Proust analyses, much that is trivial and vulgar in the world of high society he describes; people who spend the best parts of their lives worrying about which parties they are going to be invited to are ridiculous, but Proust, though he shares this weakness himself, knows they are ridiculous, and does not spare ridicule; nor does he spare the weakness, snobberies, infatuations, the pathological jealousy, of his main character. He projects these weaknesses, and his own shortcomings, too widely; everybody who is jealous in the novel is jealous in the narrator's way; too many of the characters for real *vraisemblance*, male and female, turn out to be secret homosexuals. To me the best part of Proust's novel is the first three volumes, up to the end of the *Guermantes' Way*, where the topics are, in a sense, those traditional in an autobiographical novel: family background, a young man's social and artistic education, his early lusts and romantic loves, the discovery of places, the early tremulous exploration of the grand world. The beginning of *Swann's Way* and the evocation of the sea, the beach, the young girls in *Within a Budding Grove*, has the quality of an impressionist painting, of a grand, hedonistic, high bourgeois civilization at its ripest, the fruit nodding on the branch just before it falls. But from the first pages of *Cities of the Plain* onward, we are in hell. Poetry shrivels away. More generally, the noble values, heroism, chastity, loyalty, might seem, apart from a few attractive figures like the narrator's grandmother and his friend, Robert de St Loup, to have almost no place in Proust's world (even St Loup's brightness is in the end

shadowed). But then, Proust's devotion to his art and his
eagerness to arrive at the truth within the limits of his own
experience of love and society (an 'exclusive' and interesting,
but in a sinister as well as a grand sense very 'privileged'
experience), these are heroic and chaste and loyal. But one
can understand Ezra Pound, who was impatient with a long
novel written about useless people, and the French Catholic
critic who discovered at the centre of the story a huge
spiritual void.

Proust's novel was translated into magnificent English
prose (it is said that the English version is a finer piece of
sustained 'style' than the French original) by the Scottish
poet, soldier, and scholar, Charles Scott-Moncrieff, who also
translated *Beowulf*, the *Chanson de Roland*, and much of
Stendhal. It is interesting that Scott-Moncrieff, who was a
devout Roman Catholic convert, and whose natural taste in
literature, as his verse translations show, was for the heroic
and the chivalrous, seems to have felt no moral compunctions
about translating Proust; on the other hand, Scott-Moncrieff
has also written a very interesting introduction to a new
edition of Petronius's *Satyricon*, and in that introduction he
compares the scabrous and penetrating Roman satirical novelist to Proust, seeing them both as writers who become significant and interesting in the twilight of high civilizations.
His translation of Proust was certainly one of the finest sustained performances in English prose of this century; it is
difficult to think of an original piece of English writing with
such poetically moving and supple elaborate evocations of
atmosphere and scene. Here, a debt was being paid back to
England: Proust had learned how to describe architecture
and scenery, and how to suffuse such descriptions with personal feeling, from Ruskin; just as his taste for interrupting
his narrative with serious general reflections, and profound
analyses of motive, derives also from an English and perhaps morally incongruous source, the novels of George Eliot.
The style, the mood, the manner of Proust (or possibly of
Scott-Moncrieff's translation) had a far-reaching effect on
English writing in the 1920s: Virginia Woolf (particularly

in *The Waves*, but also in the salon scenes, and London street scenes, in *Mrs Dalloway*) often, like Proust, seems to be trying to transmute impressionist experience into pure thought; and the descriptive side of Proust, the side of *bravura* accumulations of detail, had an effect on the prose of Sacheverell and Osbert Sitwell. Of younger writers, Mr Anthony Powell, in the long series of novels on which he is currently engaged, has been described as a dehydrated Proust. Some critics, notably Wyndham Lewis, have felt that this influence was a debilitating one. It can be agreed that, in spite of the sharpness of his social satire, Proust, with his feminine and yielding attitude to experience, was not an influence for blunt directness or manly briskness. It is interesting also that, on the only occasion on which he and Joyce met, they could find nothing to say to each other.

A novelist of much less importance than these, but one who also set a fashion, and who was attractive and individual as a man, was Norman Douglas. Descended from Deeside lairds on his father's side, from German noblemen on his mother's, Douglas as a young man became a diplomat, served in the British Embassy in St Petersburg, and later travelled in India. By birth and background, he belonged to the international ruling few; and a good deal of the cast of his mind, his lifelong interest in such topics as geology and botany, and his elaborate scholarship in topographical literature, was typically German rather than English. After he gave up diplomacy, his life became that of a wandering bohemian, with many friends in most European countries, but with no conventional ties. He was sometimes in funds and spirits but sometimes, as during the years of the First World War, beset both by poverty and by bad health. He remained, however, pugnaciously cheerful; his aristocratic *morgue*, combined with his mixed experience of life, made him feel as much at home drinking coffee in a Parisian railway station with an urchin who had stolen his coat, as dominating the conversation at a dinner party. He was well-served by the athletic constitution he had inherited from his ancestors; he was a hedonist, but many of his pleasures were simple, sane, and wholesome ones: long walks, sight-seeing, simple meals in remote Italian inns. He was never drawn into purely literary circles, and was neither a social nor an intellectual snob. An unconscious vein of stoicism in his nature corrected his epicurean philosophy, and kept him on the whole healthy and happy during a long life. His best books are his ones on travel and his autobiography, but *South Wind*, his most famous novel – indeed, his only 'straight' novel – set a pattern for Aldous Huxley's *Those Barren Leaves* (in which Douglas figures as a character, Gardan) and for Sir Compton Mackenzie's novels about Capri and the strange sexual practices there, *Vestal Fires* and *Extraordinary Women*. Through Aldous Huxley, Douglas could also be thought to have had a certain influence on the early novels of Evelyn Waugh and Anthony Powell. The rather thin thread of the story of *South Wind* has to do with the impact of relaxed Mediterranean morals on Anglo-Saxon respectability. But what is memorable about the novels, as about Douglas's travel books, is the gently mocking commentary on things in general, the fantastic historical digressions, and the vivid evocations of landscape. Douglas at his best wrote as good prose as any author of his time: it appears perfectly easy, informal, and conversational, but is in fact admirably terse, and never lapses into garrulity. Douglas is not always at his best, but even at his most tiresome he has a characteristic flavour. In his impatient individualism, his amusing old-fashioned anti-clericalism, his passionate interest in the details of 'natural philosophy', his cranky erudition, his bluff, hearty, enjoying temperament, and his simple-minded belief in healthy sensuality as the cure for most human ills, he belonged neither to modern nor Victorian England, but, perhaps, to the French eighteenth century. There is also something of the ancient Roman about him; perhaps the English writer he most resembles is Walter Savage Landor. His gift for mockery is based on a firm limitation of interests, untypical of the complex, uneasy modern mind; his gay rebelliousness on a social assurance is today equally strange. And the occasional touch of spleen or brutality in his writings similarly recalls the eighteenth-century traveller, like Smollett, or the Roman satirist. *South Wind,* which is by no means the best of his works, appeals sometimes to an appetite in immature readers for rather facile sophistication. Douglas was too much of an egoist to have the objective interest in character and situation a novelist needs. He is under a cloud today with many critics because he described Lawrence as having merely 'opened a little window for the bourgeoisie'. But it should be remembered that Lawrence, though he put Douglas rather mockingly in a novel, once in a letter wrote of Douglas as a completely natural man, never false to his inclinations and instincts. And Douglas is too enjoyable a writer to remain long under a cloud; his travel books, where he himself is frankly at the centre of the picture, *Old Calabria, Siren Land, Fountains in the Sand,* are probably the best books of their kind written in English during this century.

8

The 'Gay' 1920s

ONE can think of the 1920s as a decade in which the British people as a whole were recovering from the shock of the First World War and hoping desperately that things would get back to 'normal': to the material comfort and moral indolence of the Edwardian decade, to the high Victorian confidence in the steady march of human progress. Mr Baldwin, who became Prime Minister in the middle of the decade, symbolized with his pipe, his solid farmer's air, his dislike of 'abroad', his attitude towards Labour and its claims of the good old-fashioned paternal employer, his praise of the sub-Hardyesque novels by Mary Webb, this deep national wish to get back to old foundations. But it was impossible to go back. For the fighting soldier, like Sassoon or Graves, the war had left a permanent scar on the mind. To intellectuals, politics, Versailles, the Irish troubles, the General Strike, and at the end of the decade the Slump, seemed a hopeless muddle: they sought for diversion and satisfaction in the interests and pleasures of private life. At a popular level this attitude led often to a cheap hedonism (reflected, for instance, in the plays of Noël Coward and the novels of Michael Arlen), a cheap cynicism, an equally cheap sentimentalism. There was a great deal of cant in the 1920s: cant in particular about 'freedom' (meaning especially freedom of sexual behaviour), about 'youth', and about 'the old men who led us into the war'. 'Youth' became so very much of a cult that even today English reviewers generally talk of a novelist, poet, or playwright as young, new, and promising till he is at least fifty; he then becomes an established figure, and with luck may ripen into a grand old man. If he lives long enough, everything will be forgiven him.

This cult of youth was satirized, with his usual pungency, by Wyndham Lewis in his novel *The Apes of God* and in his lively polemical essay, *The Doom of Youth*: he saw behind it a cult of immaturity, which he felt was being encouraged by sinister interests for their own ends. 'Youth' has obvious romantic and attractive characteristics; but it is also very docile and credulous. The violent and silly movements of our time, as well as some of the honourable and idealistic ones, have gained half their adherents from the very young, the emotionally and intellectually immature; and a good proportion of the other half from people who 'refuse to grow old'. Lewis's satire is as applicable, today, to the cult of teen-age pop singers and to the organized flattery and exploitation of adolescent consumers as it was in the 1920s.

In the 1920s, the new sexual freedom was sometimes defended, but often treated as a natural result of the war. Mrs Viveash, in Aldous Huxley's *Antic Hay*, is excused for breaking many hearts because her own heart was broken when the man she 'really' loved was killed in the Great War; and the Great War is often, also, brought forward in novels and plays of the 1920s as an excuse for unmannerly or neurotic behaviour by young men. It was too convenient an excuse, altogether, and a great deal of the 'advanced' writing of that decade is vitiated by a soft streak of silliness and self-pity. In an early novel, *This Side of Paradise*, the American Scott Fitzgerald manages to combine almost every kind of daringness, and silliness, that mark this kind of 1920s novel. Yet plunging uncritically into this 'hectic' world – 'hectic' and 'daring' were very fashionable 1920s adjectives – equipped him, when he had cooled off a little, to stand back and write a small masterpiece about the same world, *The Great Gatsby*. An American novel of the same world, of cocktails and sleeping about, which fascinated me in my youth, and which in literary quality is somewhere between *This Side of Paradise* and *The Great Gatsby*, is Carl Van Vechten's *Parties*. I remember this as funny, sad, and rather tender. A good farcical treatment of the whole international pleasure-seeking set-up is Anita Loos's *Gentlemen Prefer Blondes*. Aldous Huxley, who in a sense is the English equivalent of these American writers of the 1920s, could never quite let himself go as they could. He is the wry observer at the party, not, like Scott Fitzgerald or Van Vechten, the man who is going to have a terrible hangover next morning.

What one finds oneself looking for in the best novels of the 1920s is not, therefore, a broad and comprehensive picture of society but a personal consistency of attitude, on the novelist's part, when faced with a confusing and fragmentary world. Thus it could be said that three of the most distinguished novelists of the 1920s, Virginia Woolf, Aldous Huxley, and D. H. Lawrence, are none of them typically novelists; Huxley being essentially a discursive essayist, Mrs Woolf a poet of mood and sensation, D. H. Lawrence the prophet of a new religion of dark emotional drive. Moreover, each of these novelists speaks not for the whole man but for a separate layer of him; Huxley for the intellect and its detachment, Mrs Woolf for sensibility and its fine discriminations, Lawrence for the emotional will, its thrust, its restlessness, its rancour, and its vulnerability. They are good writers, and Lawrence is more than a good writer; though perhaps the power within him never took a finally satisfactory shape.

Reading Mrs Woolf, we must not be primarily interested in the active clash of character or the dramatic working out of plot. What she does convey is a fine and welcoming feminine 'sensation of living', of living from felt moment to felt moment, each unit of feeling having its individual complexity of colour, texture, shape. Her characters tend not to confront each other directly; when they are together, Mrs Ramsay summing up Charles Tansley, for example, Tansley is there as a bit, a gritty and uncomfortable bit, of her general consciousness, rather than as a shy and awkward young man; and more typically still, the characters of Mrs Woolf wander through the park, look at the play of light on leaves and grass, observe the dogs and nursemaids, the

banana peel on the gravel path, the crinkled face of a be-
draggled old man on a bench, while some tenuous but intense *inner* conflict plays itself out within their own selves
through this pattern of sensation. The frontier of the self,
for Mrs Woolf, is not the edge of the skin but the outer
limits of perception; and thus it is harder for her characters,
each tightly if impalpably enclosed in a sort of envelope, to
come into contact or collision than for characters more
crudely conceived. Clarissa Dalloway is for me one of the
most wonderful evocations in fiction of the airiness and inconsequence and extraordinary charm of a certain kind of
woman, but at the same time Clarissa has no abstract ideas,
no practical purposes; she is mere charm; so also Mrs
Ramsay, Mrs Woolf's most solid female character, seems
at times to melt away into a mere atmosphere. Even when
Mrs Woolf's characters are, like Lily Briscoe, given sharp
perceptions, they remain isolated: my view of the sunset
does not (except through art, and of course Lily is a painter)
communicate with yours.

Yet *To the Lighthouse*, in which Mrs Ramsay and Lily
Briscoe appear, is perhaps the most 'realistic' of Mrs Woolf's
novels. She uses in it the experiences of her own childhood.
She was the daughter of the great Victorian scholar, rationalist, mountaineer, literary critic, and founder of the *Dictionary of National Biography*, Sir Leslie Stephen. The
Stephens, who had begun, at the end of the eighteenth century, as Evangelical Christians deeply concerned with the
abolition of the slave trade, had become one of the great
Victorian mandarin families – the Stracheys, the Huxleys,
the Darwins, the Haldanes, the Trevelyans are others –
which generation after generation produced men and women
of public spirit and of high intellectual ability. In the liberal
atmosphere of Victorian England, this new aristocracy of
talent had established itself as firmly as the old aristocracy
of blood (in fact the Stracheys, Trevelyans, and Haldanes all
came from the landed gentry, but had produced no men of
great note in the world till the Victorian age). Thus, in
everything she writes, Virginia Woolf is inescapably aware

of the rewards and responsibilities of belonging to a privileged class.

Moreover, behind all Virginia Woolf's subtle and exact sensibility to shades of mood there is something harder, her father's sturdy agnosticism. Beatrice Webb, when she met Virginia Woolf, was puzzled by what seemed a delicate and spiritual nature unrelated to religion or to any large sense of social purpose like Beatrice Webb's own. Virginia Woolf's rationalism was firm and fundamentally sad. She was one of the group of writers called the Bloomsbury school – E. M. Forster, Lord Keynes, Roger Fry, Clive Bell, Lytton Strachey, Desmond MacCarthy were others – who had nearly all been at Cambridge, and many of whom had been profoundly influenced by the philosophical methods and conclusions of G. E. Moore. I doubt, from her own writings, whether Mrs Woolf was any more capable of following an abstract philosophical argument than Clarissa Dalloway. But she would have been affected by an atmosphere. Moore's importance as a moral influence on the Bloomsbury group is that he was not interested in God, history, or politics. He thought that good and pleasant states of feeling were the only things in life that were ultimately valuable, and he thought these states of feeling arose primarily from the enjoyment of love or friendship or the admiration of beauty, in art, in nature, or in human beings. He thought such feelings intrinsically good, and he thought feelings of lust or of delight in the thought of pain, cruelty, or ugliness intrinsically evil. But most of the practical business of the world, and even most of the labours of the mind, seemed to him morally meaningless except as a way of bringing good feelings into existence and suppressing bad feelings. In all the writers who were influenced by him there is a passionate striving towards clarity and honesty of thought and feeling, and towards a perception of the passing but real beauty of the world. The good is to be found in individual experience and, though men and women are mortal, the good is not less real.

This refined and difficult but by no means sentimental philosophy gives the work of the Bloomsbury group its own dignity and pathos. They accepted death as final, they looked for no vicarious immortality in the community, and it was only in the experience of art and in personal relationships that they looked for what values there are; these values, however, being really *there* for them, not a mere projection of subjective states. This made them stringently hostile to all kinds of stupidity and failure and general sloppiness in human living. Their philosophy perhaps robbed them of the charity which accepts failure as part of the essence of the human condition. They recognize, of course, that much of life is muddle and waste; but they seem rather frighteningly to assume that only a few successful lives, those of intellectuals and artists, of truly 'civilized' people, really 'count'. The others do not matter; though the lives of 'outsiders', like Charles Tansley, may have *for* the civilized people a value of pathos or comedy. At the same time, most of these writers were liberal and humanitarian in their social attitudes. Their humanitarianism did not spring, however, from any self-indentification with the struggling and the suffering. It sprang from impatience with the irrational and untidy and destructive. Their pity was real but a little cold.

In Mrs Woolf's *To the Lighthouse* there is more warmth and body than in any of her other novels, because it is based on strong and deep memories of the sense of community in the family. When Mrs Ramsay dies, the maternal warmth that created that sense of community, that shielded Mr Ramsay from his bitter sense of disappointment with himself, shielded his children from his black moods, and soothed the children's own resentment, goes too. What can be re-created will be re-created in a ghostly way, in her memory. There is thus piety and a reverence for the spirit of a dead parent, in the book, as well as the sense of community. But a sense of community of that sort and a habit of piety of that sort were not to be found by Mrs Woolf herself. In her other novels – except for her very last one, *Between the Acts* – one is too much aware of her as a brilliant solitary, guessing at rather than grasping other lives. Thus, in her most experimental novel, *The Waves,* the characters present themselves, from childhood to old age, through a series of soliloquies; but each voice seems Mrs Woolf's own. She offers us a lyrical abstraction from the pain with which she felt the world; the quality of her mind and spirit has a distinction that will make some readers always grateful to accept the offering. There are others, the Charles Tansleys of this world (Charles Tansley, even softened in Mrs Ramsay's maternal consciousness, is a wonderful prototype of the 1950s' 'angry young man'), whom she will always fill with a sense of social resentment and unease.

Aldous Huxley was a much more uneven writer. Probably his earliest novels, *Crome Yellow*, *Antic Hay*, and *Those Barren Leaves*, are those that will wear best. They are full of wit, sadness, and fantasy; they are elegantly written; they show a zest for caricature and an extravagant youthful delight in the display of learning. Obvious models are Norman Douglas, possibly Ronald Firbank, and farther back W. H. Mallock and Thomas Love Peacock. In the phrases of the young novelist in *Crome Yellow*, Mr Huxley hates the description of 'middle-class interiors' and loves to display ideas 'bombinating in a vacuum'. The setting may be a palazzo in Italy, an English country house, or London's literary bohemia. The characters are mainly *rentiers*, writers, or artists. The men are not encumbered by routine jobs nor the women by household tasks. Everybody thus has leisure and energy for endless discussions that make many pages of these novels read less like ordinary fiction than like fragments from a parody of a Platonic dialogue. These early novels of Huxley's are not, however, by any means so arid and abstract as such a description might suggest. They have the interest of satire and sometimes, indeed, of farce. Huxley likes to show either how people's ideas and principles usually fail to square with the lives they lead or how alarming it is when they do. He displays very amusingly various types of intellectual pretension. He takes his models from life: I have a copy of *Antic Hay* in which somebody has pencilled in the fly-leaf the originals of the main characters; but since nearly all (two exceptions are Philip Heseltine and Wyndham Lewis) are still living, I cannot give the names here. In *Point Counter Point*, where the wit and gaiety begin to sag – the sharp but thin feeling for life is stretched over too cumbrous a framework – there are portraits, hardly disguised, of D. H. Lawrence and John Middleton Murry. In his handling of violent incidents (of which he becomes fond from *Point Counter Point* onwards), Huxley tends to be melodramatic. He has the feel of bright literary chatter, he can understand people through their ideas, through the things they say when they are trying to be bright, but he is at a loss when he has to deal with the more direct and simple feelings, and the tense situations that can arise from them. In the sub-articulate world, the world of dumb crises, in which his friend D. H. Lawrence was so deeply at home, Huxley is lost.

Huxley's principal theme is the search for a workable faith in a bewildering world – the bewilderment expressed as a fragmentation of ideas, rather than as profound social disorder. In *Point Counter Point*, he seems to be trying to believe in a creed rather like that of Rampion, the figure who stands for D. H. Lawrence in the novel, the creed of a 'life-worshipper'; but Philip Quarles, the novelist crippled by self-consciousness, who perhaps stands for Huxley himself in the novel, is a more convincing figure. (Lawrence himself found Rampion a bore.) More naturally and sincerely, Huxley, since *Point Counter Point*, sought salvation in a mystical attitude, which aims at renunciation of ordinary human appetites and passions and especially the renunciation of ordinary human egoism. The self, in the sense of the ego as opposed to the atman, is the great enemy, and benevolent non-attachment is the final goal. This is like Buddhism except that, unlike the earliest Buddhists, Huxley was a theist believing in a purely spiritual Ground of Being. He did not become an anti-rationalist, but kept up his science: he was interested in the possibility of obtaining visions of bliss through the use of drugs like mescalin. In his satirical fantasy, *Brave New World*, he envisaged with considerable horror the possibility of a hygienic and humane, but fundamentally inhuman, Utopia based on Pavlovian conditioning, sedative and bliss-producing drugs, and licensed, harmless promiscuity; a noble savage, who has read Shakespeare, bursts into this world, asserting the rights of guilt and remorse and tragedy. The savage is a corrective, but does not express Huxley's own point of view. In a fairly recent book of essays, *Brave New World Revisited*, much more allowance is made for the possible use of science in creating a more humane world.

Critics often complain that the scientific-cum-religious attitude at which Huxley arrived is pallid and joyless, that he was a writer who was squeamish about flesh-and-blood reality, that he found it easy to love God because he found it difficult to like men. And from a purely literary point of view, he certainly wrote too much – too many novels, essays, discursive travel books – so that his real, but not gross or abundant or overflowing, talent was spread out too thin. One is aware, in his later writing especially, of mechanical tricks of style: of the manner of the teacher pointing at the blackboard, expounding, and making at regular intervals little propitiatory jokes – not always very good ones. But in the honesty and range of his mind Huxley was a peculiarly stimulating writer, especially for young people who need their intellectual curiosity stirred and their provincial complacencies disturbed. He had an urbane, civilized, honourably serious mind; and in his earlier writing he was a genuine wit and a true artist, in a minor but valuable vein.

It is much more difficult to write about D. H. Lawrence. Huxley himself (so he tells us in his fine introduction to Lawrence's *Collected Letters*) thought Lawrence unlike any other man he had met: he had met other men superior to himself in various ways, but they were the same kind of man as himself; Lawrence, he felt, was different in kind. Certainly, what must at once be recognized in Lawrence is *power*. Let me quote a passage from a short story:

At a certain moment the men who are really living will come beseeching to put their lives into the hands of the greater men among them, beseeching the greater men to take the sacred responsibility of power. ... At last the masses will come to such men and say, 'You are greater than we. Be our lords. Take our life and death in your hands, and dispose of us according to your will. Because we see a light in your face, and a burning on your mouth. ...' Ah, but my chosen aristocrat would say to those who chose him: 'If you choose me, you give up for ever your right to judge me. If you have truly chosen to follow me, you have thereby rejected all your right to criticize me. You can no longer either approve or disapprove of me. You have performed the sacred act of choice. Henceforth you can only obey.'

That shows Lawrence's prophetic power (he is not speaking through his own mouth, of course, but through the mouth of a character in one of his stories); he is prophesying what the *morale* of a movement like National Socialism, or perhaps indeed like Stalinism, will be. The passage is beautifully written, with power and truth and simplicity – too beautifully in fact, for Lawrence either fails to realize, or is not concerned, that what he is prophesying will prove hateful to all those who wish to be neither slaves nor masters, who wish to be free. Similarly, he either does not realize, or does not feel, that there is something hateful in the motives of his hero, the German-Slavonic Count Psanek, who makes this prophecy. Lawrence recognizes a strong and sincere emotion, yields imaginatively to it, and refuses to make judgements about good or evil, right or wrong; or rather he prefers the strong and sincere emotion, very often involving either the will to hurt or the will to dominate. Thus from any more complex or more balanced point of view, from any in the widest sense 'liberal' point of view, Lawrence is objectively wrong in all his practical attitudes. One has a sense of authenticity in acting on a strong emotion; one is wiser usually to question it, and not act on it.

I would like to make a distinction here between emotions and sensibility. Sensibility is what makes one aware of other people's emotions, and makes one treat them with care and tact; emotion means a state of feeling which heightens one's sense of authentic selfhood, acts as a drive on the will, and blinds one to other people and often to one's own best interests. It is a state of feeling, and one talks about being *in* a state, enveloped in it. Love seems to me an emotion in its onset, in the state called falling in love, but thereafter it becomes a habit of the will and sensibility, a habit of awareness of, and communication with, other persons, and care for them. Love, for Lawrence, was not this, but primarily emotional, and therefore primarily self-assertive. I never 'chose' Lawrence, in Count Psanek's sense, and therefore I am free to criticize, and to say that I think he was wrong.

Lawrence's social background was very different from that of Mrs Woolf or Huxley; where they came from the intellectual aristocracy, the English mandarin class, Lawrence was the son of a miner, his mother being of a slightly higher social class than his father, who resented her 'refinement', just as she nagged at the father's rough ways. Thus he was brought up in an atmosphere of struggle for dominance between man and wife, with his sympathies tugged sometimes towards his father's strength, rowdiness, and dumb angers, and sometimes towards his mother's hymn-singing. His mother, however, was the dominant emotional factor in his life till she died, though afterwards he felt guilt at not having loved his father enough. His mother's Nonconformist piety gave him that 'gravity', as Mr David Holbrook calls it, that serious Puritan streak of self-concern, which remained with him all his life. His father's humiliations and brutalities made him turn again and again towards the theme of the man of little education, of few words, who dominates a more subtle and complex woman by the dumb force of his masculinity. As in many artists who have been dominated by their mothers, there was in Lawrence a strong streak of latent homosexuality. His friendship with Middleton Murry broke up on Murry's refusal to enter with him into a relation of 'blood-brothership'. Lawrence hated the Cambridge intellectual conception of male friendship, based on debate and argument from emotionally prepared positions; true friendship, for him, had to involve surrender. In his relationship with his wife,

Frieda, a grand maternal earth-goddess, he was in some sense a child rediscovering his mother and achieving, in innocence, the Oedipal wish; he bitterly resented Frieda's interest in her children by her first husband and seems not to have wanted children of his own. Remembering his father, he sometimes wanted to dominate her rather than be loved by her. She was a demanding woman and he was not a sexually energetic man; it is perhaps because of this that he put forward the oddest of his ideas about sex, the idea that in the act woman should be content to hold, to calm and satisfy man, and should not wish for an orgasm herself. The stress, as in *Lady Chatterley's Lover*, on the female admiration of the male, rather than the male admiration of the woman, may have sprung from his latent homosexuality. These things are not in themselves morally wrong; but some critics set up Lawrence's life history and the personal attitudes which spring from it as the norm, rather than as the special cases they obviously are.

But more important than Lawrence's feelings about sex were his feelings about class. His prose and poetry both assert his working-class origins, not in obvious ways like his skilful use of dialect, but in his use of short rather than complex sentences, his way of stopping and starting again, his conduct of an argument by way of repetition of a key word or symbol rather than by a final condensation; there is spurtiness, jerkiness, sudden tiredness, and humorous impatience, but there is always life. He distrusted the coldness, the lack of contact, the excessive cerebral articulateness, of middle-class life. Working-class couples have violent rows, have prolonged sulks, but make it up tenderly. Middle-class couples tend to avoid the rows and the sulks, 'to paper over the cracks', but often miss the tenderness. *Lady Chatterley's Lover* is essentially a plea for tenderness and for the pathos, the comedy, and the dignity of the male animal, whatever his social class, whatever his mental resources. Sir Clifford had to be castrated or paralysed, to symbolize Lawrence's sense that the English ruling classes retained their intellectual arrogance but were dead from the waist down. For

Lawrence, also, the most important thing in life was not 'character' or 'personality' but something deeper – the basic carbon which may be formed by different kinds of pressure into coal or diamonds. He would ask, not, 'What have you made of yourself?' but, 'Of what kind of fundamental stuff are you made?' His characters react towards or against each other instinctively, without argument, as animals and children do. Surface 'attitude' or 'personality' he thought of as pose and convention; he looked for the deep drives, hated invalids and cripples in whom these drives have gone sick: romanticized gamekeepers, miners, all kinds of healthy and inarticulate men in whom the expression of emotional and physical need is direct. But he did not see, in industrial civilization, any chance of permanent happiness for such men.

Lawrence wanted people to be more 'primitively' themselves than they ever can be in a complex modern society; he spent much of his life looking for the simple life in Sardinia, Italy, and New Mexico, but never appeared to find it. He was, inescapably, a complex modern man. He looked for what he called a 'wisdom of the blood' and because of his quickness of response to alien modes of being, his reverence for a living difference or otherness, no writer of our time has been able to evoke so vividly animals or children, natural scenes or the basic drives of love or hate, or the sense of blankness and separation between persons. But, though he is undeniably a writer of genius, he is also strikingly uneven. Miss Kathleen Nott, in a broadcast talk printed in the *Listener* (19 April 1962), has these remarks to make about Lawrence's purely technical weaknesses as an novelist:

It is strictly the forms of his language and his art that give Lawrence away. In his book on Lawrence, Dr Leavis had dealt with those many critics, including Middleton Murry, who have insisted that Lawrence could not create individual character: has dealt with this to his own satisfaction if not that of others. Even in the two books which, one may agree with Dr Leavis, are Lawrence's best – *The Rainbow* and *Women in Love* – the women, though treated with unwonted care and sympathy, spend far too much time talking pure Lawrencese. And the dialogue does not advance the action or develop the characters. It was unfashionable for a long time – during Lawrence's development, too – to hold that these dramatic elements are the significant structure of a novel as well as of a play. But in fact a novel is a movement in time: it is therefore about the necessity of growth: it is therefore inevitably about the interaction of a pattern of events and character. In a Lawrence novel, people do not really grow up at all: they just go on arguing to a foregone conclusion – Lawrence's: this is the prescription for monologue, not dialogue: the other side tends to turn into a sounding-board.

Miss Nott goes on to suggest that, after the Great War, 'merely to insist upon "life" instead of death may have been healing and inspiriting' and that to Dr. Leavis 'Lawrence, like Freud, may have seemed a psychological liberator'. But she adds: 'But now perhaps we should rather see "life", in Lawrence's usage, as one of the great abstractions.' And even a grand abstraction like this, not properly fused with art, will fail to be the germ of a culture – for, Miss Nott insists, 'culture is about individual lives and individual insights'.

Certainly, Lawrence does tend to shovel into his novels conversation, scenes, personalities for no better artistic reason than that these, or something like them, happened in real life. He rants at the reader, he harangues him, or he sometimes make his characters do the ranting and haranguing for him. The special vocabulary in which he expresses many of his deepest convictions, the vocabulary of the wisdom in the blood and the impulses in the solar plexus and the ganglia, is both philosophically absurd and poetically unconvincing. For all that, Lawrence's ideas, what Miss Nott would call his 'great abstractions', are not to be dismissed in a hurry any more than his art is. He has perhaps only one or two early novels, *The White Peacock* and *Sons and Lovers*, which are satisfying for structure as well as texture, but the short story was less of a strain on his powers of construction, and some of his short stories are masterpieces; his travel books and his letters are delightful. Of his two critical books, the one on Hardy is mainly self-expression, but *Classic*

American Literature, unconventionally though it is written, is enduringly vital and suggestive. His poems, T. S. Eliot has suggested, are rough and unfinished, like pages from the working note-book of a great poet; but because a freshness and intimacy comes from their very roughness, they are endlessly re-readable, and re-readable in bulk; one reads them as one would read an intimate journal. Lawrence's great strength was in instinctively putting a finger on what is alive and what is dead. His weakness was not allowing enough of a place for the life of the intellect in his total ideal picture of man. Man is at once something more, and something less happy, than a harmoniously working animal. He is rational, as well as passionate and imaginative. In modern society he can no longer live by ritual; but he still dreams of Eden, and this dream, transmuted through an imagination like Lawrence's, helps to keep him alive.

Three other minor but still very significant novelists of the 1920s deserve mention. Ronald Firbank was the grandson of a Victorian working man who had become a railway magnate and whose son, Firbank's father, was a very conventional Tory M.P.; in three generations, Ronald Firbank himself had managed to acquire the look of a decadent aristocrat. He had a lean, bony, exaggerated face, with a slightly Red Indian look, out of which started the masterful nose that had jutted ruggedly from between the broad cushiony cheeks of his grandfather and had given some dignity to his father's air of vapid complacency. Firbank's face has been perpetuated by Augustus John and Wyndham Lewis, and his high thin voice, his hysterical giggle, his pathological shyness, his wriggling walk, the mixture of brilliance and inconsequence in his conversation have been described by Lord Berners and Sir Osbert Sitwell. For those who frequented the Eiffel Tower and the Café Royal, for London's wealthier Bohemia, he became a mascot. He was very amusing for the first ten minutes of an encounter; then his inability to conduct a conversation except at a series of tangents became tiresome. The descriptions of him suggest a high-grade mental defective with a streak of genius.

Profoundly solitary, he brooded a great deal about Roman Catholicism, but seems never to have become a Catholic. He spent the Great War in nervous seclusion in Oxford; he died in solitude in an expensive Italian hotel, using what was left of his money to ward off those human contacts which at once frightened and fascinated him.

Firbank's life was one of frozen hysteria and sterile self-absorption; the saving elements in it were his deep affection for his mother (he seems to have had no real relationship with anybody else) and his sense of the absurd. His novels must have helped him to retain his precarious balance, and in them he concentrates with an almost religious earnestness on the 'amusing': for him, in life and in literature, to be obvious and to be serious were equal solecisms. His characters are seen neither in action, in profile, nor in depth, but in teasing fragments, through a haze of cocktail chatter. He scatters his pages with the oddest snatches of conversation, clues to impossible mysteries. The smart dresses, the over-heated rooms, the expensive bric-à-brac are on the same plane as the talk and the people, as real or unreal, and show the same magpie-like instinct for hoarding bright scraps. Even in his high, thin, giggling naughtiness, Firbank seems to me to have a child-like quality, that comes out in his wonderful mis-spellings; his books belong on the same shelf as *Peter Rabbit*, *Through the Looking Glass*, or even *The Young Visitors*. Alice liked books 'full of conversations' and the narrator wanders through Firbank with a wide-eyed Alician alertness.

The novels of L. H. Myers provide an indirect commentary on Firbank's world and also on the Bloomsbury of Virginia Woolf. The best known of them, those collected under the title *The Root and the Flower*, are set in India of the Moguls. But they are not historical novels in the strict sense. Their theme is the spiritual life and how far, if at all, it can be adequately embodied in social institutions. Myers's very unpleasant portrait of the Great Mogul's degenerate son, Daniyal, and his court of buffoons and flatterers, 'the Camp', devoted to art, gossip, trivial sensuality, mild malice, and amateur theatricals, is a criticism of the aesthetic 'civilization', life in terms of little 'kicks' and thrills, for which Firbank lived and died. The frivolity of this mode of life, which refuses to make a choice between good and evil, seems to Myers more corrupting than the sincere choice of evil itself. There are, he feels, worse things than stern military despotism. Yet the power politicians are also treated harshly, and it seems to have been Myers's feeling that spiritual insight is denatured or deformed when embodied in institutions. The representative of spiritual wisdom in his book, the Guru, is the enemy of institutional religion; he believes in original goodness, rather than original sin. It is interesting to learn from an excellent article by Mr Walter Allen that Myers, a very rich man, had both a certain sympathy with Communism and an intense dislike of the Anglo-Catholic Toryism of Mr T. S. Eliot. Myers was preoccupied with the nature of the good life, which seemed to him to involve both renunciation and an experience at some point of the fullness of living. He was more impressed with the fertility of the basic human impulses than depressed with the instability of institutional culture and religion; his historical philosophy might be described as optimistic fatalism. In the rich vein of its thought and the texture of its prose, combined with a certain thinness of narrative interest, and a way of turning characters into representatives of a moral or intellectual position, *The Root and the Flower* recalls Pater's *Marius the Epicurean* more than any other work of English fiction; though Myers would have thoroughly disapproved of Pater's aestheticism, ritualism, and sceptical, twilit poetics. Myers is a writer, like Pater, who gives a general impression of wisdom but his wisdom is unrelated to current problems. It may be that his wealth and his assured social position allowed him to observe life with an undue remoteness; though gloom about the state of the world eventually drove him to take his own life.

T. F. Powys, a member of a very gifted Welsh family of writers, resembles the Myers of *The Root and the Flower* in that his books are essentially didactic allegories; they have been incisively described by Empson as Buddhist death-plays with Christian imagery. The setting is always rural and the texture of the prose recalls Jane Austen and, much more profoundly, Bunyan. The characters have often Bunyanesque names, like Lord Titball, and the wicked characters, who are plentiful, embody a single personified drive, usually malice, cruelty, or lust. The good characters, who are sometimes clergymen, are hated because of their goodness and usually come to bad ends. Through all the tales there runs a melancholy mysticism: thus, in *Mr Weston's Good Wine*, the wine is death, and we drink it to escape from this vale of troubles. Powys is at his best a perfect artist, but, it seems to me, a minor one. He can achieve formal perfection because his view of life is such a sharply limited one and so perfectly pessimistic. He is a writer who is very often used by critics lamenting the decay of a fine old rural culture, which has its last embodiment in his pages. But for Powys himself, both Jane Austen and Bunyan stand for qualities, of serene order and of spiritual fervour, that have gone from English country life; he sees that life as stupid and brutal and sometimes vilely cruel, an enemy of the spirit; and much as I admire his art, I would much rather live in Subtopia than in Powysland.

9

The 'Serious' 1930s

IF the 1920s were a decade when writers tended to turn away in fatigue, boredom, and disgust from everyday problems of social living and political choice, the 1930s forced the writer's attention back on the intractable public world around him. In 1929, the great Wall Street slump had disastrous repercussions everywhere in Europe. Unemployment and social distress, as well as militant nationalism, brought Hitler to power in Germany: for a few years at least, guns *meant* butter. Hitler's policy of rearmament put Germany back to work but threatened the peace and liberties of Europe. Hitler came to power in 1933. Later in the decade the Spanish Civil War and the Italian conquest of Abyssinia forced writers to take definite political sides as no comparable events in the 1920s had. There was also a growing and fully justified fear that Spain, Ethiopia, and, in the Far East, Manchuria were only preludes to an all-out assault by the new Nazi, Fascist, and in Japan military-imperialist powers on the entrenched positions of the older liberal democracies. Of the two allies which could redress the balance of power, the United States had a strong tradition of isolationism; and Russia was much more deeply feared in many conservative circles in France and Britain than Germany, Italy, and Japan were. The liberal-democratic powers were also themselves imperialists and thus in a weak position in objecting to expansion. Inside Europe, the small succession states of the Dual Monarchy could only exist on goodwill; they were in no position to defend themselves against either Germany or Russia. And many English liberals were weakened in denouncing Hitler because they, like him, had denounced the provisions of the Treaty of Versailles as unjust.

Since 1917, Russia had been isolated from the Western

world. Her very isolation, the abundance of propaganda literature for or against her, the strong emotional colouring of most of the newspaper reporting that came from Russia, the little that was known in any exact or reliable detail about the working of her new system of government, was likely, on the principle of *omne ignotum pro magnifio*, to engage and tantalize the imagination of the young. A young man not only of the working class but also of the middle class grew up in the 1930s with no certain prospect of a job in front of him, with an all too probable chance of being caught up in another major war, with social distress and economic stagnation all around him. It was natural that many should find themselves thinking with interest and curiosity of that larger country, the Soviet Union, in which, in however ruthless a fashion, the problems of preserving full employment and keeping production swinging upwards and keeping the national morale high seemed to have been solved. Very few English writers of the 1930s actually became members of the Communist Party; many of those who did remained members only for a short time. But just as in the 1890s the Roman Catholic Church provided a focus of attraction for writers who in the end may never have taken the final step towards conversion, so, in the 1930s, Communism provided such a focus.

A well-known London publisher, Victor Gollancz, founded the Left Book Club, which, besides publishing a monthly magazine for its members, sold them every month a book on some aspect of Socialist or of militant anti-Fascist politics. But while a majority of young intellectuals were driven in these years towards the extreme Left, a minority were driven towards the extreme Right. Sir Oswald Mosley had been the most forceful and intelligent of the younger ministers in Ramsay MacDonald's second government, but, finding all his schemes blocked by middle-aged ineptitude, had left the Labour Party to found the short-lived New Party, which at first included such distinguished men as John Strachey and Harold Nicolson. Such followers left Sir Oswald when he rapidly swung, with the foundation of the

British Union of Fascists, into an imitation of Mussolini and later of Hitler. Political meetings in the years between 1930 and 1940 had often a dramatic and violent flavour which it is hard to imagine in the 1960s, when we usually get our political propaganda on television or from the canvasser at the door step, and when even at a general election it is rarely worth a candidate's while to hire a hall, hold a meeting, and make a speech. Brawls between Fascists and Communists, and the beating up of interrupters at Fascist meetings, were common. For most young writers in the 1930s, the liberal, middle-of-the-road attitude seemed a weak one.

Thus, the best English novels of the 1930s reflect a state of social tension. They can be divided into four main categories:

(1) The symbolic melodrama, or literary thriller. Novels of this sort use the mechanism of the old-fashioned tale of crime and adventure to put across the frightening state of the world. Graham Greene is the master of this genre.

(2) 'Documentary' novels, like some of Christopher Isherwood's, in which the writer uses his own personal observation of danger-spots, such as Berlin, to underline in a quieter and more exact way his sense of the world's insecurity.

(3) The social allegory, often concerned with the conflicting attractions, and disadvantages, of innovation and traditionalism in social life. Rex Warner is the notable writer here.

(4) The social farce or comedy, with elements of satire and fantasy, that lays its stress less on political disorder or social distress than on the incoherence and frivolity of contemporary manners among the upper classes. The notable writers here are Evelyn Waugh and Anthony Powell. Where the underlying mood of the other three types of novel is radical, the underlying mood of this type is wistfully or cynically conservative.

Let us take these four types of novel in order.

Graham Greene, the great master of symbolic melodrama in the 1930s, divides his novels into real novels and entertainments, which may be, like *Our Man in Havana*, comedy thrillers. The straight thrillers, like *Stamboul Train, A Gun for Sale*, and *The Ministry of Fear* are plain, old-fashioned ones, with spies, secret documents, chases in the dark, and murders. They concentrate on the hunted man, rather than the hunters, but in this they are in the tradition of John Buchan's *The Thirty-Nine Steps*. They also sometimes, like *A Gun for Sale*, involve the convention of the villain-hero, the bad man cheated by worse men, who comes out on the side of the good at the cost of his life. In the serious novel, like *The Power and the Glory*, the hero is less than bad; he is weak. The whisky priest in that novel has let his vocation down, he is being hunted by the Mexican authorities who want to suppress organized religion, but his vocation drags him back to risk his life, to lose it. In *The Heart of the Matter* a man who is not obviously weak, but perhaps excessively sympathetic and understanding, is led, though a devout Roman Catholic, into committing adultery, conniving at murder, taking the sacrament without having made a proper confession, and finally into suicide; by what one knows of the rules he ought to go to hell, but he is intrinsically a much 'nicer' person than most of us. In *Brighton Rock*, which I think one of Mr Greene's most overpraised novels, we have the vicious adolescent race-gang leader Pinkie, spiritually real because he has chosen pure evil, contrasted with the hearty, sensuous woman who believes, in a coarse British way, in 'right' and 'wrong'. For Greene, evil has spiritual glamour, and spiritual goodness is often connected with moral weakness. Goodness appears as a supernatural light which shines through unlikely people. In his more recent novels, however, this preoccupation, though still there, is less obvious. The hero of *The Quiet American* is neither weak, nor a Christian. He is a journalist in the Far East whose Asian mistress may be taken from him by an innocent and idealistic American secret agent, who has become his close friend. He discovers that the American has helped to engineer a bomb outrage. He tips off local Communists about him. The American is murdered. The Englishman is left feeling flat. Did he act out of jealousy? He has, in any case, been hunted into an act which darkens his life. In *A Burnt-Out Case*, a famous French Catholic architect, also renowned for his love-affairs, visits a French *leproserie* run by monks in Africa. He is disillusioned about his talent, tired of love, feels no religious fervour: he wants to be mildly useful, and have a rest from his reputation. His fame pursues him and a jealous husband, whose intrusions into his spiritual life he has snubbed, shoots him in revenge for an adultery he has not committed. He dies laughing at a joke which no one else sees. Greene cannot really get away from his religion; the unspoken question about the hero of *A Burnt-Out Case* (leprosy under proper treatment 'burns itself out', but leaves the cured victim a shell of a man) is whether the hero is saved, just as the unspoken question about the hero of *The Quiet American* is whether he is damned. Damnation is often, in Greene, associated with success in the world, salvation with utter failure.

A novel of the 1930s which seems to me underrated, and which displays most of Greene's powers and his typical thematic pattern, is *England Made Me*. The hero is a weak but handsome young Englishman called Anthony, with gentlemanly manners but no staying power, who has drifted about the world from one job to another, losing jobs through petty dishonesty (to have money for drink or cards), or boasting or lying (pretending to have been to a better school, to have met more important people, than he has). Anthony is a typical black-sheep hero as his friend, Minty, is a typically flawed near-saint. Minty is hopelessly incompetent, a remittance man in a Scandinavian city, not vicious, but irritating and futile, an embarrassment to the British Ambassador, an old schoolfellow, who can never quite finally 'drop' him. He has a devout religious faith, which he expresses in a ridiculously finicky old-maidish manner. He is very lonely and opens his heart to Anthony, under whose more glamorous exterior he recognizes a fellow victim of life. Nevertheless, Minty is, we discover as the plot develops, a good man but one without self-will, without malice, nursing in his weakness and wretchedness a vision of goodness, tortured by the evil around him of which he has an acute and painful awareness. He is a man crushed and almost crippled by the sense of his own inferiority.

Anthony, when the story opens, has not yet made his final choice between good and evil. He has come to the Scandinavian city where Minty lives because his sister is loved by an unscrupulous Scandinavian financier (he may be modelled on Kreuger the match-king) who for her sake gives Anthony a job. For the first time in his life, Anthony has the money and sense of social importance he has always felt he is entitled to. Then he is asked to behave brutally to some poor man whom the financier has ruined, and who wants an interview. He can lie and pilfer but his genuine sense of decency revolts at injustice and cruelty. The financier conceals his anger, but gives his orders; a henchman of his pushes Anthony into a river on a foggy night. Minty guesses that a murder has been committed, lets the murderer know he guesses, but can do nothing to bring about vengeance in this world. Evil seems to have triumphed. But, in fact, Anthony's soul is safe; in his weak way he has borne witness for goodness. And round the wicked, as the story moves to a close, unspeakable clouds of darkness seem to gather.

Greene does not heavily underline the moral implications of his stories, as I have been doing here. He is a remarkably readable writer, and yet a writer from whom it is very difficult to remember sentences and paragraphs. One remembers scenes. Greene is present in his novels as a producer is present in a film, rather than as a poet in a poem. He works in a series of sharply visualized episodes, and the frequent use of metaphor and simile to heighten description, or intensify atmosphere, is one of the few obviously personal characteristics of his style. He cuts, like a film director, from episode to episode; there are no long, dull, ruminative, or padded passages. The episodes he chooses to present are each, in themselves, a minor climax of some part of the story; something has always come to a head, life is never just jogging along. So Greene's stories translate admirably into cinema, and one may find it hard to remember whether one has read the book or seen the film. He is cinematic also in his sense of atmosphere, heat, monotony, or seediness, atmosphere always used to heighten expectation and never for its own sake. We have probably no more workmanlike novelist. What worries one about some of the recent novels is a sense that, though they are as workmanlike as ever, Greene is perhaps becoming as bored as some of his critics, not with his obsessions (all art is obsessive), but with the narrowness of their range. There is more comedy and irony in his recent books, sometimes, as in *A Burnt-Out Case*, directed against the very reader who finds a deep spiritual meaning in his works. He has lost, today, the peculiar tang he had for young readers in the 1930s – the sense of the great railway station, the tightness of nervous expectation, the poetry of uneasy departures towards unnamed danger, and the 'seedy' feeling of the modern city, peeling, stripped, shabby, deprived. The sense of the threatening in the ordinary is today commonplace: in the 1930s, Greene made it new.

In preparing this revised edition, I worry a little about the concept of the 'documentary' novel. It was a real concept in the 1930s, connected with the high achievements and great prestige of the British documentary film. The idea behind it was that detached, cinematic observation of carefully, or even of apparently casually, chosen episodes would bring out a social significance, not imposed by the novelist. The trouble is that the only really distinguished practitioner of the form one can think of now is Christopher Isherwood. There must have been others; and the phrase was also used, inappropriately, about James Hanley and other realistic novelists of working-class life, who were usually much too emotionally involved in their material to appear 'documentary' in Isherwood's sense. There was a 'documentary' quality also in much of the poetry of the time and in the travel books in which Auden collaborated first with MacNeice and then with Isherwood himself. As editor of *New Writing* and later *Penguin New Writing*, Mr John Lehmann also in the 1930s and on into the 1940s made a practice of publishing short prose pieces, often by non-professional writers, which aimed at giving a true picture of life in the mines or in the army. But on the whole Isherwood must stand alone for what is either a lost species, or one that only evolved into fully satisfying life in his own works.

Isherwood's two most obviously 'documentary' works of fiction, *Good-bye to Berlin* and *Mr Norris Changes Trains*, are, on the surface, about the everyday experiences of the narrator, who has a different name in each book, but who is in each a version of Mr Isherwood himself, a young Englishman of the upper middle class, without private means, earning a modest living as a private teacher of English in Berlin during the rise to power of the Nazis. The tone is that of the benign observer, sympathetic and detached, often politely surprised, an observer with a quiet sense of comedy. Yet in a series of small episodes, round a kitchen table, in a nightclub, on a holiday island, in a sanatorium or a brothel, Isherwood shows us a nation becoming trapped. Even Mr Norris, the absurd gentleman crook, who seems at first to belong to P. G. Wodehouse comedy, becomes an instrument of betrayal and murder, a type of the traitor self-betrayed; evil cannot be kept comic and small, will not stay still. But in showing the Germans and others around him lost and trapped, Isherwood vaunts no sense of personal moral superiority. The Communists in Berlin are shown as having courage and purpose, but are not romanticized; the narrator waves sympathetically towards them but, irremediably liberal and middle-class, will never join them. Isherwood's tone of unsentimental charity and of astringent clarity is a high achievement; it is not for nothing that his favourite English novelist is E. M. Forster.

The prose of Isherwood's novels is to me more interesting than of Greene's: Greene's clipped, vivid sentences make us see what he wants us to see, put us at the desired angle of observation, but do not, for all his frequent use of metaphor and simile, convey overtones of personality, make Greene's own voice memorable. Or, perhaps, Greene's personality has no overtones. But with Isherwood, the style is the man. The prose looks easy and even amateurish, it is exactly like somebody informally talking to us. Isherwood never seems to be taking any special pains, but there is no waste; the deceptively casual-looking sentences each define an impression, convey an idea, or set a tone. One knows many longer and more ambitious-looking books that are less packed with genuine *matter* (matter observed, selected, felt, correlated) than those two short books about Berlin. I would have said in the 1930s that Isherwood was the most exciting of the younger English novelists. He is still a writer of great attractiveness, but one cannot say that the promise was fulfilled. *Prater Violet* was a sentimental novelette about the film industry, though with a pleasing portrait of an eccentric director. The autobiographical *Lions and Shadows* and a travel-book, *The Condor and the Cows*, were better, with all the old charm of style. More recently, the long and ambitious *The World in the Evening*, even if starting from experience, like all Mr Isherwood's best writing, seems over 'fictionalized'. In Isherwood's most recent collection of stories, *Down There on a Visit*, on the other hand, reviewers, shocked by some of the sexual episodes, complained that experience had not been 'fictionalized' enough. But there is still plenty of time for him to hit the right balance again.

Let us now turn to the third type of novel I have mentioned, the 'social allegory'. The most important writer of this kind of novel in the 1930s was Rex Warner, a public schoolmaster teaching Latin and Greek, and a minor poet much influenced by Hopkins and Auden. The three best known of his allegorical novels are *The Wild Goose Chase, The Aerodrome*, and *The Professor*, and I shall deal here with *The Aerodrome*, perhaps the best of these. The setting of this story is a small, sleepy, out-of-the-way village in the south of England, on the outskirts of which the Air Ministry decide to erect a large new aerodrome for experimental purposes. In charge of the aerodrome is an Air Vice-Marshal, who is a man of driving intelligence and ambition. He takes charge of village life and starts to dominate and organize the local inhabitants in a way which would be inconceivable in real life. The whole story, indeed, is full of improbable incidents and coincidences: the hero, who thinks himself the son of the local Vicar, turns out to be the illegitimate son of the Air Vice-Marshal, whom his father, for that matter, believes himself to have murdered on a climbing holiday; and a young Air Force officer, who is appointed as chaplain to the village by the Air Force, turns out to be the Air Vice-Marshal's illegitimate son by the Squire's sister. The story sometimes recalls a fairy-tale and sometimes a Victorian melodrama; and a quality of artful simplicity in the prose also prevents one from accepting the book as a realistic story. The allegorical meaning is not hard to grasp. The Air Vice-Marshal represents the radical, organizing, planning, untraditional, irreligious mind. He does not believe in conventional morality. He does not believe in life after death. He believes in plenty of sexual pleasure, and in comradeship, for his officers, but warns them against 'love'. They need to be disciplined, alert, on their toes, to get the most out of a limited life, and the greatest possible use out of their minds and bodies. The villagers must be kept in line, too. The whole theory is one of military discipline applied to civilian society, applied also to the ruling *élite*, but allowing that *élite* a certain fullness of life. The village stands for tradition; it also stands for the guilt and gloom which dog the Parson and the Squire (perhaps the Christian doctrine of original sin and the melancholy of a dispossessed ruling class), and for primitive habits, as when, at a village bar, a man bites off the heads of live rats for a drink. The heroine, who comes from the village, seems at first merely sluttishly promiscuous. But against the mechanical heartlessness of the Aerodrome, the village asserts a pull. For all its muddle and mess, and its own kind of pain and cruelty, the village stands for habit and natural growth and the possibility of love. In the end, the Air Vice-Marshal is killed and his plans for taking over and reorganizing the whole country come to nothing. Warner balances the radical and conservative sides, or the sides of organization and natural growth, and makes the Air Vice-Marshal too attractive to be merely a villain. But it is interesting that a man who began as an extremely left-wing writer, and whose friends, like Auden and Spender, had glorified the airman as the new man in a new society, should find himself at the end of the 1930s making the dangers of innovation seem so much more formidable than the faults of traditional ways.

The fourth type of novel I mentioned was the farcical comedy with ominous undertones. The two masters of this kind of novel in the 1930s (and they are still, in the 1960s, among our most distinguished novelists) were Evelyn Waugh and Anthony Powell. The pattern of Waugh's early novels is not unlike the pattern of Aldous Huxley's early novels, with more horse-play and less intellectual conversation. There are parties, casual love affairs, there is wit and fatuity, but Waugh's bright young people belong to a different world from Huxley's, a *Tatler* world of horses, long rakish cars, spats, bowler hats, Mayfair, St James's: in fact a writer who has probably influenced Waugh much more than Huxley (though he has expressed critical admiration for both of them) is P. G. Wodehouse. Waugh's attitude to his world is, also, more affectionate than Huxley's, if not quite so benignly tender as Wodehouse's. In early novels like *Decline and Fall* and *Vile Bodies* Waugh is mocking the bright young people for their silliness, but he is also admiring them (though carefully avoiding sentiment) for their foolhardiness and dash. Thus characters who in the early novels exist chiefly as harmless fools or amusing rogues, butts for malicious drollery, in a wartime novel like *Put Out More Flags* are packed into uniform, to fight and die gallantly for their country. And Waugh's mixed feelings about his characters from the beginning are so balanced on the sympathetic side that we are not surprised when they topple from splendid fools into natural leaders. The one novel, however, which some critics at the time thought a failure, *Brideshead Revisited*, is also the one novel in which Waugh exposes his loves and his reverences, for intense adolescent friendships, for old Catholic families, for English country houses, for romantic love, and for religious loyalty. There are moving and funny passages in this novel, there is something genuinely touching in Charles Ryder's friendship for the young, utterly charming and hopelessly weak Sebastian, and there is insight in Anthony Blanche's warning to Charles that his *engouement* with English upper-class charm may be fatal to his art: the same sort of crush on Waugh's part is nearly fatal to his own art here. He indulges in various types of special pleading. His animus, for instance, against the young lower-middle-class officer, Hooper, with his total lack of aptitude, tact, responsibility, sensitiveness, seems partly conditioned by a need to reassure himself about the social position of Charles Ryder who, if several rungs on the ladder above Hooper, is as many more rungs below Julia and Sebastian. If there is venom in the treatment of Hooper – we hate those classes into which we fear to fall, and love those into which by luck or favour we might rise – there is sentimentality in the treatment of Sebastian. Sebastian is an alcoholic; his physical and emotional temperament, it is implicitly made clear, is that of a homosexual. He likes to be courted. Yet it is taken for granted by everybody in the book that his relations with the degenerate young German deserter whom he meets in French North Africa are utterly innocent, and that his alcoholism has never touched the purity of his soul, never led him, as alcoholism does lead people, to the verge of despair or deadly malice. In real life, alcoholism may preserve a certain childishness in people, but does it usually preserve innocence? It is a tribute to Waugh's art that, where Sebastian is concerned, he makes us believe something we would find hard to believe in real life.

But perhaps Waugh's great gift is for combining farce with the sense of anguish. For all the pomp and circumstance of *Brideshead Revisited*, earlier and less solemn novels like *Decline and Fall*, *Black Mischief*, and *A Handful of Dust*, in different degrees, brought anguish nearer the surface – presented disaster in a flat, non-committal way, with an effect of shocking humour, a joke at which one ought not to laugh, but nevertheless did: the white slave traffic, sexual perversion, drug taking, the lingering death of a schoolboy who has been accidentally shot in the heel at the start of a race, the death of a gay young woman in hospital while her friends hold a cocktail party in her private ward, the sinister coincidence by which a dish presented to a young Englishman by African tribesmen turns out to be the girl he is engaged to – all such incidents, in the earlier novels, are good for a laugh, or good for a wry ironic shudder. In *A Handful of Dust* the final horror which Waugh inflicts on his decent, innocent hero – the innocent always suffer in Waugh – is to read the works of Dickens aloud for ever to a mad hermit in the Amazonian jungle. Older critics, like G. K. Chesterton, could find nothing funny at all in *Decline and Fall*. It was a kind of humour, of course, on the verge of hysteria but I personally find Waugh's way of turning our obsessions with violence and disaster, our age's gift for disorder, into absurd farce more morally congenial than the archaically 'heroic' attitudes of writers like Hemingway, Malraux, or Koestler. There is a dizzying gaiety in some of these early stories; one feels that the foundations of life have been deftly whipped away but that one is still gliding briskly along a polished floor. Waugh, like the rest of us, needed something underneath the floor: he discovered his foundations in Roman Catholic dogma and in the cult of a hierarchical society, in which everybody has his correct place in an agreed pecking order. I feel that he tends to be a little breathless and starry-eyed about clubs and country houses, and old regiments, but I think also that critics have identified Waugh too much with his characters, and not seen that he is fundamentally an artist: a lonely vocation, of some of whose sorrows and pitfalls *The Ordeal of Gilbert Pinfold* gives a touching and comic account. I no longer think that Waugh ought to have extended his social range: his role is as the celebrator of the follies and nobilities of a dying order. We can make allowances, charitable ones, for what is incoherent, bellicose, irate, suspicious, in Waugh's attitude to society and still salute in him one of the most notable professional artists of our time. I have never read even a short review by him without wishing that I could write as well and carefully as that.

A writer of the 1930s, who has carried on most interestingly to our own day, and who has a great deal in common with Waugh in a drier and more bilious vein, is Anthony Powell. Born in Golders Green, educated at Lancing, Waugh has always been in some ways a romanticist in his attitude to the great world; Powell, of an old family, and an old Etonian, is at once at home and disabused in that world. At his most satirical, Waugh has always some characters with whom we are invited to identify ourselves; and others, like Captain Grimes, a comic image of the life-force 'beyond good and evil', who may be both ludicrous and deplorable, but for whom Waugh creates a generous comic sympathy. Powell's mode of comedy is Jonsonian rather than Shakespearian, corrective rather than sympathetic. In a novel of the 1930s like *Agents and Patients*, the agents are rogues and the patients fools, and (in Dryden's phrase) he makes us abhor them both alike. At the most, he will sometimes make one of his characters pitiable, like the transvestist old gentleman in *From a View to a Death*. The skilled, laborious accuracy of style, the sour pertinence of observation, the ingenious farcical inventiveness displayed in these early novels makes them permanently amusing reading. But they do display, apart from touches of romance in *Afternoon Men* and *Venusberg*, an unrelishing attitude to life – or the relish is that of olives and very dry sherry. Since the end of the Second World War, Mr Powell has published six instalments of a long novel, *The Music of Time*, which explores English social life in a much broader way, and though these novels are full of excellent comedy one feels that the driving force behind them is not, as in the early books, comic disapproval, but a peculiarly pertinacious curiosity about the ramifications of social life, displayed alike by Mr Powell and by his stand-in in the series, the narrator, Nicholas Jenkins. Jenkins is given a style which at first seems very ponderous; he likes to describe every incident or episode with which he is engaged in the most meticulous detail, and to reflect on its moral implications, laboriously, and with an odd mixture of penetration and apparent naïvety. As one critic has suggested, Nicholas is repeatedly 'politely surprised' and from this polite surprise much of the comedy springs, as indeed it does in Jane Austen. Nicholas is the hero as the ideal novelistic observer; observation is his ruling passion, and the portentousness of his style, his way of describing things in slow motion, makes him also one of the comic characters. The style is part of the comedy. But it is a style whose finesse is a little obvious, a little laborious.

The first novel of the series (and it might be contrasted, very interestingly, with the Oxford scenes in *Brideshead Revisited*) handles with notable skill two subjects that lend themselves easily to lush romanticism or to easy farce, public school and university life. The broader theme, however, is that of social demarcation, and of finding and keeping one's proper place in society. The three schoolboys, in whose study the story begins, stand for three broad divisions of the English upper middle classes. The narrator represents in a sense the norm, the type of the professional classes (though it represents a shift in the social pattern that he does not become a barrister, a member of the higher civil service, or an officer, but finds work in the film business). A wealthier but flashier young friend, who does not dream of going to a university, is the predestined stockbroker. Another friend, Stringham, reckless and charmingly ruthless, a variant of Dickens's Steerforth, who goes to a university but does not bother to work, represents old-fashioned aristocratic dash: the times are against him, and he ends up as an alcoholic, kept alive only by remnants of his own arrogance. A dull and awkward boy, Widmerpool, the butt of all the others at school, humourless and self-important, plods on, in successive novels, to greater power and influence in the world, while remaining intrinsically absurd, as Stringham remains intrinsically attractive. I have heard Powell's art, in this series of novels, described as that of a 'dehydrated Proust'. The phrase pays proper tribute to his power of working out large general implications from small incidents; and it suggests a dryness of humour that remains from his earlier phase as a satirical novelist. Nicholas Jenkins's comic vision, like Powell's own comic vision earlier, does rest very often on intelligent dislike; but curiosity, requiring suspension of judgement, is a stronger motive in him, and there is also implied in this later series of works a firmer criticism of hardness of heart than could be spelt out of the earlier novels. Powell, nevertheless, still makes very little appeal to lovers of romance or sentiment. The portraits of misfits, of the eccentric, the awkward, or the self-assertive, are very finely balanced; but if the scales were to tip it would be on the side of pity rather than contempt. In its increasing ramification, *The Music of Time* is a solid and authentic picture of London, of webs of acquaintanceship, meetings at parties, in pubs, over luncheon, gossip and discussion, scandal, decisions; a world in which, intimately or slightly, everybody knows or knows about everybody else. Powell's long novel deserves respect not only as a work of art but as a record of a casual yet intimate interlocking of very diverse social groups – the worlds of money, of fashion, of old-fashioned exclusiveness, of bohemian sleaziness, of serious and futile activities in art and literature, of busy and yet often purposeless social and political manoeuvring.

The sixth volume of the first half of *The Music of Time* has a somewhat grimmer flavour than the volumes that preceded it, a flavour that makes one wonder if – in a sense like Proust's great novel too – the long book will end up as a study in progressive damnation. We witness the growing degeneration, or the more frankly displayed viciousness, of many of the characters, a theme brought to a climax in a country-house charade where many of them enact a charade of the Seven Deadly Sins. The comedy becomes sourer, and Nicholas Jenkins's polite amusement comes closer to frank horror or disgust. On the other hand, more positive values than were present in the earlier volumes are evident in the account of Nicholas's childhood in a military family and by the patriotic and cheerful attitude of some of the more agreeable characters to the onset of the Second World War.

10

Looking Back and Forward in the 1940s

So far, taking the history of the English novel in periods of roughly ten years from the beginning of the century, we have been able to trace out a fairly clear pattern of development. It is difficult to do this for the 1940s. The years from 1939 to 1945 were years of war, in which young writers were in the army, and older ones often busy with official jobs. The times were not propitious to either the novel or the drama, though, like nearly all periods of war, they suited poets. The end of the war, moreover, did not bring with it a return to normality. The young writer, out of the army, faced the same drab problems that confronted his fellow-subjects: rationing, a housing shortage, the need to start earning a living quickly, plus the technical difficulty of a paper shortage, which meant that a novel accepted in 1945 might not be published till 1947 or 1948. On the whole, unlike the first, the Second World War neither wounded the writer's soul nor forged his talent. And the years after 1945, for the young writer trying to make his way in London, were pleasant though delusive. He thought of himself as exploring a new world but was often merely meeting his old friends again as they slowly returned to civilian life. I remember around 1946 young writers sharing sparsely furnished flats, giving parties, with mulled Algerian wine and weak bitter beer, talking eagerly through the night, trying to call into existence, as if by magic, a 'London literary world'. They would eventually meet older writers but these were as much at sea in the new post-war world as their juniors. The war had been won. The Labour Government of 1945 was bringing into existence the Welfare State. In an austere, shabby, but just era, people of all classes dressed and ate much alike, class barriers seemed blurred, life had a certain improvised, camp-ing-out quality. But it lacked colour. There were no settled tendencies or leading reputations. People did not discuss politics or religion but personal relationships and books they hoped to write. Yet there was an unworldliness about young writers at that time, even about those who had had a tough war, which one does not find now.

Thus, if much of the best writing of the 1930s was based on a clear scheme of notions, and much of the best writing of the 1920s on the proud self-assertion of the individual sensibility, some of the best stories and novels of the 1940s reflect a desire to cling, in a shifting and dangerous world, to the warmth of human relationships. This is a topic about which women write better than men, being perhaps fundamentally bored with the 'public' world which the imaginative male writer feels the need to postulate. A similar idea is expressed with elegance and skill in a long story by Miss Rosamond Lehmann, which appeared in the early years of the Second World War, *The Red-Haired Miss Daintreys*. The first few paragraphs of this story are a disquisition on the novel in general, in which Miss Lehmann says that she is very distrustful of novelists who desire to illustrate a general theme and who therefore plan out the development of their novels, in too abstract a fashion, in advance. She would have more confidence in the novelist who did not know what he was setting out to do but merely said, 'I want to write about some people.' Our most important experiences, she feels, are those of intimate and affectionate response to other people, especially imaginative response; it is from such experiences that truly creative writing springs. The experiences, and the feelings that have gathered round them, are what engage the writer's conscious attention: the abstract theme, on the other hand, emerges without the writer being at first explicitly aware of it.

Miss Lehmann's own novels illustrate this approach. One of her best novels, published in the 1940s, is *The Ballad and the Source*. This is based on a young girl's romantic impression ('the ballad') of an older woman and the contrasting, rather grim truth ('the source'), gradually revealed, about the older woman's life and character. The sour facts are like the raid or killing, hateful in themselves, which in later years the balladist will turn into an heroic tale. Miss Lehmann rightly insists that ballad as well as source has its own validity; literary 'realism' which leaves out entirely the noble fantasies we weave round other people, and the unreasonably high expectations we base on our fantasies, impoverishes the sense of life. In all Miss Lehmann's novels, there is a heightened awareness of the 'glamour' of life, or the personal charm and delightfulness of people who may be brittle, heartless, dangerous. The charm, the superficial brilliant impression, have their own reality; even if often not the reality of what appears to go with them. When people's manners are more engaging than their characters, we are not to dismiss the manners as mere hypocrisy; but to think of them as representing a genuine idea, aimed at but tragically unachieved, or, even more interestingly, as showing a streak of fineness of which somebody whose conscious aims are coarse or selfish may be quite unaware. Miss Lehmann often presents this type of situation through the fresh and expectant sensibility of some young woman, her heroine; and if this heroine is to be continually disappointed, because her vitality is perennial, she will not, when we meet her as an older and more experienced woman – as in *The Weather in the Street*, a beautiful novel about love – have dried up and gone dead but will still be riding the waves with careless zest and risking the final shock, which never comes, against the harsh rocks of the shore. In her sensitiveness to the poetry of what is transitory and pungent, Miss Lehmann recalls Virginia Woolf; but her style does not call attention to itself so much as she tells a story more straightforwardly.

Elizabeth Bowen is a novelist who has much in common with Miss Lehmann. The world they are both at home in is one with traditions of assurance, of elbow-room – perhaps, if one is making fine distinctions, an 'upper-class world' in Miss Bowen's novels, an 'upper-middle-class' one in Miss Lehmann's – and they both have gripping stories to tell, which they tell, on the whole, in what strikes the ordinary reader as a 'sound, old-fashioned way': the interest in experiment showing itself more in the shaping of paragraphs and sentences, the freshening up of the novelist's language, than in the structure of the book as a whole. Towards the end of the 1940s Miss Bowen published a novel about London life during the war, *The Heat of the Day*. It vividly evokes the tense, exalted atmosphere of the black-out and the air-raids. A woman, Stella Rodney, discovers that her lover, Robert Kelway, is a traitor and is blackmailed by a secret agent, Harrison, who offers to spare the lover if, as a reward, the lady will 'yield herself' to him. On this harsh and what might seem rather melodramatic framework, Miss Bowen has erected a structure of words which allows us to grasp, not only a particular scene at a particular time, but a general pattern running through English life. Robert's terrible family, living at a house called Holm Dene, 1900 mock-Tudor, placed 'in the middle of nothing', explain, if they do not excuse, the mood of disgust with the dregs of middle-class English life that has turned Robert into a traitor; with the Kelways, natural conversation, spontaneous intercourse, freezes dead. Behind Stella's own poise and charm there is the failure of her first marriage; the husband, broken by the First World War, who turned from her wit and charm to a commonplace kindly nurse who could give him the protection he needed. We feel sorry even for Harrison, who, like the first husband, is a wounded soul; a man without background, living in a world of intrigue and subterfuge, without friendship and without love. Robert, the unfortunate hero, saves the situation by committing suicide. Stella herself, one of the most attractive heroines in English fiction, generous and direct, is bewildered by the inner twistedness of the males she has to deal with, but has magnanimity and generosity enough to reach out and try to understand even Harrison. But there is one untwisted male in the book: Stella's son, Roderick, who represents the persistence of hope, as Stella represents the persistence of warmth and courage. Miss Bowen's heroines tend to be women with a capacity for fullness of living and loving, to which life offers only imperfect or dangerous satisfaction.

While we are dealing with female novelists, one, in particular, should not be overlooked. Miss Ivy Compton-Burnett has created a world which has a sinister and compelling power over the imagination. The setting of Miss Compton-Burnett's novels tends to be a large country house in which several generations of a family of landed gentry live together. The period is perhaps the last decade of the Victorian era, but Miss Compton-Burnett, who works almost entirely by dialogue, each of her characters announcing identity by some subtle individual variant of a highly artificial comedic prose, is not interested in physical description or local colour. She is interested in the pains of dependence and the lust for power, and on the deadly hurts which, never renouncing the most frigid conventions of politeness, the members of a large ingrown family can inflict on each other. The younger members of the family depend upon and resent their elders. Either the father or the mother is usually a tyrant, and the parent who is not a tyrant is usually a weakling or a fool. The characters exist to torment, to dominate, or to undermine each other; the obvious real-life solution of escaping from each other is ruled out, because nobody would dream of working for a living. The tension often leads to some central episode of crime or wickedness: the poisoning of a mother by her son, the exposure of an invalid to the night air so that she dies, or at the very least the breaking of a heart and the crushing of a will. But obvious consequences are, at least for a time, suspended; the son announces at table he has poisoned his mother, the remark is civilly ignored as evidence of hysteria; though perhaps everyone secretly believes him. The simplest way of describing Miss Compton-Burnett's tales is as Victorian thrillers, such as might have been invented by Miss Braddon, presented with a comic artifice that might have appealed to George Meredith. Comparisons that have been made with a much greater novelist, Jane Austen, seem to me quite off the mark. Jane Austen's world is one in which the soul can breathe, and, in its miniature range, it gives one a Shakespearean sense of life's gravity, order, and fullness. Miss Compton-Burnett's world is not sane and rich in that sense; it is a narrow, enclosed, obsessed world and though its flavour is very distinctive, a little of it is enough at a time. One cannot read two Compton-Burnett novels in succession, for her world is one of the imagination, a powerful but narrow allegory of hell in which one breathes a little more freely when she turns from the world of the totally lost, the adult members of the family, to the conversation of the servants and the children.

A writer who has something in common with Miss Compton-Burnett, in that he is inspired in some of his best work by a fastidious antipathy, a cool, intelligent dislike, is Mr Angus Wilson. He was for some time an official in the Reading Room of the British Museum, a point of vantage which gave him an intimate understanding both of real scholars and of the eccentric and obsessed; his novel about historians, *Anglo-Saxon Attitudes*, is the only English novel I know which brings the dry, prickly, tetchy, and yet at its best, honourable, disinterested, and self-sacrificing world of learned societies and research in the humanities imaginatively alive. Wilson's observation is preternaturally sharp, but acquaintance with the melancholy of reading-addicts, the indifference to time and circumstance of enthusiasts, the burrowing persistence of cranks, has probably sharpened Mr Wilson's sense of the individual as a type. I imagine that when he meets a new person he does not so much respond as classify him in a very elaborate and exact system of mental pigeon-holes; in a sense, he has met everybody already. He has a firm grasp of what seem at first totally disparate social scenes: the smugness of a Scottish university, the dignity and decay of an English country house, the sodden bonhomie of a London nightclub, the stiff self-righteousness of progressive opinions in the suburbs, the wanton extravagance of a wealthy hostess in Mayfair. He is not out after subtleties. He isolates the essence of such atmospheres by bold flat caricatures and by concentration on self-betraying tricks of speech; with this there goes Dickensian fantasy and a touch of Dickensian sentiment, particularly about the decent and inarticulate young. Mr Wilson has also a touch of what Bagehot dismissed, too contemptuously, as Dickens's 'sentimental radicalism': he sees cold and narrow, or arrogantly selfish, social sympathies as symptoms of some basic inadequacy in personal generosity; but he can also sketch in, with sardonic objectivity, the dry and doctrinaire fanaticism of the Left.

Wilson made his reputation with short stories, *The Wrong Set* and *These Darling Dodos*. But since the late 1940s he has concentrated on novels, *Hemlock and After, Anglo-Saxon Attitudes, The Middle Age of Mrs Eliot,* and *The Old Men at the Zoo.* Mr Wilson might be described as a liberal humanist preoccupied with the emotional inadequacies of a liberal humanist attitude. The hero of *Hemlock and After* is an English Gide. Though a married man, with adult children, he has allowed free play to his homosexual impulses, but he suddenly discovers that far more sinister urges than he imagines, including an urge towards cruelty, underlie his sentimental fondness for the company of handsome and clever young men; recovering from this shock, he discovers also that his tolerance has sharp limitations when it comes to abnormalities other than his own. He finds himself morally impelled to expose, and thus to drive to suicide, an acquaintance who, because of a childhood fixation on his sister, has been seducing immature girls. The hero's state can be regarded, from different points of view, as disintegration or the purgatory of self-discovery: was his new road to self-completion only the old road to hell? Yet after his death – a death rather imposed on the book for a tidy ending – there is a suggestion that his painful, on the surface often cruel, honesty may bear good fruit in the lives of others. The hero of *Anglo-Saxon Attitudes* is not wholly dissimilar. A historical scholar, gifted, but too lazy to have fulfilled his early promise, he is a failure also in his personal life. He is separated from his irritating wife, in a 'civilized' way, and politely estranged from his unsatisfactory children. His efforts to enter into a more honest relationship with his family do not bring them closer, but indirectly restore his integrity as a scholar; he investigates an historical fraud, and accepts an important editorial commission. Wilson admires very much the honesty that becomes aware of a gap or hollow, a basic inadequacy, in the inner self. His type of the good man is the stoical and unwhining emotional cripple. *The Middle Age of Mrs Eliot* is a more subtle story, of a lively, popular, not very deep woman, driven by widowhood and comparative poverty to discover both the limitations and the strength of her own resources; her awkward but tender relationship with her homosexual brother Edward is specially well done. Wilson's most recent novel, *The Old Men at the Zoo*, about a fascist invasion of England, shows how apparently 'civilized' attitudes can, under stress, and if they are not based on a real 'civilization' of the feelings, collapse into brutality and savagery.

Wilson has made enormous technical advances as a novelist since *Hemlock and After*, but, for that very reason, the first novel is interesting as exhibiting clearly not only his qualities but his weaknesses as a novelist. He is a vigorous and clear writer but his prose has not the distinction and balance of Waugh or Powell. It seems sometimes unduly prim and at other times rather coarse and obvious; there is an accumulation of descriptive detail which becomes tedious, and a tendency to go on underlining points which a more economical writer would have made firmly, just once. There is a certain cheap smartness. And there are queer shifts of presentation and focus. In *Hemlock and After*, the cosy, vulgar, horrible procuress seems to have stepped out of some unwritten, because unprintable, Victorian masterpiece; the sensitive, neurotic, saintly lady belongs to the world of Virginia Woolf; the good adolescent boy might have stepped out of a franker Talbot Baines Reed story about the dangers of London life; and the bad one belongs to the most scabrous tradition of picaresque romance, almost to Petronius. The story as a whole exists at apparently incompatible levels, perception in depth and cartoon in profile, subtle comedy and the gentle exploration of pain juxtaposed with violent melodrama and bawdy farce. Such incongruities, the lack of a moral centre or a commonly accepted code of manners, of a commanding style of life, are an objective feature of our society. And the incoherence of this society is Wilson's point. It is not his only point. His dryness, his flair for spotting self-deception, routine behaviour, sheer nastiness, by no means preclude sympathy; he has a deadly eye for the spurious and the tedious but he has also a love for painstaking, undramatic virtue and a fairness towards the good points of characters whom in many ways he dislikes. His liberalism consists of a painful checking back of the impulse to condemn, rather than of a spontaneous sympathy with the sheer variety of the human world; he does not see virtue as leading to happiness, and indeed happiness, I think, is something he dislikes, associating it with self-centredness and insensitive complacency. In so far as he is a moralist, he is busy reminding us that we cannot afford to be comfortable or self-approving. This makes him a bracing writer. There are great gaps; he cannot really describe love, for instance: it tends to be something over and done with in the past, or sensibly renounced for the future. Similarly there is no joy in his world, no simple delight in mere physical existence and well-being, and I can think of no living novelist with less of the poet in him. I cannot imagine Wilson as being anybody's favourite writer; but it is impossible to read him without interest and moral respect.

A novelist who resembles Wilson in his gift for satire and fantasy, in his sharply critical concern with the social structure, and perhaps in a tendency to see people as types rather than individuals, is George Orwell. Orwell, whose real name was Eric Blair, went to Eton and later served in the Burmese police; these experiences gave him a profound dislike both of social privilege and of imperial rule, but also left a mark on his character. His hatred of authority was that of a man who was, by training and perhaps by temperament, an authoritarian. His radicalism was rooted in a vivid, and perhaps romantic, sense of tradition. He had strong prejudices of a sort more often associated with the extreme Right than the Left: the poet Roy Campbell, who was making propaganda for General Franco in Spain while Orwell was fighting for the Republic, has saluted him as a 'valiant, generous heart'. Orwell was only in his early forties when he died of tuberculosis in 1949; his refusal ever to live soft, the deliberately chosen hardships, the injuries he had suffered in Spain, all wore down a sturdy constitution. His last novel, *1984*, was written in a remote, damp island on the west of Scotland, when he ought to have been in a Swiss sanatorium. He was not only a natural fighter, he was also by temperament a grim self-punisher.

Orwell's love of the English common people is shown, outside his novels, in books like *The Road to Wigan Pier*, published in the 1930s by the Left Book Club, in *The Lion and the Unicorn*, published during the Second World War, and many of his essays. It was perhaps not a wholly unsentimental love. Orwell believed that the British working classes were a distinct race, tending to be short and stocky whereas the upper classes tended, like himself, to be tall and thin. He believed that they had a distinct and noticeable smell. He was writing in a period, during much of his life at least, of large-scale unemployment and, for many of the poor, chronic undernourishment and bad housing. There is still a hard core of poverty, there are still slums in Britain; old-age pensioners and a number of unskilled, casual labourers still have a grim time. But whereas before the war one could tell a 'working man' from a lower-middle-class man by his clothes and his bearing, this is now impossible. Orwell thought that there were 'two nations' where really there was one, a minority of it overprivileged, and an important part (but even then not a majority) living in conditions of anxiety, deprivation, and near-despair. The coming of the Welfare State has, despite continuing problems of housing and unemployment, changed the face of Orwell's England.

Orwell writes about the culture of the working classes – the culture that reflects itself in boys' twopenny magazines and in vulgar comic postcards, in fish and chip shops, in trips and jellied eels, in miners' choirs, in charabanc outings, in street-corner oratory – without trying to make that culture seem more grand and important than it is, but with gusto. In many ways he is himself a good-hearted Philistine. He associates taste and refinement, in the Bloomsbury sense, with privilege and injustice: the qualities he admires are loyalty, courage, humour, generosity. He does not grudge the people the garish or pathetic pleasures that sweeten a drab life, but he wants them to be more responsible, and at the same time his radicalism is based on a faith in their instincts. Though something of a fanatic himself in many ways he hated abstract fanaticism, the 'smelly orthodoxies'. He thought the Left was handicapped by the cranks who supported it, the long-haired, short-sighted vegetarians and nudists, with their superior bleat. He distrusted doctrinaires of every kind; distrusted all evasion of plain fact and straight feeling, all abstract, wordy, and pretentious writing about politics. He had a fine indifference as to whether he was approved or not; he was swinging a great flail round his head, and it was as likely to knock down supporters cheering behind him as opponents cowering in front.

The two works of fiction produced by Orwell in the 1940s, *Animal Farm* and *1984*, were social allegories. *Animal Farm* was about the Russian revolution of 1917. In this story some farm animals get tired of their servitude to men and start a revolution to run the farm in their own way. The revolution starts with magnificent spirit and ideals, but things go wrong. The pigs, more cunning than the other animals, and their rough allies, the dogs, worm themselves into a position that resembles that of the old human masters. Privilege and injustice reassert themselves, made blacker by blatant hypocrisy. The old war-horse, the old revolutionary hero, is sent off to the knacker's yard. The human masters of the neighbouring farms and the pig masters get together and, sitting round a table viewed through a window, they look alike. The animals have lost. Orwell's sympathy is all with the animals, but still this is a morally ambiguous fable; the difference between the ruling few in any country and the common people is not the difference between men and animals; the motives behind Stalinism, however ugly it was, were not motives of cynical hypocrisy but of misguided 'realism', nor have the rulers of Russia come to a permanent friendly agreement with the rulers of other countries, as Orwell suggests they will, nor is there evidence that their subjects, as a mass, are profoundly disillusioned with them. Orwell would not have enabled us to foresee the 'thaw' in the Soviet Union, or the personality of Mr Khrushchev. The book remains extraordinarily charming and readable, and it makes surprisingly gay reading. Perhaps the gaiety comes from the pleasure Orwell felt in mocking solemn English fellow-travellers; but I have a feeling that *Animal Farm* might survive as a children's story, as a lively beast fable, long after its immediate topical relevance has been forgotten. In comical satire, after all, one does often look for clever and damaging oversimplification, rather than for a balanced account of facts.

There is no gaiety in Orwell's last novel, *1984*. This describes an interlocking world-society in which the driving motives, among the rulers, are hatred, the lust for cruelty, and fear, and in which the driving motives among the ruled are terror and desperation. This society has deliberately rejected objective standards of behaviour: in particular, charity, joy, truth. It is a criticism of the plausibility of Orwell's general conception that it is difficult to see how the kind of society he describes, a society rejecting the very notion of objectivity, could last long. A society organized, like the one Orwell imagines, on sadistic principles, would probably be as imperfectly sadistic as traditional Christian societies have been Christian, or liberal societies liberal, or democratic societies democratic. There are counter-balancing principles in human nature and the principles which are not officially approved of will nevertheless find some way of expressing themselves. *1984* was a book written by a sick and dying man, who had never had any religious faith or hope, and who had lost for the time being the political faith and hope which served him as a religion. He had not lost the reverence he had always felt for justice and truth, though he saw these, too, as vulnerable. His book was meant to warn but missed its mark and induced despair in some of its readers. The fine intention should be credited to him, and he remains morally a most impressive figure, built on a gaunt, haggard, and heroic scale. But he was not a great novelist, or even, in most of the ordinary senses of the word, a good novelist. He was not sufficiently interested in the varieties of human character, of human worlds, or in private life.

11

The Novel in the 1950s

THE 1940s had seen the shaping of a new society in Great Britain but for most novelists this new society had not yet taken any imaginative configuration. Orwell in the 1940s wrote political prophecy. A fine and sensitive novelist like L. P. Hartley tended to look back, as in his Eustace and Hilda trilogy, to the world of his youth in the 1920s, or, in *The Go-Between*, to an even earlier period, that of English country-house life about the time of the Boer War. His sad and comic novel, set in war-time, *The Boat*, concerns the attempt of a liberal, hedonistic, middle-aged, slightly epicene man of letters to live through the war, without letting it impinge too much on him, clinging as a talisman to a boat he wants to row on a stretch of river which is preserved by the local magnates for fishing. He fails in various ways to make his mark with the local magnates; he is tempted into a gesture of defiance which brings death and disaster, though not to himself, in its wake, and which is taken as having political implications which he never seriously intended. But, having an income of his own, he manages to slide out of this disagreeable situation, and will settle down elsewhere till things return to normal. He is both a figure of comedy and the traditional, sensitive, and cultivated observer of a Henry James story: the essence of the tale is that the war-time world offers him no point of vantage, he does not belong anywhere, and growing frustrations lead him to acts which have grim consequences and whose motives, for all his liveliness of mind, he does not understand himself.

In the Eustace and Hilda trilogy, Eustace is like a younger version of the hero of *The Boat*. He has luck, inheriting some money that enables him to go to Oxford; he has charm, which makes him aristocratic friends; he has talent, which enables him to write. A pleasant life lies ahead but his way is barred by his beautiful sister Hilda, who stands for seriousness, public spirit, unsnobbishness, for the puritan tradition of the just-upper-middle classes. Hilda is introduced to Eustace's grand friends, falls in love with a Byronic semi-fascist rake, suffers a breakdown. Eustace nurses her, cares for her, cures her by a kind of shock treatment, and then, always an invalid himself, falls ill. He dies, grateful to have sacrificed what he wanted himself to Hilda's sterner nobility. Eustace is a symbol of the aesthetic spirit allowing itself, out of its very responsiveness to passion, to be crushed and sacrificed to the moralism of English life, as represented by his sister. And, of course, if Hilda is grander, Eustace is nicer, and the necessity of the sacrifice seems sad. Both Eustace and Hilda stand for certain lines of tradition in English life. Eustace reaches back to Walter Pater, she, with her clinic, to Florence Nightingale. They are not contemporary figures; and when Mr Hartley explores the modern world, as in *My Fellow Devils* or *A Perfect Woman*, he is less impressive, he seems to be observing people as sharply as ever without quite managing to 'place' them. There is something, indeed, of this innocent bewilderment (which allows lapses into melodrama) in the handling of the villainess, the beautiful Communist plotter from London, in *The Boat*. Mr Hartley's gifts are for exploring, with fine comic and pathetic sense, the nuances and the crises of a settled society.

A writer who can be contrasted with Hartley and about whose merits as a novelist there has been a great deal of discussion lately is C. P. Snow. The son of a working-class family in Leicester, Snow went to grammar school and then to the small University College of Leicester, and won a scholarship to Cambridge where he became a don, teaching and researching into physics in the great days of Rutherford. During the Second World War, however, he became a member of the Civil Service Commission, concerned with the allocation of senior scientific and technical staff to various kinds of war work, and, though he has been writing his series of novels, *Strangers and Brothers*, for a good many years, he only recently retired from the Civil Service. Quite apart from his novels, Snow is a notable public figure. His Rede Lecture on the dangerous lack of communication in our time between men of scientific and literary culture has been much discussed and ferociously attacked by Dr F. R. Leavis; in it, he deplores what he regards as the obscurantist attitudes to science and technology of such writers as Pound, Eliot, Yeats, Wyndham Lewis, and D. H. Lawrence and the comparative illiteracy in scientific thought even of writers of more progressive views than these. He insists that there are certain massive problems, like that of raising the standard of living of the economically backward areas of the world, which the romantic conservatism of the literary world prevents men of letters from seeing. In another set of lectures he has illustrated some of the dangers that arise in war-time from the scientific ignorance and credulity of politicians, and from the inability of some scientists to pool their ideas in committee. Knowing as he does at first hand the politics of academic life, the arguments that weigh in a committee and are seldom expounded from a platform, the passions and the habits of mind that go with research, Snow has an understanding and an interest in the world of official power and responsibility that is rare in English novelists. He shows how this world, as much as the world of the artist, is not necessarily a world of gross ambition, or of idealistic self-dedication, but a world in which certain kinds of human aptitude seek their proper field. It is possible that novels like *The Masters*, *The New Men*, *The Affair*, dealing with this public world, have unfairly distracted attention from novels like *Homecomings*, which skilfully relates Lewis Eliot's private to his public world. But there is something subtle and accurate in the conception of Eliot as the just, detached, and honestly helpful observer; quick and clever at summing up people's obvious weaknesses and capacities, and yet often surprised by the very people he sums up, since he has little intuition; it is appropriate that his early private life, at least, should be unhappy.

There has been much disagreement about Snow's literary stature. Miss Helen Gardner finds a sober authenticity in his picture of college life. In his famous Richmond lecture of 1962 Dr F. R. Leavis denounced Snow's world as a cardboard one, but did not illustrate this condemnation with any examples. I have heard that Robert Graves admires Snow's sheer story-telling power; one gift which Snow certainly possesses is economy of construction. In *The Affair* we are presented with a very large cast of characters, including all the fellows of a college, and some of their wives, and a complicated plot, dealing with the re-investigation of a charge of fraud for which a former junior fellow of the college has been expelled. We have to pick up on the way a good deal about research methods and about college procedure. We are to examine an important general theme – one suggested to Snow by the Dreyfus case – that of the complicated relationships between men's personal dislikes and prejudices, and to some degree their vested interests, and their sense of justice. The feeling of suspense and impending crisis has to be maintained and yet subdued to the atmosphere of formal propriety, or of formalized casualness, which attends academic life. All this is managed unobtrusively, and we also get a sense of the outer personality, the principles, the social and political tactics, and, more complexly, the sudden unexpectedness of a wide range of characters. The prose is not memorable in itself; the dialogue is true to life, and there is just enough of it to stress character, without being, or aiming at being, profound, witty, or eloquent. For Dr Leavis, both Snow and his characters write and talk in clichés, but, in so far as this is true, a certain grey clearness is representative of Lewis Eliot's mind, and a care for amenity and precision, within a common vocabulary, is more typical of academic talk than a vital feeling for rhythm or phrase. Lewis Eliot's passionate interest in life is in small signs of character in people, which give clues to the practical decisions that people will make. There is dry light, there is no saturation. The wine, the food, the college settings, the quirks of personal character are not in the novels to be enjoyed for their own sake but as emollients to the stiff task of making group decisions. Snow understands very clearly man as a politician, man as involved in perpetual adjustments to colleagues and institutions and general codes and purposes. He understands men who attend parties with the purpose of sitting on committees; he does not understand men who sit on committees with the purpose of attending parties. This is not to say that his characters are unreal, but merely that one particular, and for fiction an unusual, facet of their reality has captured his attention. It is a facet more important for men than for women, and Lewis Eliot fails to understand inner natures of women, even when he describes their surface behaviour with his usual accuracy. However, Eliot's blank spots and blind patches, his own honesty about what he does not really understand, add to one's sense of his authenticity as an observer. What he observes may be largely the machinery of life; but that machinery profoundly affects life's quality: that is what Eliot is probing at, however indirectly.

Scenes from Provincial Life, a novel by a younger friend and Civil Service colleague of Snow's, William Cooper, helped to set a fashion, in the early 1950s, for removing the milieu of the novel away, not only from Snow's corridors of power, but also from the world of rank and fashion, from political commitment, and serious ideas. The book is about a young schoolmaster, clever but not hard-working, in a provincial city in 1939; how he coaxes along his classes and tries, not very efficiently, to placate his headmaster; how he makes love to a pleasant business-girl whom he does not really want to marry; how he and a pushful friend tormented by a homosexual love-affair make vague plans to go to America and dodge the coming war. The effect is of frank pastoral comedy, with moments of reality and pain especially for the hero's mistress, which he is too good-natured not to recognize, too selfish to heal. The people enjoy themselves and suffer a little, are bright but without coherent ideas, are hedonistic and self-centred but do not want to be unkind. The hero is the average sensual man, a little more intelligent than most, perpetually aware of the mild absurdity of his friends and of the situations in which he involves himself, worried about dodging the traps life sets, but not worried about life. This kind of hero, and this kind of sense of comedy, look forward to the world of Kingsley Amis; though without the element of social resentment and satire in Amis's books.

Cooper's quality as a novelist is his humorous simplicity and candour, which looks like, and for all I know may to some extent be, naïvety. He seems naïve in some critical comments he has made on experiment in fiction, but on the other hand he has dramatized Ladu Murasaki's great novel, *The Tale of Genji*, for radio, and he shares with Sir Charles Snow and Snow's wife, Pamela Hansford-Johnson, a passion for Proust; and unless one is a very dull sort of snob, one ought to be just as interested in the alert observation of manners in small provincial circles as at smart parties in the metropolis. Cooper had written a number of early novels under another name. Of his novels after *Scenes from Provincial Life*, I like best *Young People*, of which the setting is Leicester in the late 1920s or early 1930s. This includes a character, symptomatically named Swann, a code hero, wise, theoretically subtle about social niceties and in practice splendidly unconscious of what effect he makes, eager, physically clumsy: modelled, one gathers, on an idea of what Cooper's friend Snow will have been like as a Leicester undergraduate. But the real hero of the book is a bouncy and somehow innocent fraud, a working-class student who pretends to come from a grand family in Bath, who is thought very bright but fails all his exams, who jockeys a decent, genteel girl into marrying him, betrays her, betrays everybody, but is forgiven because his acting, his pretences, have been life-enhancing for his friends. Cooper's almost alarming moral tolerance is often bewildering: does it reflect good-natured obtuseness, a jolly moral callousness arising from never having expected much of people, or from a realistic grasp of life, more realistic and understanding than the reader's? He is at any rate a fine craftsman, a most acute observer, and a writer who always conveys vitality.

It has been general critical comment that English fiction in the 1950s has shown a very high average level of technical intelligence, but that it has not produced masters: the novelist as great man, as oracle, sage, or prophet, as lonely dedicated artist, of the type of James, Conrad, Joyce, Lawrence, seems no longer to exist. The trick or device of the successful contemporary novelist is to seem a limited person, sensitively at sea and intelligently bewildered, like oneself. Some young critics, however, have seen a major figure in Joyce Cary, a retired colonial Civil Servant who published his first novel in 1930, after retiring from his job in Nigeria because of ill health. Cary was a man of unusual generosity and range of mind, a range which comes out in *Art and Reality*, a very fine set of meditations on the art of the novel, written on a slow and painful death-bed. He had thought seriously about politics, about religion, about art, about the truths of personal and social relationship. He wrote his most successful novels in trilogies, covering a series of events in turn from the points of view of three main characters concerned in them, and with each character impersonating not only a way of speaking and of seeing, but a philosophy of life. He wrote his original drafts at enormous length and then selected from them enough material to cover, in sections, a life story. This method of dramatic impersonation (one model is the Defoe of *Robinson Crusoe* and *Moll Flanders*) had certain disadvantages as well as potentialities. A late novel, *Not Honour More*, purports to be written by a retired colonial administrator and soldier, Captain Jim Latter, when he is in jail awaiting execution for the murder of a Liberal politician who is a rascal and a lecher but also a man of genius (Cary was probably thinking of Lloyd George). Captain Latter personifies the bitterness of the ex-officer out of a job, with no real purpose in life, after the Great War. He is the type who would have become a supporter of Sir Oswald

Mosley. He thinks and talks in conventional officers' mess phrases. He is rather proud of *not* trying to analyse his own loves, resentments, and angers. He has a streak of deviousness; he is not *only* a plain, blunt man, but also partly somebody acting, and a little over-acting, that part. He gives in the end an impression of staginess, as, to me, does the much more famous Gulley Jimson of *The Horse's Mouth*. I lived in Chelsea for more than ten years, and met lots of bohemian artists, but never one like Gulley going out on all four cylinders all the time. I never met one, either, who could quote Blake's prophetic books, *ad lib.*, and in fact it is my experience of painters that they have a rational distrust of being articulate and have a double attitude to literary men, surprised that the words come out so easily, but distrustful about seeing behind the words. If you wished to deride the book you would say that Gulley Jimson was a cinematic conception, if you wanted to praise it up you would say he was a poetic conception. I suppose that these impersonative novels of Cary's worry me because I start off reading what I think is going to be a realistic story and then discover that it is a moral fable. I think Cary may well be one of my blind spots, like D. H. Lawrence; but it is a different kind of blind spot; I feel the moral size of the man and yet the novel does not seem an adequate vehicle for it. The technique, after all, of the impersonative novel is a very primitive one, that of Defoe's *Moll Flanders*: it throws the task of adding irony, of making fine moral discriminations, on the reader; it runs the risks of monotony, undue repetitiveness, a lack of real suspense, a narrative structure of a string of similar episodes, all illustrating one not very complex character. One respects Cary, but one does not feel that he was a 'master' in the old sense.

A novelist of recognized distinction, whom it is very hard to place, is Henry Green. W. H. Auden has called Green 'the best English novelist alive', while C. P. Snow, reviewing Green's *Nothing* in 1950 – which is a well-written novel about a set of people who are not only frivolous but also inane or inept – found in Green's work, according to Edward Stokes's useful study, *The Novels of Henry Green*, 'all the signs that we have come to associate with artistic diffidence and decay'. Green, whose real name is Henry Yorke, is the managing director of a Birmingham firm of manufacturers, and writes with confidence both about the very rich and idle and about working-class people from typists and clerks upwards, engaged in industry. He was in the Auxiliary Fire Service during the Second World War and *Caught*, based on his experiences, is one of the best documentary novels of the Second World War, while *Back*, published a little later, is an excellent novel about the slow and difficult resettlement to civilian life, and love, of a prisoner of war whose mistress died while he was away. Snow's dislike of Green is in this sense odd, that Green shares with Snow a wide experience of practical as well as social life, and is a most accurate observer. He is uniquely accomplished among living English novelists in his gift for creating, in a selective, condensed, and stylized, but fundamentally uncannily authentic way, an impression of how people belonging to a very wide range of social classes speak : the hesitant rhythms, the repetitions, the indirectnesses, the trailing off. He has suffered from partial deafness since his adolescence, and this may have made him attend to human speech with intentness, and may also have helped to put a slight distance between himself and other people, thus making him an acute and detached observer. He never appears in his novels as a moral commentator, but his personality appears very strongly in the extremely mannered prose, with its tendency to omit definite articles, and to run into long sentences, linked by a series of 'ands', or break into series of short ones, sometimes without finite verbs. The sentences also put recorded external incidents, unspoken thoughts, and sometimes indirectly reported speech into the same perspective. The style does call attention to itself, and that may have been in Snow's mind. Green demands alertness if one is to be clear who is doing and saying what, and to follow the threads of the story. Even at his most realistic Green gives an effect of lyricism and fantasy, and of moral detachment from general questions; there is no pastoral sentiment in his treatment of working people, but no rebellious social consciousness either; he does not represent his vacuous idle rich as glamorous, as Evelyn Waugh sometimes does, but neither is he consciously attending to their ridiculous side, as Anthony Powell often is. He has also an old-fashioned belief in love as the solution for many human problems, and a delight in the awkwardly tender. He is a novelist who appears to approach life (and this may help to explain Auden's admiration for him) without preconceptions, without 'rehearsed responses', as a poet approaches life; delighting in the odd and the unexpected, taking what is given as an addition to the richness of things, and demanding of himself, as of the reader, nothing but an extremely concentrated, and yet unfussy, attention. And the actual matter of the novel may sometimes – this would again help to explain Snow's annoyance – seem matter that could have been presented in a more broad and simple way, without asking just that degree of concentration. Nor have his novels 'morals' in any obvious sense, except the moral that life, or the segment of life being attended to, is like this; 'a poem should not mean but be', wrote the American poet Archibald MacLeish, and perhaps Henry Green feels like this about novels. But a poem (the kind of poem MacLeish had in mind) should as a total symbol imply a meaning, and perhaps Green's novels seem to imply for Snow a total, in a sense lyrical-comic acceptance of life, based unconsciously on a position of security and privilege (and based on a certain fundamental remoteness which can go with such a position), which Snow found morally or politically unacceptable. He is certainly a most distinguished artist; his novels need several re-readings, for all their brilliance of surface they do not reveal everything at once.

The 1950s seem to me to have been a period particularly rich in novels which, without being wildly ambitious, hold one's attention by their general economy, intelligence, and obviously accurate portrayal of some cross-section of contemporary life; the number of women novelists whom one would like to deal with in a longer survey, Elizabeth Taylor,

Barbara Pym, Elizabeth Montague, Penelope Mortimer, among others, is remarkably high. There are novels by intelligent women which can bog one down in the detail of tea-parties, babies' nappies, or shopping expeditions, which can verge on the flavour of *Mrs Dale's Diary*, and which can also sometimes shade off into an Angela Thirkellish defence of threatened gentilities, but which nevertheless often convey the texture of daily living, the drama of the undramatic, in a way which most novels by men fail to do. The equivalent among male minor novelists is the detailed picture of a particular world, the advertising world in Roger Longrigg's *A High-Pitched Buzz* or Bernard Gutteridge's *The Agency Game*, with more sex, drink, and satire, but with the same feeling for texture. Universities, following the success of *Lucky Jim*, have been a favourite scene for this kind of textural novel, and Malcolm Bradbury's *Eating People is Wrong* is a good example of a combination of close textural observation (the awkwardnesses of teacher-student parties in the provinces) with much more bravura, broad-wash scenes of farce or melodrama. John Bowen's *The Centre of the Green* manages to deal with the difficulties of family life, the psychological compulsions and the social malaises that lie behind promiscuity and attempted suicide, and the loneliness of London, in a way that avoids melodrama and mere documentation. The general level of compassion, intelligence, and, above all, accurate observation in a surprising number of novels of the 1950s was very high. The old distinction between the 'high-brow' novel (Virginia Woolf, E. M. Forster, D. H. Lawrence), and the 'middle-brow' novel (Hugh Walpole, J. B. Priestley, Somerset Maugham) is much less easy to draw in the 1950s or 1960s than it was in the 1920s. There is a larger intelligent reading public, and perhaps a greater readiness in both writers and readers to confront awkward and uncomfortable realities.

In spite of this high general level of achievement, there was a good deal of critical discussion in the 1950s about whether the novel, in the old sense, was a declining or decaying form, and certain writers of talent seemed to be moving away from the straight novel to fantasy, allegory, or satire. William Golding is perhaps the most famous of these. He tells, in his first novel, *Lord of the Flies*, what seems at first to be a modern version of Ballantyne's *The Coral Island*, but the boys wrecked on the island do not have a jolly time, they quickly regress to barbarism and superstition; in *Pincher Martin* a man lost overboard clings desperately for hours to a barren rock, trying not to drown; we learn at the end that he was drowned instantly, that the rock was an aching tooth, and that his clinging to the rock was an emblem of his selfishness throughout life, his clinging to his own desires, which prevented him from accepting God's mercy. *Free Fall*, an elaborate life-drama, more in the pattern of ordinary novels, again turns out to be an allegory on sin and grace, about man's fallen condition. Golding is a writer much admired, but some critics have felt that the end of *Pincher Martin*, the sudden transformation of the realistic and exciting physical detail into a metaphor, a metaphysical conceit, gives the effect of cheating. A writer who interests me more, and whose books are less allegories than moral or religious fables, is Muriel Spark. Her characters and backgrounds, and her use of dialogue, all have an authentic ring, but her purposes are not those of the ordinary realistic novelist. She is a devout Roman Catholic (Golding's metaphysics are also Christian) and Mrs Spark's gift for comedy is made portentous by her sense of the eternal significance of all human choices. In one of her grimmest and funniest books, *Memento Mori*, a set of very old people receive recurrent anonymous telephone messages, 'Remember, you must die'. It is Death (or God, through Death) who is calling them, asking them to amend their lives, to prepare their souls for judgement. They are nearly all unwilling to accept this possibility: they cling to their meannesses, their rancours, their petty vices, and Mrs Spark achieves a striking mixture of comedy and pathos. Another funny and frightening novel, *The Bachelors*, might be a sermon on the text, 'It is not good for a man to live alone,' though one of the bachelors turns out to be a saint, for whom celibacy is a vocation;

another, but he is thwarted in the end, is dedicated to the denial of life and love, to evil. Mrs Spark's novels are at once very amusing and harrowingly penetrating; she is compassionately aware of how much of life is distraction in Pascal's sense, the search for trivialities and disguises that will divert our minds from the soul's sadness and loneliness, from life's uncertainty and transcience, from the abyss.

Both Golding and Mrs Spark are strengthened as novelists by holding firmly to a faith or values which are not, at least overtly, the faith and values of most of their readers. Nigel Dennis's *Cards of Identity* is an ambitious satire, partly allegorical, which is weakened in the end by the purely negative values underlying it. The Identity Club has its yearly conference at a large country mansion and, using modern techniques of psychological persuasion, the members of the Identity Club persuade the owners of the mansion and the local doctor to accept the roles of old family servants. Papers are delivered, anecdotes about identity-changing or the assumption of fantasy identities are told, and the performance of a mock-Elizabethan play leads eventually to the murder of the Club President and his suppression by a younger and more ruthless rival. The satire is ambivalent; it is partly satire on modern means of mass persuasion, and on the uneasiness which many people feel today unless they can adapt themselves to a stereotyped role. But the cruel and frivolous members of the Identity Club seem to be regarded by Mr Dennis with a certain Nietzschean complicity, and the ruthlessness of the whole scheme is in the end distasteful. Mr Dennis lacks that basic sympathy with the human weaknesses which make up human nature – which Mr Golding and Mrs Spark possess. Nigel Dennis's first novel, written many years earlier, *Boys and Girls Come Out to Play*, about a young man's desperate escape from a family of progressive philanthropists, though imperfect in itself, may throw some light on the attitudes behind *Cards of Identity*. That remains a disagreeable and rather over-elaborated but powerful and sourly amusing book. Its nearest earlier equivalent is perhaps

Wyndham Lewis's powerful but again bitter and top-heavy satire, *The Apes of God*.

A novelist whom I much admire is P. H. Newby, a quietly industrious man who manages to combine running the B.B.C. Third Programme with a regular production of fiction of high quality. I particularly like the two novels, *Picnic at Sakkara* and *A Guest and His Going*, dealing with the relations between a lecturer in Cairo, Edgar Perry, who later runs an English language school for foreign students in England, and the baffling, violently unpredictable, but delightful young Egyptian student, Muawiya. In Egypt, Muawiya rescues Perry from a violent nationalist crowd, later makes a farcical attempt to shoot him at a picnic, but saves the situation for himself, if not for Perry, by suggesting that Perry has been trying to commit suicide. He has been told by his nationalist friends to shoot Perry, because he seems too fond of him. He is bitterly offended when Perry mocks at his ineptitude as an assassin but sees Perry off, bringing lavish wine and food, when Perry returns to England. In the second novel, it is Muawiya who is in the morally superior position, though he still behaves very oddly. He is on a British Council trip to London at the time of President Nasser's rise to power, when the feelings that brought about the Suez crisis are simmering and rising to the boil. He borrows somebody's motor car and in a panic takes refuge in the Egyptian Embassy. In a lighter way, with the comedy more often verging on farce, and with real tragedy more in the distance, these books are in the tradition of *A Passage to India* – though Muawiya in the second novel drives one explosive patriot to attempted murder and real madness. Perry is very like a Forster hero, dry but kind, with a warm heart and a cool head, ironically aware of inadequacies. Muawiya is less like Azis than like Gino in *Where Angels Fear to Tread*, the unreliable and dangerous member of an older and simpler civilization, who can teach the liberal Englishman the values of spontaneity. There are other admirable observations: of how, in the second novel, Egyptian independence can turn old Egyptian hands, who have devoted their lives and affections to the country, into violent anti-Egyptians; and of the difficulty for Muawiya himself of moving from a relation of rebellious dependence to one of equality, either hostile or friendly. The element of dryness in English life, or English professional upper-middle-class life, against which Muawiya as a remedy is reflected brilliantly throughout both books in the gradual, civilized but inexorable distancing and formalizing of the relations between Perry and his wife. These two sober, penetrating comedies deserve to be minor classics. For sheer professionalism in the best sense, for competent and patient attention to the novel as an economical art, Newby is hard to match among his contemporaries.

With Newby, perhaps because of a certain delicacy and primness in his handling of language, I find myself classifying a number of women novelists. Olivia Manning in *Artist Among the Missing* covers the Middle-Eastern scene, Palestine as well as Egypt, with vivid, exact observation, with a fine sense of comedy, but with a richness of atmosphere and a patient exploration of inner distress which, in the two novels I have mentioned at least, are not within the field of Newby's purpose. Miss Manning's novels are rich-textured and she has an admirable scenic gift, a gift, I mean, for putting a large number of characters down in a definite setting and conveying both the feel and mood of place and the tensions, and submerged harsh emotions, of what looks on the surface an ordinary social occasion. She is good at exploring complicated relationships: in *Artist Among the Missing*, between the fine-strung, creatively over-sensitive hero, driven almost to madness by his dread of hydrophobia, and his bluff, hearty *fausse bonne femme* of a wife. Olivia Manning has a strong feeling for corruption and for the sudden outcropping of callousness and cruelty in ordinary life – as when a character in *Artist Among the Missing* tells the wife of the hero that a short course of psychotherapy (probably involving shock treatment) will restore him to the world superficially normal but not with his old quality of mind and sensibility, like a tyre that has been restamped. In her excellent short stories, Miss Manning's tartness of personal and social observation sometimes becomes positively satirical.

The writers whom I have been mentioning are generally admired, but if one were asked to name novelists typical of a new mood in the 1950s, one would mention none of these, but a number of writers rather younger: Kingsley Amis, John Wain, Iris Murdoch, whose first novels appeared around 1954; and John Braine and Alan Sillitoe, whose first books of fiction appeared around 1956-7.

Amis and Wain have from the first been paired by critics, though there, too, the differences are striking. Wain is both more of a moralist and more of a romantic than Amis, and his observation of life is passionately coloured, indeed sometimes distorted, by his moral convictions. One has often a feeling that he is bullying his characters, shaking or jostling them. He is present as a person, as a voice, in all his fictions. A novel of his which never, I think, got the praise that was its due was his second, *Living in the Present*, which, under the guise of a satirical and farcical melodrama, is a very gripping and uncomfortable study in the pathology of rage. The hero, a teacher under an unbearable headmaster, is disgusted with his job, with the restaurants in which he eats, with the people in the neighbouring flat who give noisy parties, with London, with life. He decides to kill himself but kill the worst man he knows first. He pursues a pretentious crypto-fascist poet across Europe; he manages to alarm his quarry and disconcert him, but various farcical accidents, and various invitations to go on living, prevent the murder and prevent the suicide. One girl gives him the idea of pleasure; another the sense of love; a friend the awareness that, even where there is great weakness, there can be kindness and decency. There is one wonderful piece of writing, a scene where, overcome by rage, walking alone in the street, the hero imagines himself confronting and grappling with the hated headmaster; the heroine appears, her touch brings him back to reality. And gradually the world begins to take the colours of sanity; the neighbour, for instance, who gave the noisy parties proves human. What stops this novel from being a complete success is the lack of critical distancing between the author and hero. It is often very difficult, not only here but in a number of Wain's other novels, to make up one's mind when he is properly using his exceptional gift for imaginatively evoking rage, rancour, and disgust, and when he is simply himself indulging in these feelings.

It could be said that one of Wain's chief gifts as a novelist is for evoking, or expressing, violent feelings and for contriving situations that will justify the explosion of these feelings, rather than for cool observation of externals or a gift for ready, sympathetic or humorous, identification with a range of characters; his plots, after his first two picaresque novels, have tended to be very neat and very artificial. The gift of plotting, and the gift of producing concentrated and eloquent expressions of strong emotion, are gifts of the dramatist rather than the novelist, and the drama, to which Wain is now turning his attention, may be his real medium. But the novels as they stand are not negligible. The sense running through them of the author's driving energy, lacerated amusement, and scornful rage compensates for implausibilities and two-dimensional (all black and white, or black and then white) characters. But even through parody and exaggeration, Wain, like Amis, is one of the few living novelists who give us a sense of actual contemporary life.

Amis, however, is much more the novelist born. There is in the born novelist's presentation of his world and his characters a discreetness, a hesitation about final judgements, a sense of something held in reserve, which Amis has and Wain lacks; a good example is the scene in *That Uncertain Feeling* where the wealthy stick of a complaisant husband suddenly becomes toweringly formidable, not because he has been cuckolded, but because the hero's independence has reduced his wife to hysteria. The hero of *Lucky Jim* has had all kinds of topical meanings tagged on to him; in fact, he belongs to an old tradition in folk-tale, the wise simpleton or lucky blunderer. He is also a male Cinderella, for one can find in the novel bad and good magicians (Professor Welch

and the rich man from London), an ogress, a thwarted witch
or enchantress, and a defeated boaster. Jim Dixon is not fundamentally an angry young man but, like Wells's Kipps, a
put upon young man. There is, however, very little fantasy in
the sharp social and psychological observation, stylized for
comedy, but never, like some of Wain's stylizations, taking
wing from life. There are passages, of course, of sheer farce,
the blanket-burning episode and the drunken speech (modelled, perhaps, on the similar Wodehouse oration by Gussy
Fink-Nottle). But there is penetrating realism in the whole
account of the relations of Jim and Margaret, the most
thoroughly 'done' (in a Henry Jamesian sense) part of the
book. It is a pity that where the unattractive, unhappy, and
life-consuming Margaret is so wonderfully drawn, the heroine, the kindly princess, should not be much more than a
sex-object, with a verbal glow around her. Of Amis's subsequent novels, the third one, *I Like It Here*, was a misfire.
That Uncertain Feeling seemed to me a much better novel
than many critics made out, but unevenly balanced between
seriousness, pure farce, and high comedy; I also felt the
cards were a little rigged against the unfortunate Mrs Gruf-
fyd-Williams. The last one, *Take a Girl Like You*, seemed
to me near Amis's top form; a much more subtle and comprehensive treatment of the rival claims of natural randiness
and the traditional decencies than *That Uncertain Feeling*,
bringing in the idea of a code of honour (Patrick ought not
to have had Jenny, when she was drunk and defenceless),
and working out some themes quite new to me in recent
fiction: for instance, the social and sexual disadvantage at
which the physically unattractive always are, and the compunction, and helpfulness, the physically attractive can
sometimes show about this. The sadness, heaviness, and
shame that attends Patrick's ignoble triumph at the end;
Patrick's recurring fantasies of cruelty to others and death
to himself; the grimly comic monologue of the aged impo-
tent peer (he used to suck old electric batteries to see if there
was any juice left in them, but there is no juice left now in
his); all put the pursuit of sexual pleasure, which is Patrick's

main aim in life, in moral perspective: we get a glimpse of the scholar Patrick could have been, which the gay life leaves him no time to be. Full of humour, this is nevertheless on the whole a sober rather than a funny book, like Fielding's *Amelia*: Fielding believed that good nature was the core of morals but by the time of *Amelia* had come to believe that good nature without principles was not enough. The account of the visit to Fielding's tomb in *I Like It Here* is the one really moving and memorable passage in that novel. Like Fielding's, Amis's heroes are thoroughly virile, susceptible to female charm to the point of weakness, but good-natured. Patrick, in *I Like It Here*, is made to suffer for his weakness: the friend whom he most admires rejects and despises him for his moral rape of Jenny; but about his ultimate good nature we are left in some doubt. Jenny resigns herself to the situation, but probably Patrick has no intention of marrying her. Some light has gone out for both of them; many people found this novel very coarse and nasty, but, given that some lights have gone out for Amis also, I found it a just picture of some aspects of contemporary life.

Amis, then, leaves one admiring, but with a heavy and sad feeling; in one story in his most recent publication, *My Enemy's Enemy*, he took for his hero a bachelor, the platonic admirer of a middle-aged married woman, the wife of an old friend of his. She dies, he comes to the funeral. He gets into conversation, over a meal, with the dead woman's daughter, who has married a naturalized Italian. He finds himself talking about English ways, English customs, English traditions, in an implicitly insulting and excluding way. The girl is hurt but forgiving, and asks him to come back for another meal; but she does make him realize both that her mother, whom he idealized, was not very kind about her marriage and that this patient, platonic love of his, if it involves no remorses, also runs no risks. I think Amis may in future write about superficially rather dull people, like the people in this story, but bring out with the great subtlety of moral observation which he possesses both the earnestness they can awkwardly express and the reality of moral problems one thinks of as trivial and prosaic. But I hope he still sometimes gives himself over to pure comedy, even to farce.

John Braine and Alan Sillitoe can be dealt with more briefly. Critics who, in this age of sociology, look to the novel as a document were excited by Braine and Sillitoe, because they dealt not with lower-middle-class protest, as Wain and Amis were thought to do, but with genuine working-class protest. Both are of working-class background, Braine from Yorkshire, Sillitoe from Nottingham. Braine started to write when he was in hospital for a long time with tuberculosis; Sillitoe when he was invalided from the R.A.F. with a small pension, on which he could just live in Majorca. He is a poet (a more promising poet, I think, than some critics have made him out) and in Majorca he met Robert Graves; he had been writing stories with an imaginary or fantastic background, and Graves suggested to him that it would be more successful to use working-class Nottingham, where he had grown up. His book of short stories, *The Loneliness of the Long Distance Runner*, is a masterly book, and I think the short story is his proper length. It permits an objectivity and clarity of line which he has not so far achieved in his novels. His view of working-class life is classical and tragic: you cannot win, but you can fight. The hero of the title short story is a Borstal boy, a magnificent runner; the Governor of the Borstal wants him to win a race, and he wants to win it himself, but for the sake of pure defiance he forces himself not to. A streak of defiant sadness runs through all the stories. A boy watches a man preparing to hang himself, with the natural curiosity of a small boy, but without emotionally understanding what it is all about. A lonely old man, a good craftsman, but a solitary drinker, makes friends in a tea-shop with a couple of lively schoolgirls. He starts standing them tea regularly. It is all innocent, but it changes his life. The police threaten him and warn him to see no more of the girls. He goes back to beery soddenness. Disappointed about the result of a football match (football has become the one symbol of happiness in his life) a man nags his long-suffering wife till she finally leaves him. It is the loneliness, the tragedy, the defiance of working-class life that interests Sillitoe: he is not interested in the warmth, the solidarity that impress Raymond Williams and Richard Hoggart. In *Saturday Night and Sunday Morning* the hero is a piece-worker in a bicycle factory, who does as much overtime as he dares, to have money for a blow-out over the weekend, to buy drink and clothes. He has simultaneous affairs with two married sisters, one with a husband in the army. One sister becomes pregnant and procures an abortion by drinking gin in a hot bath. The army husband gets wind of what is going on, tipped off by the other husband, Arthur's mate in the factory. Arthur gets beaten up, but remains defiant, refusing to take Jack's advice and 'knuckle under', clinging to the pleasures of the rogue male, 'the White Hoss, fishin', and screwin' '. His spirit is reinforced when he sees an insulted wife break a glass on her husband's forehead. That is how to behave: '... now he was awake once more, ready to tackle all obstacles, to break any man, or woman, that came for him, to turn on the whole world if it bothered him too much, and blow it to pieces.' He is a rebel, but he softens a little to a young woman, Doreen, whom he asks to live with him, not to marry him (they have already made love). We leave him fishing by the canal, in proud solitude.

Arthur Seaton, the hero, does not correspond at all to any stereotype of working-class morality, but seems to have the morality of a Nietzschean aristocrat. Sillitoe's poems are romantic, profoundly pessimistic, and completely hostile to organized society. Sillitoe is like a working-class Byron, in the pre-*Don Juan* stage: what he teaches is that working-class individualism, where it exists, will be far more intransigent than middle-class individualism could ever be. Society, for Arthur Seaton, is simply The Enemy.

John Braine, also, cuts across the formula about working-class life one might have got from Hoggart and Williams; the formula that for the traditional working classes, money and power do not matter, happiness and group loyalty do. Joe Lampton's father, who has died before the beginning of

Braine's novel, *Room at the Top*, was one of the Hoggart men: a first-rate workman, never given promotion because he was too strong a Socialist and too staunch a Trade Unionist. But Joe himself is a working boy on the make. He has been in the R.A.F. He has got himself some education. He moves from a grim north country one-industry town to a prosperous midland mixed light-industry town, to a municipal clerical job giving him official middle-class status. He is a young man eaten up with desire for rich possessions, pricing every suit, every haircut, every car, every piece of interior decoration, every woman he sees. He meets through the local amateur dramatic society a married women in her thirties (terribly old she seems to him at times, baffy and crows-footed), begins an affair with her, and goes away on holiday with her. They are happy, though he is shocked that she has allowed herself to be painted in the nude. But at the same time he is attracting, and being attracted to, the pretty, insipid little daughter of the local rich man. He makes her pregnant, and is accepted as a son-in-law. He has broken with his older mistress and she kills herself in a car crash. He gets drunk and tries to get people to beat and punish him, but nobody and nothing wants to, and he is all set for the grim emptiness of success. Sillitoe writes in a plain, immediate, Defoe-like style, Braine in a prose of slick metaphors owing much to Raymond Chandler. But *Room at the Top* is powerful in scheme, in plotting and narrative thrust, as a moral fable about ambition. It illuminates the pattern which a lust not so much for 'material things' as for the gaudy spoils and trophies of the cash-war takes in a commercially competitive society (it had to be set in the provinces, for, whatever can be said against London, the commercial prizes there have never been the only or even the most important ones). The weakness of the book, coming out in the faintly whorish *chic* of the style, shiny-shoddy, contrasting strongly with Sillitoe's homespun if often threadbare honesty, is that Braine is not emotionally detached from Joe Lampton, but half-admires him for doing what any lad of guts or spunk would do in his place. Nor does

Braine seem to see the vacuity, but only the softness, the expensiveness, the silkiness, of the butterfly-brained little princess his hairy swineherd has married; though in the sequel, *Life at the Top*, he does see that she could easily turn into a proper little bitch. But in the first novel Braine is as much beglamoured by her as Lampton is by all articles of conspicuous consumption. Both Sillitoe and Braine are worrying if one takes them as giving real clues to what energetic young proles will be after today: they will be utterly anarchistic, Sillitoe says; and Braine, for his part, says they will be dazzled and utterly ruthless in pursuit of the most gaudy, the most intrinsically worthless prizes. Sillitoe seems to have more talent, or at least, what is perhaps a larger aspect of that, clearer self-knowledge. But Braine is not writing fantasy although much of the social truth in *Room at the Top* is exposed unconsciously. But if one agrees that social truth and aesthetic truth must coincide then aesthetic doubts arise when a social meaning is exposed without the author's full knowledge and when the reader's intelligence has to supplement certain gaps in the author's.

The question of the relation of social and aesthetic meaning also arises in one of the great successes, in Europe as well as England, of the last ten years, Lawrence Durrell's *Alexandria Quartet*. Here also is a world of fantasy, in which, for all the main characters, the cold intoxication of the maintained sexual dream is to coincide, in the end, with the fine solitude of the artist. Two characters, Darley and Pursewarden, are novelists, one, Clea, is a painter. The heroine of the first of the four novels, Justine, has been married to one novelist, becomes the mistress of two others, and exists essentially as problematic material – is she a nymphomaniac, a *femme fatale*, a woman harried by a traumatic experience, a vapid, fashionable woman, a tough Israeli patriot longing for the life of the *kibbutz*, a figment, a bore? And are men's motives fundamentally sexual, artistic, political, religious – or are all motives disguises for other motives, are there fixed characters in the world, are we all actors, is it all a fancy-dress show? Durrell takes the epigraphs for his novels from the Marquis de Sade, but one should think less of the lust for cruelty in that author than of the interest in transformations and disguises, the passion for shocking revelations, for stripping off the mask, for amateur theatricals. The Greek poet, Constantine Trypanis, complained to me once that Durrell, for all his philhellenism, has no understanding of the element of measure and of laborious sobriety, not only among Greeks but also among Arabs and Jews, in the eastern Mediterranean world: Durrell's world is one of palaces and brothels, whores and millionaires. It is also a world, with its long letters, its long descriptions and soliloquies, its set pieces, in which we are conscious of the effort of literary transformation and, in the writing, of queer alternations of amateur naïvety with high virtuosity. Pursewarden, the novelist, for instance, is quoted very often as making pregnant and pithy remarks. But these remarks are often slightly disguised platitudes to which inverted commas and attribution to a man of genius give a spurious glitter. As it were: 'As Pursewarden used to say, "It is a long cloud that has no silver turning."' Dream fantasy, of an erotic-sadistic sort, is pursued with too childish a directness and simplicity. Clea, who stands for the artistic conscience, the ruthless benignity of the pure observer, goes swimming with Darley and a friend. They are playing with a gun that shoots a harpoon, it accidentally goes off and pins her under water through her right hand, her painter's hand; to rescue her from drowning Darley has to hack off her hand at the wrist. With the new artificial hand (like Renoir, in old age, with the long brush strapped to his wrist) she becomes the great painter she has always wished to be. Durrell's gift and gusto for handling words outruns, in his prose as in his poetry, his sense of the real; he is nearest to the real, perhaps, in his fine handling of the comic-macabre, in a character like Scobie.

Durrell reminds one of Ouida (the Ouida whom Norman Douglas admired so much), Oscar Wilde (in the sense in which Yeats thought Wilde a great professional as a talker but a brilliant amateur as a writer), Frederick Rolfe, Firbank at times, Sir Osbert Sitwell in his memoirs a little. It is a tradition of amplitude, gaudiness, thick impasto, dramatic chiaroscuro, writing in which at the end of many a long paragraph the appropriate response is: 'Gosh!' The writers whom I have mentioned as constituting this tradition (and Meredith is near it often, and earlier on Beckford perhaps started it, and Kinglake's *Eothen* and Robert Byron's *Road to Oxiana* are travel books belonging to the family) have lived much abroad, have found much to bore and irritate them in England, but carry into their fantasy worlds an English assurance. They have a touch of the mad milord. It places *The Alexandria Quartet* that there is a passage in which Pursewarden grumbles about English publishers, who are always looking for another Trollope ('I like a nice Trollope', Richard Hoggart once remarked at a literary conference, 'to take to bed with me'). One sees the point, and yet Trollope's achievement, his solid beef-and-pudding world, is nearer the centre of the English tradition of the novel than Durrell. But if there is a place for the exotic, for bravura, for anti-insular panache, in contemporary English fiction, for philosophic romance rather than sober realism, Durrell's novels fill it. But Iris Murdoch is also involved in this same tradition with Durrell, though she uses English settings, and she describes it on the whole with more penetration, economy, and overall success. And it was this element of romantic fantasy and aristocratic independence of spirit, the taste for the free and the wild in her writings, which made me unwilling to group her alongside Amis and Wain.

Miss Murdoch's first novel, *Under the Net*, was often classified with *Lucky Jim* and *Hurry on Down* because it too had a rogue hero. But it was essentially a *roman philosophique* (one of the characters is modelled on Wittgenstein) and its purpose was to question and explore the whole texture of social life, from an angle of inquiring farce, rather than to make a specific gesture of social protest. Iris Murdoch is a trained philosopher, and for a time was a philosophy tutor at Oxford. She came from a family of Irish gentry, and her socialism, which she keeps out of her novels but writes about interestingly in essays, comes from her philosophical interest in Victorian and Edwardian anti-individualist moral philosophers like T. H. Green and Bosanquet. She has written a book on Sartre and was strongly influenced by Raymond Queneau, whose world is one of fantasy.

People who dislike Miss Murdoch's novels have often said to me that she offers in her fiction a world imaginatively constructed from her thinking about life rather than a world imitated, in the Aristotelian sense, from her observations of it. She presents characters who in such a world as ours *ought* to exist rather than characters whom we have met existing in it. They will have a coherence and simplicity, in the philosophical sense an essence, which the opacity of ordinary life, and the contrariness of ordinary character, does not as a rule expose to us, and this essential nature will be brought out in situations of an extreme sort, contrived with cunning artifice. The extreme situations spring from a feeling in Miss Murdoch that the ordinary current and texture of life is both more improbable, more absurd (in Camus's sense of almost insolently arbitrary), and yet more bound to some large pattern of order than we usually are ready to recognize. I see Miss Murdoch's fictional imagination as the super-logical synthesis of two contradictory propositions. The first proposition is: 'Everything must happen in accordance with the laws of logic, therefore nothing that happens is intrinsically surprising.' The second proposition is: 'Everything that happens is contingent, therefore it is free, it involves, or can involve, a total response of the human personality, therefore it is *always* surprising.' These two attitudes, cross-weaving each other, explain the ambivalent effect of her stories: something is being shown to us which is quite odd and extraordinary; something is being demonstrated to us which, in some obscure way, we knew already, but now know in a more disturbing way.

Her world, therefore, is a reconstituted one containing all or most of the elements of our everyday world, including its physical and emotional intractability, the elements of stubbornness and resistance in experience, but more heavily loaded with concrete implications of, and puzzles about, significance. There is an obvious painstakingness, a pursuit of precision even at the cost of awkwardness, in her prose, which is typical of the philosopher.

Iris Murdoch's best novel, to my mind, is her fourth last one, *The Bell.* The scene is an Anglican lay religious community. It is run by a young man called Michael, who has been deflected from a vocation as a Church of England parson by a homosexual episode – a romantic and sexually innocent one – that happened when he was a master in a public school. A young girl, Dora, an ex-art student, comes to the community before returning to her stiff, unpleasant husband from whom she has been parted for some time. The essence of Dora's character is beautifully given to us in the first chapter when, travelling by train to the community, she shelters between her hands a panicky butterfly that would otherwise kill itself against the carriage windows and, still holding it, steps out on the village station leaving her luggage behind her. Michael's character is more complex: we are to contrast a sermon he gives, seeing the essence of Christianity in love and spontaneity, with a sermon given by another member of the community, seeing that essence in rigid obedience to rules. Michael's spontaneity leads him to make casual advances, on a hot day, after a lot of cider, to a handsome boy visiting the community. Dora, also, half-consciously, helps to awaken the boy. In the end Dora finds the path to reality in continuing her training as an art-student, which she had given up for marriage; Michael, after the community has been disbanded because of his weakness, is forced to give up his religious vocation, to accept a more prosaic role in the world, and a more adult responsibility, for a girl who had pretended she had a vocation to become a nun, but was really in love with him. Very broadly the theme which links all Miss Murdoch's novels is that men naturally, and for reasons with which up to a point one sympathizes, evade self-knowledge and as far as possible build round themselves workable fantasy worlds that flatter their ideals; that shocks, threats, violences, deprivations, however distressing, lead to leaps forward in self-knowledge; but that the results of such leaps forward are usually a more complex and painful knowledge of responsibility, rather than a greater ease of life. But this fine and stern morality of self-education would not have the force it has if the richness of the fantasy-life had not, for Miss Murdoch, a compelling imaginative attraction. Her own favourite novel is her most fantastic one, and the one in which the whims and wildness of the heroine are most indulged, *The Flight from the Enchanter*. Her talent is far too individual a one for it to be likely that she will become the founder of a school. But of all the new novelists in the 1950s she has, it seems to me, the greatest penetration and the most striking individuality.

PART THREE

THE DRAMA

12

The Weakness of the Victorian Age
and the 1890s Revival

THE nineteenth century in England, although rich in other
kinds of literature, was weak in drama. Between Sheridan's
The School for Scandal, written towards the end of the
eighteenth century, and the early comedies of Oscar Wilde
and Bernard Shaw in the 1890s, no English working playwright produced a prose comedy of lasting literary value. On
the other hand, though almost every major English poet of
the nineteenth century, Wordsworth, Coleridge, Shelley,
Keats, Byron, Browning, Arnold, Tennyson, Swinburne, even
Hopkins (who has left us a fragment) tried his hand at poetic
drama, usually either in the manner of Shakespeare or in
imitation of classical Greek, these poetic plays make dull
reading and when they were put on the stage, as some of
Browning's and Tennyson's were, failed to establish themselves in the repertoire. The working playwrights were often
professionally connected with the theatre, but had little or
no literary culture or ambition; the poets were too far away
from the theatre to understand the difference between words
to be read on the page and a play as a structure to be
enacted, of which words are only one element and, compared
to action and character, a subsidiary one. Nineteenth-century critics from Lamb to Swinburne concentrated, in dealing with Shakespeare, and even more in dealing with minor
Elizabethan dramatists, on scenes taken in isolation, and,
within these scenes, on passages displaying peculiar verbal
felicity: the stress was on intensity rather than structure.
The nineteenth century was a great period of Shakespearian
scholarship; but there again the emphasis was on establish-
ing and elucidating a text, and on relating the text to its

literary sources, rather than on the play as a dramatic whole. A minor poet, Thomas Lovell Beddoes, managed to produce many striking isolated passages of dramatic verse: what he could not do was construct a play in which there was any cumulative dramatic tension, or any sustained interest in plot or character. The tendency to be fascinated by detail at the expense of structure, to proliferate in ornament, is a general weakness of Victorian prose, poetry, painting, and architecture; but only in the poetic drama was it a fatal weakness. Even a very great novelist, Henry James, who had been a dramatic critic, who constructed his novels like plays, and who had a vivid 'sense of theatre', failed as a practising playwright: he failed to achieve the directness and gross sense of audience which a playwright needs. He was battling against a theatre dominated by the actor, and therefore dominated by convention and spectacle, and against an audience conditioned to character acting and the star system. The examples of Wilde and Shaw suggest one of the mysteries of the theatre; the theatre is recurrently mechanical, childish, immature, a place of the silliest make-believe, the most blatant machinery. The notable dramatist, when he comes along, rarely rejects all this; he sees what actors can do, and what audiences can take; he uses all this, demurely pretending to be turning out the standard article, and he transforms it. No good dramatist has ever despised stock responses or made his appeal to the select few in an audience. The dramatist knows that a common range of easily accessible, socially held feelings are what he must manipulate, however much he hopes to transform them; and he knows that the audience, if it is really to be held by a play, is not a large committee that will be guided by its most intelligent members but one single great beast.

It is interesting that the two men who brought life back to English comedy in the 1890s were both Irish; so, before them, were Congreve, Farquhar, Goldsmith, and Sheridan, and so have been a number of novelists who have handled comic dialogue and situation in the novel with special vitality, Sterne, Maria Edgeworth, Charles Lever, Sheridan

Lefanu, Somerville and Ross, Elizabeth Bowen. These writers, it should be noted, were all members of the Protestant minority in Southern Ireland, tending to think of themselves as a kind of aristocracy, morally bound to display in their speech and manners a certain gaiety and style. Apart from these special attitudes of a minority group, the Irish people in general have a feeling for speech as a social art, a raciness, wit, and fluency, and a taste for rhetoric which are much less typical of the English.

Both Shaw and Wilde came from, and in a broad sense belonged to, the Anglo-Irish Ascendancy, though Shaw's family was so poor and disreputable that he was never even invited to garden parties given by his baronet relation. Wilde was the swaggering amusing Irishman of the old comedies. Shaw, though with his own swagger, represented the dour and puritan side of the Irish tradition: the pride that bites on the bullet of poverty. Wilde was a man of the world, who needed a life of luxurious ostentation, and whose vanity and appetites, combined with some deeper need to take perpetual risks, to shock, to destroy himself, finally landed him in disaster. He was perhaps in his own way just as serious a thinker as Shaw. *The Soul of Man Under Socialism* is as good a piece of excited rhetoric as any of Shaw's prefaces, and if it draws mainly on insights from William Morris, Matthew Arnold, and Walter Pater, so much of Shaw is drawn from Carlyle, Ruskin, and Nietsche. Wilde's *The Ballad of Reading Gaol,* shoddy and sentimental as it is in parts, has largeness of spirit; it is not the work of a fundamentally frivolous or heartless man. Yet, though Wilde is full of witty paradoxes, his originality is not so much in his thinking as in his personality, in a grace and impudence that enabled him to deploy second-hand material with a striking social effect.

Yeats, another contemporary of Wilde's, and an Irishman of a similar social and religious background, said of Wilde that he should not have been a writer but a man of action and certainly he usually aimed, as the rhetorician does, not at the greatest depth and finish, but at the most flashing immediate effect. His success both as man and writer, though there was so tragically much more to him, was that of the social entertainer. It is as 'entertainment' that his plays have survived. Three of them, *Lady Windermere's Fan, An Ideal Husband*, and *A Woman of no Importance*, are really melodramas peppered with epigrams. Wilde's last and his only perfect comedy, *The Importance of Being Earnest,* is modelled on the typical late Victorian farce, deliberately nonsensical in its characterization and motivation, delightfully innocent in its appeal to the audience to connive at the most extreme improbabilities. Wilde urges this farcical form, which in itself has no detachable literary value, which exists for escapism and belly-laughs, to express his own criticism of life, his own flippant, detached, and dandified attitude. He also uses it to make his own contribution towards Victorian dream- or child-literature, like *Alice in Wonderland*, to create a world of innocent libido, where lust is expressed in a greed for cucumber sandwiches, and where children are born, not under gooseberry bushes, but in Gladstone bags. Lady Bracknell, too, is somewhere between the Queen and the Duchess in Alice.

From Wilde descends the whole comedy of entertainment in our century, Somerset Maugham, Noël Coward, Frederick Lonsdale, the lighter plays of Terence Rattigan, the Aldwych farces of Ben Travers, the comedies of William Douglas-Home. What all these successors of Wilde lack, however, is the perfect finish, the almost Mozartian gaiety, which having laid melodrama and the desire to shock aside, Wilde was able to achieve with such grace and charm in *The Importance of Being Earnest.* Shaw had failed respectably as a novelist, though he had made a reputation for himself as a critic of music and drama, before he had any success as a dramatist. As a dramatic critic, he helped to create the taste by which he was to be appreciated: he attacked Irving and the star actor-manager system, mere spectacle, and what he thought of as romantic escapism even when he found it in Shakespeare. He was a great dramatic critic, the only Englishman, apart from Hazlitt, with a mind

one can fully respect, who has ever devoted himself to that
chore. His book, *The Quintessence of Ibsenism*, put across
his own special interpretation of that rugged, bleak honourable talent. Shaw was very much more a conscious partisan
of his own ideas than Ibsen, and less interested than Ibsen
was in individual human character. Yet, however much a
partisan in his prefaces, he loved in his plays to give opposite
ideas a free counterpointing interplay, so that he not only
reminds one, as Robert Graves has suggested, of Lucian, but
at his best (as in the dialogue of Don Juan and the Devil in
Man and Superman) of some of the earlier dialogues, the
dialogues with sophists, the *Gorgias* or the *Protagoras*, of
Plato. But he lacked Ibsen's and Chehov's sense of the confused, obscure poetry of life. He never wrote a play that
rouses us as deeply as *The Cherry Orchard* or *The Wild
Duck*. What he does have is a greater mastery of incisive
and rebounding combative dialogue than any other English
dramatist since his countryman, Congreve. Combined with
this was a gift for lucid and graceful speakable exposition
of ideas that remind one of earlier philosophical dialogues,
especially of Berkeley's satirical *Alciphron*. In a way, to echo
Byron on Berkeley, it is often no matter what Shaw's characters are saying: we enjoy a splendid intellectual tennis-
match, with real not imaginary balls, the slammings, the
cornerings, the swift unexpected returns across the net. In
an age like our own, which seems to prefer intoning responses
to enjoying dialectic, the sense of free play of mind in Shaw's
plays is wholesome. At his best, he loves the game, and is
not rigging the score. Because his approach to ideas is
through the aesthetics of dialectic, not, like that of his rival
and contemporary, H. G. Wells, a fundamentally sentimental one, we can read his passages of abstract discussion
(the very sound and solid arguments for burning Joan of
Arc presented with such dry relish in *St Joan*, for instance)
with a very lively pleasure even when the topics are no
longer controversial.

At his best, however, he is no mere artist in dialectics, but
a dramatist. An early comedy, *You Never Can Tell*, with a

seaside setting, seems to me one of the few modern plays (Goldsmith's *She Stoops to Conquer* is another) with the generosity, the sweetness, the verve of Shakespeare's golden comedies. I used to hate *Candida* because I thought the way in which the young poet in that play spoke, his embarrassing bits of purple, showed Shaw's vulgar ignorance both of poetry and of what poets are like. Having seen one of two good performances of the play, I now wonder: the poet was probably modelled on De Quincey, on what Shaw might have heard about Francis Thompson, and on his acquaintance with the threadbare, awkward, but splendidly arrogant young Yeats. *John Bull's Other Island*, Shaw's only long play devoted to Ireland, has an accuracy, a bitterness, a distressed love, hard to match elsewhere in his work: in a visit to Ireland a couple of years ago it was borne in on me that it has also a worrying continuing truth. But a more famous play, *St Joan*, fails to be a tragedy and becomes an inspirational pageant. *Heartbreak House* uses, or caricatures, Chehov's devices, and fails utterly to catch the refinement of his spirit.

There is something lacking in Shaw, the deep sense of which came to Yeats in a dream when he saw Shaw's face transformed into a sewing machine, grinning, grinning, grinning, and clicking, clicking, clicking. There is something brittle and heartless in his optimism, his assumption that some immanent spirit – he calls it the 'Life-force' – is somehow or other, through all the disasters of history, working towards greater good. His belief in the 'Life-force' made him far too ready to welcome the 'men of power', from Napoleon through Stalin to Hitler. He was too ready to explain sympathetically the excesses and inhumanities of political institutions from the Inquisition to the Ogpu, which impose officially-approved points of view by terror. For that splendid English liberal tradition, which gave him his own platform, he never expressed any respect; though plays like *The Apple Cart* and *Good King Charles's Golden Days* suggest that, hating the idea of rule by committees, by compromise, by variously solicited free consent, he felt sometimes almost as attracted to the romantic conservative ideal of monarchy as to radical dictatorship. He was a brilliant imitator of speech and a mimic. But having transformed himself into a public puppet, a Jack-in-the-Box, he was a performer of, rather than a listener to, his own self: certainly he was not an open listener to others. But he was a great orchestrator, at a light opera level, of simple but surprising and interesting intellectual themes. And, however inhuman one considers his general philosophy, he fought valiantly for many good causes. And there remains behind all the pother, a master, who too seldom fully achieved himself, of romantic rather than realistic, of sympathetic rather than satirical comedy. He is at his best when, as in *Heartbreak House* or *Pygmalion*, he creates characters which are more than mere mouthpieces for ideas.

The history of the comedy of ideas after Shaw, like that of the comedy of manners after Wilde, is one of decay. No follower of Shaw's is really a success; neither Galsworthy nor James Bridie nor J. B. Priestley nor Arnold Wesker (these are the names that immediately suggest themselves, but Wesker will be dealt with in Chapter Sixteen) has Shaw's swiftness and suppleness and incisiveness of dialogue. Compared to the lean quickness with which his thought moves on the stage, they seem all suet pudding. Galsworthy's plays are carefully constructed and well-meaning, but the dialogue is stilted and dull, the characters wooden, and one is too much aware all the time of Galsworthy's intention to present an example and state a case. James Bridie, on the other hand, a Glasgow doctor who became a professional dramatist in middle life, had something of Shaw's sense of the dialectic clash of ideas in the world. But he had also too much of a Scottish feeling that all oppositions can finally be resolved over an intimate talk and a good dram. His writing has a touch of that couthness and cosiness, that snug self-warming, self-approving quality, which has done so much to damn Scottish literature over the last hundred years, just as the opposite quality, a politely despairing irony, has done so much to make Irish literature interesting. Apart from that,

Bridie never really learned how to construct a play: his three-act plays often resemble three brilliant first acts of three quite different ideal plays, none of which he has had the courage to push through to an end along a single line of development. But partly because of this very digressiveness, his *language* is much more alive than Galsworthy's, or indeed than Priestley's.

Mr Priestley might be described as a very good and solid working replica of that desirable type, the eighteenth-century all-round man of letters. He has written novels, essays, critical books, travel books, many of which I have read, particularly when I was young, with some enjoyment once, but none twice; and now, for instance, I find that I remember much more vividly the 1930s film version of *The Good Companions* with fine performances by John Gielgud, Jessie Matthews, and Edmund Gwenn than I remember any page of the book. Yet I do find myself remembering in detail those of Mr Priestley's plays that I have seen, and perhaps his main gift has been for the theatre. The plays that aroused a great deal of discussion were those about Dunne's theory of serial time, like the exciting thriller, *Dangerous Corner*. I think myself that he was not really at his best in these, nor in a modern morality play like *An Inspector Calls* (though when I saw this it was helped by a magnificent performance by Sir Ralph Richardson), which used a detective story formula to labour the sound but unsurprising moral that there are skeletons in the most prosperous cupboards and that we are all members one of another. Priestley, I think, was at his best in a farce full of rich northern local colour like *When We Were Married* or in solidly sensitive studies of middle-class life like *Eden End* (which had a magnificently funny drunken scene) or *The Linden Tree*, about the obstinate loyalty of a professor due for retirement to the provincial city, the university, the students, from which his family want him to cut free. If Mr Priestley had not been so diversely gifted, he might have done more in drama than he has and might have carried on the very solid tradition of the realistic Manchester dramatists of the 1910s.

Weakness of the Victorian Age and the 1890s Revival

Mr Priestley's *When We Were Married* is a farce, of a broad and hearty sort – so is Shakespeare's *The Merry Wives of Windsor* – but it has a rich, racy quality about it, the quality of a provincial life more solid and settled than that of London. It is the lack in the broadest sense of thickness and substance that one must complain about in much of the English drama of this century. For all Shaw's greatness, there is often a gasping thinness in the air his characters breathe, a lack of the sense of life's pressure, except for *John Bull's Other Island*. A certain rootlessness in the personal lives of many English dramatists has reflected itself in a lack of body and richness in their work. I thought when I wrote the first version of this book that the revival of the poetic drama, associated with Eliot and Fry, and in a different way with Auden and Isherwood, might bring back more fullness and life; but I would now look elsewhere.

13

Suburban Domestic Drama

NEITHER the drama of ideas nor the high comedy of manners, neither the tradition of Wilde nor the tradition of Shaw, made in the first fifty years of this century an appeal to the typical suburban audience. About Shaw, the remark might be: 'Very clever, no doubt, but a bit above my head', or about Noël Coward in his friskier moods: 'Very amusing, if you like that sort of thing, but frankly I'm old-fashioned.' One can imagine this conversation taking place in one of those dormitory suburbs about an hour by train from London.

The suburb, which is neither town nor country but parasitical on both, has no function other than that of residence. It is insulated from the sharper pressures of English life: from the liveliness and competition of the working class and from true urban sophistication. The people who choose to live in the suburbs are usually quietly prosperous: they are intelligent without being intellectual, polite but incurious, and industrious without being innovators.

These negative virtues are not the source of profound drama or literature, and the suburb with its wariness of involving itself in intellectual complications or getting out of its emotional depth is not a deep appreciator of literature or drama either. In the 1920s and 1930s when suburban people went to the theatre in London or in their nearest large town, they chose a play that would reflect, perhaps with a certain flattering enlargement, the rigid boundaries, the comfortable humours, and the safe certainties of their own lives. And since a demand, on a free market, always creates a supply, they got what they wanted. One reason why the British theatre is less stuffy now than it was then is that since 1945 classes or groups who in the 1930s would not often have gone to the theatre, the discontented young (who may include the young from the suburbs), the students, the more articulate layers of the working classes, the people of working-class origin who have got degrees but do not see suburban cosiness as their goal, have all more money in their pockets.

One can give a generic description of the old-style suburban domestic drama, which, now that it has almost completely vanished, arouses in one antiquarian sentiments, like Victorian melodrama. In retrospect it is hard to differentiate one play from another. The setting is ideally the living-room of a large suburban villa, with french windows opening out on the garden, through which young people in white flannels carrying tennis rackets often wander in and out. The curtain rises on a comic servant dusting the furniture and describing to a curious visitor the various endearing characteristics of the family. The younger people in the play are probably minor characters. The heroine is as likely as not a sweet, fluttering, managing mother (in her forties but still very attractive) with whom every suburban matron in the audience can identify herself. The young people's problems and awkward complications are put in to show her powers of tactful management, but the main plot is usually the wistful revival and gracious laying to rest of some romantic ghost from her own past – perhaps the return of some admirer, bronzed and still handsome, from the Far East. Nothing will come of his return except that it arouses her husband, who is such a nice man but who has been taking his wonderful wife a little too much for granted, to a new attentiveness. Or perhaps the admirer can be shunted off (with enormous generosity and just a twinge of sweetly concealed heartache) on a difficult daughter. The dialogue does not aim at wit or incisiveness, but at an effect, in the heroine, of sweet absent-minded charm, in the husband of pipe-puffing gruffness, and in the other characters of pleasant natural chatter.

The author? At various times between the two World Wars and, indeed, for a time, after the Second World War it might have been (though it is invidious to single out a few names, where so many have been successful in this genre) A. A. Milne, Dodie Smith, Esther McCracken, John Van Druten, Merton Hodge, Daphne du Maurier, even (in spite of his Chehovian touches) N. C. Hunter. But however often one saw it, and whoever the author was, it was always 'a very nice play'. Of course, the local colour altered, the emphasis shifted from time to time; there might even be a delicious, though thwarted, expectation that somebody was going to do or say something 'naughty'. The plot was often a bit thin; but the very cushioning of the action by the conventions of middle-class decorum allowed one to sit back in one's stall with a reassuring sense of safety. After all, it was a privilege to meet these nice people and to be allowed, through the convention of the fourth wall, to be with them, in that summery, chintzy room: it would be sacrilege to demand that they *do* or *say* something exciting.

In dealing with the work of writers who would not claim to be more than honest entertainers, and who have given many people a lot of harmless pleasure, one should not be heavy-handed. Yet if we look back at the play which seems to me to be the moral ancestor of suburban domestic drama, Goldsmith's *She Stoops to Conquer*, it is impossible to avoid an impression of profound decadence. Like the plays I have been talking about, *She Stoops to Conquer* is notable for its too amiable golden mellowness of mood – one thinks of Yeats's phrase about Goldsmith 'sipping from the honeypot of his mind'. Yet we feel nevertheless that the rural society which Goldsmith sentimentalizes and idealizes is at once more fully integrated, more vital, and less genteel, than the suburban society of the plays of A. A. Milne or Dodie Smith. Tony Lumpkin is alive in a way in which the young man with the tennis-racket under his arm is not; Mrs Hardcastle, compared to the modern managing mama in her forties, is almost an *unkind* portrait; the servants and the drinkers in the tavern are part of a single community with the squire and his lady, not comic relief keeping a respectful distance. Lastly, the dialogue of *She Stoops to Conquer* is in the tradition of Farquhar rather than Congreve; for the eighteenth century it is almost naturalistic, avoiding stylized repartee, point, and antithesis. Goldsmith's gift is humour, not wit. Yet the play remains alive on the page as well as the boards: a contribution to literature, as its successors are not.

The suburban domestic drama is a special instance of a phenomenon of the inter-war years which is worth touching on – the phenomenon of what Virginia Woolf, and also Mrs Q. D. Leavis in *Fiction and the Reading Public*, called 'middle-brow literature'. By this term these and other writers meant the abundance of books and plays into which a certain professional talent had gone and which might claim to seriousness of theme or originality of treatment, but which were really standard articles, soothers, not intended in any way to unsettle feelings or convictions. The popularity of middlebrow literature went with the limitations of the suburban background as a place for learning discrimination. Great drama or literature is generally aristocratic in its regard for finish and form, but has its roots, on the other hand, deep in popular culture. Suburban domestic drama was killed by changing social conditions. In the years before 1939, the inhabitants of the suburbs could think of themselves as the junior officer class; they were at the bottom rank of top people; today, they are at the top rank of the bottom people, and, if they are professional people on fixed salaries, have been since 1945 at an economic disadvantage both against working men who can bargain for higher wages and business men who can make higher profits. This has been a discomforting experience for them, but in the long run a bracing one, both giving them a wider sense of the total community they belong to, and a greater readiness to respond to even painful explorations of social change and tension in literature, drama, and the other arts.

14

The Irish Dramatic Revival

IN the last chapter, I was suggesting that the very comfort and placidity of English life for large sections of the middle classes is responsible for the insipidity of a great deal of the English drama of this century. Some of the criticisms I have been making of the weaknesses of the modern English naturalistic tradition in drama have also been made by Irish dramatists like Yeats and Synge; and one reason, certainly, for the distinction of the Irish dramatic movement in this century is that life in Ireland was not during its greatest days, and can hardly now be said to be, comfortable or complacent.

In the preface to his most famous play, *The Playboy of the Western World*, J. M. Synge has given a classic description of certain advantages enjoyed by the Irish dramatist:

When I was writing *The Shadow of the Glen*, some years ago, I got more than any learning could have given me from a chink in the floor of the old Wicklow house where I was staying, which let me hear what was being said by the servant girls in the kitchen. ... In countries where the imagination of the people, and the language they use, is rich and living, it is possible for a writer to be rich and copious in his words, and at the same time to give the reality which is at the root of all poetry, in a comprehensive and natural form. In modern literature of towns, however, richness is found only in sonnets, or prose poems, or in one or two elaborate books which are far away from the profound and common interests of life. One has on the one side Mallarmé and Hüysmans producing this literature, and on the other Ibsen and Zola dealing with the realities of life in joyless and pallid words. On the stage one must have reality and one must have joy; and that is why the intellectual modern drama has failed, and people have grown sick of the false joy of musical comedy, that has been given them in place of the rich joy found only in what is superb and wild in reality. In a good play every speech should be as fully flavoured as a nut or apple and such speeches cannot be written by anyone who works among people who have shut their lips on poetry. In Ireland for a few years more, we have a popular imagination that is fiery, magnificent, and tender; so that those of us who wish to write, start with a chance that is not given to writers in places where the springtime of local life has been forgotten, and the harvest is a memory only, and the straws have been turned into bricks.

Synge died still a comparatively young man, having written only a few plays, but these few, or the best among them, do combine a sense of reality, of the profound and common interests in life, with joy in language, with speeches as fully flavoured as a nut or an apple. It might be questioned, however, whether Synge's plays genuinely belong to the English tradition or even whether the beautiful language they are written in, the language of peasants speaking in English but thinking in Irish, using Irish idioms and tricks of syntax and word order, is 'English' in any strict sense. Certainly, Synge's diction could not provide a model for a young man setting out to write plays in Birmingham or Manchester. His tricks of language could easily become mannerisms, as they do to some degree in his own last unfinished tragedy, *Deirdre*, or in the Kiltartan comedies of Lady Gregory. Again, admitting that *The Playboy of the Western World* is a masterpiece, one wonders whether it might be described, in William Empson's sense, as a masterpiece of 'pastoral' writing: of writing, that is, which projects the complex feelings of contemporary life into an ideally simplified, and therefore manageable, setting. James Joyce, at least, who was as great a master of language as Synge, did not dismiss the intellectual drama of Ibsen as a failure and did not see the solution of the Irish writer's problem as involving a retreat from urban complexities to peasant simplicities. One of Joyce's earliest writings was a tribute to Ibsen and his play, *Exiles*, though it is on the whole a failure, is an attempt to explore a confusing and painful situation in his own life, a complex interweaving of love, jealousy, and friendship, with stark Ibsenian honesty.

One may say then that Synge's 'programme' involved an undue degree of artificial and artful simplification (this comes out in the long, moving, but certainly very mannered prose passage I have quoted from him). It may be that it is the central task of the dramatist today not merely to look for the raw poetry of rustic speech and life, where that survives, but to make a poetic and dramatic shape out of what seems ugly and intractable. The weakness of Synge's 'programme' can be seen not only in the rather too 'couthy' kitchen comedies of Lady Gregory but in the plays of Yeats. Here an absolute mastery of language, a speculative mind playing profoundly with symbols, a deep and real feeling for Irish tradition and its folk roots, somehow fail to compensate for a lack of that dramatic 'body' which we tend to look for in the action and characters of a 'real play'. Yeats's plays are very beautiful but also, with some exceptions like *Purgatory*, deliberately remote; some of them might be very moving in performance, as Japanese Noh plays are. The drama arose from primitive ritual and it is legitimate to develop it, late in its history, back to very sophisticated ritual; but something gritty and alive in between is left out; and in the ordinary sense of the word Yeats's dramas are far less 'dramatic', in force, tension, concentration of language, than his poems about his personal life and the life of Ireland in his time.

The most promising Irish dramatist after Synge, in Synge's own direction of combining 'richness' with 'reality', was Sean O'Casey. In his earlier plays, O'Casey seems to have realized (born and brought up in the Dublin slums he could hardly help realizing) the dramatic inadequacy of the pastoral attitude. O'Casey's view of the Dublin slums is a warm and generous one, but also harshly realistic, and not in the least sentimental. His earliest and best plays, *Juno and the Paycock*, *The Shadow of a Gunman* (which is somewhat slighter than the first), and the splendid *The Plough and the Stars* (this was the flag of the Irish Republic for which the

Irish patriots rose at Easter in 1916) are essentially tragedies. They are shot through, nevertheless, with a broad, deep and effective humour – the vital humour of the Irish poor. The Irish 'troubles' give O'Casey a background which enables him to introduce plausibly the acts of violence which he needs to resolve, in a tragic sense, what might otherwise be merely static scenes of pathos or humour. Thus the atmosphere of these wonderful plays is sometimes like that of a music-hall cross-talk act (but of a kind that could be invented only by a man of genius) interrupted by a murder. Like Synge, the young O'Casey listened to the language of the Irish poor, but looked not for beautiful cadences, only for the unmistakable ring of truth. One is less aware of O'Casey's 'style' in these early plays, than in the case of Synge. One thinks, in an Aristotelian way, of the appropriateness of speech to character. A critic who sharply disagrees with me here is Raymond Williams, who insists that O'Casey's dialogue consists of 'naturalistic caricature' plus a 'few simple tricks', including the use of keywords like *shining, dread, darkness, death, shroud,* and what he calls 'adjectival drunkenness'. Williams is shocked that Nora should be led away in *The Plough and the Stars* in her distraction to the music of *Lead, Kindly Light,* that Bessie Burgess should die singing *I do believe, I do believe, that Jesus died for me,* and that the final emotion of the play should be expressed by the Cockney soldiers' rendering of *Keep the Home Fires Burning.* He sees a degeneration, in comparing the language of Synge with that of O'Casey 'from the speech of isolated peasants and fishermen, where dignity and vitality of language were directly based on an organic living process, to the speech of townsmen, normally colourless and drab, containing the undiscriminated rhythms of the scriptures, popular hymns, and commercial songs.' I think he is quite wrong: that most or indeed nearly all of the things that he objects to in the early plays at least are not 'naturalist caricature' but true naturalism, and that what he thinks of as O'Casey's coarseness and extravagance is the uncondemning naturalist imagination.

O'Casey, certainly, is not a 'lord of language' as Synge and Yeats are but is more of a dramatist of our own age than either of them. Williams's objection is not really to the language of the people in these early plays, but to the people themselves, and to O'Casey's full sympathy with them. Nora and Jack parting speak, says Williams, in the 'language of the novelette': but this is a play representing real life and, in real life, in emotional crises, trite but sincere language is often all that people have to use. Williams misses a specific sensitivity to a sharply defined milieu. But it can be admitted that in these early plays O'Casey was a young man working spontaneously rather than a conscious artistic theorist. The sad history of his later plays is the history of a growing, and inappropriate, ambitiousness about language and a loss, partly connected with his settling in England, of that specific sensitivity to the life of a particular place and time. In his later plays, *The Silver Tassie, The Star Turns Red, Within the Gates, Red Roses for Me*, and *Oak Leaves and Lavender*, he deserts the poetic realism of the earliest plays for a broad-brushwork, poster-coloured expressionism whose failure lies, precisely, in a lack of genuine poetry. His characters no longer talk in their own style, but in a style that O'Casey has invented for them, a florid and rhetorical language always aiming at, and always falling short of, high impersonal eloquence. Moreover, his later characters are no longer, except in snatches, real people – they are symbols of social or moral attitudes that O'Casey disapproves of or admires, like figures in a medieval morality play. The melodrama is now obvious, the pathos overweighted; and even the earthy music-hall humour creaks a little. We can no longer believe in the detail of what is happening at the 'realistic' or 'naturalistic' level. And O'Casey, a brilliant imitator of speech rather than a superb creator of it, has not the verbal art that would make us believe in it at any other level. (A brilliant imitator: O'Casey's volumes of autobiography, full of interesting raw material, fail as art for me because they are a character performance, an imitation of O'Casey talking about O'Casey and acting out O'Casey, rather than the creation at a distance of new words to embody a new vision of life.) In a country of poets, O'Casey was, in his beginnings, a great prose dramatist with the sense of the poetry of the ordinary, the trite, which also belongs to Ibsen and Chehov. It is his personal tragedy that he has attempted to transform himself into the kind of dramatist he was least fitted to be. It is possible that he had exhausted his early vein even before he left Ireland; certainly since he cut apart from his roots, he has lost his way. Yet even today he is a better dramatist than Mr Brendan Behan, whose play *The Hostage* is simply late O'Casey with more music-hall knock-about, less grandiose rhetoric, and a touch of honest cynicism – about Ireland, about England, about whether anything matters anyway, about just how much blarney and horseplay an audience will take – of which O'Casey himself has always been finely free.

Another Irish dramatist who, for reasons that it is harder to divine, has never quite fulfilled his splendid early promise is Denis Johnston. He is a younger man than O'Casey and his second play, to which he mainly owes his reputation, *The Moon in the Yellow River*, had its first production in the Abbey Theatre in Dublin in 1931. In some ways, Johnston belongs less to the Irish theatrical revival than to what could be called the Auden generation of the 1930s. A very fascinating non-realistic play of his, *A Bride for the Unicorn*, a poetic fantasy in prose with much incidental social satire and some verse choruses, very much resembles in flavour Auden's and Isherwood's *The Dog Beneath the Skin*. The hero, again, of Johnston's *Storm Song*, a play about the making of a film in the Aran Islands, is very much a hero of the great decade of the documentary film. He very much resents the commercial interests that are strangling his attempts to make a film of pure social documentation; at the end of the play, symbolically, he deserts the heroine (an emancipated representative of the old landed aristocracy) to go on studying the art of the film in Russia. 'Like many of his type,' Johnston tells us, 'he would probably call himself an anarchist, while meaning that he was a communist, though in fact he is neither, being an artist – which is the last thing he would admit.' Johnston's background is obviously quite different from O'Casey's. He touches in lower-class humours and patches of local colour with a masterly hand, but he has not O'Casey's intimate feeling for the tragedies of Irish working-class life, and in his best play, *The Moon in the Yellow River*, the main characters, a disillusioned Catholic, a romantic rebel, a practically-minded German engineer, are all extremely articulate in a Shavian way. They could argue their problems out for ever, in fact, but the one inarticulate character in the play, Commandant Lanigan, a gunman turned policeman, brings about a *dénouement* by shooting the rebel dead and thus shaking the disillusioned Catholic back into a belief in love and life. I think Mr Johnston one of the most powerful and neglected of recent dramatists, but he is specially interesting in the difficulty he seems to find, even in this his best play, in reconciling a wish to handle themes of universal, or at least European, modern concern with his feeling for the special circumstances of Ireland. He is torn similarly between three disparate gifts, for Shavian dialectic, for poetic fantasy, and for straight realism. He is a dramatist who never quite fulfilled his promise or made up his mind what he wanted to do, and in this perhaps he is Ireland's equivalent for Scotland's James Bridie; but his talent was more distinguished than Bridie's, and he could have done more with it than he has. Since his time, Dublin has ceased, on the whole, to be an important centre for new drama; Ireland has achieved and is now sure of keeping her independence, her problems are the real but not the intensely dramatic problems of a small agricultural republic on the verge of Europe, and it is likely that her drama and her literature both may go through a period of calm provinciality. The notable plays come from the days of aspiration for freedom, the struggle for it, and the contemplation of it in its raw newness. These tensions are gone, and Yeats's Abbey Theatre is burned down and not likely perhaps to be soon built again in a small country where neither the state nor individuals have much money to lavish on culture, and where Yeats, Synge, and O'Casey in their time all aroused the bitter suspicion of the respectable and the conventionally religious. It may be that Synge's 'few years more' of a 'popular imagination that is fiery, magnificent, and tender' in Ireland are now over.

15

The Revival of Poetic Drama

WE have seen that by the 1930s all the various types of prose drama we have been considering might have been said to have reached a dead end. Prose drama, on the whole, had simply failed to grasp the depth and tension and complexity of contemporary living; nor was it usually on a very distinguished level as mere *divertissement*. It was in these circumstances that a number of writers who had made their first reputations not as dramatists but as poets decided to see if they could revive, even if at first in 'little theatres' or for specialized audiences, the tradition of the verse play. They were doing something very daring. There had not been a verse play that could claim both to be 'good theatre' and to have value as poetry since Thomas Otway's *Venice Preserved*, in the Restoration period; and for that matter, even Otway's play is melodramatic and sentimental and his blank verse cannot claim to be great poetry but merely to be humanly speakable. Yeats's verse dramas had never enjoyed popular success, had rarely been performed out of Ireland, and seemed to have little direct relevance to the contemporary world. The attempts of T. S. Eliot, Christopher Fry, W., H. Auden and Christopher Isherwood, and a number of other writers to revive the verse drama, to give it a topical and popular impact, deserve, therefore, great respect, however limited we may now judge their ultimate success to have been.

It is interesting that verse drama, as revived in the 1930s and 1940s, had a much closer link with religious and political beliefs than the prose drama of the time. Some of it was performed first in churches; some of it in 'little theatres', to small and largely politically committed audiences. T. S. Eliot had shown in the fragments of *Sweeney Agonistes* a powerful gift for combining farce with horror and the rhythms of jazz with the penetration of major poetry. But *Sweeney Agonistes* was fragmentary and, though produced effectively by Rupert Doone for a small audience, never reached a large stage. Eliot really commenced his practical career as a dramatist by writing the choruses for *The Rock*, a pageant-play written to raise money for new London churches, produced, and largely devised, apart from the choruses, by E. Martin Browne. Eliot struck up a friendship with Martin Browne, who was to produce all his subsequent plays, and whose practical knowledge of the theatre, its possibilities and limitations, were to be of inestimable use to the dramatist; he would warn Eliot, for instance, that a passage of fine poetry was of no use in a play unless in some way it definitely forwarded or illuminated the action.

Eliot's first full-length play, *Murder in the Cathedral*, was written to be performed in Canterbury Cathedral, to commemorate the martyrdom of St Thomas à Becket, who had been murdered there. In spite of its primarily religious purpose, the play has considerable purely dramatic power; though, since the origins of drama are religious, and since for Eliot himself the Mass is the greatest of dramas, this is perhaps a superficial distinction. Yet oddly the chorus of the women of Canterbury, who illuminate the action rather than forward it, have a richer *theatrical* impact than the dignified and impressive but rather thin, flat, sharply outlined character of Becket himself. St Thomas is the area where a crisis occurs rather than a living person; and the other characters, the Knights and the Tempters, are even more formalized. The real 'action' of the play lies not in the violent killing of St Thomas at the end but in his confrontation of various temptations, of which the most serious is the temptation to accept his martyrdom for the wrong reason; not out of Christian humility and obedience and the need to bear witness, but out of spiritual pride. The play is not a tragedy but a passion-play and a playwright might find the real drama of Christ's Passion not on the Cross but in his wrestling with Himself in the Garden of Gethsemane.

The true drama here also is 'interior': the crucial moment being when the most dangerous tempter tempts Thomas in his own words. The 'outward' value of the action is that of an edifying spectacle, a commemorative ritual, and here and there a direct monition to the audience.

All Eliot's plays are works of edification. But he has become progressively more interested in pure theatre after realizing the need to get across his Christian themes to a large, neutral, or only tepidly Christian audience, without direct use of any Christian symbols. Eliot's third play, *The Family Reunion*, has a modern setting, one of English aristocratic country-house life, and the plot is concerned with the return of a young nobleman, Harry, Lord Monchensey, to his ancestral home, of which his widowed mother, Amy, wishes him now to become the head, taking up his proper duties as a local magnate. It is soon obvious that Harry is tormented by private doubts and fears and is both indifferent to, and indeed almost unaware of, his mother's plans for him. These doubts and fears are personified not only for Harry but for his chauffeur and for the audience as the Eumenides or Furies who pursue Harry (who has murdered, or is under the illusion that he has murdered, his wife) as they pursued Orestes after he murdered his mother, Clytemnestra: and these archaic and frightening beings, with their glittering eyes, do in fact occasionally stare through the french windows of the manorial drawing-room. (Mr Eliot now feels that their visibility was a mistake, and that there is no satisfactory way of staging them.) Gradually in a conversation with a sympathetic aunt and cousin, Agatha and Mary, the story about Harry's wife (he asserts that he pushed her overboard off a passenger steamer on a dark night and has been 'on the run' from the Furies ever since) comes out. It is not made explicit but we are led to believe either that Harry's belief that he has killed his wife is a hallucination or that what is haunting him is something more complex and rooted than a single violent act. In an attempt to help Harry to recover his balance, Agatha reveals to him the tragic circumstances connected with his own birth. Harry's father had hated his wife Amy and passionately loved her sister Agatha. He had wished to murder Amy but Agatha, though returning his love, had persuaded him not to commit this crime, partly because Amy at that time was about to have a child. The child, of course, turned out to be Harry. Harry can thus feel that his own sense of guilt may be perhaps an inherited, unconscious memory of his father's desire to kill his mother. Even if he did kill his own wife, he may have been, as it were, unconsciously acting out his father's story; the guilt he is expiating is not merely personal. Agatha also lets Harry know that she feels that she, rather than Amy, is spiritually his mother; she had genuinely loved Harry's father, where Amy had loved only his place and possessions. Harry begins to understand that the Furies are not instruments of blind vindictiveness but of purification; and he is like Orestes, too, in that when he is driven finally to the place of his purification, the internal divisions that have rent his family and are embodied in him will be healed. But the place of his peace will certainly not be his ancestral home; so he sets out again on his travels, in his expensive car, to confront, instead of fleeing from, the Furies, and this shock, and the disappointment to all her hopes, kills his mother.

The verse in this play has fewer easily memorable or obviously eloquent passages than that of *Murder in the Cathedral*, but the reason is that Eliot is now aiming at catching the tones, idioms, and rhythms of contemporary speech; instead of the rich, highly coloured language of the choruses in *Murder in the Cathedral*, we have minor characters – less important uncles and aunts of Harry's – who occasionally express their thoughts in unison, or in a succession of parallel observations, giving an ironical choric effect of well-intentioned dimness and well-mannered incomprehension. To this chorus, Harry's sufferings are disturbing for their very lack of everyday palpableness: if only these sufferings were something that an aspirin, a hot-water bottle, a day in bed, a drink after a tiring journey, an understanding talk with an older man of the world, or, at the very outside edge, a consultation with a nerve specialist could put right! This was the first play of Mr Eliot's about which critics began to complain that he was flattening out his poetry, his poetry of language. But a richer use of language would have destroyed the play's grey, tense, edgy contemporaneity of atmosphere. Paradoxically, Eliot was looking for exactly the verse equivalent of what Synge called Ibsen's way of 'dealing with the realities of life in joyless and pallid words'. He needed a grey kind of poetry, and some critics, indeed, had already found that in his non-dramatic poems. 'Eliot,' says Yeats, in every way temperamentally Eliot's opposite, 'has produced his great effect upon his generation because he has described men and women that get out of bed or into it from mere habit; in describing this life that has lost heart his own art seems grey, cold, dry. He is an Alexander Pope, working without apparent imagination, producing his effect by a rejection of all rhythms and metaphor used by the more popular romantics rather than by the discovery of his own, this rejection giving his work an exaggerated plainness that has the effect of novelty.' One does not expect one great poet to be fair about another great poet of contrasting temperament, and this seems to me very unfair; but it is closer to part of the truth about the plays, which Yeats was not thinking about, than to the truth about the poems. From *The Family Reunion* onwards, one effect in drama that Eliot is aiming at is 'unexaggerated plainness'; indeed, in *The Cocktail Party*, when for purely dramatic reasons he needs a passage of strikingly 'poetic' writing, he has to make one of his characters quote Shelley.

Not only is the poetry of language submerged in *The Family Reunion*; drama, in so far as drama involves a violent or crucial *action* of some sort, is submerged too. Miss Helen Gardner in her perceptive study, *The Art of T. S. Eliot*, thinks that this play lacks complete effectiveness on the stage because it sets out to dramatize not guilt but the sense of sin. Now, it is true that there is in the past perhaps no guilt on Harry's part: he may not really have murdered his wife, he may have merely wanted to, and had an hallucination about an accident. But it could be said that Harry is guilty in another way, in a way of which Mr Eliot is quite unconscious, and that his guilt, running across the sense of ancestral sin, makes the real drama. Harry does make one dramatic decision in this play, the decision *not* to stay at home and assume his traditional family responsibilities, and this decision kills his mother. Eliot has obviously no sympathy with Amy, but it is my experience from watching the play performed that she arouses a good deal of sympathy in the audience. It is not her fault that her husband wanted to murder her; her desire to have her son accept the responsibilities of a great position is not an irrational or immoral one. Harry, Agatha, and Mary are intended to be much more 'spiritual' than she, but there is something very 'materialistic' about the stage, and the spirituality of these characters often presents itself as self-absorbed introspectiveness. By contrast, Amy's selfishness about the estate and who is going to look after it, and after its traditions – a selfishness, after all, concerned with responsibility as well as pride and self-importance – has something sympathetically ordinary about it. Just because Eliot is not interested in Amy's 'inner states', she acquires by her very opacity a solid theatrical power. Her death is the most moving thing in the play, at least when one sees it acted: much more moving than Harry's departure towards a reasonably cushioned purgatory. Harry's general attitude of indifference or absentmindedness towards Amy is also estranging. All this tends to dislocate the moral pattern of the play.

I find the same kind of dislocation in the next play, a much more effective piece of theatre, *The Cocktail Party*. The equivalents of Amy here are a husband and wife who get on each other's nerves, who have each been having a love affair, who are in different ways humanly inadequate – the husband can arouse love in others, but not give himself to them; the wife can give herself, is generous, but knows she never arouses a really deep response of feeling in others. Both husband and wife are naggingly aware of their inescapable mediocrity of spirit and indeed the husband's coldness, timidity, and irritable self-centredness drive the girl who was in love with him to a psychiatrist, who sends her off on a mission which leads her to martyrdom among savages. The psychiatrist also brings back to the husband his strayed wife. The plot is that of the Alcestis story, in which Alcestis went down to Hades as a substitute for her husband, and Herakles brought her back again, but the role of Alcestis is doubled between the mistress and the wife. With its cunning use of light comedy dialogue, of interruptions at crucial moments, this is a more skilful play than *The Family Reunion*, but morally in some ways even stranger. The husband and wife are meant to represent average humanity, as opposed to its spiritual guardians, a psychiatrist, a gossipy old lady, a rather irritating man-about-town, and the potentially exceptional person, the future saint, the husband's mistress, Celia. But the guardians as characters on the stage seem thin, type-cast, and self-important; Celia also seems self-centred, and priggish. The unsatisfactory husband and wife, involving less of Eliot's personal approval and sympathy, seem, perhaps for that very reason, more fully human. The psychiatrist's speech, a fine example of the sparse, grave rhetoric of Eliot's dramatic verse, about the kind of 'ordinary' happy marriage to which he wishes husband and wife to settle down,

> They may remember
> The vision they have had, but they cease to regret it,
> Maintain themselves by the common routine,
> Learn to avoid expectation,
> Become tolerant of themselves and others,
> Giving and taking, in the usual actions
> What there is to give and take. They do not repine:
> Are contented with the morning that separates
> And with the evening that brings together
> For casual talk before the fire
> Two people who know they do not understand each other,
> Breeding children whom they do not understand
> And who will never understand them,

seems, even in the total context of the play, insufferably patronizing. Again, perhaps theme cuts against plot structure. The theme is that, even to achieve mediocre happiness, the married couple in the play need to be spied on and helped, and that even so Celia's martyrdom is necessary, to atone for her own sin, as an act of general atonement, and to mend the marriage; but what the action of the play rather suggests is the deeper strength of the married relationship, in itself, and at a natural level, in re-establishing itself against mutual irritations and infidelities.

But it is a strength rather than a weakness of these two earlier plays of Eliot's that an almost unwilling, or only partly consciously sympathetic, awareness of the strength of natural habits and motives cuts across the conscious pattern of insistence on the primacy of the spirit. The spiritual is in the natural, too. The two succeeding plays, *The Confidential Clerk* (modelled, even to its title, on farces of the 1890s, like *The Private Secretary*) and *The Elder Statesman* (modelled on *Oedipus Coloneus*) are more harmonious, less tensed, in the play of plot against theme, and for that reason lack the impact of the earlier plays. One is at first worried, in *The Confidential Clerk*, to find certain images, of the moving stillness of the Chinese jar and of the secret garden (Eden, but also *Alice in Wonderland*'s garden), which are used with such effect and concentration in Eliot's poems, put across on the stage in a thin, didactic manner. But we should realize that Eliot, a master of pregnantly obscure concentration in his poetry, is not aiming at that effect in his dramatic verse. Much of the verse in *The Confidential Clerk*, for instance, sounds on the stage like ordinary speech slowed down a little, so that we become aware of its recurrent rhythms and repeated phrases. Eliot uses this effect of articulate transparency quite deliberately. It allows him to modulate deftly from passages of light or vapid conversation, in the key of comedy, to passages expressing grave disquiet or, as at the end of *The Elder Statesman*, grave serenity. It holds the audience at a greater emotional distance, and it makes them concentrate more on the implications of what is being said, than ordinary prose dialogue would. But it does not quicken and excite attention or suddenly transform a situation or a mood: Eliot has done what he set out to do in his poetic drama, but, compared to what he was doing in his non-dramatic poems, he had a complex aim. He wanted to invent a kind of verse that would be speakable, without self-consciousness, in a play with a modern setting, to an ordinary audience by ordinary actors. He wished to invent plots which would be interesting in themselves but which would also allow him to put across a Christian vision of the world without appearing didactic or sentimental. He wanted to use verse to explore and dramatize, at least at peak moments in his plays, not complex characters but complex, and yet important and dramatically recognizable, states of moral or spiritual being. He has done all this; but his *comparative* failure as a dramatist (it is only comparative) is that he has not done this in a way that extends our consciousness at its finest, but only in a way that makes more widely accessible, in a slightly simplified version, the results of some, not all, of his explorations of life in his poems. What is most moving and convincing in the plays is already there, in a more concentrated way, in *Four Quartets*; what is weak in the plays, and some things *are* weak, lessens the effect of what is moving and convincing; and there is no exactly comparable weakening element in *Four Quartets*.

A striking contrast to the spareness and transparency of Eliot's dramatic language is to be found in the earlier verse dramas of Christopher Fry. I shall quote a speech from one of them, *A Phoenix Too Frequent*, in which the abundant richness of fanciful detail ironically decorating rather than developing a simple idea makes an interesting contrast with the sparse development of *argument*, in the speech already quoted from *The Cocktail Party*:

> For me
> The world is all with Charon, all, all
> Even the metal and plume of the rose garden,
> And the forest where the sea fumes overhead
> In vegetable tides, and particularly
> The entrance to the warm baths in Arcite Street
> Where we first met; ... all! ... the sun itself

Trails an evening hand in the sultry river
Far away down by Acheron. I am lonely,
Virilius. Where is the punctual eye
And where is the cautious voice which made
Balance-sheets sound like Homer and Homer sound
Like balance-sheets? The precision of limbs, the amiable
Laugh, the exact festivity? Gone from the world . . .

There, our essential feeling is one of playfulness; the lines
gently mock the woman who is mourning, a little more elo-
quently than her feelings justify, for her dead husband,
while at the same time they allow a lyrical quality to her
grief; as in such lines as

Trails an evening hand in the sultry river . . .

There is a great facility of phrase and image, and if I were
to quote the whole of the long speech from which this is an
extract the reader would have the sense of how many ways
a single topic can be turned. What surprises one about Mr
Fry is how many words he can squeeze out of one idea. In
the early verse comedies, *A Phoenix Too Frequent*, *The
Lady's Not for Burning*, and *Venus Observed*, this playful
and fantastic wealth of language seems to be modelled on
Shakespeare's early comedy, *Love's Labour's Lost*, for it is
full of conceits and quibbles and verbal parodies and paradoxes, full of speeches written not as drama but as exquisitely artificial exercises in sophistry or lyricism. These
early plays have the air of being brilliant improvisations, and
though I enjoyed the only one which I have seen performed,
The Lady's Not for Burning, assisted by the excellent acting
of John Gielgud and Pamela Browne, I would find it hard
to compress my series of vivid and pleasant impressions into
any very coherent account of the plot. Watching this play,
I felt, about episodes as well as speeches, that Mr Fry, like
somebody telling a story to children, was 'making it up as
he went along'.

One does not expect our age to produce the copious and
florid talent. I associate the early impact of Fry's plays upon
me with the bleak and austere years after 1945, and in that

sparse time his lavish and careless abundance of episode and epithet, his festival spirit, may have been one of the factors in his success. But it is also the reason for recent critical recoil from him. The sheer brilliance and exuberance of lines like these from *The Lady's Not for Burning*,

> ... the river
> Where the water gives those girlish giggles around
> The ford ...

> I, the little heretic as he thinks,
> The all unhallows Eve to his poor Adam ...

> Such white doves were paddling in the sunshine
> And the trees were as bright as a shower of broken glass ...

> I've an April blindness,
> You're hidden in a cloud of crimson catherine wheels,

may also be their vulnerability: to quote L. C. Knights on Restoration comedy, the words 'have an air of preening themselves on their acute discriminations'. The language is self-regarding, exists too much for itself, blurs the distinctions between characters, and thus also blurs plot and theme, though theme less than plot. One was left at the end of *The Lady's Not for Burning* with a sense that death awaits us all, but that life is joyous and fresh and miraculous, that our coming here and going hence are mysteries. Like Eliot, Fry is a Christian dramatist, but moving, to use Charles Williams's distinction, by the way of acceptance rather than rejection of images; he praises the Creator indirectly by exulting in the creation. But the exultation often seems lyrical rather than dramatic.

Ironically, a growing sobriety and maturity in Fry's work has coincided with a falling off in popularity. A later play, *The Dark is Light Enough*, is much more disciplined and chaste than the earlier works; the speeches reflect character, and further the plot. The dominant figure is an old countess, caught up in a war between Austrians and Hungarians. She shelters her daughter's former husband Gettner, a moral reprobate, from soldiers who are pursuing him; she allows the daughter's second husband, Peter, a good man, to be taken as a hostage; when the soldiers suffer a defeat, she hides their Colonel, once her enemy, and finally brings about before she dies a complete moral change in Gettner. She is an ideal figure of Christ-like goodness and generosity and seeking of abiding peace, a beautiful *dea ex machina* making lives by divine non-interference. But it is a weakness of the play that, existing merely to illustrate the perfection of the countess's character, it is not properly in Aristotle's sense 'an imitation of an action'; it lacks dynamic thrust. Fry seems to lack, it has been suggested, a basic theatrical sense, 'a feeling for those actions which demand enactment, not description'. The even barer style of his latest play, *Curt-mantle*, about Henry II and Becket, exposes this structural weakness very clearly.

It is not for me, even if I felt I could speak with any authority, to judge whether the Christian faith is true or, a slightly different question, whether a morality of love and non-resistance, which could be called Christian, is the highest morality. It may be that Fry like Eliot follows a true light, where many of the rest of us are blinded. These are not questions of literary criticism. Fry and Eliot may be in the right, and our age as a whole in error. But really powerful dramatists in any age will be profoundly immersed even in the errors of their age. That is why Samuel Beckett, with his acute sense of agony and meaninglessness, his use of Christian symbols to underline mockery and desperation, is not only a more powerful dramatist but also, whatever his personal beliefs, a more powerful Christian dramatist, a dramatizer of the Christian sense of dereliction, than either Eliot or Fry.

Eliot and Fry are the two verse dramatists of our time who have broken through from the special 'little theatre' audience to the big audience. Other poets who have attempted verse drama in the last thirty years or so have never got beyond the 'little theatre'. I would like to see a revival some time, in a big theatre, of Stephen Spender's play of the 1930s, essentially about the rise of Nazism, *The Trial of a*

Judge. This is a play on the same theme, the weakness of the honest liberal, as Rex Warner's novel, *The Professor.* The Judge, the hero of the play, is that honest old liberal, caught, in an imaginary country modelled on Germany, between the rival fires of Communism and Fascism. He is a man who, though he hates the Communists and probably thinks that the Fascists are in their way 'patriots', is determined to administer the law without fear or favour. This gets him into trouble with the Fascists, who want Judges to be mere instruments of policy, and so for trying to hold the scales level he is in the end treated as if he were a Communist himself, disgraced, imprisoned, and killed. Even his fellow-victims, being passionate Marxists, keep assuring him that the idea of 'impartial justice' for which he is dying is a bourgeois illusion. Fire must be fought with fire, they say, lies with lies, crime with crime, violence with violence: but for the Judge it seems that revolution, when its principles are stated in this way, becomes merely the other face of tyranny. Thus, as in Warner's novel, the man who in a violent time stands for abstract justice is weaker than the man carried away by passion; and yet he has greater human dignity, he stands for certain permanent human values, which will have their demands to make when the storm has passed away. I have never seen this play acted, but Spender's fluent and sincere rhetoric, which sometimes made his earlier poems sound like harangues, exactly suited the excited, exalted tones of the dialogue in this noble melodrama. Spender is often 'rhetorical' in his non-dramatic poetry, in the sense in which T. E. Hulme defined rhetoric: the vigorous expression of an emotion unrelated to anything firmly grasped in the outer world. But what makes for stridency or confusion in the personal poem often, in *The Trial of a Judge*, makes for conviction in dramatic speech.

The plays in verse and prose written in the 1930s by W. H. Auden and Christopher Isherwood (Auden concentrating on the verse, Isherwood on the prose dialogue) made more of a stir than Spender's play, but perhaps not a lasting stir. They have an air of clever improvisation: and it is interesting that

Auden called his first independent short verse play, *Paid on Both Sides*, a cryptically topical exploration of the feud theme from Norse sagas, a 'charade'. The gay, knock-about, satirical expressionism of an Auden-and-Isherwood serious farce, *The Dog Beneath the Skin*, is still engaging; a compound of pageant play, pantomime, modern morality play, improvised school theatricals. But in the graver Auden-and-Isherwood plays, *Across the Frontier* and *The Ascent of F6*, expressionism gets out of hand, one is too much aware of symbolic situations and type characters; the types are perhaps local and temporal rather than permanent (typical Englishmen of that time, rather than typical recurrent men), and the symbolism also is topical, the docile absorbers of vicarious heroism on the wireless, the awful mother figure at the top of the last mountain, the argument between political activism and religious pietism or life-denial. There are some eloquent and witty pieces of writing in these three plays of Auden and Isherwood's, but taken as wholes they have neither the value of tragedy (that is, the statement of human predicaments which are permanently insoluble at the human level but nevertheless enhance our idea of our dignity), nor of comedy (that is, of the statement of human predicaments which are permanently soluble but which the run of men, through silliness rather than wickedness, never solve). The tone of these plays has a bright evangelical knowingness, hearty, smart, in the end – though some of the jokes are good, and some of Auden's choruses are beautiful – spurious. They are the work of two very skilful writers, and a sense of enjoyment in charade is perhaps the most permanently vital thing about them. They give one a sense, as much of the most interesting writing by the younger poets of the 1930s does, of a mixture of brightness and quickness of the mind, with genuine goodwill, and, finally, with a strange immaturity of the heart.

There are other interesting poets, Norman Nicholson, Ronald Duncan, Anne Ridler, who later attempted verse drama – these three in a Christian vein deriving largely from Eliot. One welcomed these plays, saw them or heard them over the air, perhaps reviewed the texts, when they first came out; but it could be said of all of them that an honourable didactic intention was much more in evidence than a properly dramatic grasp of situation or character. Living drama must explore life in its intractable and embarrassing thickness; it must echo back to us from the stage a critical or agonizing sense of our own situation, in our own actual world. From that point of view, the attempt to revive the poetic drama by Eliot, Fry, and others must be pronounced a failure, though a distinguished and honourable one.

16

The Wind of Change in the 1950s

I HAVE spoken in the first part of this book of the various European and American influences – Brecht's theatre of epic or moral fable, Beckett's and Ionesco's theatre of the comically or tragically absurd, Eugene O'Neill's and Tennessee Williams's angry naturalism, tinged sometimes with romance as well as protest, and the didactic naturalism or realism of Arthur Miller – which have been fed into the notable revival of prose drama in England since 1955. So many new dramatists have come up since that year that I could make this section a mere catalogue of names. It seems to me more useful to give a detailed discussion of three dramatists, each of whom 'stands for' a number of others: John Osborne, Harold Pinter, and Arnold Wesker. Osborne owes something to Tennessee Williams, of whom he has written an appreciative review, and something to Brecht (Tennessee Williams's attitude to women comes out in *Look Back in Anger*; *The Entertainer* reminds one of Brecht's *Threepenny Opera*, and *Luther* of his *Galileo*). Pinter owes much to Beckett and perhaps something to Ionesco (marriage of comedy and terror, drama of non-communication, sense of the madness of the common world). Wesker is morally akin to Arthur Miller, whether or not he owes anything technically to him. Of these three, John Osborne has been the most notably successful. He and Pinter, both trained in the theatre as repertory actors, are much more 'professional' playwrights than Wesker, who makes many technical mistakes. But Wesker is committed, even if naïvely, to a clearer and more coherent social philosophy than the other two; like Miller, he is *extremely* didactic.

It is very hard to arrive at a measured judgement about John Osborne. Ionesco has attributed the English regard for

him to 'patriotism, politics, or intellectual mediocrity', and
yet the first night of Osborne's *Look Back in Anger*, at a
small, exploring theatre (Granville-Barker's and Shaw's
theatre once), the Royal Court, in Sloane Square, Chelsea,
was one of the great occasions in contemporary English
theatrical history. It must be admitted that in this play
Osborne is very little of a technical innovator. His dialogue
is traditional naturalistic stage dialogue, with a rather personal, but also slightly Shavian, use of the long harangue.
He is not like Harold Pinter, whose dialogue is a highly stylized imitation of natural speech in all its inconsequence;
Osborne's personages speak like stage people. Osborne's
figures, also, strike one as stereotypes; though in both Jimmy
Porter, in *Look Back in Anger*, and Archie Rice, in *The
Entertainer*, Osborne had, as it were, patented the stereotype before one became aware of its replicas in ordinary life.
Jimmy and Archie are stock figures, but stock figures who
have not been done in exactly that way before.

In the same way, in manipulating the audience's reactions,
Osborne uses not the stock-response, but the anti-stock-
response. About the royal family, for instance, he is simply
like the women's magazines in reverse. Patriotism, religion,
the reticence and the decent forbearance which are at the
heart of what is best in English upper-middle-class morality,
elicit not gruff, silent, sentimental approval but a Bronx
cheer. Osborne is in no sense a thinker. He is a man with a
wonderful emotional wobble, he might have been invented
to help us to understand the meaning of the term 'love-hate'.
Certain confusions in his attitudes – the confusion of a
hatred of genteel snobbery with a brutish wish to squash
women, of vocal, vague, all-over-the-target radicalism with
sentimentality about cheap beer, free cheese, all the gaieties
of the Edwardian music-hall *Pink 'Un* world – he has never
sorted out. He is a more powerful dramatist for not having
done so. *Look Back in Anger* was not really about the sex-
war or the class-war but about repertory actors crowded together in uncomfortable lodgings in awful provincial towns
(Osborne started as a repertory actor) and getting badly on

each other's nerves. Whatever else he is, Osborne, like Noel Coward in his early days, is a man of the theatre, and an extremely competent one.

Jimmy Porter, in *Look Back in Anger*, embodied that un-articulated resentment which I have sometimes found in male students at a provincial university: a rage for action and enthusiasm; for some heroic role which contemporary society does not offer young men. But there is also in him some of the baffled frustration of the energetic mediocre man, unwilling to confront his own mediocrity. Jimmy feels that he is the only person around in his world with any vitality, that other people are half-dead. He rages against his wife, Alison, because he cannot arouse her to fight back; though in fact through most of the play she does fight back, very effectively, using his compulsive and humiliated sexual desire for her (he feels that making love to her is a kind of self-castration, that she snaps him off and gobbles him up) and her silence, her upper-middle-class training in polite inattention and withdrawal. Is the play about the sex-war, the class-war, or the sex-war as an image of the class-war? Jimmy perhaps stands in some ways for working-class male self-assertion. He only reluctantly and occasionally shows tenderness or gentleness towards Alison. She herself, though no intellectual, represents upper-middle-class liberalism; she had given up a great deal to marry Jimmy, and she finds that he has not so much married her, as married an oppor-tunity for revenge, for stamping on her tribe, and married, also, an imaginary uncritical audience. It is hateful to him that she should still remain a potentially independent human person. Alison had wanted to love Jimmy as a lover, a friend, a person, an intimate equal; Jimmy had wanted to dominate, hurt, in a sense destroy her as a symbol of her class. He had not perhaps consciously wanted to do this; but merely to transform her into the working-class wife, who is docile and subservient, who listens with assumed interest to what her husband has to say, agrees with it or pretends to agree with it, is the last prop of his battered ego. Jimmy wins in the end, he has utterly broken Alison; but his true friend, Cliff, who recognizes that the class-war (in which he believes) cannot be fought or forwarded by an individualistic, sadistic destruction of persons, leaves Jimmy. Jimmy no longer belongs to any outer social world (Cliff stands for the social world he should truly belong to), and the defeated Alison is smashed in spirit and, even physically, sterile. There is a way, indeed, of reading this play as a very powerful, because unconscious, counter-revolutionary tract.

It is a powerful play, and so important in the history of the recent English theatre that it is worth giving a summary of what happens. The curtain rises on Jimmy and his friend Cliff reading the *Observer* and the *Sunday Times* in a furnished room in a provincial city while Alison irons Jimmy's shirts. Jimmy keeps up a steady flow of vituperation about the vapidity of the posh Sunday papers, about the snobbishness of Alison's family, about her own hateful apathy. His violent verbal clowning suddenly transmutes itself into real violence. He pushes Cliff against the ironing board, knocks it and Alison down. She burns her arm on the iron and when he tries to apologize she cries out, 'Clear out of my *sight*!' In act two, a friend of Alison's, a repertory actress called Helena, is staying in the same lodging-house. It is again Sunday, Helena wants to take Alison to church, and this starts off an anti-religious outburst from Jimmy. Alison, alone with Helena, confides to her friend that she is pregnant and afraid to tell Jimmy; she thinks the news will merely intensify his mood of rage. A telegram has meanwhile arrived for Jimmy, to tell him that the mother of an old friend, a working-class woman to whom he is devoted, and to whom Alison is indifferent, is dying in a London hospital. He dashes off to be with the dying woman, further infuriated against Alison because she refuses to accompany him. Here, a little, he regains our sympathy; he has already partly regained it, and half-silenced Helena, by following his anti-religious outburst with an account of the slow painful death of his father, a Spanish Civil War veteran. When Jimmy has gone, Alison's father turns up to take her away. He is a sympathetic person, who seems to understand, as

Alison does not, just what Jimmy's rage is about. Helena remains to face Jimmy when he comes back. She has been overtly hostile to him, but she has other, deeper feelings. They have a verbal row, Helena slaps Jimmy's face, then falls into his arms.

That is a good curtain for the second act, and the opening of the third act is even better. Jimmy and Cliff are again reading the Sunday papers and a woman is ironing Jimmy's shirts, but it is Helena, not Alison. Cool, crisp, and intelligent, Helena, unlike Alison, knows exactly how to handle Jimmy, though Cliff instinctively dislikes her. She knows just when to stop his aggressive clowning from turning into real rage and Cliff, depressed by her humorous self-discipline and school-prefect jolliness, hating the new emotional tidiness of the situation, wants to leave. Suddenly, Alison, utterly shattered, comes back. Pale, ill, she has had a miscarriage, and will never be able to have another child. Helena now decides, like Cliff, to leave, partly out of compassion for Alison, partly on grounds of Christian morality: she loves Jimmy, but is sure they have been doing wrong. Left alone with Jimmy, Alison grovels, broken as he wanted her to be broken; the curtain falls when Jimmy and Alison, after he has lifted her up, are playing their childish love-game, their refuge from quarrelling in the past, of bears and squirrels. They have both cut their moorings: Jimmy is cut away from Cliff, representing working-class humour and decency; Alison from her father, from any right to be treated with the respect due to a lady. Yet Alison has perhaps conquered as much as Cliff. Jimmy, with nothing left now to fight or to protest against or to show off in front of, is now surrendering himself to that devouring sexual need of hers, hidden by primness and coolness, in which he had earlier seen the destruction of his manhood.

What was it that made Jimmy Porter the spokesman of a generation? The psychologist who explains Jimmy is not, I think, Jung or Freud, but Adler; he represents what Adler called masculine protest. His failure in two of the three main fields of human activity, finding satisfying work, and fitting into a community, has channelled all his urge to dominate into the third, marriage. The defeat of Alison is his revenge for the impregnability of the world. He blows off his top about everything, because he has to blow off his top; he devises factitious targets for a necessary anger; the anger is focused not on its cause but on Alison as a symbol. Alison's surrender at the end – 'I don't want to be a saint. I don't want to be a neutral. I want to be a lost cause. I want to be corrupt and futile' – is full of meaning. Saintliness means the Christian tradition; neutralism means liberalism; being a lost cause means – Alison is pandering to Jimmy's wishful thinking – that the upper classes are on their last legs; being corrupt and futile means that, even if they retain power, they do not deserve to. What Alison *says* here contrasts sharply with what one has observed in the play, that a traditional code and belief give Alison's father and her friend Helena virtues that are not to be found in Jimmy himself or the deracinated Alison. The working-class man has also traditional codes, beliefs, and virtues; but it is Cliff rather than Jimmy who exemplifies these. Jimmy has not convinced us that he is more fitted to rule the world than Alison's father or Helena. He has won his symbolic, domestic social revolution, but at the cost of a retreat from reality into a fantasy bear-and-squirrel world that is outwardly tender but inwardly horrible.

This still seems to me Osborne's most powerful play. It was followed by *The Entertainer*, which, in a more jerky and episodic fashion, played skilfully on the idea of a (largely imaginary) 'Merrie England' in decay, combined with the very mixed feelings of most Englishmen – distrust of jingos, distrust of the more hysterically self-righteous sort of liberal, a feeling that a carpet had been whipped from under one's feet – about the Suez crisis. This was followed by an attack on gossip-column and scandal-sheet journalism, a musical comedy called *The World of Paul Slickey*, which failed. Two very recent plays, one a satire on the cult of royalty, the other a study of fetishism, were also generally judged to have failed. Osborne's most ambitious play to date is an historical one, *Luther*, owing a great deal in its episodic construction and detachedly didactic intention to Brecht's *Galileo*. Confused, timid, rash, obstinate, but a man with power in him, Luther is a natural Osborne hero. The play takes the story of his life from 1506, when he was received into the Augustinian order, to 1530, when, having brought about the German Reformation (and indirectly inspired, and then repudiated, the Peasants' Revolt) he was a married man living in the country with his wife and son. Osborne manages to get across vividly some of the main features in Luther's character: self-disgust, partly springing from chronic constipation; obsession with sins committed only in fantasy; fear; hatred of joy. Perhaps it is just this kind of man, hurt and ugly, who always does bring about great revolutions. Osborne's Luther is a powerful figure, earthy, groaning, alive; he suggests that, even if he goes on learning from Brecht, Osborne's central interest will never be the movement of society as a whole but the individual, the powerful, suffering, partly creative, partly destructive individual, who refuses to play the game according to the ordinary rules.

Arnold Wesker is a much more politically and intellectually articulate and committed dramatist than Osborne, but much more naïve (or naïve in a different way) as a person and craftsman. He is an accurate observer of special segments of life; life in Jewish families in the East End of London, where he himself grew up; life among cooks in the kitchen of a restaurant (he has worked as a restaurant cook); life among Norfolk farm-labourers (whom he got to know as a pastry-cook in Norwich); the vividness of his latest play, *Chips with Everything*, about the training of R.A.F. servicemen, owes much to his own period of national service. His first play, a one-acter, *The Kitchen*, is an extraordinarily crowded one in which a cook goes mad. Next came his trilogy, *Chicken Soup with Barley*, *Roots*, and *I'm Talking About Jerusalem*, based on the personal and political history of a Jewish family, the Kahns, resembling his own; a history full of courage and desperation, idealism and cynicism, push and restlessness and occasional apathy, arguments, reconciliations, humour, harshness, and generosity. It is natural, because politics is the salt of life, that Sarah Kahn, the matriarch of the family, should have forgotten about leaving her children with the neighbours in the excitement of demonstrating against the Fascists; it is natural, because politics is the bread of life, that Aunt Cissie should be a trade-union organizer in the garment industry. To talk politics is to the Kahns as natural and instinctive as gossip is to most people. We should acclimatize ourselves to this in Wesker from the first, as we should get used to an overtly emotional, self-dramatizing way of talking in his characters that might otherwise embarrass us. In writing about Jewish family life, Wesker is drawing on his own intimate experience, and is often too stickily close to it, but his account of Norfolk farm-labourers in the second play of the trilogy, *Roots*, comes from acute outer observation, and deserves high marks both for accuracy and fair-mindedness. Whatever he does with the Kahns, Wesker refuses to sentimentalize or idealize his farm-labourers. They are not noble savages, or quaint characters, or rough diamonds with hearts of gold, or down-trodden victims of ruthless landlords – the landlords may behave ruthlessly, because the system makes them do so, which is another thing. The Norfolk farm-labourers are taciturn, unresponsive, greedy, inarticulate, shrewd in spotting pretence. But Beatie, the daughter who has been living away from them, shows in her own struggle with the realities of life and with what is at first a mere mimicry of culture and thought, how much more there is in them.

Wesker is fiercely and overtly political. This is the driving force behind his plays, the impulse behind his rhetoric, the source of the strongest emotions in his characters. Yet he is not political in a narrow sense. His plays are pleas for an extreme Socialist political attitude to extend into, and to permeate, all aspects of life, work, the arts, leisure. One would have to re-define the word politics to describe Wesker's conception of it, and think not of the art of rule or the struggle for power but of a broad, brotherly concern for other men. (All politicians, usually rather perfunctorily, *profess* this, but it is actually at the heart of what Wesker is saying.) But it is, on the other hand, only within a framework of evangelical Socialism that Wesker can imaginatively envisage that concern. He could not have, or he has not so far, depicted in his plays a good individualist or a good believer in tradition and hierarchy.

Chicken Soup with Barley, the first play in the trilogy, starts out in 1936. The Blackshirts are marching and most of the Jewish East End has turned out to demonstrate against them. Sarah Kahn, the mother of the Kahn family, is rushing about, making tea, and urging people to march. Ada, her fourteen-year-old daughter, is marching. Her brother, Hymie, is wounded in a scuffle with the police. The only character who shows no enthusiasm is Sarah's husband, Harry, who likes a quiet life, his slippers by the fire, a smoke, but who is doomed to live in the maelstrom Sarah creates around her. Harry cannot keep a job, he is physically weak, he tells lies and steals money from his wife's purse to buy cigarettes. But Sarah cannot let him alone; she batters at him constantly to become another kind of man, be strong, brush the cigarette ash off, but all without effect. In the middle of one of her tirades he has a stroke, which eventually paralyses him. He can shuffle about and get occasional odd jobs, never kept for long. Then, in the second act, it is 1946, the war has come and gone. Sarah is still full of fiery enthusiasm, but her daughter Ada is disillusioned. The attempt of Ada and her husband to opt out of industrial society and build up their own William Morris world is the theme of the third play of the trilogy, *I'm Talking About Jerusalem*.

It is difficult to keep up ideals. In 1946, one of the anti-Fascist demonstrators of the beginning of *Chicken Soup with Barley*, Monty Blatt, is now a small but prosperous greengrocer in Manchester. He talks of the liquidation of the Trotskyites and of the Jewish Anti-Fascist League Committee in Russia: 'There's nothing I can do any more. I'm too small; who can I trust? It's a big lousy world of mad politicians – I can't trust them Sarah!' Sarah is the one who keeps blindly fighting on, a real old-style idealistic Communist, fighting less because she is intellectually clear about the issues than because fighting keeps her alive. She is one of Wesker's most powerful characters, not particularly sympathetic, but always tremendously vital. One by one towards the end of *Chicken Soup with Barley*, her family and friends fall away. There remains her son, Ronnie – who appears also in *I'm Talking About Jerusalem* and who is an important unseen character in *Roots* – who seems to be a stand-in, often with a choric role, for Arnold Wesker himself. In 1956, Ronnie too has lost his faith, because of the Russian suppression of the Hungarian uprising. He says: 'Political institutions, society – they don't really affect people that much.' Sarah reacts violently; terrified that he too will become a drifter like his father, she rises to a fine eloquence. This final scene is powerful and dignified, but the construction of *Chicken Soup with Barley* as a whole is weak. The theme of gradual changes in political beliefs and attitudes in one family over twenty years is more suited to a novel; too much is described rather than enacted; and the characters often describe themselves, their ideas, or their aspirations in a way which is not necessarily false in feeling but certainly gross in tact. Ronnie, the artist of the family, says: 'I want to write a novel tonight. ... Faith, Mother, faith! I am one of the sons of the working classes, one of its own artists.'

Roots is regarded by most people as the most successful of these three plays, and I think the reason is that Wesker has translated his theme here not, as in the other two plays, into episodes stretching over a number of years but into one tight and unified dramatic situation. Briefly, the story is this. Beatie Bryant, who has been working in London as a waitress and has fallen in love with Ronnie Kahn, and with his cultural line of talk, comes back to visit her family in a Norfolk village. She has never met anybody like Ronnie before and his words are constantly on her lips. She quotes him on everything, and he seems to have pontificated on everything – comics, football, the Bomb, Trade Unions, painting, music, politics, culture, his idea of the good life, in fact. This con-

stant quoting of Ronnie's words is a subtle device. It makes
us see Ronnie through Beatie's dazzled and bewildered eyes
and the pompous pronouncements that would be intolerable
from him are bearable and even touching when repeated,
perhaps without real understanding but with real love, by
her. Most of the play is taken up with Beatie's half-comic
and half-pathetic efforts to sell her family 'culture'. There is
something childlike about her enthusiasm that makes her
preaching forgivable. Even while she is standing on a chair,
addressing her mother as if she were at a public meeting,
she is caught off her guard by a cloud of wasps and excitedly
joins in a wasp-hunt with her mother. Wesker shows her
enjoying ice-cream and home-made bread, wallowing in her
bath, and wanting to rush out and see a new litter of pigs.
Her desperate attempt to get her family interested in ideas
and music must, of course, come to little. They are prepared,
however, to welcome Ronnie. A magnificent spread has been
prepared for him – tomatoes, cheese, pickles, sausage rolls,
tinned fruit, the whole works. He does not arrive, and Beatie
is growingly nervous. The family situation gets tenser and
tenser, with Beatie trying to impress a growingly bored
family, and finally the postman comes with a pompous letter
from Ronnie, breaking the whole thing off. Of course, Beatie
is shattered and her family react badly. In her despair,
Beatie confesses that she has been too lazy ever to learn
anything from Ronnie; she has merely been parroting him.
She storms at her mother, who slaps her face and says: 'You
say you know something we don't, so why don't you do the
talking? Talk – go on, talk, gal.' Beatie says she cannot,
because she has no roots, she is 'just a mass o' nothin' '. And
then suddenly eloquence comes to her. She talks suddenly
out of her own pain about how the mental laziness of the
workers does, in fact, invite commercial artists to exploit
them and true artists to despise them. Nobody is listening,
but Beatie realizes that at last she is not echoing Ronnie,
not copying, but creating: her own thoughts are coming at
last out of her own life. This is a grand moment in the contemporary theatre, and Joan Plowright, with her sudden

dance of triumph at this climax, bringing rough art and natural strength together, suddenly gave symbolic actuality to the theme that had been so much, and sometimes rather abstractly, talked around all through the play. The theme of the almost blind striving of the culturally dispossessed to break through inner barricades, to learn to trust their own spontaneity, is vitally topical. At the same time, it should be noted, in the manner of the Hoggarts, the Holbrooks, and the Williamses, that knowing how to make home-made bread, how to prepare a grand high tea, with cold meats and scones and jellies, or how to look after pigs, how to handle proverbial and colloquial language, all these things are in a wider sense part of 'culture', too. Culture is not merely abstract ideas and literature, music and art. Are Beatie's family – their instinct that her Ronnie-ideas were second-hand was not unsound – quite so barbarian after all? Wesker depicts them realistically, but not unsympathetically.

Wesker's other plays do not require such detailed treatment. The third play in the trilogy, *I'm Talking About Jerusalem*, is generally admitted by critics to be the weakest. It has no real dramatic tension, and the presence of Ronnie as a chorus at a number of moments that might have dramatic tension is embarrassing. Dramatic critics praise highly Wesker's most recent play as I write, *Chips with Everything*, about the breaking in of an idealist in the R.A.F. I have not yet seen a performance or a text. Wesker has been praised highly for his political sincerity and his intimate knowledge of Jewish family life. I think he has the potentiality of being something more than a latter-day Galsworthy, a writer of documentary uplift and propagandist plays, of being a humane artist, and *Roots* and *The Kitchen* show this potentiality. The words, like Osborne's, have hardly any independent literary distinction; but they come across well on the stage.

Harold Pinter is the only one of the three dramatists who are my main topic in this section who seems to me to have a literary quality as well as a powerful sense of stagecraft; yet, paradoxically, his dialogue is very much nearer to straight demotic speech, to what you might hear from a tape-recorder put down on the top of a bus or in a public bar, than Osborne's or Wesker's. But it is not only that: it is demotic stylized. And he is the only one of these three dramatists whom I enjoy reading as well as seeing or hearing. His plays have working-class settings, but they are not naturalistic plays of social or emotional protest, like Osborne's, nor naturalistic and didactic plays, like Wesker's. They are about people for whom explicit and rational discourse about ideas or purposes, and for whom the sense of community, is impossible. Our society produces an increasing number of such people, so Pinter's plays, though not 'realistic', are by no means irrelevant to 'real life'. Pinter's characters are obsessives, who do not want to listen, or to understand, but who want to be listened to or at least to be allowed to speak; if communication is something they evade, silence would also frighten them. They are very simple-minded characters, working throughout a play to untie one little knot, and leaving it at the end still tied. And they exist in an atmosphere of undefined menace, move through situations which are farcical but sinister and threatening. Pinter obviously has read his Beckett and his Ionesco. He claims, however, not to be a symbolist dramatist, and says he would not know a symbol if he saw one; he starts many of his plays with an image, or a vision, of two people in a room; he then tries to find out what they are doing or saying, what is happening to them – to try to find out, without necessarily trying to understand. Symbolism, however, can be none the less powerful for not being consciously intended; a deep sense of something absurd or desperate or latently threatening in human life is all the more helpful to a dramatist for *being* deep and obscure, for not having been schematized, discussed, or turned into an explicit philosophy. Pinter, as a dramatist, through *not* analysing out his imaginative experiences, has retained a gift for frightening himself, which enables him to frighten us.

Pinter's most powerful play is *The Caretaker*. It invites comparison with Beckett's *Waiting for Godot*, less rich for those who like to play hunt-the-symbol, but a play with more of the sense of the particular and concrete, rather than abstract, misery of humanity in it. There are only three characters in *The Caretaker*. Their initials down the list of characters, Mick, Aston, Davies, spell out the word *mad*. Aston is in his early thirties. He lives in a room which is part of a dilapidated house owned by his brother Mick. He has had electric-shock treatment in a mental hospital and is incapable of earning a living. He goes out occasionally and buys pieces of wood and carpenters' tools with the idea of building a shed in the back garden. He comes in near the beginning of the play with a tramp, Davies, whom he has helped to get away from a brawl in a café, where Davies had a temporary job. Davies is elderly, malignant, falsely effusive, but somehow pathetic. He clings to his dignity. He is evasive about his age and identity. He has some papers left years before at Sidcup, with a friend, which would prove his identity and enable him to get a job, if he had sound enough boots to enable him to walk to Sidcup. He has various vague ideas about getting jobs, but they are very vague, and having found a place to sleep, and a man to lend him money from time to time, he obviously means to stay there. The place is no paradise. The roof leaks and a draught comes through the window. Davies is frightened of the gas-stove, in case it might asphyxiate him, though it is disconnected, and no gas is laid on.

Aston's brother Mick surprises Davies, when Aston is out on his pointless daily wanderings. Mick jeers at Davies and frightens him, but in the end offers him a job as caretaker in the house, so that his brother may have company. Mick, who is in the building trade in a small way, with his own van, is quick, sharp, and mocking in speech. He plays up to Davies's self-importance while at the same time keeping him frightened. Davies does stay on, grumbling at the rain which comes in from the window on to his bed; Aston has to keep the window open, since the old man smells so bad. At the end of the second act, Aston gives a long account, talking more to himself than to Davies, of his shock treatment in hospital and of how he wants to find the doctor who gave it to him, perhaps to kill him, possibly to confront him and protest; we are not told. But first he must build a shed in the garden. It has been suggested to me by an actor interested in psycho-analysis that the cruel doctor stands for the Freudian father-image, and the shed in the garden for a Freudian mother-image; Aston must re-create the mother and enter into her, before he can kill the father. I feel doubtful about any intention, or actual theatrical implication, as specific as this. Aston's soliloquy, however, does have an effect of enormous loneliness and pathos – a four-page soliloquy, delivered in a low, gentle voice, which keeps an audience absolutely still and expectant.

The last act begins a fortnight later, with a long talk between Davies and Mick. Aston has said almost nothing, it appears, to Davies since his long soliloquy. Mick is depressed by Aston's accumulation of useless junk. He indulges in fantasies of turning the room into an expensive furnished apartment. Aston comes back and complains about Davies's noisiness in his dreams and when settling down to sleep. Davies turns on him and taunts him about the mental hospital and the danger of being sent back. Mick is the boss, he says, and Davies is Mick's, not Aston's, caretaker. But when Davies appeals to Mick the next day Mick will not countenance any sneers at his brother; they are sneers at himself. Sick of the whole situation, Mick smashes a Buddha (image of patience and passivity) which is the only one of Aston's pieces of junk that has a symbolic meaning. If Davies wants to stay, he must make his peace with Aston. Davies tries to do so, constraining himself to an unwonted humility. He would help to put up the shed. The shoes which Aston has given him, which he had been grumbling about, were all right. Could he stay if he did use them to go down to Sidcup and get his papers? But Aston seems firm in rejecting him, and more sure of himself than he has been. Perhaps the smashing of the Buddha means that he is going to stand up for himself in future. He has been fiddling all through the play with some small electrical appliance, a plug or a two-way switch, and now at last he seems confident that he sees how to mend it.

I have mentioned a possible Freudian interpretation of this play. The actor who outlined this for me (he had been acting Davies in a repertory production) also described the play as a drama, not of non-communication, but of non-affective communication – the actors can convey at least simple ideas to each other, but cannot get into emotional *rapport*. Each character in turn makes, for a moment, his feelings come alive to himself but never alive between himself and the person he is talking to. The three characters are all in different ways desperately lonely, and they all nourish what might be called fantasy-projects, substitutes for rational life-purposes: Davies's papers at Sidcup which he never really intends to get because they are not really there, or, if they were, would not solve any of his problems; Mick's scheme for turning a broken-down slum room into a smart furnished flat out of *Woman and Home* or *House and Garden*; Aston's shed, his patient accumulation of junk that may prove to have some use, some time. The play could, of course, be given a Christian interpretation, with Aston as Christ (the emphasis on carpentry and the electric-shock treatment as a sort of crucifixion), Davies for ungrateful Man, still unregenerate Adam, and Mick either as God's servant, the Archangel Michael, or as the Devil tempting Davies to further acts of impiety and ingratitude, and then leaving him to God to judge. But I feel that this kind of interpretation, though it is helpful with Beckett, with Pinter would be facile and cheap; it is not irrelevant that where Beckett was brought up as an Irish Protestant, Pinter's background is Jewish. Mick, Aston, and Davies exist as stylized and slightly simplified but real individuals in an extreme but not impossible situation, where Didi and Gogo and Lucky and Pozzo seem, by contrast, personified ideas. And in a Pinter play the detail of the action itself takes up most of one's attention, whereas in a Beckett play a lot of one's attention is spent in trying to work through the action – which may seem pointless, bizarre, or nonsensical – to an underlying thematic pattern. A critic has described one of Pinter's other plays, the comic-macabre one-act thriller, *The Dumb Waiter*, as 'interior without being intellectual': another way of putting this is that the world of Pinter's plays may seem at one level remote, fantastic, perhaps nonsensical, but it has also – and its power comes from this – a very uncomfortable and gripping feeling of sinister familiarity. Lacking the breadth of human appeal of either Osborne or Wesker, Pinter is much more distinctly the creator of an imaginative world of his own, a world, however, which has a disturbing nearness to some extreme aspects of actual life. We are often now aware of Pinter situations in real life, though they are not situations on which we would consciously have focused before Pinter had written.

This chapter is already disproportionately long in relation to the rest of Part Three, but I think this is justified, because it is the most recent literature which we find hardest to get into any sort of perspective and it is the most recent literature which, even in a book of this sort, demands an exploratory rather than a summary judgement. We are not at the stage of 'placing' Osborne, Wesker, or Pinter in the whole English dramatic tradition: we are at the stage of asking ourselves what exactly is there. And even so, much must be left out. There are very intelligent playwrights, such as John Whiting and Robert Bolt, who have not received the amount of critical attention that Osborne, Wesker, and Pinter have, because their attitudes to life seem 'traditional' and their handlings of words 'literary'. There is, on the other hand, a specifically 'non-literary' theatre, the theatre of Shelagh Delaney or Brendan Behan, which has an air of charade or improvisation about it, and which has owed its success partly to the vigorous use of common speech in the dialogue, and partly to brilliant production by Miss Joan Littlewood. Then there are dramatists such as John Mortimer, who in his subtle, tender, and funny, but also in places unconvincingly melodramatic, *The Wrong Side of the Park*, still finds shabby-genteel middle-class life a rewarding subject. There are novelists, such as Doris Lessing and Angus

Wilson, who write Chehov-cum-Shaw plays about middle-class intellectuals and who make one aware, by their sacrifice of clarity of line to novelistic detail, how much easier, just as a sheer task of construction, is the composition of a novel than that of a play. But one of the encouraging signs about the new situation in the English theatre is that distinguished outsiders are being coaxed into having a try.

It would be easy, nevertheless, to be too cheerful about the present situation. I have emphasized already that no literary form more readily becomes stereotyped than the drama. The drama of the absurd, the epic drama, the naturalistic drama of social revolt, the didactic naturalistic drama, all these, like all dramatic models, are already creating their own conventions. We have become too ready, today, to praise a new play because it insults something that used to be praised, takes place in a kitchen or a leaking basement or a public lavatory, uses cockney slang or provincial dialect with no patronizing comic intention, echoes progressive sentiment, or has been written by a schoolgirl or a bus-conductor; yet the last five or six years of the 1950s in the English theatre were an exciting time and the weather so far seems set fair for the early 1960s. The best new plays are, at least, nearly always in touch with something which disturbs us all.

PART FOUR

POETRY

17

The 1890s to the First World War

THE 1890s saw the emergence into the English poetic consciousness of that sense, which had been long alive in France, of the great gulf fixed between the world of poetry and everyday life. The Pre-Raphaelites had also felt that gulf, William Morris had called himself 'the idle singer of an idle day', but he had revolutionary social enthusiasms, he hoped to transform the world of everyday life. The poets of the 1890s lacked that energy; like Baudelaire, one of their heroes, they accepted the world around them with the bored, indifferent attitude of the dandy; like Gautier, another of their heroes, they adopted the creed of 'art for art's sake'. It was not a very nourishing creed and many of them, pursued by melancholy, by ill-health, by remorse for the excesses of their lives, ended by becoming Roman Catholics. Their approach to religion was through sadness and the sense of sin, through the weariness of life which Dowson expresses:

> Labour and longing and despair the long day brings;
> Patient till evening men watch the sun go west;
> Deferred, expected night at last brings sleep and rest:
> *Sufficient for the day are the day's evil things,*

and through that sense of personal struggle with the Adversary that is the theme of Lionel Johnson's most sustained and powerful poem:

> Dark Angel, with thine aching lust!
> Of two defeats, of two despairs:
> Less dread, a change to drifting dust,
> Than thine eternity of cares.
>
> Do what thou wilt, thou shalt not so,
> Dark Angel! triumph over me:
> *Lonely, unto the Lone I go:*
> *Divine, to the Divinity.*

The note that is heard with intensity in these two quotations is, at a more subdued and muted level, the common note of much poetry of the 1890s, particularly of the poetry of those whom we call the Decadents, the members of the Rhymers' Club, Yeats's 'companions of the Cheshire Cheese'. Yeats, who was neither a drunkard nor a Christian, whom life never defeated, has that note himself:

> We who are old, old and gay,
> O so old!
> Thousands of years, thousands of years
> If all were told. . . .

The Irish folk there are supposed to be rejoicing over their earthly immortality: they sound very glum about it, indeed. With the note of muted sadness, still authentic in the best poems of the 1890s, there went a taste for the dainty and the quaint, and for the grotesque and the sinister, exemplified by Theo Marzials'

> The griffins grinned in the moonlight green,
> The hound by the thin red embers slept;
> I scraped a chord on my mandoline,
> A chord, pardie, that might ruin a queen,

or Wilde's

> Like wire-pulled automatons
> Slim-silhouetted skeletons
> Went sidling through the slow quadrille.
>
> They took each other by the hand,
> And danced a stately saraband;
> Their laughter echoed thin and shrill.

These stage properties, the griffins, the mandolines, the skeletons, and the sarabands, have not worn well; though if we remember that the poets of the 1890s had a very strong influence on the young T. S. Eliot, we may remember the 'pleasant whining of a mandoline' in *The Waste Land* when we read Marzials' passage and we may even wonder whether the whispering, straw-stuffed dummies of *The Hollow Men* may not have had obscure, remote ancestors in Wilde's 'wire-pulled automatons'. Another poet of the 1890s, Arthur Symons, anticipated Eliot in his fascination with London street scenes. Eliot has expressed a particular debt to John Davidson, too robust and prickly to be a member of the Rhymers' Club for more than a brief period, who in his poem *Thirty Bob a Week* explored the stoical world of the small clerk just hanging on to respectability, and vividly reproduced, as the pub scene in *The Waste Land* does, the idioms and cadences of common London speech. When I wrote the first version of this book, critics thought my interest in the 1890s eccentric. If one is interested in the sources of great literature, in the soil from which it grows, however, one cannot forget that Yeats 'learned his trade' among these minor poets, that Eliot heard in them, alone among the poets writing in his youth, the cadences, for all their affectations, of the natural speaking voice. It was Arthur Symons's book on the French symbolist poets that put the young Eliot, about 1910, on to Laforgue, and that book had also had its influence on Yeats.

Eliot's elder countryman, Pound, went back even farther in his early poetry to the ancestors of the aesthetes or decadents, to the Pre-Raphaelites, William Morris, Rossetti, Swinburne. The sense of the isolation of the poet from society, and the melancholy that goes with that sense, is as integral a part of the early work of Pound and Eliot as it is of Dowson or Lionel Johnson. It might be said that, after the great and often untidy expansiveness of the major Victorian poets, of Tennyson or Browning or Clough, the poets of the 1890s rediscovered, through deliberately narrowing their scope (or because their scope was naturally narrow), the possibilities of economy, of the working out in a short poem of a single mood. What their more robust contemporaries noted was the sadness or perversity of the mood, and often the perversity of their lives: and 'then in 1900', says Yeats, 'everybody got down off his stilts; henceforth nobody drank absinthe with his black coffee; nobody went mad; nobody committed suicide; nobody joined the Catholic Church; or if they did I have forgotten.'

The Modern Writer and His World

In poetry as in prose, what the Edwardian decade witnessed was the false, fitful afterglow of the sturdy self-confidence of the earlier Victorian age – but with the sweep and range of high Victorian poetry adapted now (and inevitably somewhat cheapened in the process) to a wider and less critical audience. The central figure here was Kipling, whose qualities and defects I think I have sufficiently exhibited in my first chapter: the ballad tone, the hymn-book echo, the jauntiness, the coarseness of texture and the contrived cheap effects, and yet the undeniable sincerity. Kipling has something in common with another poet and publicist of the Edwardian age, Chesterton, but where Chesterton writes rumbustious and sonorous verse,

> Before the Roman came to Rye or out to Severn strode,
> The rolling English drunkard made the rolling English road,
> A reeling road, a rolling road, that rambles round the shire
> And after him the sexton ran, the parson, and the squire,

he somehow never gives us, as Kipling quite often can, the authentic little shiver up the spine which, if it does not always mean that we are reading great or even good poetry, means that we are confronting poetic power. Chesterton's *Lepanto* one would admit as poetry on the same terms as one admits Macaulay's *Lays of Ancient Rome*. It 'stirs the blood' as these do, it is splendid stuff for declamation: but two lines from a ballad of Kipling's about Queen Elizabeth plucking up her courage to look at her face in the glass somehow put *Lepanto* in its place,

> Backwards and forwards and sideways did she pass,
> Making up her mind to face the cruel looking-glass. . . .

Kipling's rhythm there may seem at first as crudely emphatic as the rhythm in the lines already quoted about the rolling English road; the difference is that it is a genuine dance-rhythm, it somehow enacts the sidlings, the backwards and forwards movements of a dance; we are enacting a ritual. The *purely* declamatory rhythms of Chesterton and Macaulay do not enable us to do this.

Belloc, unlike Chesterton, excelled in the short poem, the epigram, the sonnet, sometimes the song. He, again, like Kipling, can hear tunes, can make verse move in dance-rhythm, as in the unforgettable last portion of *Miranda*:

> Never more,
> Miranda,
> Never more.
> Only the high peaks hoar:
> And Aragon a torrent at the door.
> No sound
> In the walls of the Halls where falls
> The tread
> Of the feet of the dead to the ground.
> No sound:
> Only the boom
> Of the far Waterfall like Doom.

But, like Chesterton, Belloc was too busy diversifying: journalism, controversy, politics, history, novels, essays, topography, churning the stuff doggedly out to support his family, ever to give his full concentrated energy to poetry, his best gift (it was not Chesterton's best gift). Belloc's comic poems for children and his long comic-satirical poem, *The Modern Traveller*, are classics of their kind: a kind that depends on very neat form, shocking and surprising incidents related in a very calm tone, surprises in rhyme and turns of verse as well as in incident, and a gravely sustained mock-solemnity of manner: the avuncular poet must never let on to the children that he himself sees the joke. But Belloc's serious poems, aiming at a classical terseness and rotundity, or sometimes at a carol or folk-song effect, somehow give an effect again and again of *pastiche*, or at least of mannerism – there is an affectation of robustness, a false sturdiness. He remains a great man of letters who, acquitting himself creditably in everything he attempted, is never or very rarely *final* in his achievement. Belloc is like Dryden in rarely doing his best, because he can always do remarkably well; one feels that the potential talent was grander than the poetry it achieved.

The tendency of the Edwardian age to dilute can be seen, also, in the verse narratives of John Masefield, which have often a real interest as stories combined with a fluent rough and ready handling of verse. For poets without the unfastidious direct greed for an audience of Kipling, Chesterton, Belloc, Masefield, the tendency was to retreat to scholarship, myth, history, or, as in the case of one of the best poets of this age and one of the most difficult to criticize adequately, Walter de la Mare, into a fairy-tale, nursery-rhyme, folkish yet fantastic world, a world of 'magic'. The retreat, as in Bridges, could lead to pedantry, as in this attempt, in a version of the *Aeneid*, to naturalize the quantitative hexameter in English :

> They were amid the shadows by night in loneliness obscure
> Walking forth i' the void and vasty dominion of Ades;
> As by an uncertain moonray secretly illumin'd
> One goeth in the forest, when heaven is gloomily clouded,
> And black night hath robbed the colours and beauty from
> all things.

One admires the skill, and yet feels that the whole thing is against the grain – 'loneliness obscure' – of natural English. The same scholarly delicacy, yet with a feeling of thinness, oddness, quaintness, can be seen in Sturge Moore's variations on Rimbaud :

> The cow eats green grass;
> Alas, alas !
> Nothing to eat
> Surrounds my feet,

or of Ronsard :

> Time flits away, time flits away, lady :
> Alas, not time, but we
> Whose childish limbs once skipped so fairly
> And still to dance are free.

These are not fair examples of either Bridges or Sturge Moore at their best; but even at their very best, in a poem like Bridges's *London Snow* or in Sturge Moore's poem on a swan which Yeats admired so much that he quoted it at the back of his *Collected Poems*, there is a chilled, Parnassian air, which one finds also in a slightly younger poet, Laurence Binyon, or in R. C. Trevelyan's original poems and versions from Greek and Latin verse. If Kipling and Chesterton have a flavour of Fleet Street at midnight, Bridges, Sturge Moore, Binyon, Trevelyan, suggest the atmosphere of the British Musuem or the Bodleian: books, dignity, silence, a certain remoteness. The retreat from vulgarity is also a retreat from life.

Yeats describes himself as at one time seeking to be a poet of this scholarly school, the school of Sturge Moore and of the younger 'Michael Field'; but there is a vitality in his use of myth lacking in his contemporaries, simply because the figures out of his 'old mythologies' come directly out of the 'book of the people'. Yeats in the end, also, came to distrust the direct use of myths, especially as providing a decorative and emblematic account of his love for Maud Gonne, and turned instead to themes taken straight from his own life and from contemporary Irish history:

> I made my song a coat
> Covered with embroideries
> Out of old mythologies
> From heel to throat;
> But the fools caught it,
> Wore it in the world's eye
> As though they'd wrought it.
> Song, let them take it.
> For there's more enterprise
> In walking naked.

One should compare what Yeats says there with the words of his younger friend, Synge,

The poetry of exaltation will always be the highest; but when men lose their poetic feeling for ordinary life, and cannot write poetry of ordinary things, their exalted poetry is likely to lose its strength of exaltation, in the way men cease to build beautiful churches when they have lost happiness in building shops. Many of the older poets, such as Villon and Herrick and Burns, used the whole of their personal life as their material, and the verse written in this way was read by strong men, and thieves, and deacons, not by little cliques only. Then, in the town writing of the eighteenth century, ordinary life was put into verse that was not poetry, and when poetry came back with Coleridge and Shelley, it went into verse that was not always human. In these days, poetry is usually a flower of evil or good; but it is the timber of poetry that wears most surely, and there is no timber that has not strong roots among the clay and the worms. . . .

That poem of Yeats's – published at the end of a volume that came out in 1914, called *Responsibilities* – and that phrase of Synge's about 'strong roots among the clay and the worms' both foreshadow great changes that were to come over English poetry between 1910 and 1920. But these were Irishmen, and in England itself the two great innovators in these years, Ezra Pound and T. S. Eliot, were expatriate Americans, who had not yet created their public. The movement that did seem innovating and liberating to ordinary readers in England in these years was what is called Georgianism. It was not a movement with a programme or manifestos. It reflected the taste of Edward Marsh, a civil servant with a small private income which he used to encourage young painters and young poets. Marsh's series of anthologies, each called *Georgian Poetry*, came out annually from before the Great War to some years afterwards, and included work by many young poets who were to serve and some of them to die in the Great War, Rupert Brooke, Edmund Blunden, Robert Graves, Siegfried Sassoon, Edward Thomas, Wilfred Owen. Marsh also admired and included a very different poet, D. H. Lawrence. And yet Lawrence perhaps was not so utterly different after all. After Kipling and after Bridges, the great quality of the best Georgian poetry was a lack of the strident and the remote or the precious, a certain intimate plainness of tone. There was a deliberate avoidance, of what Synge calls 'the poetry of exaltation', sometimes a conscious slight prosiness. A recurrent, though not the only, topic was the familiar scenes and incidents of the

English countryside, treated (as by Edward Thomas) not from the point of view of the countryman, but of the hard-worked Londoner getting away for a weekend. Perhaps in the years before 1914 many of these young poets had some unconscious premonition of the disaster that was going to overwhelm them. Some died in the war (though, ironically, war service gave Edward Thomas, a natural poet who had been supporting himself for years by high-quality literary hackwork, the leisure and lack of worry he had always needed to get down to writing his own poetry); some, like Graves, Blunden, and Sassoon, survived the war, but were left nervously disturbed. Each of them wrote his prose book about the Great War, laid its ghost, about ten years after 1918. And in all their later poetry there would be a sense of trouble. The guns in France had ripped off the green surface of the world. Blunden has put this splendidly:

I saw the sunlit vale, and the pastoral fairy-tale;
The sweet and bitter scent of the may drifted by;
And never have I seen such a bright bewildering green,
But it looked like a lie,
Like a kindly meant lie.

When Gods are in dispute, one a Sidney, one a brute,
It would seem that human sense might not know, might not spy;
But though nature smile and feign where foul play has stabbed and slain,
There's a witness, an eye,
Nor will charms blind that eye.

Nymph of the upland song and the sparkling leafage young
For your merciful desire with these charms to beguile
For ever be adored: muses yield you rich reward:
But you fail, though you smile –
The other does not smile.

One oak of a poet stood over all these younger writers. Graves, Sassoon, Blunden all at one time or another visited Thomas Hardy at Max Gate, and received his poetic blessing. They were drawn by his love of the English country-

side and a pure English tradition, by the rugged honesty of
his mind and verse, his unsmartness, his fine old-fashioned-
ness, and the spirit in his work of high anguished doubt
about the heart's and the world's destiny. Hardy is the most
uneven, as he is also the most excessively copious, of great
poets, but has a special magic that comes out of the very
awkwardness of glumly prescient innocence. He was aware
of the decay around him of the settled Victorian world:

> The bower we shrined to Tennyson,
> > Gentlemen,
> Is roof-wrecked; damps there drip upon
> Sagged seats, the creeper-nails are rust,
> The spider is sole denizen;
> Even she who voiced those rhymes is dust,
> > Gentlemen.

Yet, especially in his own lovely south-west country (still the
least altered and spoiled part of England) the outer scene,
with its natural magic, remained. But for how long? He was
old, he was mortal, the world was given over to change:

> When the Present has latched its postern behind my
> > tremulous stay,
> And the May month flaps its glad green leaves like wings,
> Delicate-filmed as new-spun silk, will the neighbours say,
> 'He was a man who used to notice such things'?

So we can see Hardy as a brooding, presiding spirit inspiring
these Georgian poets; younger men, lesser men, but with
their proper share of his plainness, his honesty, his inner
disquiet, his countryman's eye for 'noticing such things' –
we can see them, as well as him, as in some sense 'the last of
the English'. The Great War was to help to make this kind
of poetry of local mood and habit and brooding recollection
impossible: the pastoral scene was henceforth to look

> like a lie,
> Like a kindly meant lie.

There were to be no more workable weekend retreats from
anxiety. And behind the new poetry that was about to be

born, and to alter the sensibilities of more than one generation, there was not to be an English genius, old or new, but
the work of two Americans and an Irishman. Yet Hardy's
influence has never wholly died. Lytton Strachey, not usually
a good critic of literature, has an excellent essay on Hardy
in which he notes how Hardy's poetry is

full of ugly and cumbrous expressions, clumsy metres, and flat
prosaic turns of speech. ... In the second of the following lines,
cacophony is incarnate:

> Dear ghost, in the past did you ever find
>
> Me one whom consequence influenced much,

while a line like,

> And the daytime talk of the Roman investigations,

trails along in the manner of an undistinguished phrase in prose.
Hardy is incorrect; but then how unreal and artificial a thing is
correctness. He fumbles; but it is that very fumbling that brings
him so near to ourselves. In that 'me one whom consequence
influenced much' does one not seem to catch the very accent of
hesitating and half-ironical affection? And in the drab rhythm
of that 'daytime talk of the Roman investigations' does not all
the dreariness of long hours of boredom lie compressed?

Strachey there puts his finger on the central technical paradox of Hardy's poetry, the paradox of expressive clumsiness;
if it is so fully and finely expressive, can you call it clumsy?
Of course, Hardy in both prose and verse could be inexpres-
sively clumsy often enough. But a passage that seems in-
expressive on a first reading may not seem so on a second.
Certainly, a number of poets who seem much more consistently skilful than Hardy, poets of different generations
and schools, Robert Graves, W. H. Auden, Philip Larkin,
have all acknowledged a debt to him; he was admired also
by two poets who might seem very unlike him, D. H. Lawrence and Ezra Pound.

Pound is, for many reasons, an extremely controversial
figure, but even his most hostile critics would admit his importance as a technical innovator in poetry and as a direct

influence, through precept or example, on other notable poets, including Yeats and T. S. Eliot and, among much younger men, the American poet, Robert Lowell. A good poet and a very honest and original American critic, Yvor Winters, thinks him a powerful influence but a disastrous one. The figure with whom it is most easy to compare Pound is the great painter, Pablo Picasso. Picasso started painting in provincial nineteenth-century Spain, in an old-fashioned style, he came to Paris and gradually brought his style up to date, and then became one of the great technical innovators and inventors of our time. Pound, born in Idaho, came to England in 1907, similarly old-fashioned and provincial. His early poems are modelled on Swinburne and Rossetti, on Pre-Raphaelite medievalism; in 1907, in London, he must have seemed a country cousin, thirty or forty years out of date.

Even Pound's earliest poetry displays, however, a magnificent sense of cadence and rhythm. In his years in London he became associated with various *avant-garde* groups, with the Imagism of T. E. Hulme and F. S. Flint, with the circle which gathered round Ford Madox Hueffer's *English Review*, with Wyndham Lewis's Vorticism, which was in some ways an English equivalent of the German Expressionist movement in art and poetry. A passion for technical experiment in verse was allied to a passion for translation, which led to versions or adaptations of medieval Provençal and Italian poetry, the Anglo-Saxon *Seafarer*, Chinese classical poetry, Japanese Noh plays, and the Latin elegiac poet, Propertius. Pound knew little of the languages he was translating from, and Chinese and Japanese, which he rendered from the notes of a great American expert on Japanese art, Ernest Fenollosa, he could hardly be said to know at all. Yet he had an intuitive understanding of Chinese and Japanese aesthetics and his short imagist poems, in particular, owe much to the Japanese *haiku*. His early poems are those of a man in love with the past and with the multifariousness of human culture but a man also seeking to renew English versification. He had an infallible sense of

where the new was going to come from. He helped Yeats to
harden and sharpen his middle style. He managed to get
T. S. Eliot's earliest poems published, when they had been
rejected by baffled editors for about five years. He helped
Joyce to get *Ulysses* published. He was encouraging in the
same way to young artists of promise in other mediums than
literature, such as the composer Georges Antheil and the
sculptor, Gaudier-Brzeska. He praised the verse techniques
of a poet whose attitudes he disliked, D. H. Lawrence. Few
men of major talent have been more unselfish handmaids
to the talents of others. Yet when he left England for good
in the early 1920s, to settle in Paris, then in Italy, he had
not really made a reputation for himself. Except in small
avant-garde circles he was treated as something of a joke,
and even friends and admirers, like Ford Madox Ford
(Hueffer had changed his German surname, when the Great
War loomed) or Wyndham Lewis, write about him in a jocu-
lar fashion. He seemed to them to combine enormous technical gifts with a peculiar human naïvety, so that Wyndham
Lewis dubbed him 'the revolutionary simpleton'. Yet the
longest poem of his English years, *Hugh Selwyn Mauberley*,
is not naïve in the least, but a bitterly subtle and acute
survey of the decadence and isolation of the poet in a predominantly commercial society.

Mauberley is an account, also, of Pound's own isolation
and bitterness in such a society :

> For three years, out of key with his time,
> He strove to resuscitate the dead art
> Of poetry; to maintain 'the sublime'
> In the old sense. Wrong from the start. . . .

Pound there bids farewell to London, which he feels has let
him, and art, down :

> Conduct, on the other hand, the soul
> 'Which the highest cultures have nourished'
> To Fleet Street where
> Dr Johnson flourished :

> Beside this thoroughfare
> The sale of half-hose has
> Long since superseded the cultivation
> Of Pierian roses.

Pound also notes the waste and destruction of the Great War, in the death of the young and brave, in defence of a 'culture' that has become itself a dead thing, of libraries and museums:

> Charm, smiling at the good mouth,
> Quick eyes gone under the earth's lid
> For two gross of broken statues,
> For a few thousand battered books.

Mauberley is one of the most penetratingly sad (though at the same time one of the wittiest) poems of our time; yet out of its account of the artist's defeat it wrests art's own ironic victory.

But the bitterness that was to overtake Pound and was to be even more notable in the early poems of his brilliant young fellow-countryman, T. S. Eliot, was not the new important aspect of their poems. Bitterness, in poetry, is sometimes important but is never new. The new and important point was their revolutionary use of language. Hardy, as we have seen, was a rustic poet, both in a good and in a bad sense; rootedly English as hardly any important poet since him has been rootedly anything (Yeats, for instance, did not really grow out of Irish culture, but rather drastically re-created Irish culture as a backcloth for his own gestures). One imagines Hardy as speaking and thinking very slowly, groping even for simple thoughts; but the early verse of Eliot and Pound, where it has the tone of speech, suggested the quick, light, glancing, incisive, and malicious talk of intellectuals in a capital. Pound's little poems of three or four lines struck contemporary readers as jokes. Many of them *are* jokes, and good ones:

> Phidon neither purged me, nor touched me
> But I remembered the name of his fever medicine, and died.

Others are more than that. The wife or concubine of a Chinese Emperor, neglected by her lord, paints three lines of verse on a fan:

> O fan of white silk,
>   clear as frost on the grass-blade,
>   you also are laid aside.

An Alexandrian poet meditates on women:

> Woman? Oh, woman is a consummate rage,
>   but dead, or asleep, she pleases.
> Take her. She has two excellent seasons.

Pound, in his own guise for once, considers the crowd in the Paris underground: this is his own exemplary imagist poem, gradually condensed to two lines from an original draft of about thirty:

> The apparition of these faces in the crowd:
> Petals on a wet, black bough.

It is a rainy day, we are to imagine the underground station full of drab figures in dark clothes, and suddenly, in the crowd, the pale, flower-like faces of a small group, perhaps only a couple, of beautiful girls. 'Apparition' suggests a startlingness, a word used of ghosts, which are pale like blossoms, but also of visions. Then we are presented with the other image of the petals or blossoms, soon to fall, perhaps, on the wet, black branch. Beauty grows out of the crowd, triumphantly, though perhaps, like the petals, only in the end to fall on the ground and be trampled heedlessly under foot. Nothing of all this is *said*: it is all, as in Japanese *haiku*, beautifully *implied*. When one first reads these little poems of Pound's, one thinks how frail and slight they are, but finds that they last a life-time.

That Eliot learned much from Pound is common knowledge, though the earliest influences on his poetry were different ones, the decadent poets of the 1890s, and Jules Laforgue. And even when, from about 1915 onwards, he came strongly under Pound's technical influence, he had other sources of his own, the English metaphysical poets and the Jacobean dramatists, for whom Pound did not really share his admiration. And from their very beginnings, it might have been guessed that Eliot was going to be the verse dramatist in verse, not Pound. Pound, in fact, has done versions of the Noh play and of a tragedy by Sophocles, but nobody rates these among his best work. When we can compare them on a similar theme, Pound is much more static. They have both written poems on the theme of the middle-aged literary lady, who likes to act as a hostess and sympathizer to young poets. Here is part of Pound's *Portrait d'une femme*:

> Yes, you richly pay.
> You are a person of some interest, one comes to you
> And takes strange gain away:
>
> Trophies fished up: some curious suggestion;
> Facts that lead nowhere; and a tale or two,
> Pregnant with mandrakes, and with something else
> That might prove useful, and yet never proves,
> That never fits a corner or shows use,
> Or finds its hour upon the loom of days:
> That tarnished, gaudy, wonderful old work,
> Idols and ambergris and rare inlays,
> These are your riches, your great store; and yet
> For all this sea-board of deciduous things,
> Strange woods half-sodden, and new brighter stuff:
> In the strange float of differing light and deep,
> No! there is nothing! In the whole and all,
> Nothing that's quite your own.
> Yet this is you.

And here is a part of Eliot's *Portrait of a Lady*:

> Now that lilacs are in bloom
> She has a bowl of lilacs in her room
> And twists one in her fingers while she talks.
> 'Ah, my friend, you do not know, you do not know
> What life is, you should hold it in your hands';
> (Slowly twisting the lilac stalks)
> 'You let it flow from you, you let it flow,
> And youth is cruel and has no remorse
> And smiles at situations which it cannot see.'

> I smile, of course,
> And go on drinking tea.
> 'Yet with these April sunsets, that somehow recall
> My buried life, and Paris in the Spring,
> I feel immeasurably at peace, and find the world
> To be wonderful and youthful after all.'

Pound is ruminative and reflective there, teasing a concept from a metaphor; the lady's room and her mind are the same sort of fascinating, though finally unorganized, uncreated junk-shop; the elusive core of her personality is to be sought in the end in the sense of her unordered riches or perhaps, more kindly, her rich disorder. She is not there herself, except as something for the reader to infer. Eliot's technique is much more bare, dramatic, and direct. The lady is there in her voice, full of its 'definite false notes', its little cadences of genteel and sighing aspiration; the voice gives her away, but even more her hands do, twisting the lilac stalks, savagely, the lilacs which in Eliot's poems are always associated with the headiest onsets of sexual desire. She *wants* the young poet, for something more than tea and sympathy; and smiling and drinking his tea, controlling his embarrassment, he 'sees the situation' – or thinks he does, for this fine poem has a twist and a surprise at the end.

Yet in a broader sense both these young poets, in these passages, are using a similar approach. They are making a tentative, exploring use of verse, using poetry to edge nearer to the hard, and perhaps hostile, shape of a real situation: not starting off with a preconceived notion of what the situation is or with what Auden calls a 'rehearsed response' to it. What made readers in the 1910s puzzle over passages like these – the *sense* of both passages is perfectly straightforward – was that Eliot and Pound habitually presented in verse situations quite as puzzling as those of real life, without giving the reader any reassuring guide about what he ought to feel about them. What does Eliot feel, in particular, about the talkative, romantic lady nearing the menopause, twisting lilac stalks? What does the reader feel? Certainly, not mere contempt and amusement; Eliot is not writing satire, and he handles the lady's speech rhythms so exquisitely that, though we are aware of what is tired and faded and conventional in her words and sentiments, we are not estranged from what lies underneath. 'Paris in the spring', as a phrase, is a cliché, but Paris in the spring, as a fact, as a symbol standing for what she wanted from life and has lost, is something to be respected. It is the poet in the poem who is made to look gross, in the end, in his too easy pity and contempt, in his failure to realize that, while he was taking the lady's measure, she was taking his: the poem insists in the end that she *was* a lady, and the young poet not quite a gentleman. So this hesitant, tentative, apparently rather flat use of language gave a new and complex psychological immediacy to poetry; those who admired this new mode would obviously find, by comparison, the diction, attitudes, and situations of much Georgian poetry unreal. Eliot himself has admitted that he was never able to give Georgian poetry a fair consideration because what he himself was after, when young, was so different. It was this disturbing, uncomfortable use of language, the supple closeness to the rhythms of intelligent speech, that poets of a later generation, like Auden and MacNeice, were to take over from Eliot and from the Pound of *Mauberley*: a way with words, rather than attitudes or themes.

As far as themes and attitudes were concerned, the young poets of the 1930s were at the opposite pole from Pound's sympathy with Mussolini and Eliot's sense of drift and hopelessness up to *Ash Wednesday* and his subsequent Anglo-Catholic Conservative piety: they found a moral inspiration rather in Wilfrid Owen's fragmentary preface to his war poems:

> Above all, I am not concerned with Poetry.
> My subject is War, and the pity of War.
> The Poetry is in the pity.

Yet these elegies are to this generation in no sense consolatory. They may be to the next. All a poet can do today is warn. That is why the true Poets must be truthful.

Owen's techniques, not at all like those of Eliot or Pound, were to compete with theirs for influence over young poets of the 1930s like Stephen Spender:

> But cursed are dullards whom no cannon stuns,
> That they should be as stones;
> Wretched are they, and mean
> With paucity that never was simplicity.
> By choice they made themselves immune
> To pity and whatever moans in man
> Before the last sea and the hapless stars;
> Whatever mourns when many leave these shores;
> Whatever shares
> The eternal reciprocity of tears.

There is a directly grandiose quality in that passage which is not to be found, and was not aimed at, in the oblique early stances of Pound and Eliot. And perhaps the unashamed openness of feeling might make one question even the tone of Yeats's wonderful *Easter, 1916*:

> Hearts with one purpose alone
> Through summer and winter seem
> Enchanted to a stone
> To trouble the living stream.
> The horse that comes from the road,
> The rider, the birds that range
> From cloud to tumbling cloud,
> Minute by minute they change;
> A shadow of cloud on the stream
> Changes minute by minute;
> A horse-hoof slides on the brim
> And a horse plashes within it;
> The long-legged moor-hens dive,
> And hens to moor-cocks call;
> Minute by minute they live;
> The stone's in the midst of all.

Is the complex symbolism of that – the stream as the flow of daily life, the stone as the relentless purpose of the Irish revolutionaries – too much 'concerned with Poetry' in Owen's sense? Is Yeats, also so much preoccupied with myth and fantasy, one of those of whom Owen is thinking when he says 'the true Poets must be truthful'? Would Owen have thought (probably he had never read anything they wrote) of Pound and Eliot, working on translation and satire while men were killing and dying in the trenches, as 'dullards whom no cannon stuns'? If he had thought that, he would have been taking an intense but narrow view of poetry; just as Yeats himself was taking an intense but narrow view when he excluded Owen's work from *The Oxford Book of English Verse* on the grounds that the poetry of war may be heroic or ribald but must not be concerned with 'passive suffering'. It may be a chief *secondary* duty of a poet today to warn, but his primary duty today as at all times is to be a poet. And the poetry of life is not *only* in the pity, but in the delight and exultation, the beauty and absurdity, in what Eliot has called 'the boredom, the horror, and the glory', in the whole grand complex. Owen is demanding, certainly for noble reasons, an over-simplification of the poet's task. Yet that Preface, and that stanza, both have about them the stern and simple authority of the English puritan tradition; the tradition that embraces duty joyfully, and turns dutifully from joy; and they will be listened to, generation after generation, by earnest young men who have turned away in exasperation from more balanced and sophisticated but, for that very reason, to them less inspiring masters.

18

The 1920s

In the 1920s, and indeed in the 1930s and up to our own time, poets like Pound and Eliot, whose early experimental work I have dealt with in the last section, were, of course, continuing to develop their gifts. Eliot's most famous poem, *The Waste Land*, came out in 1922 and expressed better than any other poem of that decade the sense of hopeless drift which afflicted all the more sensitive members of the post-war generation. Herbert Read, with that simplicity, dignity, and candour which are his great qualities as a writer of prose, has explained in the preface to his autobiography, *Annals of Innocence and Experience*, the background against which *The Waste Land* was written:

These pages will make sufficiently clear that I consider the no-man's years between the wars as largely futile, spent unprofitably by me and all my kind. I do not pretend to know how we could have made them more positive: the forces against us were not human, but satanic – blind forces of economic drift, with the walls of faith and reason turning to air behind us.

The Waste Land, however, did not express merely this negative sense of blind satanic drift; it expressed poignantly a desperate sense of the poet's, and the age's, lack of a positive spiritual faith and the great need for one. The feeling of personal anguish and dereliction, of menace and sterility everywhere, which is at the root of *The Waste Land* achieved a narrower, but even more intense expression, in its successor, *The Hollow Men*; a poem which is like a confession of final defeat or an act of final surrender. If *The Waste Land* is the dramatic crisis of a fever, *The Hollow Men* is the terrible weakness that succeeds a fever, when body and soul both seem drained of life. Up to *The Hollow Men*,

Eliot can be said to have explored in poetry, with growing power and penetration, a sense of the disintegration of life. In these early poems, he does not figure as a person; he assumes masks, Prufrock, Gerontion, or uses pronouns that suggest a point of observation, a mood, 'he', 'one', 'we', 'they', rather than a stable personal attitude. He is less, in a semi-imagist poem like the early *Preludes*, saying that this is how he sees the world than that this is how the world looks from certain angles of observation. He thought of the poet not as somebody expressing emotions, a personality, a point of view, but rather as a sensitive area in which levels of experience, usually kept separate, fuse. The brilliant impersonality of technique nevertheless merely masks a growingly intense personal distress. After *The Hollow Men*, *Ash Wednesday*, a very beautiful but also very difficult poem, is at last frankly personal, an account of the slow and painful purification of the inner self, after religious conversion. He is seeking to reintegrate himself through submission; and his final series of great long poems, the *Four Quartets*, are philosophical meditations on the relation of time to eternity, or of human history to the will of God, and again much of the material in these poems is personal, reminiscent, and reflective.

The imagery in these later, Christian poems of Mr Eliot's has fewer flashes of isolated vividness than that of his earlier poems like *Prufrock* or *The Waste Land*. The tone is more consistently grave, the rhythms more slow and solemn, the transitions less strikingly abrupt; there is not the same disquieting use in a 'serious' context of flippant wit or heroic burlesque or sardonic anticlimax. And though the later poems are mature and profound as the earlier poems are not, they have not had the same revolutionary effect on younger writers. *Prufrock*, *Gerontion*, *The Waste Land* had their enormous influence because they were a young man's poems, with something of a young man's restlessness and savagery in their handling of language and, paradoxically, even at their gloomiest, with something of a young man's high animal spirits. *The Waste Land* had its enormous influence also partly because it expressed so perfectly the disquiet and bitterness of a whole generation, and more specifically the sense of sterility and hysteria in sexual relationships which is a recurring theme in novels as well as poems of the 1920s; and partly because of the range of technical invention in it; the use of abrupt cinematic cutting from one scene to another, the shifts of tone, the sharp and glaring contrasts, the juxtapositions of sordid and colloquial phrases from modern urban life with allusions to, or parodies of, the splendour and formality embodied in the poetry of the past. The poem has a dreamlike, irrational vividness even before its thematic pattern has been grasped; a vividness which resembles, perhaps more than anything else in English literature, the first impact of that other profound and phantasmagoric poem, Coleridge's *The Ancient Mariner*. And just as, according to Livingstone Lowes, *The Ancient Mariner* embodies all sorts of fragments from Coleridge's multifarious unsystematic reading, sent up from his subconscious memory at just the poetically appropriate moment, so the quotations and allusions and passages of *pastiche* which make up so much of *The Waste Land* are the product of Eliot's equally ranging and adventurous reading, more consciously employed.

It is possible to read *The Waste Land* and feel its impact without grasping the underlying theme of the barren land which can only be reclaimed to fertility by a ritual sacrifice. This theme underlies the legend of the Grail and it is behind the myths of Adonis and Osiris, the young men or young gods, slain in the springtime, and mourned by those who slew them. The sacrificial victim was a sacred king and the representative of a god; the fertility of the land was magically involved in his own youth and strength; and so he had to be regularly sacrificed in case, with his own old age and decay, the land should wither too. But the Grail legend is Christian, though with pagan undertones, and the sick king cannot be slain; he can be cured through the instruments of the passion of the greatest of the sacrificial kings, who is Christ, as God incarnate; and the barren land which has to be reclaimed to fertility is the human heart, full of selfishness and lust, choked with the tares of sin. But there are strong elements in the poem that have very little direct connexion with this pattern. The puritan tradition in New England, indeed, the Christian tradition at its severer levels everywhere, associates the idea of sin intimately with sexuality, and it is in cruel, heartless, or unfulfilled sexual episodes, vividly presented, that Eliot finds his recurrent symbols of sterility. In these sexual episodes, also, there is an emphasis on the (possibly redemptive) suffering and patience of women, a topic which has little to do with the Grail theme, though it has strong Christian associations of a different kind. There is something neither pagan nor Christian, but Manichean, in the poem's failure to set anywhere, against images of sexual débâcle, images of sexual fulfilment. Nobody would guess from *The Waste Land* that people enjoy making love. The thematic pattern of the poem, and its vivid topicality, its presentation of the London scene, perhaps disguise some very deep complex of personal feelings in the poet, a disgust, a desperation, a temporary withdrawal from life. *The Waste Land* certainly today looks both a more personal and a more romantic poem than it did when it first came out. Yet, for all that, it expresses now as when it was first written a deep malaise about contemporary society, which can be shared by people who do not otherwise share either Eliot's social and moral attitudes, or his religious beliefs.

The Waste Land, for all its impressiveness, is, when compared to earlier poems of Eliot's like *Prufrock* and *Portrait of a Lady*, an imperfectly unified structure. It does not quite stand up on its own. We need Eliot's notes at the back; we need the help of the many commentators who have expounded the poem; we know also that it started as a much longer poem and was cut down to its present size and shape by Ezra Pound, to whom it is dedicated. The worry we feel about the form of *The Waste Land* is intensified when we consider Pound's own very long and still unfinished poem. *The Cantos*, a poem which uses a technique rather like that of *The Waste Land* – progress by juxtaposition – but on a very much larger scale. The poem begins with a translation from a famous passage in the *Odyssey* (or, to be accurate, from a Renaissance Latin version of the *Odyssey*) in which Odysseus visits the underworld and, sacrificing a black ram, calls up the ghosts of the mighty dead. Throughout the poem this is what Pound himself is doing, and so we switch in a bewilderingly zigzag fashion from Greek mythology to Confucian wisdom, and from Renaissance bravos to modern armament manufacturers, and from these to the Founding Fathers of the American Revolution. The structural pattern, as R. P. Blackmur has noted, is that of the interrupted anecdote; Pound starts telling a story, breaks it off in the middle, and starts telling another story about somebody else belonging to some quite different place and time; the dropped threads may or may not be picked up later in the poem. In some of the later cantos, however, this kaleidoscopic method is dropped. There are two long and straightforward sets of narrative cantos, one about John Adams, the second president of the United States, the other about the annals of China. And in *The Pisan Cantos,* drafted when Pound was in a prison-camp in Italy after the Second World War, accused of high treason, there are again a number of consecutive, though always rambling and digressive, passages of description of his experiences as a prisoner and of anecdotes and judgements about old friends.

It becomes clear, after one's first bewilderment has died away, that the contrasting fragments of history, legend, and anecdote of *The Cantos* have been assembled not just with a magpie eye, not just as assorted bright old bits, but as documentations for a thesis (never itself, since Pound hates abstractions, made abstractly explicit) about society. The long sections about John Adams and China make the thesis clearer. Adams is the type (one should not say the symbol, for Pound will have no truck with symbolism in the ordinary sense) of the good ruler; he stands for an American culture based on the independent farmer and craftsman and the wealth of the land, as against Alexander Hamilton's vision (the vision that was to become truer in the end) of concentrated financial power and growing industrialism. Jefferson is the more usual symbol of the anti-Hamiltonian attitude, but probably Pound thought the supple and evasive Jefferson a weaker man than the downright, sometimes surly Adams. Adams, also, unlike Jefferson, was the founder of a family dynasty. China, again, is the type of a stable agrarian society, held together by respect for a traditional code of wisdom, that of Confucius; Pound wants us to contrast China's long, stable, and coherent history, achieved in spite of Mongol and Manchu invasions, and changes of dynasty, with the short and violent history of Europe since the Renaissance and certainly since the Industrial Revolution: he wants us to set the serene wisdom of Confucius against our own hesitations and anxieties and uncertainties, our lack of firm standards. We are meant to see usury and other-worldliness – if Pound admires Confucianism, he hates Taoism – as the great evils that destroy society. We are to ask ourselves where we have got to with all our industrial 'progress'.

Pound's ideas have a great deal in common with those of English 'distributists' like Belloc and Chesterton, who also dreamt of a return to a society of small peasant proprietorship and respect for traditional wisdom. One practical weakness of all such philosophies is that, after all, our industrial world and our industrial population are here: they cannot simply be abolished with the wave of a wand. Pound, like Lawrence or like Yeats, or like such a contemporary social theorist as Richard Hoggart, is raising his voice against an inexorable, mechanical process of detribalization, delocalization, a 'processing' of society like the 'processing' of cheese. You cannot bind living trees together in bundles, only dry sticks. Yet here we are. History can never go back to a simpler state of affairs when its problems had not arisen; its present problems are what it has to solve – it must go forward. But in Italy, which in Pound's time was still an agrarian country, apart from its pockets of heavy industry in the north, these ideas no doubt seemed more plausible to Pound than they might have done in the smoky and rainy labyrinth of London. He became an admirer of Mussolini, thinking, to give him his due, not of Mussolini's role as a militant nationalist – Pound has always detested war and war-mongering – but of his big public works, like the draining of malarial marshes and the settling of landless peasants on them. He also thought that he might manage to interest Mussolini in the economic notions of Major C. H. Douglas, who could perhaps be considered as an amateur forerunner of Keynes. Pound's general ideas and his fondness for Italy, where he had lived for seventeen years, his belief also that Mussolini had the root of the matter in him in economics, led him during the Second World War to broadcast from Italy, though he had never relinquished his American citizenship. And so at the end of the war he was arrested by the American forces and would have stood his trial as a traitor to his country if a medical board had not certified him to be mentally unbalanced. He was confined for some years to a public mental hospital in Washington, where he managed to go on writing new instalments of *The Cantos* as well as translations of a play by Sophocles, Confucian texts, and the classical Chinese *Book of Odes. The Pisan Cantos*, largely taken up with Pound's meditations in his prison camp near Pisa in Italy, won the Bollingen Prize as the best volume of poetry published in the United States in 1949 – a fact which is a remarkable tribute to the liberality and tolerance of the best American critical opinion. Since his release from confinement, Pound has lived in the Italian Tyrol with his married daughter, continuing to publish instalments of *The Cantos* which become increasingly hard to understand without back-references or independent commentary.

It is very difficult at the moment to make any final judgement either on Pound as a man or on *The Cantos* as a large-scale poem. Very many critics would agree that there are passages of splendid poetry in *The Cantos*, particularly in the first thirty, in the very personal *Pisan Cantos*, and in a more sustained though less concentrated way in the two sets of continuous narrative *Cantos*, about China and about John

Adams. One main critical question is whether Pound's ideas about society and its organization have the wide and deep human relevance of Mr Eliot's ideas about the emotional sterility of modern society in *The Waste Land* or his later Christian ideas about history and about redemption, in and out of time. Mr Eliot's ideas are emotionally meaningful for non-Christian as well as Christian readers. But Pound's economics, which are central to his thesis, have for uninstructed readers at least an air of crankiness about them. They are also very technical: he has quoted both in verse and in prose the mark of an acquaintance of his, 'Can't move them with a cold thing like economics', and it must be admitted that, for instance, the fiscal reforms of the late-eighteenth-century Habsburg-Lorraine Grand-Dukes of Tuscany, however admirable in themselves, do not lend themselves particularly felicitously to heroic verse. Much of Pound's economic and political material, presented in disconnected fragments, is precisely the material which, to be understood, needs to be presented in connected prose. The direct attacks on usury are, however, fine and moving rhetoric. Yet, when we look at the world around us, so full of unhappiness and aggressiveness, we find it hard to believe that it is *only* the banking-system which is at the root of all our troubles or that everything could be set right by any manipulation of the currency, however ingenious. There seems to be a disproportion not merely rational but both moral and aesthetic, between the complicated disease Pound diagnoses and the simple remedy he suggests. And he seems also, with a touch of American pragmatism, perhaps even of American philistinism, to reject a great deal in the Western tradition including Platonism (though there is some neo-Platonic mysticism in *The Cantos*, equating the divine intelligence and light), Christianity, and the development of science and technology since the seventeenth century. Without all of these things, European history would no doubt have been more static, like the history of China. It would also have been, at the least, less interesting. One possible reaction to *The Cantos* is summed up in Tennyson's phrase:

'Better fifty years of Europe than a cycle of Cathay.' Pound's notion of tradition is a fragmentary and selective one, more concerned with beginnings than ends. He likes the sense of something starting, he is bored by ripe (to him nearly always overripe) periods. In the end, *The Cantos* are one man's personal anthology of the things that have moved him or distressed him in human history; they are an epic of man's quest for a stable civilization; and they are an intellectual autobiography, Pound's own search for order amid the rich chaos of his impressions. A judgement on the poem is a judgement not only on the skill of Pound the artist, but also on the wisdom, or unwisdom, of Pound the man. Whatever the final verdict, there is plenty of great poetry in *The Cantos*.

William Butler Yeats in his development in the 1920s as indeed earlier (Pound had acted as his secretary around 1912) was stimulated, influenced, and irritated by Pound; Eliot, on the other hand, he saw as a writer temperamentally alien to him, grey and controlled, a master of satire like Pope, rising to greatness only in the last stanza of *Sweeney Among the Nightingales*. Yeats expressed his irritation with Pound when he described Pound in a letter to Dorothy Wellesley as 'a sexless attitudinizing American professor'. His appreciation he expressed when he prefaced his famous book of occult philosophy, *A Vision*, with a section called 'A Packet for Ezra Pound'. Of Yeats's greatness, there can be no doubt at all; he is the only modern writer I know of whose reputation has steadily risen in the twenty years since his death. The usual reaction to a notable writer's death is a lull in his reputation, followed perhaps by reappraisals thirty or forty years later. There was such a lull after D. H. Lawrence's death; he was not much read or written about in the 1930s or 1940s; Joyce has been written about a great deal since his death, but his appeal is much more to a public of specialists, of experts. Yeats wrote as a man to men. His work is likely to retain its popularity when Pound and Eliot have undergone a temporary lapse from favour, when the very daring of their experimentalism begins to seem (as Donne began to seem to Dryden and seemed wholly to Pope) historical and quaint. Yet it would be hard to explain to a young reader of a liberal, rational, scientific turn of mind in just what Yeats's greatness consisted. In politics, for instance, Yeats might appear even more of a 'reactionary' than Pound; though in fact he was a very moderate nationalist, never fierce or bigoted enough for Maud Gonne's taste, and as a senator, and a spokesman for the Protestant minority of Irishmen interested in art and literature, he did take up, on subjects like divorce and censorship, a very unpopular liberal attitude. Though he flirted in later years with General O'Duffy's Blueshirt movement, he had a dislike of the mob, or the herd, that would have prevented him from ever becoming a genuine Fascist. He can, unlike Pound, write great political poetry, realistic, tragic, ironical, because he had always a background in a sense in which Pound, a wanderer and an exile from his native country during the best years of his creative life, never had.

Yeats, moreover, unlike most of his younger contemporaries, rode rather loosely to his age. For younger poets like Auden the choice was between a religious and a scientific attitude to life; Yeats was neither orthodoxly religious, in the sense in which both Eliot and Auden are now orthodoxly religious, nor orthodoxly scientific, or would-be scientific, in the sense of the young radical Marxist and Freudian poets of the 1930s. His attitude might be more properly described as a magical attitude; or one might say that Yeats had both a science of his own and a religion of his own, united, as primitive science and primitive religion are, at the level of magic. The science and religion are beautifully expounded in *A Vision*. Here they are woven into something that must be called, using the older and more ambitious associations of that word, a philosophy. It is a philosophy in which pious or rational readers can pick many holes; there is no reason at all to suppose that it is true, and Yeats's tone of voice does not ask us to do this; he thought that the notion of believing, or not believing, was irrelevant to his speculations in *A Vision*. But from the poet's point of view these speculations have the advantage, which most modern philosophies lack, of being at once inclusive and systematic. The only meaning of 'true' that is relevant to our criticism of Yeats is not 'true' as 'corresponding, point by point, to known facts' but 'true' as 'fitting together into a broadly meaningful and aesthetically satisfying pattern'. *A Vision* is a coherent book. At his occult or magical level, Yeats does reconcile his own 'facts' and his own 'values', even if to the ordinary reader the facts seem very dubiously factual and the values odd and arbitrary; but these questions arise only after the book is closed, for Yeats's masterful rhetoric, in prose as in verse, carries conviction *while* one is reading him. The obvious comparison here is with Blake. It is a mistake, I think, to regard Blake as an inspired religious teacher (in his shorter poems, he is an inspired religious poet, and in *The Marriage of Heaven and Hell* an inspired precursor of Nietzsche, which is another matter) and to accept the Prophetic Books as a new gospel; but it would be a worse mistake to dismiss them as ravings. It would be a mistake similarly to swallow *A Vision* whole; but a worse mistake to dismiss it as merely odd and eccentric, having no relationship to the greatness of Yeats's poetry.

As I have said in the first part of this book, Yeats owed a great deal to Vico and to Nietzsche and a leading idea in many of his poems is that history is a fated and recurrent eternal pattern (Troy, in an image that recurs in his poetry, is always being burned down), in which like actors we must again and again play the particular parts assigned to us. Believing in reincarnation, he believed also that, like actors in a repertory company, we are offered a wide range of parts, so there is something liberal even in his fatalism. For, however painful our parts may be, we should play them with style: 'Hamlet and Lear are gay.' There was a mixture, in fact, in Yeats's temperament of a passionate lust for the life of blood and bone and the 'devil between my thighs', and another wish for the remote contemplative immortality of a withdrawn spirit; and it was his occult philosophy of history which enabled him to reconcile these warring wishes.

He saw death first as the road to the life of pure contemplative wisdom, but ultimately as the road back, both through personal reincarnation and through the returning wheel of major historical patterns, to our own life here. For the physical life of the body in the world, he had a deep lust, at any level – even at that of 'a blind man battering blind men'. On the other hand, his sense that our life here is play, even a charade, that we wear a formal mask and perform the symbolical outward show of a hidden supernatural reality, saved him from being really battered down, as so many fine writers of our age have been, by the spectacle of the misery, the extensive meaningless squalor and ugliness, and the bitter injustice of the world.

It is a common criticism of Yeats that he lacked pity. His dismissal of the poetry of the First World War as a poetry of 'passive suffering' indicates hardness. Human experience that will not take a strong and stylish mould of form Yeats tended temperamentally to neglect; and there is probably a large range of contemporary experience where his general advice to put a good face on things and swagger seems silly and futile. But if he lacked the humanitarian spirit, he certainly did not, in any sense, lack humanity. No poet of our time has loved and admired his friends more, or incised their profiles in more firm and enduring verse. And even in regard to his lack of pity, one must make qualifications; it implied no lack of *pietas*. In the bitter and violent Ireland of his time, 'great hatred, little room', the Ireland of heroes, fanatics, assassins, and also of the most ignoble spites, envies, and jealousies, Yeats was always, for all his grand romantic airs, a moderating influence, indeed, in an aristocratic eighteenth-century way, as has been suggested already, a liberalizing influence. He admired barbaric energy and the strength of primitive emotions but, as a highly civilized humane modern man in spite of himself, he hated barbaric waste and destruction.

Yeats's own temperament was gentle, humane, moderate, and, oddly, exceedingly sociable – he described himself, when he received the Nobel Prize, as an 'extremely social

man', but he assumed often in verse, as the aesthetic antithesis to his natural temperament, the heroic mask. One
reads him certainly not merely, or even primarily, for his
'ideas'. One reads him more for the reflection in his verse
of a traditional culture with a tragic dignity about it: a culture still unified, still vital, still rooted in the soil, which no
English poet of comparable stature expresses with comparable eloquence. There is, of course, the work of Hardy; but
what Hardy has to say he expresses, if we compare him with
Yeats, in a clumsy and stammering way, even though the
clumsiness can become on occasion a positive technical asset.
And Hardy's regretful rejection of the Christian faith, and
the grey semi-pantheism which takes the place of the lost
faith in his mind do not provide him with that framework
that Yeats's occult philosophy and his aristocratic attitudes,
that his nonsense and his poses, to put it as harshly as possible, provide for Yeats. The mythological background of
The Dynasts, with its Spirit Sinister and Spirit Ironic, its
abundance of awkward philosophical neologisms, is handled
without any of the tact with which Yeats handled much
wilder ideas; and one should not forget either what Yeats
owed to traditional folk beliefs and legends, still alive in his
youth to the countryfolk around Sligo, but not alive to the
same degree to the quieter countryfolk of Hardy's Wessex.

One might say that Yeats, unlike almost all the other poets
we have been considering in this chapter, had not had to
digest the Industrial Revolution. The only great, shapeless,
modern commercial town he had ever lived long in was
London, and his London, after all, had been the London of
the Rhymers' Club, of gatherings of poets like Johnson and
Dowson, Plarr and Davidson and Wratislaw in the Cheshire
Cheese in Fleet Street, and the London, also, of Oscar
Wilde's witticisms at the Café Royal. It is possible even today to live in London and hew a romantic city out of it.
Moreover, he had been rescued from the drabber side of
London, from journalistic drudgery, by Lady Gregory just
in time. And in Ireland he had a direct experience of that
traditional, aristocratic culture, based on the land and on

direct relations between landlord and peasant, which other poets with the same romantic, 'reactionary' notions knew only as a remote ideal. In the small literary community of Dublin, moreover, he stood out as a giant and could be on intimate terms, of affection or dislike, with all the most significant of his contemporaries; where in vaster London, the writer, however distinguished, tends to be lost in an anonymous mass, or in a bundle of competing talents, and gradually to have what is distinctive and individual in him rubbed away. Also, Ireland escaped the direct impact of the First World War and its aftermath. The Easter Rising of 1916 and the subsequent Irish 'troubles', harsh and painful as they were, were very different in quality from the trench warfare in which English poets like Edmund Blunden, Robert Graves, Siegfried Sassoon, or Richard Aldington stood up for years in the filthy mud and from which they returned with war neuroses which it would take the rest of their lives to cure and resolve into art. One can see the bias which made T. E. Lawrence write, from Oxford, to Ezra Pound, in 1920 or so: 'Surely Yeats is no good?' The truth was rather that fate was against the writers of T. E. Lawrence's generation and had very greatly favoured Yeats, giving him the temperament and the background and the intellectual power that would enable him to become a major English poet and also the last very great English poet, and perhaps, next to Wordsworth, the most mature English poet, in the romantic tradition. He is also, of all the English romantic poets (unless Tennyson is to count as one) the most consistently splendid craftsman and artist in verse.

Though Eliot, Yeats, and Pound seem in retrospect to dominate the poetic world of the 1930s, this was not necessarily how it looked to readers at the time. The poets who are rather roughly and confusingly called the Georgians attracted a much wider audience; some of these had appeared in Sir Edward Marsh's anthologies; others were published in J. C. Squire's monthly *The London Mercury*, and like the original Georgians were interested in country life, often rather from the weekender's point of view. The young

South African poet, Roy Campbell, in a brisk and vigorous piece called *Georgian Spring* wrote:

> But still the air is full of happy voices,
> All bloody: but no matter, let them sing!
> For who would frown when all the world rejoices,
> And who would contradict, when in the spring,
> The English Muse her annual theme rehearses
> To tell us birds are singing in the sky?
> Only the poet shuts the door and curses
> And all the little sparrows wonder why.

But there were interesting and original poets in the 1920s who did not belong to the Georgian tradition and at the same time were not merely followers of Yeats, Pound, or Eliot. A book like this cannot do justice, for instance, to poetry written during these years in Ireland or Scotland, against a very different social background and developing from another tradition. Yeats's reputation has overshadowed that of witty and scholarly poets like F. R. Higgins and Austin Clarke, of a translator from Erse like Frank O'Connor, and of poets like Patrick Kavanagh who write, unlike Yeats, from a peasant and Catholic background; even today, young Irish poets of considerable distinction like Richard Murphy, John Montague, and Thomas Kinsella do not often get the degree of attention from reviewers that can be obtained by English poets, often of smaller talent, writing in a more immediately accessible tone of voice, about more familiar topics. In Scotland, a man with the gifts of a major poet, C. M. Grieve, who wrote his poems under the pseudonym of Hugh MacDiarmid, was at once helped and hampered by the need to create not only a body of poetry but also a sympathetic audience for it. His earliest volumes like *Sangschaw* and *A Drunk Man Looks at a Thistle* were the most vigorous poems in Scots that had been written since the days of Burns, using the archaic literary as well as the living colloquial resources of Scots with an extraordinary mixture of lyrical grace, robust humour, and intellectual force; but the old bottles would not, in the end, contain his new wine, and as he came more and more to use poetry, in a sense like

Pound in *The Cantos*, as a medium for thinking aloud in, he turned to an English vocabulary, knotty with learned words, and to freer forms, and, as in his powerful *First Hymn to Lenin*, to a more revolutionary content. For MacDiarmid, England was the enemy of Scottish culture, which he saw as perfervidly intellectual and hard, rocky and masculine in its primitive force; his genius was recognized by poets like T. S. Eliot and Dylan Thomas, but his writing has been, quite deliberately, too much against the grain of the English tradition ever to have had a wide or a deep influence on younger English poets. It is only in the last year, as I write, that his *Collected Poems* have been published; and, like Hopkins, he may begin to have an influence on young poets many years later than the writing, and first publication, of his work.

With MacDiarmid it is not wholly absurd to group D. H. Lawrence as a poet. Lawrence, like MacDiarmid in his later work, thought of poetry as a medium for thinking, feeling, perceiving aloud in, rather than of the single poem as something to be given a final shape; he writes in gestures, in spurts of perception, in repeated stresses on a key idea, rather than in modulated impersonal lines and verse paragraphs. His poems, like his prose at its best, convey an extraordinary sense of immediacy. Each tends to stress fiercely one feeling, one response, and for the sense of complexity and balance, the play against each other of opposite feelings, one has to read a great many poems, one after the other, rather than any single poem; the technical quality is a contempt for any kind of 'dead' finish. The most fervent admirer of Lawrence's prose, Dr F. R. Leavis, has not, in anything I have read of his, committed himself to any admiration of Lawrence's poetry; much younger critics, like Mr A. Alvarez, admire it very much. The best essay on it is by a very different poet, W. H. Auden, in his brilliant volume of collected criticism, *The Dyer's Hand*. It is poetry in which the successive spurts and lapses of sensibility create, or fail to create, form : whereas in most of the great poetry of the world form, or an idea of form, if it does not create, at least

conditions and channels sensibility. Both MacDiarmid and
Lawrence look forward to a raw, uncooked poetry, startling
in its freshness or embarrassing in its baldness, which a
number of young poets can be seen beginning to write just
today. Their influence in the 1960s on the poetry that young
men are writing is important; in the 1920s, it was negligible,
except in so far as MacDiarmid inspired a number of
younger Scotsmen, then and subsequently, to start writing
in the plastic or synthetic Scots which, as his own poetry
became more intellectual, he was gradually to drop himself.
MacDiarmid's most notable disciple is probably the younger
poet, Sydney Goodsir Smith, whose most important works
are an ironic set of meditations on literary and amorous life
in Edinburgh, *Under the Eildon Tree*, and a powerful, plain
chronicle play, harshly treated by English critics when it
was put on at the Edinburgh Festival, *The Wallace*. But
none of MacDiarmid's disciples has achieved that almost
Lawrentian nakedness and bareness, that lack of any sort of
defence or pretence, which is the individual mark of Mac-
Diarmid at his most masterful.

In England itself the Sitwell family formed a little group
in themselves and gathered around them in the magazine
Wheels young poets who shared some of their tastes and
sympathies, like Aldous Huxley and Sherard Vines. The
early work of all three Sitwells, Edith, Osbert, and Sacheverell, shows a strong family likeness, a common range of
themes and attitudes. Edith, in particular, was interested in
exercises in pure technical virtuosity, as in the set of poems,
Façade, for which Sir William Walton wrote music. Influenced by Rimbaud, she, like her brothers, was interested in
the use in poetry of subtle associations of perception – a particular intense shade of green would be described, in terms
of sound, as *shrill*: a particular effect of light, again in terms
of sound but also partly in terms of imagined muscular
effort, as *creaking*: rain falling at a certain angle might be
described, partly in terms of sight but also in terms of
imagined tactile sensation, as *wooden*. This idea of a correspondence between different kinds of sensation, and this trick

of transforming, with the rapidity of hallucination, one complex of sensations into another, led to vivid effects, but sometimes also to an air of affectation, and to what looked like purely arbitrary associations. There was an amusing correspondence in the *Observer*, a dozen or more years ago, about Dame Edith's use of the adjective 'Emily-coloured' as applied to primulas and hands.

As a practising poet and a technical critic of poetry, Dame Edith has been especially interested in what she calls the 'texture' of verse, the emotional effectiveness of certain combinations of vowels and consonants in themselves, and as arranged and contrasted in a line of verse. Here, too, one has sometimes, when one reads her critical writings (for her practice is self-justifying) a sense of arbitrariness: for her particular vocabulary of 'light' and 'heavy', or of 'light' and 'dark' vowels, of 'gross' and 'thick' or 'thin' and 'shrill' syllables, or syllables that 'leap' is, however sensitive, very subjective compared to the duller but more methodical vocabulary of scientific students of phonetics. I am not sure, also, if Dame Edith's approach allows for the fact that the same line of verse can be read aloud in a number of different accents – standard Southern English, the accent of Dame Edith's native Yorkshire, that of Ireland, of various regions of Scotland, and of the United States – without being robbed of its beauty. A poet whom Dame Edith rightly admired, Roy Campbell, seemed when one read him on the page to have a perfect ear, but nevertheless Campbell himself read his poems *aloud* with a nasal South African twang, and using Cockney vowels and diphthongs, that turned them into burlesque. We can feel the beauty of Chaucer and Dunbar without reproducing their pronunciation in more than an approximate fashion; and modern scholars think that Shakespeare's plays were spoken aloud in what now sounds to us like a rather rich, burring rustic Midland dialect. Wordsworth, who had a northern burr in his speech, sounded, as Mr F. W. Bateson has pointed out, all the r's in 'earth's diurnal course'. This is not to say that sound effects in poetry can be ignored, but that the structure of a line of

verse on the page corresponds to a whole range of phonetic
possibilities, all or most of which may have an aesthetic
validity; and that there is a danger of the poet's attributing
to combinations of sounds, as to combinations of sensation,
which are specially moving to himself – because, perhaps, of
his own way of speaking and hearing, or because, perhaps,
of arbitrary and irrelevant associations – an absolute value
which they do not necessarily possess. A pupil once asked
me whether the Sanskrit word *Shantih* at the end of *The
Waste Land* did not seem to me to have a peculiar magic
of sound: I asked her whether she found the same magic
of sound in the compound words 'sea-shanty' and 'shanty-
town'. Miss Sitwell's experiments in working out correspon-
dences of sensation and patterns of verbal texture, though
they have obviously been very important for her own development, have been too personal, subjective, and sometimes arbitrary to be usefully taken over by other poets. Her
poetry, in its very individual sound effects, is, as it were, the
medium for her own voice, the expression of her own physique.

Like her brothers, Miss Sitwell was an early devotee of
the Russian ballet, and from that devotion comes a tendency
in her earlier work to describe landscapes or personages in
terms of formal theatrical décor. That earlier work was more
interesting from such purely technical points of view than
for its subject-matter, which, if we compare it with the
subject-matter of Yeats, Pound, or Eliot, seems repetitive
and thin: a sophisticated child's story-book world or, more
simply, the world of an enclosed dream. In a long poem,
however, *Gold Coast Customs*, written shortly before the
outbreak of the Second World War, Dame Edith seemed to
awaken sharply to a vision of the distress and evil in the
outer world, and since that war she has become much more
massive, simple, and direct in what she says and in the techniques she uses. Her later poems are a sustained protest in
the name both of Christian belief and of the natural rhythms
of life against everything that is cruel, mechanical, and destructive in the modern world. Dame Edith has been sharply

taken to task by Geoffrey Grigson among others for a lack of 'truth to Nature' in the Wordsworthian sense and for a certain largeness or looseness in the structure of these later poems. But the former criticism is irrelevant to Dame Edith's heraldic and emblematic world, and the latter criticism is irrelevant to the particular form of these later poems; a form which has, for instance, something in common with that of Whitman, expansiveness and iteration being an integral part of the intended effect. It could be agreed, certainly, that there is not in Dame Edith's work the intellectual tautness which is one of the central qualities, in different ways, of both Eliot and Yeats; her approach to the world is not through concepts but through feelings and images and the emotional associations of favourite words, like the word 'gold'. And it does remain a critical question whether the symbolist method, as used by Dame Edith, can provide a modern poet with a way of handling the total complexity of our modern world, and whether today a temperamental response, massive but necessarily confused, can integrate a major body of work. That question must be asked but, however it is answered, Dame Edith will still have made her distinctive and memorable personal contribution to the poetry of our time.

The poems of Dame Edith's brother, Sacheverell, have in their texture a family likeness to his sister's but have a touch also, like the prose of many of his books on art and travel, of that coldness and remoteness which belong to all works of art whose inspiration is other works of art rather than the life of the poet's time. Sir Osbert Sitwell, in later life, has confined himself mainly to prose, as in his vivid autobiographies, though he has used verse to re-create scenes and odd characters of the Scarborough of his childhood and, in *Demos the Emperor*, to gibe, in a confused and petulant way, at what seemed to him, when he wrote that poem at the end of a period of post-war austerity, the bleak and levelling tendencies of the contemporary world. One might say that the aristocratic background and the strong family loyalties of these gifted writers have at once helped and hampered them. The background gave them rich material (Sir Osbert's portrait of his father, in his autobiographies, is one of the comic masterpieces of the world's fiction) and their mutual loyalty sustained them in early days of struggle for recognition, but the background may have cut them off from the common life, even the common literary life of their time. Good English writers, now as in the past, tend on the whole to come from neither the aristocracy nor the very rich, nor from the very poor, but from the minor gentry; to be the children, for instance, of clergymen or dons or head-masters. Their mutual loyalty has made them peculiarly and excessively sensitive not only to hostile but to detached criticism. Not, for that matter, that detached criticism is easy. A reader of the Sitwells has to surrender himself to a peculiarly intense and individual family atmosphere. It is difficult to compare this atmosphere, in a critically useful way, with anything outside it. It is doubtful whether the Sitwells, therefore, have had the same direct influence on the techniques and attitudes of younger writers as Eliot, Pound, or Yeats, whose themes have had a much wider general relevance. At the same time, modern English litera-ture would be much poorer without their intense self-concentration, their diffused curiosity, and their defiant and unfashionable amplitude.

Roy Campbell is another poet of a now unfashionable kind whose approach to the world is through his senses and emotions, and one should add emphatically his passionate will, rather than his intellect. He was notable among poets of his time for a strict traditionalism of form and of vocabu-lary, only mitigated (but more often in his satires than in his 'straight' poems) by expansiveness and a vigorous use of colloquial expressions, especially army slang. His rhetoric had more in common with early French and English roman-tic poets – with Victor Hugo and Byron – than with that complex and allusive diction of modern poetry which we examined in some detail in the last section. His descriptive imagery, when he writes about zebras or wild horses on the Camargue, has a vividness of colour, a dash and directness that again might remind one of the Romantic period, of great painters of the exotic, like Delacroix. In his more strident and garish moments one remembers Keats's snarl at Byron,

> ... large self worshippers
> And careless Hectorers in proud bad verse.

He was able to write in this romantic-pictorial-rhetorical tradition without affectation, because he did not really belong to the modern world of great grey cities, but rather to the traditional pastoral communities which still survive, if only precariously, relatively undisturbed on its edges. Born in South Africa, Campbell lived an adventurous life as cowboy, fisherman, farmer, hunter, soldier, in many parts of the world, before being killed about ten years ago in a motor accident in Portugal, where he had finally settled. He was apt to exaggerate his own pastoral simplicity; he had also been to Oxford and had shared a flat in London, at one time, with Aldous Huxley. He was a learned man, and an excellent translator of verse and prose from French, Spanish, Portuguese, and Provençal; but he had learned these languages by living and working among the people who spoke them rather than out of dictionaries.

Campbell's great gifts as a poet tended to be denigrated in the 1930s, because, almost alone among the English poets of his generation, he espoused the cause of General Franco in Spain, and was indeed believed to have fought on that side, though it seems that his activities were rather those of a propagandist and roving reporter. He did serve, very gallantly, as a sergeant, in the Second World War. The word 'Fascist' is a vague word; in its looser senses it could probably be applied to Campbell, but he used himself to insist that he was not a Fascist, but rather a strong traditionalist (he was a fervent Roman Catholic convert) with an instinctive dislike for political interference with what he thought of as healthy local habits and customs. His feeling about politics, he once wrote, was that there should be as little politics as possible. He liked the common man, especially the soldier, and when he was once asked in a questionnaire in what ways he differed, as a poet, from the ordinary man, he wrote: 'In nothing at all ... in which, however, I differ very much from *the ordinary poet.*' He had a strongly combative temperament, which was at once his strength and his weakness. He has, as a poet, wonderful vigour, wonderful 'go', but everything he writes is very much in one tune, and his rapidly moving verses never slow down, as those of Yeats and Eliot and Graves do, to a halt from which we can take in his whole landscape. Campbell presents himself dramatically, as a figure in action, in conflict with others, but if the man on horseback (*Talking Bronco* was the title of a post-war volume of poems) has any doubts or worries, they are not communicated to the reader (except, sometimes, very indirectly, through a certain stridency in the assertive tone). A lack of inwardness and the concentration this brings breeds hardness. One of Campbell's most striking lines is 'I learned to inflict and suffer pain.'

In spite of his Christian beliefs, there are few passages in his poems which suggest that he had learned to inflict or suffer forgiveness.

Campbell never sufficiently chastened his irascible appetite, or his taste for over-acting, to make the tenor of his thoughts and feelings a sufficiently noble content for the grandly sonorous vehicle of his verse.

A more important poet who makes an interesting contrast to Campbell, for he has a certain similarity of natural temperament, is Robert Graves. Like Campbell, Graves is vigorous and combative, and he had an excellent record as a fighting soldier in the First World War. He began to make a reputation very early, and he was stunned by shell-blast, thought for some hours to be dead, and was able to read his own obituary in *The Times*, before he was twenty-one. After the war, like many of his more imaginative contemporaries who survived it, he suffered from shell-shock, or delayed war neurosis, for for about ten years, till he laid the ghost of the war, and also explosively criticized the literary and social conventions of the upper-middle-class world in which he had been brought up, in his magnificent autobiography, *Good-Bye to All That*. Much of his writing, like the famous *Pamphlet Against Anthologies* written with Laura Riding, displays the same polemical vigour as *Good-Bye to All That*. But Graves writes polemics in the clipped, dry voice of the officers' mess, whereas Campbell's polemics have the rumbustious, belching beeriness of the sergeants' mess. Like Campbell, Graves is a traditionalist in his metres and diction, but without Campbell's taste, French rather than English, for the florid, the heightened, and the highly coloured, and with a much more subtle feeling for delicacies of implication and proprieties of usage – he reminds one of the old definition of a gentleman, as a person who never *unintentionally* gives offence. Graves began his poetic career, again rather like Campbell, as a poet of the natural world, and then became one of the most typical, though not one of the best, poets of the First World War (he has excluded all his poems set in the trenches from the various editions of his *Collected Poems*). His post-war poetry, after an attempted retreat to what he called 'a bucolic Arcadia', became increasingly sharper and subtler in its expressions of a painful and complex inner struggle, which reflected itself in the difficulties of his first marriage to Nancy Nicholson and of his later relationship with the American poet, Laura Riding; but which was to some degree resolved after a second marriage, in middle age, with a wife much younger than himself. After publishing *Good-Bye to All That*, Graves left England to live in Majorca, where, apart from a return to England during the Second World War, he has since made his home. Being out of range of the English literary scene, which profoundly irritated him, was obviously, like his second marriage, soothing to his exacerbated nerves. He belongs to that generation of literary exiles and wanderers, Eliot, Pound, Joyce, Lawrence, who seem to have found it easiest to be creative away from home. Yet his long exile, punctuated by occasional visits to see publishers and friends, has paradoxically crystallized certain engagingly old-fashioned literary mannerisms and attitudes, extremely English

ones, which if he had stayed at home would have been
eroded.

Graves, all his life, deeply though humbly confident of his
vocation as a poet, has been searching for his proper poetic
theme, and that theme, as his work has matured, has gradually revealed itself as that of a sense of complex maladjust-
ment between the mind and the body, between the human
spirit and outer nature, between the sexual appetites and
romantic love, between the joy of romantic love itself and
the vague and dark forebodings that accompany it, between
the special importance which the poet, as such, sets upon
the experience of romantic love and his sane if prosaic wish
as a man for ordinary, stable domestic affection and happiness. In his important book (which has the same place in
his work as *A Vision* in Yeats's), *The White Goddess*, Graves
asserts that the true traditional theme of all good poetry –
and by good poetry he means essentially the short poem, of
the type that is usually called, though he does not like the
term, lyrical – is the love and fear of the poet for a beautiful
woman, who is for him the Muse, the representative of a
primitive nature Goddess; this Muse will return his love if
he is a true poet, but in the end she will betray and destroy
him. Graves traces this theme back to Greek and Celtic
mythology and ritual, and suggests that it is ultimately the
theme (which we have touched on already in connexion
with *The Waste Land*) of the sacrificed God, Adonis or Attis
or Osiris, who, after having become for a short time the
Sacred King and lover of the Sacred Queen, representing the
Goddess, was sacrificed, so that the fertility of the land,
magically bound up with his youth and strength, might be
preserved and not weakened by his growing sick or old. The
poet is the lover who will be sacrificed and supplanted, the
God of the Waning Year, and one of the themes of true
poetry is his perpetual vain struggle with his supplanter, the
God of the Waning Year. This 'prehistoric or post-historic
theme', based partly on obscure racial memories and garbled
traditions, and partly on a natural, or supernatural, mixture
of love and awe which man feels for woman as the mother

who bears him, the lover who awakens him to manhood, and the old hag who closes his dead eyes, is, for Graves, the one true theme of poetry. A great many poems seem not to be on this theme, but Graves gets out of this dilemma quite easily by describing all poetry which does not fit his specification as rhetoric, dedicated to Apollo, the masculine usurper of the Muse's prerogative, and not poetry. True poetry has in it an element that is dark, earthy, and terrible – Orpheus being torn to pieces by the wild women – and some of Graves's ideas are closely related to Nietzsche's famous distinction in his great essay, *The Birth of Tragedy*, between Dionysian and Apollonian art. Apollo, for Nietzsche, stood for the element of *art*, of formal control and distance, in all poetry, whereas Dionysus symbolized the element of wild primitive orgiastic dance. Paradoxically, Graves is in one sense a very Apollonian writer, who rarely publishes a poem before having worked over about six drafts of it, and who revises and polishes poems very carefully in each successive collection of his work; he is also a fine classical scholar who handles the English language, both in verse and prose, with a terseness and rotundity that are becoming rare in contemporary English writing. Yet Graves denies that poetry is in the strictest sense of the word an art at all. The poet should write out of love, not love of art, and poetry is essentially an attempt to tell the truth, lovingly.

The themes of Graves's own poetry are more contemporary and more complex than the 'single prehistoric and posthistoric theme' which, in *The White Goddess*, he imagines himself to have discovered; he does not ignore history; much of the interest of his poetry comes from its exhibiting so sensitively the *malaise* of a fine traditional poet amid the mechanical and destructive complications of the contemporary world. His poetry lacks, however, the immediate, obvious social relevance of Eliot's or Auden's because the *malaise* is related strictly to the poet's personal rather than to man's general situation; though, for that very reason, Graves could be considered a 'purer' poet than either of his two more famous, or once more famous, contemporaries.

For the skill and integrity of his poetic workmanship, in particular, and for his sensitive and exact restraint of language, he is an ideal example of poetic character for young poets; it is these qualities of character which enable him to handle, and to transform into material that gives us the highest poetic pleasure, what might otherwise be the almost unbearable sadness of his themes. Feeling controls feeling in his poems, sensibility controls emotion; wit, irony, urbanity march side by side with terror and awe; for all his principles, he has not disdained to offer, even if furtively, at some time, at least a pinch of incense to Apollo. The attractiveness of his own character, the masculine strength of his own mind, suggest that there is more to be said for the purely male element in poetry than *The White Goddess* allows.

19

The 1930s and the Second World War

BEFORE we look in detail into the poetry of the 1930s, we should say something about one dominating, though anachronistic, technical influence on the younger writers of that decade. Gerard Manley Hopkins was born in 1844, of a prosperous, middle-class professional family, showed poetic promise even in his schooldays, went to Oxford where he took a very good degree, was caught up in the aftermath of the Oxford Movement, left the Church of England and was received into the Roman Catholic Church by Dr Newman, entered the Society of Jesus, and after the usual long novitiate became a Jesuit priest mainly employed in teaching. When he died in 1889 he was Professor of Classics at the new and not then very illustrious Roman Catholic institute of higher education in Dublin, University College. He published nothing in his lifetime, but corresponded about poetry with his Protestant friends, Canon Dixon and Robert Bridges, and sent Bridges copies of all his poems. After Hopkins's death, Bridges published some of his poems in anthologies and in 1919 published a selection of them (omitting much early and unfinished work) with a rather patronizing editorial preface in which, while stressing Hopkins's genius and originality, he had also a good deal to say about his obscurity and oddity, his bad rhymes, and his 'faults of taste'. Bridges's point of view was that of a highly moral but rather chilly agnosticism with a faint Broad Church Anglican flavour, therefore he found 'faults of taste' in Hopkins because the latter took his own religion seriously, and, in the tradition of Jesuit devotional writing, attached his expressions of devotion to vivid concrete traditional images. But for Bridges's Protestant prejudice, it would be hard to see what he could find amiss (given that a dove is the traditional image of the Paraclete) in such a phrase as 'the Holy Ghost with warm breast and with ah! bright wings'. The 1919 edition, though a very small one, took ten years to sell out; during the 1920s, Hopkins was regarded mainly as an interesting curiosity; in 1927 or so, while conducting the experiments that led to his famous book, *Practical Criticism*, I. A. Richards exposed a class of Cambridge undergraduates to one of Hopkins's most beautiful and least difficult short poems, 'Margaret, are you grieving', and their response (they were not told the author's name) was almost uniformly hostile or uncomprehending, or both.

In 1930, however, a second edition of Hopkins with a much more enthusiastic though much less scholarly preface by Charles Williams hit a generation of young poets, of what came to be called the Auden generation. Hopkins's influence was both a technical and a moral one. In his poetic theory and in part of his poetic practice he emphasized the importance of counting the stresses rather than the syllables, or the combinations of stressed and unstressed syllables called 'feet', in English verse. His theory of sprung rhythm allowed for the use in a line of verse of either monosyllabic stressed feet or of stressed feet 'with any number of weak or slack syllables'. Broadly, this meant that any two lines in sprung rhythm could be considered as equivalent, however much they might differ in syllabic length, if they both contained the same number of primary stresses; in a homely image, not Hopkins's, one can count the stresses as stepping-stones, and what matters is the number of stepping-stones one has to land on with a bump, not the distance one has to leap or step between them. But Hopkins did not write all his poems, or even all his best poems, in sprung rhythm; his other innovation, 'common rhythm counterpointed', allowed for the use not only of the normal variations in an English iambic line (roughly, not too frequent anapaestic substitution and the substitution of a trochee for an iambus in any foot but the 'sensitive' second and fifth feet), but also for the deliberate mounting of a trochee, or strong-weak, metre on a basic iambic, or weak-strong, pattern: to quote an example given by Dr W. H. Gardner, in the third and most scholarly and inclusive edition of Hopkins's poems,

Gene/ *rat*ions/ have *trod*/ have *trod*/ have *trod*.

The two trochees followed by the three iambic feet have an effect rather like soldiers changing step in unison, or breaking step, half way over a bridge, or like a sudden harsh but effective change of gear when a car that has been climbing a short steep slope suddenly adapts itself to a level surface. The peculiarity of Hopkins's use of metre is a physical muscularity, a sense of the employment of strength against resistance.

Hopkins was also influenced in his poetic technique by the elaborate alliterative devices of Welsh poetry (the Jesuits, for some years, stationed him in Wales); and his fondness for Latin and Greek poetry, and his distaste for unemphatic and uncoloured particles of speech, led him to take bold liberties with English syntax (particularly, as Bridges noted, in omitting relative pronouns) for the sake of a forcible concision.

The total effect of Hopkins's technical innovations was to give his verse a quite unusual concentration of energy, at the expense, however, of the conversational suppleness or the subtlety of cadence of which the ordinary iambic line is capable; Hopkins's verse can neither be intoned dreamily, like much of the early verse of Yeats, nor spoken in an imitation of the conversational voice, like some parts of Yeats's later poems and like much of Eliot's poetry. It has to be declaimed, in a series of long sinuous pounces on the main stress, alternated with short, staccato hammer-beats. To young poets of the 1930s it seemed to offer a fascinating combination of freedom and order, of an easy and expansive handling of the line, with strong and regular rhetorical emphasis. The voice behind it is one with certain high and shrill notes, and a voice also which gives the effect of breaking forcibly through obstructions.

To young poets, also, reacting against the more immediate influences (the muted despairs or defeated ironies of Eliot's work) the positive assertive force of Hopkins's poetry was inspiring. It is probable that Eliot himself, coming late to Hopkins's poetry, never really *heard* Hopkins's voice: his remarks, in his critical writings, on Hopkins's verse technique are niggling and grudging. The faith of most of the new young poets of the 1930s was very far from being that of Hopkins; but they were in need of *a* faith of some sort, and they wanted to hold to their beliefs, as he had held to his, with a concentrated fervour. There was, of course, very much more in Hopkins's poetry than his very individual rhetoric. He was both a very great nature poet and a very great poet of personal religious devotion, and his special interest in Christ as the Logos, as the force that sustains the universe and expresses itself through the individual pattern of everything in the universe, allowed him to express the traditional romantic sense of an immanent spirit behind the beauty of nature without lapsing either into vague generalities or into semi-pantheism; his poetic vision is unique in the English tradition in its striving, grasping, individuating quality. But it was not so much his vision as his rhetoric, what Hopkins himself called the 'common, teachable element' in English poetry that a new generation strove to learn from him. It was rhetoric, not vision, not the spirit of poetry, that he himself thought weak in the English tradition. His own rhetoric, splendid as it was, had its limitations; the limitations of firm and definite emphasis that cannot comprise half-tones. The crudity as well as the vigour of some of Auden's earlier work derives from that rhetoric. In less technically various and supple poets, like Rex Warner, the influence is even more obvious. It was because they could not also learn from Hopkins the *unteachable* element – the peculiar vividness of Hopkins's vision, his sense of the individual stress and distinction of things, the joy and agony of his wrestlings with the angels – that a fair amount of work by the young poets of the 1930s tends to strike us, today, as Hopkins-and-water. Auden's own larger development, by which he surmounted this danger, was mainly in the direction of wit and humour, qualities which Hopkins displayed abundantly in his prose, but which he considered out of place in poetry: Auden's models here were very different ones, like Byron's *Don Juan*.

The 1930s in poetry as in the novel are a decade easier to characterize, and more completely dominated by a single group of figures, than any of the previous periods with which we have been dealing. When people talked about the younger poets or the new poets in those days they meant Wystan Hugh Auden, Stephen Spender, Cecil Day Lewis, and Louis MacNeice, and with these there was associated in the public mind the novelist Christopher Isherwood, because he collaborated with Auden in plays and in a travel book about China. I remember seeing in an evening paper a photograph of Auden and Isherwood setting off, at about the time of the Japanese invasion of Manchuria, for their Chinese trip and thinking that the 1930s must have been the first period in English history when the comings and goings of poets had become news. The poetry and the journeyings of these young men fitted in very closely with the things one was reading about in the papers: unemployment, the Spanish Civil War, the rise of Hitler, the Munich crisis. At the same time, the popular notion of these poets going about in a 'gang' was very much exaggerated. Spender has written that he and Auden and Day Lewis were never in one room together at any time throughout the 1930s. The public also exaggerated both the similarity and the radicalism of the views of these young men. They were all thought of as Communists or on the verge of becoming Communists, and Auden has been reproached for toning down, in subsequent revisions, his earlier poems to disguise the degree of his commitment, in the 1930s, to the extreme Left. The accusation was unfair. In the 1930s, Auden described himself as a 'pink Liberal'; there was always a religious element even in his earliest poetry ('Sir, no man's enemy, forgiving all') and a careful reader would not have been surprised by his definite commitment to Christian belief in the *New Year's Letter* of the early 1940s. MacNeice made it very clear in his pre-war poems that he was not a Communist, though like his companions a strong anti-Fascist, and that in many ways he was an old-fashioned individualist. Day Lewis was nearer at times to an orthodox Communist position. Spender has told us that for about a week he was a party member – his joining up coincided with the publication by him of a sharply critical article about some aspect of Communist policy, and so, after paying his admission fee, he was not asked for any further dues or asked to join a 'cell'. His membership quietly lapsed. Today Auden still very critically and sharply discusses the failings of society in his poetry, but from a fundamentally religious point of view. Spender, who has written less frequently than his admirers would like in recent years, has become, what by temperament he was all along, a lyrical and meditative poet of the inner life. Day Lewis continues, today, the tradition of ruminative and ironic Victorian poets like Clough and Hardy and Browning.

MacNeice altered less than any of the others, his attitude remained that of a sceptical and humane 'liberal progressive'; but in his later poetry this attitude expressed itself through a handling of historical or personal rather than political themes. The journalistic immediacy which was one common quality of all four poets in the 1930s was imposed by the immediate tensions of the time rather than by common qualities of temperament or talent.

The temperaments and talents were quite notably contrasting. Auden and MacNeice shared a fondness for colloquial language, topical allusions, urban imagery, a certain monitory tone. But MacNeice was much more of a sensualist, making precise catalogues of sensation:

Euston, the smell of soot and fish and petrol,

and holding, in another phrase of his,

the moment cradled like a brandy glass.

His poetic attitude was that of the tough, learned, and witty Epicurean, shocked by the political wickedness and folly of the world into proud contempt and wry indignation.

For Auden, the outer world was interesting not so much in itself, as for the symptoms it presented of dangerous social and psychological decay. Auden, unlike MacNeice in this, always prefers, even in a lyrical poem, to stress the moral idea rather than the sensuous image,

> Lay your *sleeping* head, my love,
> *Human* on my *faithless* arm . . .

where a more sensuous poet might perhaps have written

> Lay your *golden* head, my love
> *Heavy* on my *cradling* arm . . .

Spender was a less intellectual, more emotionally subjective poet than either of these two. Auden and MacNeice typically used either a fairly regular if slightly roughened or jolting blank verse, or fairly strict stanza forms, made modern-seeming by a certain amount of rhythmical syncopation, but avoided free verse; Spender liked free verse and often gave the effect of writing it even when he was attempting to write in blank verse or rhymed stanzas. His verse was a slow-moving, rather dense medium in which long and contorted sentences, expressing a painful groping of the mind, would lead suddenly up to lines of great lyrical concentration and poise:

> Eye, gazelle, delicate wanderer,
> Drinker of horizon's fluid line. . . .

Day Lewis does not seem to me, in the 1930s, or at any other time, to have had a distinctly individual voice, or indeed a distinctly individual personality, like these three writers. He is a chameleon-poet who takes the colour of whatever style stronger than his own he has been in touch with. His poems of the 1930s often seem exercises in the manner of Auden or of Yeats, two obviously very strong influences on him, just as his post-1945 poetry reads like an exercise in revived Victorianism. But as the range of his imitations spread, so his tact and suppleness in handling tone has increased, and so has his fluency. Paradoxically, perhaps his most 'original' poems are his translations of Virgil and of Paul Valéry, where he had no immediately relevant model of English style to draw on.

It is hard to find between the styles and temperaments and attitudes of these four poets the obvious affinities that reviewers found so easily in the 1930s. Yet the habit of grouping them together made sense in relation to their beginnings. They did work in couples and influence each other. They appeared in the same magazines and anthologies. Their work first became familiar in an anthology, *New Signatures*, edited by Michael Roberts, an important critic and interesting poet, who died prematurely in 1949. Roberts did more for them than merely publish their work. To many of them he was an elder brother figure, whose approval and admiration mattered a great deal to them. Roberts was a skilled mountaineer and it was largely under his influence (though both Auden and Spender also had brothers who were well-known climbers) that the image of the hero as pioneer or explorer played such an important part in the group. Some of their typical imagery also comes from a close attachment to the atmosphere of English public-school life; there is sometimes what might be called a 'boy scout' flavour about their writing, an emphasis on the small group and its daring leader with a background of the boy's adventure story. Another image that gripped them was that of the solitary airman (a famous early line of Auden's was, 'As the hawk sees it or the helmeted airman'), a hero of the machine-age who has, however, escaped from mass-discipline or mass-despair. Isherwood, in his fascinating autobiography *Lions and Shadows*, has brought out the degree to which the imaginary world in which these poets lived *was*, in their youths, a world of fantasy. It is worth noting that Isherwood took no degree, and Spender and Auden very poor degrees at Oxford, because the continuation of schoolboy fantasy-attitudes, or of the habit of escape and rebellion through fantasy, prevented them from acquiring the mental discipline, the provisional acceptance of conventional frameworks of thought, and the willingness to work hard over small areas, that makes for student success. They make an interesting contrast in this way with the poets of the 1950s, Philip Larkin, Thom Gunn, John Wain, Kingsley Amis, Alfred Alvarez, and others, many of whom came from a grammar-school background – which is less emotionally engrossing than a public-school background – who tended to be sharply distrustful of the private fantasy and group legend, and who tended, also, to take First Class Honours in their final examinations.

But the fantasy of Auden and Spender, even at its most extreme, was a symbol of, a metaphor for, reality. They saw around them a world of apparent safety and real drift from which they turned to images of danger courageously faced and of conscious human purpose. They felt that England was flabby and dead so they wanted to awaken those around them to the tensions and dangers of the time, to its strength and beauty. Machinery with its controlled power fascinated them: Spender in particular wrote about pylons and railway engines with simple lyrical enthusiasm, as an older poet might have written about clouds, swans, or roses. Machinery signified energy, and what a weak and drifting time needed was to 'Drink here of energy, and only energy': Spender's phrase summed up the central drive of the whole group.

What is also notable about Auden and Spender is the masculine tone of their poetry which almost excluded family life, domestic affection, or the great traditional theme of unhappy romantic love. Tenderness or awe for a woman as a person hardly appears; for they idealized a thinking, acting, group of male leaders. Love to Auden meant the larger social love of man for man, the love of which it can be said

> Hunger allows me no choice
> To the citizen or the police:
> We must love one another or die.

Thus Auden's attitude towards man and society is strict and clinical. He diagnoses the disease of weakness of purpose and drive and he suggests as a remedy energy and vitality: the old ruling class must be replaced by the rising managerial élite, the product of the machine age. Auden was not therefore a Communist but rather a middle-class intellectual radical who approached the situation in the 1930s from a militant anti-Fascist viewpoint.

The decade of the 1930s is still a critical bone of contention – a number of young poets of the 1950s, Donald Davie and Thom Gunn, for instance, wrote poems suggesting that they were reacting violently *against* the influence of the 1930s, where a reader with a long memory would feel that they were often *going back* to the tone of the 1930s – and I do not think that there is much purely literary criticism of the decade that is of great value. Everybody who writes about the Thirties is partisan one way or another, few have been able to forget the poets and look at the poems. I will, however, take Auden, Spender, Day Lewis, and MacNeice in turn and attempt to define some aspects of each poet's individual quality.

Auden, to generalize, likes to start with a concrete situation; likes to draw a general moral lesson from that; but likes to convey the lesson in a concrete fashion, less by abstract statement than by the use of emblematic or allegorical images. He prefers fairly strict verse forms and the regularity of the movement of his poems may even become a little mechanical. The very regular metres are used to lull the reader and to take him off his guard: the reader can be reassured also by the use of slangy, colloquial, or sometimes deliberately trite phrases, and thus Auden, having established a situation of confidence, is able gradually to shift the reader's perspective and make him criticize his previous point of view. Auden is a poet of wide and various gifts, but these generalizations apply at least over a considerable area of his work. Other qualities of Auden's are a certain impersonality or transparency of personality – such that the poet's more intimate feelings may indeed be exhibited, but not for their own sake, merely as a striking example of some paradox or oddity about human behaviour – and the perpetual and strikingly effective combination in his work of an assertive and questioning, of a religiously serious and a playful or mocking mood, of the note of the sermon and the lithe gestures of the virtuoso, of the poetic athlete.

Auden was so important as a focus for England's malaise of the 1930s that critics find it difficult to estimate his purely poetic achievement in detachment from his representative qualities. A recent reviewer of his collected essays described him as the best poet born in this century, and though the phrase at first seems to make a startlingly large claim, one is left admitting its justice: the great innovators, whom we have dealt with earlier, were born towards the end of the last century. Has any other poet born around 1909 anything like Auden's copiousness and technical versatility, his intellectual suppleness and range? Like most copious and also versatile poets, like Dryden or Byron or Tennyson, he is startlingly uneven, always professional, but certainly not always at his best. His virtues are hard to exhibit by brief quotation, since what one admires is the sustained dancing or singing movement of a short poem as a whole or the dialectic movement of thought, and the supple shifts of feeling, over a longer one, rather than the sudden concentration of emotion in two or three memorable lines. Auden pays for his size with an occasional coarseness of texture, for his ease with an over-assurance. What also makes him hard to judge is that he combines a gift for 'argufying', for memorable didactic comment on the current scene, with a habit of transforming the figures and scenes of that current scene into myth or allegory; even historical figures, like Housman or James or Freud or Yeats, become in his poems allegorical types. His own work, with its transformation of so much unpromising material, its balance of remoteness and urgency, is perhaps itself an allegorical representation of his concept of poetry as 'a Serious Game'. Nobody is quite sure that he is a major poet; and nobody is quite sure, if not, why not.

Stephen Spender expresses in dignified and moving rhetoric his sincere and deep emotions about a general concept, but the application of the concept to examples is left to the reader: what is being praised is not the actual but an ideal at which the actual aimed. Spender has a grave, rhetorical manner which seeks to arouse our emotions but does not give us the full detailed situation. This is in great contrast with Auden, who is often dense and factual, but who leaves the reader in doubt as to the exact response he is intended to arouse.

Spender therefore puts out of his reach certain devices which Auden can use with great effect – flippancy, humour, irony, and in particular *ambivalence*, the device by which, judged by different standards, the same set of events can be seen as funny and sad, ignoble and heroic, touching and silly, petty and significant, at once. Yet in some personal poems, about his mixed response to the Spanish Civil War (he wanted to feel stirred by heroism, but instead felt a strong desire to get away, and also that all war, even for the best causes, is horrible), and about his first wife's leaving him for another man (he wanted to feel forgiving and magnanimous, but felt intolerable spite and jealousy), Spender achieves not an intellectual but an emotional ambivalence, through his fine and painful intimacy with his own feelings. He is a poet, like Hardy (whom he does not resemble in any other respect), who is often most adroit when he looks most gauche.

Day Lewis's special quality as a poet is a gift for handling abstract ideas and their relations to each other poetically, and a subtlety, conscious or unconscious, of complex statement that, if it is not quite metaphysical 'wit', has something in common with the probing ruminations of more thoughtful Victorian poets like Clough or Hardy. His weakness is a certain thinness of imagery, idiom, and verbal texture. He has neither the physical reality of Auden nor the emotional density of Spender. He is too ready to accept current jargon without asking himself whether it is readily translatable into poetic metaphor. His later poetry, slower and richer in movement, marks a definite advance on his poetry of the 1930s, technically, but it is also marked by a growing archaism of tone and language and a conscious retreat from topical concerns.

MacNeice was the most concerned with the merely personal, or the truly immediate: with what we see and feel, our particular ties to places and people, and the complicated momentary knots these form. Though MacNiece lacked Auden's range and unexpectedness, lacked also Auden's various and carelessly abundant technical mastery, he was the most common-sensical, the most balanced of these four poets. He was the least scared of the pleasure principle, the least self-punishing. His special weaknesses (which appear in his early work more than his later) are a too conscious smartness and sophistication, the knowing insider's tone; a failure, again more noticeable in the earlier work, to make vivid images or witty lines cohere in a convincing whole; and, more in his later, longer poems, a tendency simply to improvise, to go on too long, using technique and ingenuity as a substitute for the growing slow pressures of feeling by which lasting poetry is built up; a tendency also to moralize, in a wholesome but rather obvious way, without proper application or qualification, and again sometimes at great length. But sharp observation and sardonic wit, as well as an occasional finely Irish direct rudeness, mark the later poems as much as the earlier ones.

Two other poets of the 1930s who had not such a wide public, who were thought of mainly as clever writers of light verse, but who tend today to be taken much more seriously than that, were William Plomer and John Betjeman. When I wrote the first version of this book Betjeman was the special taste of a minority who hugged their appreciation to themselves; he was very much of a clique highbrow taste; he has now, with his *Collected Poems*, become a best-seller and in liking him as I still do, one is likely to be thought of as a sentimental middlebrow. However, Betjeman appealed to the most notable younger poet of the 1930s, Auden, and still appeals to a poet who might be claimed as the leading younger poet of the 1950s, Philip Larkin. One is not in such bad company after all. One element in Betjeman's popularity in the 1950s was probably that he expressed the mood and sentiment of a recrudescent conservatism that went far wider than politics; a tendency for many people to look sentimentally and narrowly back towards older elements of the English life, because it seemed uncomfortable to look realistically forward. Betjeman is certainly not very likely ever to have a wide international or even American reputation. He is too local. He requires his readers to carry in their heads a map of London, so that 'the curious Anglo-Norman parish church of Kentish Town' or the now vanished trolley-buses diminishing towards Highbury, or the polychromatic wall of a Victorian church, St Saviour's, Aberdeen Park, at once ring a bell; it is period flavour not intrinsic beauty he is looking for, so that it might be said that not only in his attitude to English architecture, but also to English life, he has become something he once denounced in a prose essay, a 'sentimental antiquarian'. Yet no perception of the world so exact and specialized as Betjeman's can finally be dismissed as merely sentimental. In their Cornish seaside bungalow, the children of Mrs Hanks (sometimes in the late 1920s or early 1930s) are preparing for a dance:

> Norman and Gordon in their dancing pumps
> Slide up and down, but can't make concrete smooth.
> 'My Sweet Hortense. . . .'
> Sings louder down the garden than the sea.
> 'A practice record, Phoebe, Mummykins,
> Gordon and I will do the washing-up.'
> 'We picnic here! we scrounge and help ourselves,'
> Says Mrs Hanks, and visitors will smile
> To see them all turn to it.

For an expert in popular music 'My Sweet Hortense' probably dates this episode precisely. So the Christian names Norman, Gordon, and Phoebe, the expression 'mummykins', and Mrs Hanks's perhaps faintly forced cheerfulness about doing without servants and the family lending a hand, are enough for a sufficiently informed English reader to place the Hanks family in their exact social stratum. There is a wealth of implication, of digested and implicit knowledge, behind Betjeman's deceptively simple surfaces, and the feelings he arouses in us are often not simple. At a first glance this passage might appear almost cloyingly sympathetic; at a second glance, we see that the Hanks *ménage* is 'placed' as coolly and distantly as a satirical novelist might place it. We are left with a complicated feeling of recognizing both an element of comic pretence and one of human grit and decency in a milieu we might have been tempted to feel merely cheaply superior about. Such a complicated feeling cannot be dismissed as 'sentimental'; though a readiness to be unembarrassed by natural sentiment, whether his own or that of his characters, is one of Betjeman's strengths.

Betjeman's appeal is probably, in spite of his very wide public, predominantly a class and age-group appeal: to the lower-upper middle classes, especially those living on pensions or fixed incomes in a time of rising prices and notable social mobility, up and down. It is also an appeal to latent and inarticulate Christian and conservative sentiments, which are often particularly strong in those, like some of his more intellectual admirers, who call themselves agnostics and regularly vote Labour. Any reader of Betjeman, who wants to enjoy him, must at least provisionally accept this profound conservatism of his, even when it is concerned with what is no longer there to conserve. Thus in *Sunday in Ireland* the 'native Irish', the Julias, Maeves, and Maureens going to Mass, are summed up with an almost harsh statement:

> Stone-walled cabins thatched with reeds,
> Where a Stone Age people breeds
>   The last of Europe's stone age race.

Betjeman's deep and poignant regrets are not for all the things the native Irish, now resurgent, suffered under long oppression, but for the dead and buried, narrow and stiff and proud Protestant Ascendancy:

> There in pinnacled protection
>   One extinguished family waits
> A Church of Ireland resurrection
>   By the broken, rusty gates.

> Sheepswool, straw and droppings cover
> Graves of spinsters, rake and lover,
> Whose fantastic mausoleum
> Sings its own seablown Te Deum
> In and out the slipping slates.

The conservatism comes out again in the moving poem on the death of King George V:

> Old men who never cheated, never doubted,
> Communicated monthly, sit and stare
> At the new suburb stretched beyond the runway
> Where a young man lands hatless from the air.

'Communicated monthly': the reticent, precise, very Anglican phrase reflects the quality of Betjeman's own religious experience, a bleak, dutiful, puzzled, and nervous one. One of his most moving poems, *Before the Anaesthetic, or a Real Fright*, distinguishes it sharply from his aesthetic experience:

> Illuminated missals – spires –
> Wide screens and decorated quires –
> All these I loved and on my knees
> I thanked myself for knowing these
> And watched the morning sunlight pass
> Through the richly stained Victorian glass
> And in the colour-shafted air
> I, kneeling, thought the Lord was there.
> Now, lying in the gathering mist
> I know that Lord did not exist;
> Now, lest this 'I' should cease to be,
> Come real Lord, come quick to me ...

And in one of his most directly moving poems, *On a Portrait of a Dead Man*, he distinguishes with a similar honest sharpness between the consolation which is formally present in religious belief and that which, faced with a real loss, we actually find there:

> He would have liked to say good-bye,
> Shake hands with many friends,
> In Highgate now his finger-bones
> Stick through his finger-ends.

You, God, who treat him thus and thus,
Say, 'Save his soul and pray.'
You ask me to believe You and
I only see decay.

Betjeman is also, of course, an acknowledged master of humorous light verse, but it is on his more serious side, his poetry of personal attachment, that I have preferred to dwell. The seriousness does, of course, also express itself through humour and the humour even in a piece like *The Arrest of Oscar Wilde at the Cadogan Hotel* intended for mock-melodramatic recitation is never wholly shallow. John Sparrow, in his excellent essay on Betjeman, speaks of that poem as 'an attempt to create an atmosphere of "period" by wheeling on the old stage properties – the astrakhan coat, the hock and seltzer, *The Yellow Book* – all too conscientiously into place': he might have added that the third and second last stanzas (entry of the police) are pure burlesque; but the very last stanza, even while we are laughing our heads off, does suddenly remind us with the lines,

He staggered – and terrible-eyed,
He brushed past the palms on the staircase ...

that poor Wilde's farce was after all a tragic one. We are suddenly a little ashamed of ourselves for having been so heartlessly amused. Betjeman can be facile and his blank-verse autobiography, *Summoned by Bells,* seems to me to have very little poetry in it and to be primarily a bit of over-ripe character-acting, for an over-indulgent audience. But at his best Betjeman is a subtly sincere writer, light in hand but true in feeling, in the tradition of Prior, Praed, Thackeray, and in the tradition indeed of the more intimate and domestic side of greater poets than Praed or Thackeray, Tennyson, Browning, even Hardy. He is, at his best, too skilful a poet ever to have been effectively parodied or to have found an effective imitator or competitor.

William Plomer is neither an imitator nor a competitor, he is as cosmopolitan as Betjeman is insular, a South African who has lived in Japan and Greece, but who has a knowledge of London as intensive as Betjeman's, and who shares with Betjeman a fondness for the oddities and minutiae of the Victorian and Edwardian past. He started as a friend and contemporary of Roy Campbell's in South Africa, writing poetry of hot tropical directness:

> Limpopo and Tugel churned
> In flood for brown and angry miles
> Melons, maize, domestic thatch,
> The trunks of trees and crocodiles. ...

Even in that early poem there is a certain detachment, the powerful, primitive force of the romantic landscape is grasped with admiration but also with a certain ironic detachment, as a mindless splendour, a churning indiscriminate destructiveness. Plomer, who is also an excellent writer of prose, is above all the civilized observer, never surprised, never frantically enthusiastic or condemnatory, often wryly amused, but never wholly unsympathetic. His Spanish Civil War poem is an epitaph for a character like himself:

> He was rash enough to go out for a breath of fresh air;
> He loved freshness and was tired of the nerves and cigarettes
> Of partisans and non-partisans crowded in rooms
> And the priggish claptrap of the doctrinaire know-all.

When he looks back on the 1930s, as in a fine poem *Father and Son: 1939*, there is wry clear-sightedness but affection:

> With a firm grasp of half-truths, with political short-sight,
> With a belief we could disarm but at the same time fight,
> And that only the Left Wing could ever be right,
> And that Moscow, of all places, was the sole source of light:
>> Just like a young hopeful
>> Between the wars.

He likes to make poems out of odd and slightly off-colour characters and incidents: the haunch of a horse blown during the war by bomb-blast into a vegetarian guest-house; an Edwardian stockbroker shot at in the park by a mad post-office clerk; an absent-minded Victorian naturalist who has eaten almost every conceivable kind of food and who ends by gobbling up the heart of a dead Bourbon king; a German woman refugee who vanishes after going out with a basket to gather mushrooms; Daisy Princess of Pless, in a smart sailor suit at Kiel in 1903, wondering if she is dressing too young, though her figure is still perfect, for her twenty-nine years. Plomer, one might say, is a connoisseur of the odd which is also the touching, of strikingly queer and eccentric episodes that help one to realize how bizarre all social conventions, and all actual personalities, are to a detached view. He is a much more grown-up writer than Betjeman, he can at least seem an unkinder one, he does not go in for quite such broad farce or such direct sentiment, and therefore has never attained Betjeman's popularity. Yet for a quality of spare, witty, urbane intelligence, and for perfect manners in poetry as in prose, he deserves to be much more widely known than he is. E. M. Forster has described Plomer as his 'favourite contemporary poet' and he resembles Forster in combining a cool head with a warm heart, tolerance with vigour.

Auden and his group were all, as young men, at Oxford, and began to make their first reputation as poets there. Cambridge in the late 1920s also had a group of brilliant undergraduates, William Empson, Ronald Bottrall, Charles Madge, Kathleen Raine, who began in the 1930s to make their names as poets, but who never, as it were, hit the headlines quite in the same fashion as Auden's group, and who were not themselves a 'group' in the same sense. Young writers at Oxford have always tended to have a closer hold on the world of London literary journalism, the world of literary fashion, than young writers at Cambridge. Cambridge has traditionally been famous for the attention it pays to mathematics, to science, to the analytic faculties of the mind. It might be said that Oxford is romantic and worldly, Cambridge unworldly and yet realistic. Two teachers at Cambridge in the late 1920s and early 1930s had a notable influence on young poets there, Dr I. A. Richards and Dr F. R. Leavis. Richards was more scientific in his approach, striving to base critical methods and principles on a theory of psychological balance which was his own personal invention, Leavis was more literary, using his literary findings to reinforce moral and cultural judgements, but both insisted on students paying a very close attention to the given text of a poem, to the 'words upon the page'. Like Richards, Leavis tried to instil into his pupils the feeling that a good poem is a complex and delicately balanced structure, and that success in writing a poem is related to the complexity and delicate equilibrium of our grasp of the world around us; but he also insisted, perhaps more vigorously than Richards, on the rootedness of good English poetry, that its strength springs out of common speech and common feeling. Both Richards and Leavis felt that in poetry a gross appeal to stock sentiments, a flattering use of familiar images, a mechanically lulling and hypnotic use of metre, are immoral: it is not the business of poetry to waft us away into dreamland but to make us more intensely, and alertly, awake. The young poets who were exposed to the influence of Richards and Leavis, bracing but sometimes rather bleak as that influence was, tended, therefore, to have an extreme self-consciousness lacking in Oxford poets of the same generation. The Cambridge poets were very much aware of the necessity for a complex intellectual structure to underpin the direct emotional impact of a poem. They wrote, as it were, 'as ever in the great taskmaster's eye'.

This extremely sensitive but in the end almost self-defeating self-consciousness was very well represented in the work of Ronald Bottrall, whom Leavis regarded as by far the most accomplished and the most promising of the younger Cambridge poets of the late 1920s and early 1930s. Bottrall seems to me to be a poet of very real talent who has crippled himself by a fear of over-simplification, and a back-breaking worry about how several audiences at once, the severe Cambridge one, the smart London one, and so on, will take him:

> Eager to embrace every fresh manifestation
> Of intellectual and political snobbery,
> He was nevertheless too watchful for the revelation
> To outlast more recent and more successful jobbery.

His material home was a neutral country,
His stock-in trade litmus paper,
His spiritual home a Laodicean chantry,
His badge a chameleon couchant on a cloud of vapour.

Careful to avoid undisciplined enthusiasm,
He always watched for the week-end reviewers
Before committing himself to a criticism
Of new works by even solidly established authors.

Not that he was behindhand in appraising
A really *épatant* technique
Once he had got the appropriate phrasing
From the impresario of the clique. ...

These excellent stanzas take over the technique of Pound's
Mauberley, to which the young Bottrall may well have been
introduced by Leavis. They are admirable both as satire and
also, I take it, as admirably honest self-irony. At the same
time one has the sense of the poet caught up in a spider's
web; the literary world of pretence and chatter at once re-
pels, frightens, and fascinates him. The skill in the writing of
these stanzas, and the amused, painful complexity of feeling
behind them, is not being applied to something of very wide
or deep human relevance; this is the poet as a professional
talking to other literary professionals, not the poet as a man
talking to other men. Bottrall is a copious and various poet,
equipped both for experience and for the delicate measuring
of experience, but sometimes lax or rough in his writing,
and sometimes over-intricate. On the whole, comparing his
promise with his achievement, he must be judged an interesting failure, but, at its most uneven, his poetry reflects
the masculine strength of his mind.

William Empson is a much less copious poet, whose great
reputation is based (apart from his better-known prose critical writings) on two short volumes of verse, one published
around 1930, the other, *The Gathering Storm*, in 1940. A
Collected Poems in the early 1950s, long expected and long
delayed, added only three or four new poems, mostly short,
and part of the versification of a playlet put on by Sheffield

students when Her Majesty the Queen visited Sheffield University, where Empson is now Professor of English. Empson's style is much less overlaid with contemporary mannerisms than Bottrall's, whose work often suggests the direct influence of Pound or Eliot. The strongest influence on Empson's verse has been Donne, whom he does not, however, in the movement of his verse or the tone of his voice, very closely resemble. He reminds one rather of later poets, of the Caroline period and the early Restoration, Waller, Marvell, Rochester, the young Dryden. Empson aims at a tone sharp and exact, fairly near that of lively conversation or good prose. His thought is extremely condensed, his feeling, which is deep and strong, conveyed by restraint and compression rather than by an expansive flow. Nevertheless, in spite of the admirable decorum and poise of his poems, the bluff, no-nonsense air of their tone of voice, Empson is an extremely puzzling poet, more difficult, for many readers, than even Eliot. The difficulty is not of Eliot's kind. It comes largely from the abundant use in Empson's poetry of references to scientific theories or experiments or to mathematical ideas which are unfamiliar to the ordinary reader; from a fondness for setting the reader puzzles, rather like crossword puzzles, of which Empson is a great addict. He has a great taste, also, for seriously used puns and his longest and most ambitious poem, *Bacchus*, works on a series of puns on all the key words. The poem can be read, according to which senses one stresses, as an account of the myth of Bacchus; a scientific description of the processes of fermentation and distillation; and as an interpretation, a melancholy and pessimistic one, of human history, in terms of the progressive or successive stages of drunkenness in the individual. The reader ought to grasp all these implications simultaneously; but without the entertaining prose notes which Empson provides for this and other more difficult poems, even an intelligent and well-informed reader would often be justified in feeling lost.

Empson thus obviously makes a rather narrow and corrupting appeal to those who like to plume themselves on their knowingness and cleverness, on being on the inside rather than the outside; and indeed one of the less agreeable features both of his verse and his prose, though it can melt down into an innocuous and disarming facetiousness, is an effect like a snicker, the snicker of someone who knows, and revels in knowing, a nasty secret. But there is more in Empson than this. He can seem all affectation; but there is no real affectation about his *tone*, everything that he writes, both in prose and in verse, has the run of his speaking voice, an odd, sad, snarly voice, rising now and again to a very high pitch, the Cambridge voice of the late 1920s. This voice, pouncing and drawling, is natural to him and it is an excellent instrument for expressing anger, scorn, and melancholy despair. In can be heard at its full range in these lines, contemplating, in 1938 or so, war-theatened Europe from the vantage of war-torn China (the Japanese had just invaded Manchuria):

> I slept, and blank as that I yet would lie.
> Till you have seen what a threat holds below
> The heart of standing is you cannot fly.
>
> Tell me again about Europe and her pains,
> Who's tortured by the drought, who by the rains,
> Glut me with floods where only the swine can row
> Who cuts his throat and let him count his gains.
> It seemed the best thing to be up and go.
> A bedshift flight to a Far Eastern sky.
> Only the same war on a stronger toe.
> The heart of standing is you cannot fly....

The plot of the poem from which these lines come is that the young Empson, in bed in a flimsy Japanese house with a Japanese lady – he was teaching English in Tokyo – is suddenly awakened by an earthquake and confronted with the depths of fear. The earthquake stands in the poem for the general insecurity of modern society – which opens under our feet in wars, slumps, and revolutions, so that our human courage seems unable to face it. Empson would like to escape from the earthquake, and from our modern world, into deep dreamless sleep. There is no prospect of that or of escape from the world-wide human crisis and in any case the essence of courage – 'the heart of standing' – is usually simply that one cannot fly away. Empson had thought he could fly away from 'Europe and her pains', but in the Far East had found 'only the same war on a stronger toe' (dancing on its toes, I think, like Shiva the Hindu God of Creation through Destruction). But the poet's very attempts to escape, his experience in the earthquake of the individual helplessness before the forces of nature (and before also, it is implied, the equally ruthless and impersonal forces that are shaping history), has taught him a sardonic and paradoxical courage, the courage and the sense of freedom based on the knowledge of necessity: 'The heart of standing is you cannot fly.'

Perhaps one central quality of Empson as a poet is his sense of the attractiveness and fruitfulness of contradictions, his sense of the human situation as paradoxical. He likes the illogicality of the human species, its ability to eat its cake and have it too. He sees this as a source of moral strength. Thus he praises in John Donne, a sincerely Christian poet, 'the secret largeness of outlook' which enables him to transfer in two famous poems the praise usually lavished on Christ – that he is the Logos, the divine force that gives the universe its shape and holds it together – on an unknown young woman. Empson has the same largeness of outlook, but there is nothing 'secret' about it in his case. He differed, for instance, from Auden and Auden's group in having, throughout the 1930s, a deep confidence in the basic soundness of the British people; whenever that had been tested, as by the Hoare–Laval agreement, it had 'answered like a gong'. Yet part of this social sturdiness of his came, also, from taking a much more pessimistic view of the individual human life than was common among Auden and his group. Partly influenced by Buddhism, about which he had learned a great deal during years of teaching in China and Japan, Empson was more aware than any of his contemporaries of the failures of energy and desire, the swallowed bitterness and humiliation, that are involved merely in growing older, in growing towards one's death:

> Not to have fire is to be a skin that shrills.
> The complete fire is death. From partial fires
> The waste remains, the waste remains and kills.

The idea there is that human life is a struggle against natural inertia, which is bound to conquer in the end. Yet it is the struggle, foredoomed in the individual case to failure from the start, that carries the race along, and gives human life its dignity and value. Empson's strict scientific training, and perhaps the general climate of Cambridge in the 1920s left little foothold in his mind for orthodox belief – in much of his later prose writing, particularly in his book *Milton's God*, he has insisted on what he sees as the cruelty and the wickedness of the orthodox Christian concept of Hell and Damnation – but on the other hand he has a strong sense that most of our human values are very intimately bound up with our religious attitudes. And he sometimes seems to be advocating Buddhistic, or life-renouncing, religious attitudes in the place of Christian attitudes which rest on the wish for eternal life, but also overshadow men's minds with the fear of eternal pain.

Empson might be thought of as believing (with one of those ambivalent attitudes of which he is so fond) both that the human aspirations traditionally bound up with religion are directed towards a fiction and yet that fictions of this sort are what give life meaning. Something like this seems to be expressed in these magnificent early lines of his:

> All these large dreams by which men long live well
> Are magic-lanterned on the smoke of hell:
> > This then is real, I have implied,
> > A painted, small transparent slide.

> These the inventive can hand-paint at leisure
> Or most emporia would stock our measure
> > And, feasting in their dappled shade,
> > We should forget how they were made.

The theory expressed in these two stanzas is similar to that expressed by Empson's old tutor, I. A. Richards, in his famous short pamphlet, *Science and Poetry*. Richards suggests there that poetry, unlike science, does not make 'statements' but rather 'pseudo-statements': that is, by the emotive gestures and allusions it makes, it enables us to integrate our inner lives, but we must not look for 'truth' in it in any scientific sense. (This is an early and crude pamphlet of Richards's on which he himself now looks rather askance; and if Empson himself, for instance, is not making 'statements' in these lines I have just quoted, I do not know what he is doing.) More subtly in this poem, starting from such a theory as Richards's that all poetic and religious language is 'pseudo-statement', is merely 'emotive', Empson asks himself whether supposing that the poet is merely playing a trick upon himself, and he knows it to be a trick, the trick will still work. He decides that it just will. If our 'large dreams', by which we hope to live nobly, are mere projections, can we really, when trying to live by their inspirations, 'forget how they were made'? Yes we must 'imagine ... by miracle ... what could not possibly be there' and 'learn a style from a despair'. The poise in these lines between scientific objectivity and imaginative creativeness, and in a deeper sense between rational denial and poetic assent, must have been very difficult to sustain, and perhaps partly accounts for the paucity of Empson's poetic output after *The Gathering Storm* (in which, for that matter, the style is more relaxed than in *Poems*, and in which the themes are moral or political rather than metaphysical). Empson continued to develop in the most interesting way, as a critic, but the poetry that he might have written since 1940 and has not is a great loss to the English poetic tradition. Empson's poetic output is small; of the poets of his own generation, Auden had a more various invention, a greater range of tones, a generally wider scope. I do not think he has greater depth or, in spite of his wider and more supple range, a more penetrating mind than Empson. But Empson's further development as a poet is perhaps prevented by some sort of clash in his temperament between what in the broadest senses could be called disgust and appetite, or horror and amusement, or individual despair and social hope. The distinctively, sometimes disturbingly individual note of Empson's poetry is the way in which a hearty and jovial tone, as of convivial masculine humour, is laid on top of a statement, or vibration of feeling, that could result in a scream of rage or fear.

20

The War Years to 1953

LITERARY history, particularly recent literary history, is always oversimplified. The current legend about the 1940s is that the Second World War, and the appetite for poetry that springs up in a war, caused a great deal of bad poetry to be published and so critical standards were swamped. Young poets without the courage to take up a clear position on political or social matters imitated Dylan Thomas and George Barker, two poets who themselves lacked a formal academic education and whose attitudes, however great their natural talents, were weakened by self-indulgent romanticism; poetry thus, by the later 1940s, had become an affair of Bohemians and little magazines, a poor relation of more serious literature. Then, in 1953, with the death of Dylan Thomas, a powerful but evil influence, clarity and good sense, it is suggested, returned to English poetry with the group of poets who are usually lumped together as 'the Movement'. These were sane and sober young people, critically alert (a number of them were university teachers, or librarians), and they reacted against unnecessary obscurity and worked for an intellectual and moral discipline of feeling, as well as subjecting themselves to the other discipline of strict traditional forms. Poetry thus once more became intellectually respectable; and if these young poets reacted against the sloppy Bohemian neo-romanticism of the 1940s, they did not, on the other hand, return to the naïve political enthusiasms or the equally naïve *engouements* with Marx and Freud of the 1930s. They represented the poetic equivalent of the empirical, analytic tradition in English philosophy, and they also stood for moderation and good sense. They saw the function of poetry not as blindly expressing emotion, but as critically examining and evaluating it. They stood for cool, insular poise. For the enemies of these Movement poets, on the other hand, they stood either for frigid pedantry or for an attempt, socially admirable but poetically disastrous, to discourage all strong emotions, because the recent history of Europe had shown mass emotion to be bloody and dangerous; or they stood for a *petit bourgeois* attempt to arrest social change at a point where it suited a certain particular group of *petit bourgeois*, not intellectual rebels or explorers, but intellectual functionaries.

What a true judgement on the Movement should be will be one of our topics in the next section. What must be emphasized here is that the official Movement portrait of the 1940s is a very biased and selective one. It was during the 1940s, for instance, that Edwin Muir, Robert Graves, and Kathleen Raine began to reach a wide public, and not one of these three can be described as an undisciplined poet. The influences and attitudes of Auden were not yet dead; Roy Fuller, who first became well known with his poems on war themes, owed a great deal technically to Auden and shared the sharp radicalism of view, the Marxist or near-Marxist coloration, of some of Auden's early poems. Older poets like Roy Campbell were producing some of their best work, and younger poets like David Gascoyne and Vernon Watkins were writing poetry, as were John Heath-Stubbs and Sidney Keyes, which was indeed deliberately romantic, but which was also scholarly and controlled. War poets like Keith Douglas (a man of very great promise, killed in his early twenties in the Normandy landings) and Alun Lewis wrote poems of fine, strict honesty arising directly out of their war experiences. A sentimental, documentary poetry of war experience was much more typical of the new poetry by younger writers at that time than attempts to imitate Dylan Thomas. In the Middle East a group of poets, of whom the most important were Lawrence Durrell, Bernard Spencer, and Terence Tiller, wrote poetry expressing the reactions of the civilized English exile to the decay and splendour, the comedy and pathos, of Eastern Mediterranean life. Historic-ally, the 1940s were a broken-up period, five years of war, followed by five or more spartan years of Crippsian peace. For young poets, these years offered a wide range of experience, a variety of companionship and scene, but very little opportunity to put down roots. It is fair to say that in the 1940s many potential talents were nipped in the bud (Douglas, Alun Lewis, and Sidney Keyes died in the war) or ran to seed or to waste. It is also true that there were no dominating figures nor generally accepted standards; but this open-textured world, with no rigid groups or fixed allegiances, was not hostile to good poetry, even if it let some imperfect poetry through. Nor were the little magazines like *Poetry London* and *Poetry Quarterly* wholly absurd from a critical point of view; they contained, for instance, articles on American poets like Wallace Stevens or John Peale Bishop, whom the more academic critics of the 1950s were to discover ten or fifteen years later. They were up to date also in their appreciation of English poets; Eliot's *Four Quartets*, the greatest poetic achievement of the 1940s, were welcomed as soon as they appeared. In *Poetry London*, around 1941, I wrote a long review of Empson's *The Gathering Storm*; towards the end of the decade, in 1949 or so, John Wain wrote a much longer article on Empson in *Penguin New Writing*. Wain's piece set a younger generation of poets reading Empson, which was excellent, and imitating some of his more imitable mannerisms, which was not so good. Mine, so far as I know, though it made many of the same points as Wain, had no effect on anybody at all. But it would be possible, I think, to make an anthology of poems, and also of critical articles, written in the 1940s that would compare very well with a similar compilation that one could make to represent the 1950s. The reputation of a decade is often an agreed fiction. It is part of literary tactics for every new generation of young men to run down their immediate predecessors.

Yet behind an agreed fiction there are always at least some facts. Those who criticize the 1940s as a spoof decade in poetry are probably thinking of a movement called the New

Apocalypse. This was an unfortunate title; it lent itself all too easily to jokes about epileptic, apoplectic, elliptical, and apocryphal writing. Indeed, as the movement widened, and drew in new adherents like the pacifist and anarchist poet, Alex Comfort, it became more usual and more tactful to describe it as Neo-Romanticism. Three great influences behind it, though of these three probably only Read *approved* of it, were Herbert Read, Dylan Thomas, and George Barker, all in their different ways poets of the image rather than the statement; more broadly, there was a wish to get away from the colloquial diction and urban imagery and topical slant which Auden was felt to stand for towards something more florid, more savage, more lavishly ornate. The poets connected with the New Apocalypse at or near the beginning included Henry Treece, J. F. Hendry, Nicholas Moore, Vernon Watkins, Tom Scott, and myself. But like many 'movements' this one existed more as a concept than a reality; I only met Treece long after the party was over, and never met Hendry. I think a number of the other poets, including perhaps Watkins, Moore, Scott, and myself, were already writing the sort of poetry we would write anyway, but were pleased to be anthologized and too naïve, then, to realize the disadvantages of being given a label.

One strong, more general influence, however, behind both the New Apocalypse and the wider Neo-Romantic trend, was the influence of Surrealism, which in the late 1930s had been introduced to England in two attractive books, one written by David Gascoyne, the other edited by Herbert Read. What interested young poets in Surrealism was its experiments in automatic and semi-automatic writing, its contempt for obvious logic and traditional form, its use of unrelated, or violently incongruous, apparently meaningless juxtapositions of phrase. The English Neo-Romantics however did not, except in a few deliberately *outré* experiments like some of Dylan Thomas's dark prose poems and Hugh Sykes Davies's *Petron*, go all, or perhaps much, of the way with Surrealism. They felt rather that there was an inner logic, or a dream logic, in the images that emerged from the unconscious mind and that it was not the business of the poet to analyse these images intellectually (or at least, it was not his business in the poem), to reject those among the presented images that appeared to him trivial or incoherent and to mould the rest, by tact and intuition rather than some reasoned principle, into a pleasing poetic shape. 'In the destructive element immerse – that is the way': the Neo-Romantics, like the earlier poets who interpreted it differently, might have taken this phrase from Conrad's *Lord Jim* as their watchword. It was the business, they thought, of the poet to communicate rather than to interpret a message from the dark; and to let feeling and imagination, working on the message, help it to take a poetic shape. The usefulness of this idea was that it could enable young poets to tap a great deal of rich if confusing material; its weakness was that it slackened the poet's grip on the reins and made it too easy for him to deceive himself, if not to deceive others. Yet this approach to poetry, if it lent itself too easily to imitative or weakly associative writing, could produce interesting results. I would like now to illustrate these in some detail. And I would like to say something more about Surrealism, which was a European movement of great importance, however minor its influence on English art and literature may have been.

The Surrealists were interested in a total revolution in the consciousness of man by which he might transcend the everyday world. Outer reality (that is to say, the physical world around us, our perception of that, the social world around us, our adjustment to it through habit and language) was of no interest in itself to the Surrealists but was only material for transformation for various acts of creative fantasy or radical metamorphosis. Perception was to become hallucination, emotion paranoia, thought the most arbitrary and obscure set of private associations; and though the Surrealist had to start off, like the rest of us, from brute fact or crude reality, his ambition was to reach a stage where he would be cut off from it, or would have transcended it, for good.

For the true Surrealist, 'aesthetic' or 'formalist' demands were just another bourgeois superstition; a Surrealist text or picture has not the purpose of being a beautiful object to be contemplated or a psychologically harmonious whole. On the contrary, it aims at disruption. It has the purely practical purpose of loosening the reader's or the spectator's grip on everyday reality, boring a hole, as it were, that will let the great floods through, and thus playing its small part in the grand task of the total transformation of the world. It is there to remind us how near we are to madness and to push us nearer to that brink. Once the concepts of form and control are introduced, the case is altered; a poet like Dylan Thomas, who used very confusing dream material, very like that of the Surrealists, did not see himself as embracing confusion for its own sake but as pushing up through it towards the light.

The main scientific basis of Surrealism is the psychology of Freud, according to which dreams, verbal errors, neurotic obsessions, accidents, and so on, are all means by which suppressed sexual and homicidal desires, based on the archetypal Oedipal situation, force an awareness of their presence, in a disguised form, on the conscious mind. The conscious mind rejects them because they are disgusting and criminal (in the archetypal case we want to make love to our mothers and murder our fathers) and seem to bring with their conscious admission the threat of the direst punishments. The neurotic condition can be cured when the patient becomes conscious of his suppressed impulses, conscious, on the other hand, that he does not *really* want to act on them and therefore becomes ready to cease punishing himself. The difference between Freud and the Surrealists was that he wanted the rational part of the mind, the Ego, to keep the Super-ego, the punisher, and the Id, the criminal, in so far as possible in control. The ideal of the Surrealists was something like a fusion or mating of Id and Super-ego, what Blake called a 'marriage of Heaven and Hell', and a total disappearance of the rational Ego. There was, as I have suggested already, a mystical element in Surrealism; in its own odd way, it wished, like some of the great religions, to deliver man from the burden of selfhood.

English poets, even if they have at one time admired the Surrealists, have on the whole been less influenced by Freud than by his one-time disciple and later rival, Jung. Jung thought that dream-imagery and much traditional poetic imagery does not so much represent the suppressed desires of the individual as a latent race memory; in some obscure way we each recapitulate at our deeper levels the whole history of the race, and that explains the universal validity of what Jung calls archetypal images, in particular the effectiveness of mythological imagery in poetry long after we have ceased to believe in myths. The poetic use of images in Jung's sense takes the poet back to symbolism, no longer, however, the enclosed and 'literary' symbolism of Mallarmé, which we considered in an earlier chapter, but the symbol as a way of expressing certain universal emotions or aspirations (the Mourning Mother, the Crucified God) which can indeed be put into abstract language but which are most powerfully and simply expressed for the emotions in archetypal images. It should be added that there are poets, like Robert Graves and Kathleen Raine, who would deny that in the best poets these archetypal images spring unexplained from the unconscious mind; rather the best poets gather from their predecessors, and from certain sacred texts on religion or philosophy, a traditional language of symbols, with agreed and rigorously fixed meanings.

Let us illustrate these points by considering a number of texts which illustrate in turn (i) the pure Surrealist method; (ii) the 'neo-romantic' attempt, in the 1940s, to impose a formal or aesthetic order on the Surrealist method and to struggle up to light out of the confusion of dark images; (iii) the conscious use of images as lucid symbols of some human experience not otherwise so simply and forcibly expressible.

Here are some examples of (i):

(a)   Sisters of nothing ready for everything
     sisters of flowers without roots

sisters of rebel children
tiny
indifferent
reduced by the intellect
to reason to die of it
reduced in your secrets
abandoned strangers
my distant companions
with sentimental flesh
beautiful hardly beautiful but always beautiful
more simple than misfortune
more precious than the beauty
of your slaughtered lips
of your undermined smile
you entrust your poisons to me
O mithridatized ones
   and I oppose to love
   ready-made images
   not images to be made

             PAUL ÉLUARD

(b) The aeroplane weaves the telegraph wires
     and the stream sings the same song
     at the pull-up for cabmen they drink orange drinks
     but the railway mechanics have white eyes
     and the lady has lost her smile in the world

             PHILLIPE SOUPAULT

(c) Last night the wind blew so hard that I thought
     it was going to batter the rocks into pasteboard.
     Throughout the time of darkness the electric lights
     burned like hearts;
     in my third sleep I awoke near a lake
     where the waters of two streams were coming to die.
     Around the table women were reading.
     And the monk was silent in the shadow.
     Slowly I crossed the bridge and at the bottom of the turbid
         water
     I saw the slow passing of big black fish.
     All at once I found myself in a big square town.
     All the windows were shut, there was silence everywhere,
     Everywhere meditation.

And the monk again passed beside me. Through the holes
    of his rotten robe
  I saw the beauty of his body pale and white like a statue
    of love.
On waking happiness once again slept beside me.

GIORGIO DI CHIRICO

(d)   give tear twist and kill I traverse illuminate and
     burn caress and lick embrace and look I sound at
     every flight and bells till they bleed frightening
     the pigeons and I make them fly around the dovecot
     till they fall to earth already dead of weariness
     I will raze all the windows and doors to the earth
     and with your hair I will hang all the birds that are
     singing and cut down all the flowers I will take the lamp
    in my arms and give it my breast to eat and will
    go to sleep alongside the song of my solitude
    by *Soleares* and I will etch the fields of wheat and
    hay and I shall see them die supine with their faces
    to the sun and I will wrap the flowers in the newspaper and
    I will fling them through the window
    in the gutterstream that is hurrying by with all its
    sins on its back but laughing all the same to make
    its nest in the sewer and I will break the music of
    the woodlands against the rocks of the waves of the
    sea and I will bite the lion on the cheek and I
    will make the wolf cry for tender pity in front
    of the portrait of the water which is letting its arms
    fall slackly into the wash-hand basin.

PICASSO

None of these passages is completely uncontrolled
(Picasso's, for instance, however wild and formless it seems,
has a density that suggests it has been carefully worked
over). Éluard is almost classically lucid and the passage I
have quoted from him is rather a meditation on the bewildering nature of the image than an evocation of the bewildering image itself. The 'sisters of nothing ready for
everything' *are* the images often apparently meaningless
and not even strikingly and obviously beautiful ('beautiful
hardly beautiful but always beautiful') that come to the poet

quite spontaneously, that are 'given'. If he tries to explain them rationally he destroys their poetic power ('reduced by the intellect to reason to die of it'). The images come from the depths of the mind, from our repressed sufferings and desires there, and therefore from the point of view of the punishing conscience, or Super-ego, are 'poisonous', though, like the eastern king Mithridates, who in fear of ultimate assassination took small daily doses of arsenic and other venoms, they have gradually become accustomed to the poisonous atmosphere around them and immune to it. That is to say, the fact that dream images may, from the point of view of the Super-ego, have a sordid hidden meaning does not prevent them from also having a true and mysterious poetic beauty. The poet equates these 'images still to be made' – images, that is, which have not yet been poetically destroyed by being given too firm an outline or set in an intellectual context – with the idea of love, which he opposes to the 'ready-made image' (our conventional perceptions, and, more widely, the traditional images of mere rhetoric, mere literature, as opposed to the sacred poetic mystery). Love, that is to say, is for the poet the sense of endless potentiality, as opposed to any limited act. Here, still active, we can see Rimbaud's leading idea of the transformability of the world through poetry. One might compare an English poem by Robert Graves:

> He is quick, thinking in clear images;
> I am slow, thinking in broken images.
> He becomes dull, trusting to his clear images;
> I become sharp, mistrusting my broken images. . . .

In Soupault's little poem, on the other hand, the images have been a little too consciously 'broken'. It is a series of statements of the type, 'The X is Y', or 'The X does Y', where Y is a property one does not think of X as having or an action one does not think of X as performing. The effect, here, is one of lyrical fantasy, but obviously with sufficient repetition the trick would become unbearably monotonous. In many Surrealist poems it does.

Chirico's poem, on the other hand, has the same atmosphere as many of his early paintings, the transformation of dream-material into a solid and objective-looking landscape which conveys, however, a strong feeling of loneliness and frustrated desire. Picasso's passage is an imitation in language of some state of delirious excitement, probably erotic in origin: 'Picasso's dazzling and disconcerting flow of colours and materials,' says Georges Hugnet, 'is transformed in his poems into aggressive, highly coloured, flamboyant images used in continuous passages worked and reworked until they become a strange kaleidoscopic saraband.' There is the same formal drawback to this type of writing as to Soupault's: at first vivid, startling, and bewildering, it gradually loses impact, since, however richly reworked to thicken its texture, it is not a development but an endless repetition. One short passage is exciting; a longer passage would soon become unreadable; a series of short passages, once the reader had grasped the trick, would become a bore. Chirico's description of a dream landscape has not these faults, it is evocative and as a series of statements about an imaginary scene perfectly clear; but it can only be written by the poet whose imagination is *primarily* that of the painter, for whom words serve merely for transcription. Thus of all these passages only Éluard's is primarily poetical and formally satisfactory; and it is untypical of the Surrealist purpose.

Here are some examples of (ii):

(a)   Turn on your side and bear the day to me
      Beloved, sceptre-struck, immured
      In the glass wall of sleep. Slowly
      Uncloud the borealis of your eye
      And show your iceberg secrets, your midnight prizes
      To the green-eyed world and me. Sins
      Coil upwards into thin air when you awaken
      And again morning announces when amnesty over
      The serpent-kingdomed bed. ...

               GEORGE BARKER

(b)   The season's anguish, crashing whirlwind, ice,
      Have passed, and cleansed the trodden paths
      The silent gardeners have strewn with ash.

      The iron circles of the sky
      Are worn away by tempest;
      Yet in this garden there is no more strife:
      The Winter's knife is buried in the earth.
      Pure music is the cry that tears
      The birdless branches in the wind.
      No blossom is reborn. The blue
      Stare of the pond is blind.

      And no-one sees
      A restless stranger through the morning stray
      Across the sodden lawn, whose eyes
      Are tired of weeping, in whose breast
      A savage sun consumes its hidden day.
                                DAVID GASCOYNE

(c)   The force that through the green fuse drives the flower
      Drives my green age; that blasts the roots of trees
      Is my destroyer.
      And I am dumb to tell the crooked rose
      My youth is bent by the same wintry fever.

      The force that drives the water through the rocks
      Drives my red blood; that dries the mouthing streams
      Turns mine to wax.
      And I am dumb to mouth unto my veins
      How at the mountain spring the same mouth sucks ...
                                DYLAN THOMAS

Sprung on the reader without warning, these three passages might appear obscure, but, read immediately after our selection of Surrealist texts, they probably seem to have, at least by comparison, a refreshing clarity. They are composed, like the Surrealist texts, in images rather than in conceptual statements, but they have a conceptual background; it is fairly easy to relate them, where it is difficult or impossible to relate the Surrealist text, to the world we ordinarily live in. They start from that world, they look at it in a new way but do not attempt to transform it utterly, and they can be referred back to it. In a certain brilliant incoherence of imagery, George Barker, here, is most like the Surrealists and it would be useful to compare his passage with the earlier one by Picasso. We do not see why a result of being sceptre-struck should be being walled up in glass though we see how glass could suggest the iceberg image – Barker wrote these lines before Francis Bacon had begun to exhibit his paintings of screaming paranoiacs frozen into great blocks of ice – and how the iceberg image in its turn could suggest the green-eyed world (we remember the ice as green as emerald in *The Ancient Mariner*). The fact that sins 'coil upwards' in one line prepares us for the serpents in the next line as does the poet's remembering that a serpent introduced sin into the garden of Eden. And 'kingdomed' in the same line refers back to 'sceptre-struck' in the second line, and makes it look less arbitrary. It is not *really* arbitrary, for the sceptre like the serpent is a phallic image, the bed is the male's kingdom, but his maleness can seem to him both the image of kingly and godlike power, like Aaron's rod, and the image of primal rebellion. Where in Picasso's passage there is nothing but arbitrary associations of imagery, held loosely together by the theme that love is both delightful and sinful, here the argument is coherently worked out in such a way that the images, a set of loose word associations if we take them one by one, justify themselves in detail in relation to the arguments taken as an articulated whole.

It is early morning, the poet is awake in bed, waiting for his loved one to wake also. He is worried by a sense of the sinfulness of his love, whose kingly vigour has struck his lady so deep asleep. He is worried by the jealousy of the green-eyed world and by the thought that his sceptre is that of a serpent king, a kingdom of sin, or is itself the primal serpent. He is worried also because of her remoteness from him in sleep, worried perhaps because of some deep frigidity he has not been able to conquer; she seems remote from him as if in a wall of glass, seven-eighths submerged (as she would be under the sheets) like an iceberg, and he thinks of the world of sleep as a remote and icy one of which he will catch a glimpse when she opens her eyes on a world that is jealous of the lover's delight, as the lover perhaps also is jealous of her distant beautiful self-containment, of that coldness of hers, which is part of the quality of all beauty. But when she wakens all these night-waking worries of his will coil upwards and vanish into thin air, though his ability to forget it for a time will not make sin any less real; the bed remains serpent-haunted. . . .

Gascoyne's poem, on the other hand, should be compared with the landscape piece from Chirico. It is a more solid poem, in that the landscape is a real, not an imaginary one, a garden or a public park in winter, and what it symbolizes for the poet is not some special obsession of his (as the monk, the ladies, the pond do for Chirico) but rather the general weariness, sadness, and barrenness of our time, the theme of Eliot's *The Waste Land*. Everything that is said about the garden is true of the poet's state of mind, and on the other hand everything that is said about the poet's state of mind is true about the garden. It is a harsh winter in the war years. Nature, and the poet, and perhaps human history itself, are at the saddest stage of mid-winter deadness and longing for a new spring. Thus this poem is more than a mere transcription of a possible painting; it expresses a set of complex interrelations which can be expressed only in words.

Dylan Thomas's passage can be compared with Soupault's in that its form is a set of statements of the type, 'The X is Y' or 'The X does Y'; but Thomas is aiming not at trivial surprise but at a massive identification. The forces, he is saying, that control the growth and decay, the beauty and terror of human life are the very same forces that we see at work in outer nature. This is a statement which most of us would accept up to a point or with qualifications but the fine, strong shape of Thomas's stanza and the wonderfully active nature of his imagery ('drives', 'blasts', 'dries', 'mouthing', 'sucks') gives it a freshness of discovery and an emotional force, and it also gains in strength from an exchange of qualities between man and nature: we feel a *human* pity for the 'crooked rose' (crooked like a hunchback) and on the other hand the 'wintry fever' of the young man's unsatisfied desires acquires something of the impersonal dignity of a *natural* process. This equation of the human and the natural, and the celebration of both as divine, are Thomas's central themes and they enable him to confer on the adolescent sexual turbulence out of which most of his earlier poems grew, a surprising impersonal dignity (in his later poems he was often more concerned to recapture a childish non-sexual vision of nature as the Garden of Eden). The religious feeling, which has a great deal to do with death, has been described by Empson as a pessimistic pantheism, but it had Christian roots and overtones, and often makes a powerful use of Christian imagery.

It is wrong to dismiss Thomas merely as a good rhetorician, who wove variations on the commonplaces of love and death. He used his fire, his passionate dense imagery in the celebration of all human and material experience. He wrote genuinely for the glory of God, as he understood God, and for the love of man. The celebration of the act of love

> Bird he was brought low,
> Burning in the bride bed of love in the whirl –
> Pool at the wanting centre, in the folds
> of Paradise, in the spun bud of the world.
> And she rose with him flowering in her melting snow

suggests the mystic, not the wild romantic of popular imagination.

Thomas's thematic unity gives to his poems, for all the deliberate tangle and play of his imagery, a heavy central weight, which is not to be found in the work of his imitators. What Barker, Gascoyne, and Thomas, in these extracts, and perhaps generally, have in common, however, is an approach to the theme through the clash of contradictory images rather than a choice of images to illustrate a predetermined theme.

The third kind of poetry of the 1940s we are to consider, poetry of the mythological symbol of the Jungian archetype, is much more transparent in its texture, because the theme, here, does predetermine the imagery: the poet starts not from a rich confusion, but from a clear abstraction.

Here are some examples of (iii):

(a)   There is a fish that quivers in the pool
itself a shadow, but its shadow, clear.
Catch it again and again, it is still there.

Against the flowing stream, its life keeps pace
with death – the impulse and the flash of grace
hiding in its stillness, moves, to be motionless.

No net will hold it – always it will return
when the ripples settle, and the sand –
It lives unmoved, equated with the stream,
as flowers are fit for air, man for his dream.

KATHLEEN RAINE

(b)   Strange that the self's continuum should outlast
The Virgin, Aphrodite, and the Mourning Mother.

KATHLEEN RAINE

(c)   Swordsman of the narrow lips,
Narrow hips and murderous mind,
Fenced with chariots and ships,
By your joculators hailed
The mauled wonder of mankind,
Far to westward you have sailed.

ROBERT GRAVES

(d)   So soon as ever your mazed spirit descends
From daylight into darkness, Man, remember
What you have suffered here in Samothrace,
What you have suffered.

After your passage through Hell's seven floods,
Whose fumes of sulphur will have parched your throat
The Halls of Judgement will loom up before you,
A miracle of jasper and of onyx.
To the left hand there bubbles a black spring
Overshadowed with a great white cypress,
Avoid this spring, which is Forgetfulness;
Though all the common rout rush down to drink,
Avoid this spring.

To the right hand there lies a secret pool
Alive with speckled trout and fish of gold;
A hazel overshadows it. Opinion,
Primeval serpent straggling in the branches,
Darts out his tongue. The holy pool is fed
Run to this pool, the pool of Memory,
Run to this pool.

ROBERT GRAVES

(e) O Dionysus of the tree – you of the beard, you of the
     ripeness
     Among the branches of my arms and hair
     As the boughs of the vine hold the plane-tree
     You came like the wind to the branches.
     'And to the earth of my heart, O golden woman
     You are the corn goddess.'
      'O wind, come again to my branches.'
      'O darkness of earth – O ripeness.'

DAME EDITH SITWELL

(f) I who was once a golden woman like those who walk
     In the dark heavens – but I am now grown old
     And sit by the fire, and see the fire grow cold,
     Watch the dark fields for a rebirth of faith and wonder,
     The turning of Ixion's wheel the day
     Ceased not, yet sounds no more the beat of the heart
     But only the sound of ultimate Darkness falling
     And of the Blind Samson at the Fair, shaking the
          pillars of the world and emptily calling.

DAME EDITH SITWELL

(g) The ultimate dream. Arms, eagles, broken banners,
     And the blind battle in the naked wood
     Over the brazen birds
     Those with black shining feathers that scream and tear:
     The angels rending their bright hair
     Amid the fog and babel of crying voices,
     Where Cyril and Methodius clutch at their split hearts.
     Look now, this
     Is the last Emperor, whose crown of iron and gold
     Drops diamonds like frozen tears, like those smooth stones
     The glacier bears from mythological mountains ...

JOHN HEATH-STUBBS

(h)   Since I emerged that day from the labyrinth,
      Dazed with the tall and echoing passages.
      The swift recoils, so many I almost feared
      I'd meet myself returning at some smooth corner,
      Myself or my ghost, for all there was unreal
      After the straw ceased rustling and the bull
      Lay dead upon the straw and I remained. ...
          ... since I came out that day
      There have been times when I have heard my footsteps
      Still echoing in the maze, and all the roads
      That run through the noisy world, deceiving streets
      That meet and part and meet, and rooms that open
      Into each other – and never a final room –
      Stairways and corridors and antechambers
      That vacantly wait for some great audience,
      The smooth sea-tracks that open and close again,
      Tracks undiscoverable, indecipherable,
      Paths on the earth and tunnels underground,
      And bird-tracks in the air – all seemed a part
      Of the great labyrinth. And then I'd stumble
      In sudden blindness, hasten, almost run,
      As if the maze itself were after me
      And soon must catch me up.
                    EDWIN MUIR

Here we have not the puzzles about detail, the bewildering associative growth of imagery, that confront us in the Surrealists and in the English neo-romantic poets, like Dylan Thomas, George Barker, and David Gascoyne, who partly derive from them. The structure of language and thought is logical and one might almost say there is no imagery, for the image has ceased to be something that enriches the texture of a poem, it has become instead intrinsic to the poem's structure: a complex symbol, what the poem *as a whole* presents. We are given the myth in itself, not the comparison of private experience to the myth. This is objective rather than subjective poetry and there might be reasons for describing its mood, tone, and stance as neo-classical rather than neo-romantic: it represents a classicizing of romanticism, like the feeling of Keats on first looking into

Chapman's version of Homer. Puzzles are likely to arise only out of the unfamiliarity of the myth, or the unfamiliarity of the poet's interpretation of it. Thus Graves, in our first quotation from him, is writing about Perseus who slew the Gorgon: but the Gorgon for Graves is merely one terrifying aspect of the triple Goddess (mother, lover, and destroyer of man) who for him is the inspiration of all true poetry; and Perseus represents a spirit of male dominance, hostile to all true poetry. He represents the northern invaders, fierce and barbarous, who destroyed the woman-dominated civilization of Crete. Hence the tone of satire:

> Swordsman of the narrow lips,
> Narrow hips and murderous mind,

And hence the fact that Perseus, type of the conqueror, is surrounded not by true poets but by flatterers, 'joculators'. He has sailed 'far to westward' – as far as the Americas – in the sense that his man of action's philosophy today dominates Western civilization. Feminine magic is at a discount in our world and obtuse male vanity, masculine 'practicality' and 'realism', and the male urge to dominate, leave almost no place for poetry. The true poetic theme, 'the theme of woman as goddess, creative, lovely, and fatal', is, according to Graves, a 'pre-historic or a post-historic theme'. It has been carried on through the centuries by an unconscious conspiracy of true poets who may occasionally pay lip-service, often of a subtly mocking or ironical sort, to the current beliefs and standards of post-matriarchal civilization, but never accept these in their hearts. All these ideas are, of course, worked out in detail in Graves's *The White Goddess*. The second quotation (which is largely a translation from Orphic texts) I cite partly for its great intrinsic beauty; partly to show how, to somebody with an attitude like Graves's, mythology is far more *true* than history. Mythology preserves the memory of ancient rituals, it is concerned with the regular repetitive activities of many people, under a very deep emotional compulsion, whereas history is what a few people happened to do *once*. The poetic 'truth'

of the myth of the Orphic heaven, which Graves preserves
here, lies in the psychological efficacy of the rituals of purification on which the myth was based; what seems permanently valid in the passage is the advice that, if we wish to
be pure, we must *remember*, not *forget*. Psycho-analysis is
a similar modern purifying ritual, and indeed the tendency
of some post-Freudian psychiatrists, who believe in behavi-
ouristic conditioning of neurotic patients rather than in
insight-producing therapy, is to dismiss Freudianism as
itself a mythology, to see the Id, the Ego, and the Super-ego
as belonging to the world of poetic or religious symbols, not
to the true scientific world of measurement and prediction.
Freudian theory, from this point of view, is a 'myth' (much
less beautiful than the Orphic myths) derived from the
Freudian 'ritual'.

In the quotations from Kathleen Raine and Dame Edith
Sitwell, we see the other side of Graves's picture. If the male
poet is the votary of woman as the goddess or the Muse, the
female poet is the actual representative of the goddess. Thus
Dame Edith, in the second of our two quotations from her,
identifies herself with the Corn-Goddess who is one of the
characters in her first; she is using familiar material from
such sources as Frazer's *The Golden Bough*. Miss Raine
rather sees the various aspects of the goddess as stages
through which the individual woman grows:

> Strange that the self's continuum should outlast
> The Virgin, Aphrodite, and the Mourning Mother,

and which she may outgrow but which nevertheless have
more poetic meaning than her mere psycho-physical identity, 'the self's continuum'. They are perhaps not *actual*
except when embodied in the individual woman, but they
are nevertheless more *real* than she. They are archetypal
roles that give individual existence shape and meaning. That
is the sense of the first, very simple, elusive, subtle poem
quoted from Kathleen Raine – a poem which again and
again slips through the fingers, like the fish it describes. The
fish is neither the abstract idea of a fish, which one knows

one cannot catch, nor the individual fish, which one knows one can; it is rather the archetypal role of the fish, which every fish assumes, but loses when it is caught. Similarly, if one were to domesticate a poet, and then to ask him his secrets, he would be able to tell one nothing; the god that had once inhabited him, the youthful Dionysus in love with the Corn-Goddess, would have left him for ever.

In the quotations from John Heath-Stubbs and Edwin Muir we can see this same pursuit of archetypes working outside the strict pattern of poet as worshipper and woman as goddess, which for Graves is the only true pattern of poetry. Muir takes the story of Theseus in the labyrinth as an archetype of our bewilderment in the maze of the world (his long blank-verse sentences themselves twist like labyrinths), and gives the story a new twist by suggesting that the maze is the clue to the story of Theseus, that Theseus never really escaped from it, and neither do we; either the maze was a reality and the real world a hallucination, or the maze was a hallucination that expressed the essential nature of the real world. We seek a way out of the limitations of the real world, as Theseus sought a way out of his labyrinth, and perhaps there is no way out and yet the whole 'meaning of life' is probably in our seeking. Relevantly, in Muir's beautifully written prose autobiography, we learn that he first felt this sense of being in a labyrinth while walking to work through the slums of Glasgow – and, he says, 'if I was tired or ill I often had the feeling that I was deep down in a place from which I might never be able to climb up again.'

In Heath-Stubbs's passage, we see a simpler use of historical rather than mythological material – though historical material so ancient and picturesque that it has acquired a mythological flavour – to illuminate the present state of the world: the powers of light and darkness are perpetually arrayed against each other, it is always a time of crisis, every great battle might be the Last Battle. The Roman Legions making their last stand, their brazen eagles cast down, the barbarians closing in on them, the ravens closing over, the distress of the Christian Fathers, the angels weeping in the Christian Heaven, are in one sense frozen and archaic symbols, in another sense topical and monitory. When one compares the poets of the 1940s with the new voices that were to be heard in the 1950s, one has often a sense that English poetry, in these years, was taking a last look at the past, and a last look, particularly, at the Mediterranean roots of European culture. What Heath-Stubbs got from books (though he was later to teach in Egypt), other poets got by being stationed in Egypt, whether as soldiers or civilian public servants. Alan Ross described the poetry that was written during the war years by writers like Keith Douglas, Bernard Spencer, Lawrence Durrell, and Terence Tiller as 'moving poems about the Mediterranean world; poems that reflect classical values, that observe the death of a civilization, but are predominantly affected by the beauty of its diseased and amoral culture'. There were, for the strongest of these poets, Keith Douglas, other things than beauty: as in his rough, angry, blurting poem, *Cairo Jag*, comparing the sordidness of Cairo, as a soldier on leave sees it, with the horrors, different but equivalent, of the Western Desert battlefield:

> But by a day's travelling you reach a new world
> the vegetation is of iron
> dead tanks, gun barrels split like celery
> the metal brambles have no flowers or berries
> and there are all sorts of manure, you can imagine
> the dead themselves, their boots, clothes and possessions
> clinging to the ground, a man with no head
> has a packet of chocolate and a souvenir of Tripoli.

Terence Tiller, similarly, expressed the pathetic abjectness of the Egyptian beggar:

> Only a sad and humble motion keeps
> the little space he is, himself: to row
> his mindless caves with ritual hands and lips,
> and wonder dimly at his guilt: with no
> memory of it now: it was perhaps
>   too fearful, or too long ago.

The haunting beauty of the Eastern Mediterranean scene, however, was what chiefly concerned Bernard Spencer, a poet, very unjustly neglected, for whom the sadness and beauty of the world is enough. He writes of the Aegean islands:

> Where white stares, smokes or breaks,
> Thread white, white of plaster and of foam,
> Where sea like a wall falls;
> Ribbed, lionish coast,
> The stony islands which blow into my mind
> More often than I imagine my grassy home ...

With the same exact perfection, Spencer catches the look of olive trees,

> The dour thing in olive trees
> is that their trunks are stooped like never dying
>   crones,
> and they camp where roads climb, and drink with
>   dust and stones.
> The pleasant thing is how in the head
> their plumage brushes the sight with a bird's-wing
>   feeling:
> And perhaps the gold of their oil is mild with
>   dream of healing.

Durrell had perhaps a richer talent, certainly a flashier one, and one more destined to achieve vulgar success. If Spencer offers us a pure vintage, Durrell offers us a heavy and spicy blended wine. Perhaps it sooner tires the palate. He uses many more epithets than Spencer:

> Only we are held here on the
> *Rationed* love – a landscape like an eye
> Where the wind gnashes by Mareotis,
> Stiffens the reeds and *glistening* salt,
> And in the *ancient* roads the wind,
> Not *subtle*, not *confiding*, touches once again
> The *melancholy* elbow cheek and paper.

Here what is conveyed is less a scene than a mood, and all the epithets in italics, except one, tells us more about the poet's mood than about the scene he is considering. Does the landscape resemble an eye because of some resemblance to the shape of an eye in the lake's outline, or because he feels it looking at him? How does the wind stiffen the glistening salt? Thus, with Durrell the landscape is very much a 'personal landscape', a subjective one, in so far as he succeeds in making us see it at all. But as a mood poet he can be very rich. Thus he reads Horace, a Loeb edition with some earlier reader's comments pencilled on the margin, and notes

> Here, where your clear hand marked up
> 'The hated cypress' I added 'Because it grew
> On tombs, revealing his fear of autumn and urns,'
> Depicting a solitary at an upper window
> Revising metaphors for the winter sea: 'O
> Dark head of storm-tossed curls': or silently
> Watching the North Star which like a fever burns
>
> Away the envy and neglect of the common,
> Shining on this terrace, lifting up in recreation
> The sad heart of Horace who must have seen it only
> As a metaphor for the self and its perfection –
> A burning heart quite constant in its station.

These stanzas of Durrell's have some relevance to his own attitude to poetry – for him, too, for all the sensuous richness of his verse, the outer scene is ultimately 'a metaphor for the self and its perfection'. Perhaps he resembles his own imaginary ancient Greek painter, Hero of Corinth: 'Style is the very cut of the mind. Hero was not so much interested in his landscape, but by a perpetual self-confession removed both himself and his subject out of the reach of the people. Thus one day there remained only a picture frame, an empty studio, and an idea of Hero the painter.' Some of Durrell's poems have the beautiful opacity that suggests, but others have exorbitance. He has a schoolboy gluttony for words and objects. He also resembles his own very different imaginary painter, Alexander of Athens: 'Alexander was in love with Athens. He was a glutton and exhausted both himself and

344

his subject in art. Thus when he smelt a flower it was quite used up, and when he painted a mountain it felt that living on could only be a useless competition against Alexander's painting of it. Thus with him Athens ceased to exist, and we have been walking about inside his canvases ever since looking for a way back into life.'

With the 1950s, all the things we have been considering in this section, the desire to transform the world, the cult of the image and the archetypal symbol, the recreation of mythology, the sense of beauty in the classical past, and of our culture's Mediterranean roots, were to be rejected not only in practice but even in theory by many of the new poets. And the 1940s, a decade, as I hope I have shown, of extremely various and interesting production in poetry, were to be dismissed as a decade dominated by Dylan Thomas. To attempt to write contemporary history, as I am doing here, is to realize how little contemporary history is ever to be trusted. Yet it is true that much weak poetry was published in the 1950s and that after 1953 there was a revival of intellectual respect for the poet: Dylan Thomas's early and sad death raised the curtain on a new scene.

21

The 1950s: The Movement and the Group

THERE had been a boom in the publication of new volumes and new verse magazines between 1940 and 1945, and between 1945 and 1950 there was something of a slump. The larger publishers, seeing no dominating figures and no clear directions in contemporary verse had become on the whole chary of taking risks. Many of the best-known younger poets of the 1950s thus made their first appearance in flimsy formats or limited editions. Mr Oscar Mellor's Fantasy Press at Oxford published a series of ninepenny pamphlets of about six pages each: in this poets now very well known, like Elizabeth Jennings, Kingsley Amis, or Thom Gunn, made early appearances. The Fine Art Department of Reading University also in the early 1950s published a number of handsomely produced, small paper-backed volumes for subscribers, including John Wain's *Mixed Feelings* and Kingsley Amis's *A Frame of Mind*. Philip Larkin has been generally considered as ranking with Thom Gunn as one of the most distinguished poets of this generation, and it is interesting that his volume *The Less Deceived*, which in 1955 established his reputation, was similarly brought out by a small firm in Yorkshire, the Marvell Press, which has since been a pioneer in publishing LP records of poets reading their own work, and which publishes also an excellent poetry magazine, *Listen*. Reviewers took note of these fugitive publications, some of them, like Elizabeth Jennings's Fantasy Press *Poems*, won literary awards, and the bigger publishers, and the larger public, took notice. Robert Conquest's anthology, *New Lines*, in 1956 brought together the 'Movement' (the label was not his, but the invention earlier of some journalist on the *Spectator*) rather as *New Signatures*

had represented 'the new movement' of the 1930s. This led
to a great deal of publicity, little of which was critically
useful. What, in fact, *was* the Movement? The poets who
appeared in Conquest's anthology – Conquest himself, Elizabeth Jennings, Kingsley Amis, John Holloway, Thom Gunn,
Philip Larkin, John Wain, Donald Davie – did not obviously
share a common set of beliefs about life or principles about
what poetry should be. What they do seem to me, in retrospect, to have shared is a new attitude to their audience.
They were no longer writing for a 'poetry-loving' audience,
or for a set of kindred spirits, or for the ideal reader, or for
the Muse. They were not acting as spokesmen of beliefs or
causes. Nor had they, though this is a more tricky question,
a common 'class' voice. Some were of working-class or *petit
bourgeois* origin – Conquest alone of them belongs strikingly
to the gentry* (though in a mocking way) – but all of them
had been to Oxford or Cambridge and represented a young,
alert, professional middle-class attitude, not revolutionary,
but certainly not reactionary, and on the whole rather indifferent to politics. A critic of their own generation, Alfred
Alvarez, was to condemn them for being 'genteel'. Their
poems have the tone of being addressed, with sometimes
slightly conscious unaffectedness, to an ideal 'plain reader'.
There may have been an *unconscious* class or professional
tone, springing from a sense of social security and intellectual competence. Of the poets in *New Lines* (many of the
same group appeared in an anthology, *Poets of the 1950s*,
edited by D. J. Enright in Japan), Amis, Holloway, Enright,
Wain, and Davie were university lecturers at the time the
book was published; Thom Gunn was doing research and
part-time teaching in an American university; Larkin was a
university librarian; Elizabeth Jennings, now in publishing, worked in a library in Oxford. Only Robert Conquest
himself, then in the Foreign Office, was unconnected with
the academic world (he has since done some teaching in

* In fact, I cannot find his family in Burke or Debrett; but he had
a public-school and Foreign Office, rather than a grammar-school and
provincial-donnish training.

America). There is a sense in which both the virtues and the vices of the academic mind – precision and balance on the one hand, caginess and a muffled (or muffed) awareness of the world on the other – were the virtues and vices of Movement poetry. The background of some of the poets – one thinks of Wain particularly – led to a vice of tone, the teacher's vice of uncalled-for condescension, of talking *down* always, rather than as to equals.

The Movement poets shared a common attitude, modest and craftsmanlike, to the craft of verse itself. Many of them thought, like the American critic Professor Yvor Winters, of the ideal poem as the expository poem: a situation is clearly presented, a judgement is made upon it, the reader is invited to agree with the poet's judgement. People who disliked this kind of poem complained that Movement poems were thin in images, in what F. R. Leavis calls 'enactment', in appeals to perception or the sensory imagination. They were also, and quite deliberately, thin in associational appeal. Philip Larkin denounced what he called 'the myth-kitty', Amis's poems about cities, pictures, ideas (the poem as it were that is parasitical on, gets a false prestige from, other works of art). Gunn was an exception, in his devotion to myth and history recalling Graves, and so was Elizabeth Jennings; so, in a different way, was D. J. Enright, with his disabused, unsentimental impressions of much sentimentalized places, like Japan. The poets, apart from Miss Jennings, were on the whole agnostic, though not actively anti-religious: even so the Movement's prize poem, Philip Larkin's famous *Church Going*, a poem with claims to greatness, is about an agnostic's reluctant recognition of what the Church has meant. Amis's militant Philistinism perhaps unfairly stamped the others. Enright, on the other hand, did write about foreign places, because he lived and taught in Egypt, Japan, and later Bangkok and Singapore, and did not share, either, the fondness of the others for strict iambics or their dislike, on the whole, of free verse. He was the only one of the set who seemed to show some affinity, in his vivid, bitty, sometimes spurtingly angry poems, with D. H. Lawrence. On the whole, the Movement poets were anti-romantic and anti-sentimental, at least in intention. But Thom Gunn, from the first, was unashamedly romantic, in love with the violent or the tragic gesture, and very ready to make a romantic use of classical mythology, Elizabethan tragedy, or some foreign scene. A Cambridge, not an Oxford man, he had little direct contact with the other Movement poets, since after completing his degree he went to continue his studies in California under Yvor Winters, and later, with a Somerset Maugham Award, spent some time in Italy (a country which also, however, attracted Elizabeth Jennings). The anti-sentimentalism was real, but sometimes tended to bite back on itself: it was strong in the early poems of John Wain but in these poems the use of the word 'love' seems sometimes sentimental and in one more recent poem I find phrases, recalling Stephen Spender, like 'prodigal idleness', 'terrible strength', 'beautiful strength', 'terrible hard head', where emotive adjectives seem to be doing work that ought to have been done by precise observation. Yet, when all these individual reservations have been made, I suppose the broadly accepted picture of their poetry as restrained, lucid, concerned with teasing out clearly small or at least manageable moral problems, rather insular, traditionally formal (the poetry of, in John Wain's famous phrase, a period of consolidation), keeping its emotions well under control, given to distancing and irony, is a true picture. Very broadly again, one rightly felt about the Movement that it reflected a certain emotional withdrawal, or a distrust of emotions not filtered through a discriminating sensibility or controlled by the rational will. The kind of poem that became famous as a *sample* Movement poem, like Wain's deservedly admired poem about not writing traditional landscape poetry or his less successful squib about reading love poetry in the dentist's waiting-room, would often be an ironical, though sympathetic questioning of the very emotions it was rooted in. Yet these generalizations, though useful, have little to do with the poems of the Movement that one finds oneself remembering and still admiring: like this beautiful short early poem, *Winter Love*, by Elizabeth Jennings:

> Let us have winter loving that the heart
> May be in peace and ready to partake
> Of the slow pleasure spring would wish to hurry
> Or that in summer harshly would awake,
> And let us fall apart, O gladly weary,
> The white skin shaken like a white snowflake.

Only the rhyme 'hurry' and 'weary' and perhaps the tension of stresses which rhyme again forces on the word 'snowflake' would enable a reader to date that as a modern poem. Its substance would be at home in the Greek anthology or in a volume of Elizabethan or Caroline short lyrics. The historical approach, though it is such a necessary one, should not rob us of the perception that what is moving in literature, in poetry particularly, is often not what is topical, or what is strikingly symptomatic of a period, but what is perennial. I think the best poems of the Movement, like that one, like Philip Larkin's impressive *Church Going*, like Thom Gunn's *A Wound*, are poems which, even if starting from the topical, explore perennial situations. The Movement, in that sense, was essentially a conservative, or at least a liberal-conservative phenomenon, and those who have most disliked and distrusted it have been those who feel that we are living in an age of tragic violence and that to be balanced and urbane, and to confine oneself to minor grumbles about the minor nuisances of life, is merely to evade the crisis. This, no doubt, was what Christopher Logue meant when he described Larkin's poetry as 'genteel bellyaching' and what Alfred Alvarez meant when, in his preface to the recent Penguin anthology, *New Poetry*, he wrote:

I have a feeling that a good deal of poetic talent exists in England at the moment. But whether or not it will come to anything largely depends not on the machinations of any literary racket but on the degree to which the poets remain immune from the disease so often found in English culture: gentility.

He wants poets to rub our noses more in the mud of our condition. And the reaction against the Movement has been just that.

Almost as soon as the Movement became a public phenomenon reaction against the Movement started in still younger poets, notably a group of Cambridge poets connected with the magazine *Delta*, including Philip Hobsbaum, Peter Redgrove, and Christopher Levenson. Ted Hughes, though I think a slightly older man, had connexions with this Group (the name soon became an informal title) and David Holbrook, though again older and not intimately connected, wrote poetry which some of the members approved of. The Group transferred from Cambridge to London, and used to meet weekly in the flat first of Philip Hobsbaum and then, when Hobsbaum went to a university in the provinces, in the Chelsea flat of Edward Lucie-Smith. At each meeting, a group of poems by one member would be circulated in typescript and stringently and soberly criticized (only coffee was served during the reading and critical sessions; the company might adjourn to a pub or open some bottles only after the critical session was closed). The Group have never made any public statement, unlike some of the Movement poets in this respect, about what they think poetry should be, but Hobsbaum and Redgrove and Levenson, all at Cambridge, came strongly under the influence of Dr Leavis, and some of the Leavisian criteria for a good poem, concreteness, rootedness, and enactment, for instance, are very important to them. They are not in any sense a closed circle, so it is difficult to characterize them socially, but I think there is a stronger infusion of poets of working-class origin than in the Movement, more school teachers and fewer, if any, university lecturers, but on the other hand more worldliness (a number of poets who attend the Group meetings are high-salaried advertising copywriters). There is a greater mixture of nationalities. Peter Porter for instance, one of the best of the younger Group poets, is an Australian, and another good poet in the Group, Taner Baybars, is a Cypriot Turk. There is more political radicalism, a sympathy with the New Left. But the main importance of the Group is in providing young poets with a milieu, friendly, but stringently, though not destructively, critical. If the Movement think of themselves as addressing the ideal plain reader, the Group think of the creation of poetry as owing a great deal to cooperative criticism, and aiming at an actual intelligent audience, varied enough in its beliefs and attitudes to stand for an outside audience. Both sets of poets would certainly agree with Wordsworth that the poet is a man speaking to men.

The Group poets are too various to come under any slick generalization, but what one does notice in the work of some of them and some of the most promising of them, that of Ted Hughes, Peter Redgrove, George MacBeth, and Philip Hobsbaum, for instance, is a positive taste not only for emotional violence but for the ugly, the grotesque, and sometimes indeed for the cruel. Both Redgrove and Hobsbaum, for instance, have written poems, in which there is in the end more distress than humour, about being a fat man. Hobsbaum has written a powerful poem about the premature decay of his teeth. Redgrove is fond of poems about insects, slugs, or spiders, and about squashing them, usually accidentally; he has a poem about watching his wife struggling into, or out of, her girdle, an exercise during which it is difficult for any woman to appear attractive; George MacBeth writes poems about finding and having to kill a small bird outside his kitchen, and also about torture chambers and concentration camps; Peter Porter has a very powerful poem about Auschwitz in which he sees broiler-chickens turning on their spits in a restaurant window, as expressive of the same ruthless human efficiency as the German gas-chambers. It is almost as if the horrors of the Second World War, from Auschwitz to Hiroshima, having failed to penetrate very deeply into the imaginations of men in their forties who served through that war (we anaesthetized that, and we were on the right side) had pierced through, twenty years later, to the imaginations of a younger generation. I think the attitude of these young poets to this somewhat sinister material is mixed. To rub our noses in horrors might make us more humane, but again it might not: as Donne wrote in his satires, about a famous Renaissance pornographic artist, 'Aretine's pictures have made few chaste.' What Alvarez calls the 'genteel' attitude may have more to be said for it than he allows; if you do not allow your mind to dwell on nasty things, you are less likely to be fascinated by them, or to want to do them yourself.

The Group could, on the whole, be called anti-genteel in Alvarez's sense; though Edward Lucie-Smith, the moving spirit among them, is both so gentle and so elegant a writer that one of the early Movement poets, Donald Davie, described him, when reviewing Lucie-Smith's first volume, *A Tropical Childhood*, as the last Movement poet. But certainly Alvarez, one of the best critics of contemporary English poetry, feels that the Movement suffered from being self-controlled and restrained and, in his Penguin introduction, comparing a very good poem about horses by Larkin to what he admits to be a less good one by Ted Hughes, he likes the second one better for its greater violence: likes it 'because it is a serious attempt to recreate and clarify, unfalsified and in the strongest imaginative terms, a powerful complex of emotions and sensations'. Alvarez feels that the world is moving on to a condition of general break-down. He feels that the English people have been unnaturally protected from violence and that this accounts for what he sees as the anaemic quality of Movement poetry. He feels that poets like some of the Group poets and like the American Robert Lowell, whom he admires very much, and whose poems partly spring from the experience of mental break-down, offer us useful imaginative warnings of a state of affairs which we may all have to face some time. He sees poetry, and perhaps art in general, as what he calls an early warning system – a trip-wire. Ingeniously, he suggests that the Cubist movement in painting foretold the geometrical inhumanity of Auschwitz.

I have made this section briefer than the others, because one finds it hard in judging very recent poetry to see the wood from the trees, and I thought it might be most useful to draw a simple map of two large woods, the Group and the Movement. There are, of course, some fine trees that are free-growing. But I think all young contemporary poets of merit have felt the tug of war, which I have been attempting to outline, between the attraction of restraint and control and the attraction of exploring, and perhaps exploiting, violence. In a good new poetry magazine called *The Review*, in a dialogue with Donald Davie, Alvarez recently laid much stress on what he called the 'seriousness' of poetry. The poet, he said, should feel what the Australian painter Sydney Nolan felt when he visited Auschwitz with Alvarez: 'It's a bastard being human!' Davie, a very thoughtful and sensitive critic, pointed out that, though it is true that the poet should try to bear the pain of things, and still remain sane, still there is something other than the pain. In art (if poetry is indeed an art) we create and confront something objective. This imaginative confrontation has always been a solace to the soul of man even in the worst times. If one likes to put it so, it is, or it is sometimes, a bastard being human, but it is also a high privilege; if our state is tragic, it is also noble. And Davie went on to suggest that poetry may have a function which he called metaphysical or ontological.

I think Davie meant something like this. Most younger poets today, though by no means all, are probably agnostics or atheists. If they feel a sense of dependence or contingency, they would not, like a traditional Christian poet, take that as evidence of the existence of a God. If they feel a sense of oneness with Nature, they would not, like Wordsworth, take that as evidence of an immanent and sympathetic life in nature, a spirit attuned to ours. If they feel happy or intensely in love, they would feel it a dishonesty to take that feeling as evidence that the world is good. But nevertheless poets may still be making, as it were unconsciously and implicitly, some sort of assertion like that – may be saying, even when confronting the worst: 'Rejoice that all things are!' The human image, the image of nature, the image of social man is, in other words, not always ugly and shattering. There is beauty. In the art of sculpture, the dead and tortured birds of Elizabeth Frink have no more claim to be a *final* statement about nature and life than the great serene goddesses, with their calm, massive, rounded limbs, of Maillol. Our images of ourselves, of the world, of our destinies, can be serene and there is something in us that forces us to take the serene and noble, rather than the hysterical and abject, as the normal.* I feel that Alvarez underestimates the power of the dead to bury their dead, and the extraordinary recuperative force of the human appetite for the normal. And I think also that the more we allow ourselves to go on brooding with a lingering perverse pleasure on the nasty things that can happen in the world, the more likely they are to happen. If all contemporary poems were, in vivid detail, about cruelty and madness, I would not take that as a happy sign. There are many hellish things that have happened in the world about which the best advice is still Dante's: Take one look and move onwards. I hope that the race will move onwards, and that poetry will help it make its path.

* C. S. Lewis, whose fictions have an avid sensationalism and a coarse bullying tone that I detest, nevertheless makes this point very powerfully in his striking work of evangelistic science-fiction, *That Hideous Strength.*

PART FIVE

THE TRENDS OF CRITICISM

22

The Victorian Tradition

THE romantic revolution in English criticism, like many revolutions, resisted effective consolidation. It represented too complete a shift of the traditional point of view. For the critics of the eighteenth century, notably for the greatest of them, Dr Johnson, the question about any poem was how far it satisfied the reasonable expectations of the reader. There was a hierarchy of kinds of poetry, with epic at the top, tragedy not far below, didactic poetry and serious satire fairly high up, and the slight lyric and the epigram at the bottom, well below that extinct bird 'the great ode': each kind had its own appropriate beauties. There were accepted standards of good sense and truth to nature, of good taste, of correct, easy, and forcible expression. There were rules. For the great romantic critics, the rules had vanished. It was no longer the poet's business to satisfy expectation; it was the reader's business to strive to comprehend the workings of the poetic mind. The mind in creation, 'like a facing coal', was what interested Shelley or Coleridge and the poem itself was thought of almost as a by-product. Where criticism had been social and external and concerned with particular works, it now became psychological, subjective, concerned with a general poetic process.

The history of Victorian criticism, as a consolidation of and partly as a reaction against the romantic revolution, is the history of various attempts to restore external standards, to find generally acceptable methods of judging particular works, without reverting to the rigidity and pedantry of the eighteenth century. The natural tendency, in an age which was both full of doubt and anxious to believe, was to seek these external standards in moral and religious principles, but to adapt these principles, as far as possible, to the direction of social change and to new scientific knowledge. In criticism, as in other fields, the Victorians were looking for a working compromise. But a latent fear that social change and new scientific knowledge might prove *all* moral and religious principles to be illusory, a fear that everything might be swept away, led in many of the great Victorian sages, in Carlyle and Ruskin particularly, to a strained and excessive emphasis; they have the preacher's tone because they are seeking to convince themselves. They have not the critic's tone; men in the grip of such a fear cannot be detached and objective.

Matthew Arnold strikes us as the great and central Victorian critic because, unlike so many of the others, he has that detached and objective tone. Yet he shared the doubts, the hopes, and the fears of men like Carlyle and Ruskin; for him as for them the criticism of literature was only one aspect of a wide 'general censure' of the age. He, too, was a preacher and even a prophet in his own way – 'an elegant Jeremiah'. But Arnold was at least less insular and flurried than Carlyle or Ruskin, and had not their fear of detachment. He did manage to state, not philosophically, but in lucid and common-sensical terms, what was emerging as one central problem for the Victorian mind. Standards of criticism, for him, depended on standards of conduct; our perception of fineness or coarseness in literature was not essentially different from our perception of fineness or coarseness in life. But, to breed respect for, and imitation of, moral fineness, the Victorian emphasis on political and economic liberty, on freeing the individual from unnecessary restrictions, on 'doing what one liked', needs to be balanced by an emphasis on social order, and also on the wider, and perhaps more vague order of what Arnold called 'culture' – the influence everywhere, on educated minds, of decent and handsome surroundings (Arnold was sharply aware of the ugliness and pretentiousness of much Victorian architecture), of not being exposed to silly speeches and vulgar newspapers, of being exposed, on the contrary, to 'the best that has been thought and felt'. Arnold suffered, like his contemporaries, from mid-Victorian religious difficulties, but being a genuinely religious man his own solution was to believe neither more than he felt reasonably able to, nor less than he felt emotionally inclined to. He thought that the educated man should adhere to the outward usage of established Christianity, but should interpret the meaning of these in his own way; he should adhere to the old words and forms, which meant so much to him, without feeling bound by their hard literal sense. The letter killeth, but the spirit giveth life.

It was not the position itself which was new but Arnold's frank statement of it, combined with his vagueness about what it ultimately implied. To men whose belief or unbelief was more definite than his own, he appeared to be anxious to preserve a mere empty shell of Christianity; to himself he appeared to be preserving its essence.

However, a similar fundamental individualism, combined with an outward deference to authority, is to be found in Arnold's purely literary criticism. Though he is always wishing that outward sources of authority, like the French Academy, existed in England, he does not really need an Academy to tell him what to think and feel, but merely to lend his own judgements its moral support. The function of Arnold's ideal Academy, as of his ideal Church, would be to assure him that he was always right. The importance of such imaginary props in Arnold's inner life explains, perhaps, the calm assurance of his tone of voice, so different from the passionate, emphatic assertions of Carlyle or Ruskin, or the dogged grey argumentation of Mill.

How far does this implicit claim to an unarguable personal authority weaken Arnold's criticism? It certainly weakens it logically, though for merely logical, as for merely metaphysical, arguments Arnold himself had always a certain contempt. One of Arnold's most famous notions, for instance, is that of the 'touchstone' – the short passage, even the single line, from the great poetry of the past, against which we can test the ring of the poetry of the present. But, as Lytton Strachey, in an otherwise cheap and presumptuous attack on Arnold, sensibly pointed out, if we can immediately recognize the quality of these touchstones from the past, might we not similarly immediately recognize a comparable quality in contemporary poetry? And if we cannot recognize the quality, if we must accept the fact of its presence on Arnold's authority, will the touchstones be of any real use to us? More widely, this approach to poetry through the quality of the detached single line or very brief passage has obvious critical dangers. It prevents Arnold from ever considering a poem as a complex living structure; it narrows his field of practical appreciation to poets like Milton, Gray, and Wordsworth who can offer him the moments of concentrated elevation he is looking for. He ridiculed the ballad style, dismissed Dryden and Pope as 'classics of our prose'; considered Chaucer too homely; Burns too plebeian. Not even Dr Leavis, among critics of our own day, has been more thorough in his rejections. Like Leavis, Arnold is fundamentally a moralist who believes good conduct to be nourished by an alert and chastened sensibility. The 'highest' poetry is that which can nourish the 'highest' life, but high can also mean thin and narrow. Arnold's horror of bad taste is like a horror of sin and for him vulgarity is the root of all evil.

In spite of Arnold's genuine effort to be detached and objective, he is never impersonal. Although conscious of his prejudices, he does not feel it necessary to make more than an outward, polite, and slightly ironical allowance for them. Arnold was a great man; but it is not unjust to say that that strange complacent self-assurance of the Victorians, that self-assurance whose obtuseness he mocked so wittily, does in an indirect and unconscious way express itself in his own criticism.

Yet Arnold remains a much better critic than Walter Pater, who, neither accepting the everyday Victorian world, nor, like Arnold, seeking to improve it, beat a conscious retreat to a realm of subjective sensibility, a realm which it became fashionable among some of his successors to call the aesthetic realm. The great romantic critics of the beginning of the century, poets like Coleridge and like Shelley in his *Defence of Poetry* and Keats in his letters, were perhaps equally subjective; but they communicate to us the subjectivity of the creator; Pater communicates the much more sterile subjectivity of the *connoisseur*. The life of his mind was a secondary life, drawing strength from works of art which more primary energies had created. Comparing him to Coleridge, Dr Richards brilliantly describes him as a 'supple' rather than a 'subtle' mind. Pater, too, like all the great Victorian 'thinkers', was, as T. S. Eliot pointed out, fundamentally a moralist; but a moralist for disciples who were willing, withdrawing from the ordinary duties and interests of life, to exist enclosed in their own sensations. Pater's refined hedonism, his cult of the intense moment, burning with a 'hard gem-like flame', is a practicable morality only for sheltered minorities: dandies of life and literature will soon find their schemes upset if policemen, soldiers, shopkeepers, artisans, and servants, all those who prop up the gross outer framework of life, begin to live for the intense moment too. Any non-universal scheme of morality must always be extremely vulnerable; the mere existence of an attitude like Pater's in a sense justified, as a counterbalance, the he-mannish jingoistic crudities of Kipling or Henley. More specifically, it can be objected to Pater's criticism that even writers so very different from him as Wordsworth and Shakespeare tend to be made over again in his own image; and in his cruder disciples, like Oscar Wilde and George Moore, his cult of subjective appreciative sensibility becomes one of gaudy self-display. The only first-rate mind that nourished itself on Pater was the mind of Yeats.

It is, of course, of Pater's influence, and of writers like Wilde and Moore – and of the rather false heartiness of Henley and Charles Whibley as a counterbalance – that one first thinks when attempting to sense the critical climate of the 1890s. Yet perhaps the really new, or at least the continuingly fruitful, tendencies of the period are to be found rather in the work of George Saintsbury, by no means a typical '90s man at all (Frank Harris, for instance, was a typical '90s man, and one of *his* first steps on taking over the *Saturday Review* was to remove Saintsbury from the regular panel of reviewers). Yet Saintsbury was the first and in many ways the greatest of the long line of academic critics who, in the last sixty years or so, have turned the study of English literature into a humanistic discipline for undergraduates which may, in the long run, replace Latin and Greek. Saintsbury, after failing to get an Oxford fellowship, and after some unsuccessful schoolmastering in Jersey and Scotland, had become in the 1890s a hard-working London literary journalist, almost a hack; in early middle age, with Henley as one of his rivals ('The red-nosed one has got it!' said Henley bitterly, when he failed), he became Professor of Rhetoric and English Literature in Edinburgh University. The traditional interest in rhetoric, or the art of writing as opposed to the history of literature, of those who held that chair encouraged him to do pioneer work in examining in detail the metres of English poetry and the rhythms of English prose. For Saintsbury, the first great 'professional' in this field, literature, particularly though by no means exclusively English literature, was itself a sufficiently exacting field to demand a lifetime's devotion; with nothing of Pater's finicky subjectivism (though, like Pater, he was ultimately an aesthete, believing that the criticism of literature is ultimately the criticism of form) he had nothing either of the Victorian moralist in him, nothing of Arnold's urge to relate purely literary criticism to a wide general 'censure of the age'. He could not repress a certain contempt for Arnold's 'wide-ranging scatter of sometimes rather haphazard arrows'. Saintsbury himself was an old-fashioned Church-and-State High Tory; almost a pre-Victorian in temperament, he had nothing at all of the common Victorian taste for adapting oneself gradually to broad changing views; from his youth onwards, he must have disliked the general tendencies of his time; but he was much too 'professional' to wish to impose his critical authority outside his chosen field. In thus narrowing his range, Saintsbury knew what he was doing. Of Arnold's own effort of 'general censure', he remarks that 'it underwent the very curse, on speaking without qualification and without true culture, which Mr Arnold, himself, had so freely pronounced'. Arnold himself, without meaning to be, and indeed meaning the opposite, seemed to Saintsbury to have been the enemy in literary criticism of scholarship, seriousness, and simplicity. Unlike Arnold, Saintsbury had the historical sense; he judges any work of literature in its setting, and according to its intentions and its kind. Perhaps this makes him spend too much time and sympathy on interesting minor writers. The fact that reading was the main business of Saintsbury's life gives his critical approach an almost alarming leisureliness; Arnold's school-inspecting, the busy, worried life he led, did, at least, force on him a drastic necessity of choice.

Saintsbury, on the other hand, seems to write as if he had been set down in the British Museum with eternity before him. Thus, his style, with its long, loose, outstretching sentences, is parasitic on the literature it deals with; in its way it is lively, but its life is less in its own rhythms than in the quotations embedded in it, or in its appeal – oddly foreshadowing T. S. Eliot's appeal in some of his poems – to the reader's alertness to spot an oblique allusion. Henry James's splenetic description of some great Russian novels as 'fluid puddings' might apply aptly to Saintsbury's prose, with the proviso that the plums in the pudding are almost never Saintsbury's own. No ideas or sentences stand out; the writer's personality, though it comes over strongly, comes over largely through an old-fashioned formality and reserve. Thus, John Galt, we are told, 'had some of the national characteristics which have not always made Scotsmen popular'; and we are left wondering: 'Was he quarrelsome, dogmatic or pragmatic, a heavy drinker, mean about money, did his manner combine servility with insolence?' It is too late to know now: a friend of Saintsbury's, the Scotsman Andrew Lang, would probably have caught the allusion at once. Today we are exasperated by these knowing hints and that rigid courtesy. Yet within Saintsbury's labyrinth, a young student may hit on something to fire his imagination

– I remember, for instance, a phrase about the 'sad clangor' of Donne. And a great modern American critic, Edmund Wilson, finds, in the middle age of a life devoted to literature, that he has reached a point where he finds Saintsbury pleasant light reading.

Saintsbury does remain (for all the distinction, the greater expertness or sensitiveness in particular fields of his worthy successors, Raleigh, Ker, or Grierson) the greatest of the professorial critics. Perhaps, paradoxically, this was because, being the first of the really notable 'professionals', he always remained at heart so much, in the good sense, an amateur: reading for pleasure; covering enormous fields, of which a more cautious man would have ploughed only one strip; refused to be trammelled either by theories about the best methods of research on the one hand, or by doubts about how much the average undergraduate can absorb on the other. As a textual scholar, for instance, as Sargeaunt's scathing introduction to the Oxford 'Dryden' shows, extremely vulnerable; as a lecturer in Edinburgh, by all accounts, besides having an unimpressive delivery, he conveyed to his students too many brute facts and too few leading ideas. But for the ordinary reader Saintsbury and his successors performed an inestimable service. It is thanks to them that we instinctively think of literature as part of a complex historical process; and thus, by being able to place them, however approximately, in their real settings, are also able to attempt to see them as they are 'in themselves'.

23

The Edwardian Interval and the
Revolution of the 1910s

THE Edwardian decade was not a period of major criticism.
It saw the consolidation in the universities, particularly in
the Scottish and English provincial universities (classical
studies still dominated Oxford and Cambridge) of the professorial tradition; but freelance men of letters were briskly
reacting against the melancholy and decadent atmosphere
of the 1890s, and unconsciously reacting, at the same time,
against the critical attitude too. Perhaps the typical literary
critic of the period was G. K. Chesterton, for whom criticism
was a sideline; he was essentially a journalist of ideas. Gide,
giving qualified praise to Chesterton's book on Browning,
noted one of Chesterton's most irritating mannerisms: a
habit of setting up dummies for the sake of knocking them
down. He would often begin a paragraph with some such
phrase as, 'It is a commonly accepted opinion that ...' and
the 'commonly accepted opinion' would be some obviously
absurd point of view of his own invention, whose absurdity
he would then proceed to demonstrate. About writers with
whom he was in sympathy, Dickens, Browning, or Stevenson,
Chesterton could write extremely well; and he also writes
extremely well about Chaucer, without quite convincing one
that he has really *read* Chaucer. His little book on Victorian
literature is a sparkling performance; but it is, like all his
writings, a 'performance' in more senses than one – we can
see what the young T. S. Eliot, a waspish young critic in the
1910s, meant by describing it as a 'Lord Mayor's Show'. Eliot
added: 'Mr Chesterton's brain swarms with ideas: I see no
evidence that it thinks.' (One of Chesterton's really shocking
weaknesses as a critic is that he hardly ever gets a quotation

exactly right; but it is a weakness he shares with other notable critics, Hazlitt and Empson.)

Eliot, in later years, after his own conversion to Christianity, spoke, and rightly, of Chesterton with more respect; but in his youth he regarded the 'ideas' of Chesterton as a very poor substitute for the 'observation and inference' which he admired in Henry James, whose sensibility he saw as too fine to be contaminated by 'ideas' in this sense. Eliot was thinking of the critical sense which James shows in his fiction, and since his introductions to the collected editions of his novels belong to this period – though he had been writing reviews and articles about fiction since the late 1860s – something should be said about his critical achievement here. It is very much a criticism of the workshop. There are these rich retrospective prefaces to the novels; there are the equally rich prospective notes and sketches in which he blocked out or roughed out ideas for stories and novels before he wrote them; and there are formal essays and reviews about other novelists, ranging from his rather cold notice of Dickens's *Our Mutual Friend* in 1865 to a round-up of novelists of the 1910s, written for *The Times Literary Supplement* towards the end of his life, in which he saw D. H. Lawrence as 'hanging somewhat in the dusty rear'. The criticism of novels is a far more difficult task than the criticism of plays and poetry. When we are criticizing a short poem, we can have the text before us on our desk, we can, in a sense, have the text in our heads. A great play, like one of Shakespeare's great plays, is like a musical score, which we come to know almost by heart, and which we in a sense carry in our heads when we watch a performance; we also carry in our heads the memory of other performances. Both in reading poems and in reading or watching plays we also attend, quite consciously, as much to the manner of expression as to what is being expressed. But the novelist seeks to create in us the illusion that we are attending not to words upon a page but to actual scenes, episodes, concrete experiences which the words represent or enact. We remember the characters, scenes, and incidents in a great, or even in a minor but vivid novel, in a way that much more resembles our memory of something that has happened to ourselves than it resembles our attempt to recall the words of a poem which we almost know by heart or to call up an image of how Gielgud or Olivier delivered some speech of Hamlet's. Our experience of novels, when we try to recall the total impression of a novel for critical purposes, is massive and imprecise. James's gift as a critic of fiction was to take us into the workshop, to give us, without disillusion, a sense of the structure of the massive whole, of the growth of the 'germ' or seed, and to make our imprecise sense of felicities of detail more precise. He makes us notice, for instance, how a novelist 'dramatizes' or 'specifies'. His great felicity as a critic is his unpremeditated exactness. He uses language with creative condensation: Grandcourt, in *Daniel Deronda*, represents 'refined brutality': Dickens in *Our Mutual Friend*, and in all his novels, fails to work out the full potentialities of a dramatic scene, because he can create 'figures' but not 'characters'. In such phrases or such distinctions, James, with no systematic or deductive forethought, spontaneously creates concepts. One may often disagree with his judgements; with his contemptuous view of Hardy, his encouragement of the young Hugh Walpole, his excessive admiration for Stevenson. But in the criticism, as in the novels, one is wholesomely exposed to the Shakespearian richness, the pouncing swiftness, the gliding, gay subtlety, the leisurely amplitude of cultural resource, of a mind and spirit so much grander than one's own.

But let us return to Eliot's strictures upon Chesterton. James, as a novelist, draws out of a situation not more and not less than what is implicit in it; Eliot no doubt felt that Chesterton as a critic drew out of a situation very largely what he had put there himself. Chesterton's critical level of discussion is, as Eliot had shrewdly noted, that of 'ideas' in detachment from both their social setting and their philosophical basis; ideas as irresponsible forces in themselves. What Eliot failed to notice was the massive coherence of Chesterton's own 'ideas', which crystallized slowly from his earliest writings towards a statement of Roman Catholic orthodoxy; Gilson, the greatest French expert on scholastic philosophy of this century, thought that Chesterton's little book on St Thomas Aquinas – which must have been based more on guessing at Aquinas, or even inventing him, than on any detailed scholarly reading – was a better book, and nearer the essential truth about Aquinas, than any book by a genuine philosopher or scholar. Perhaps 'ideas' in themselves often are irresponsible: but Chesterton's playfulness with them, his tossing them about like balloons, was based on massive and solid inner certitudes. Yet it must be admitted that Chesterton's approach precludes his getting to grips with actual complex problems. The famous description of Hardy as the village atheist brooding and blaspheming over the village idiot is unforgettable but it is far removed from what Hardy was really like. The notions discussed by Chesterton would often seem very abstract (and partly false, because so abstract) in this way, but for that fanciful felicity of phrase. Yet even that felicity leads, in the long run, to a somewhat wearying effect. Every sentence, as in Emerson or Wilde, has to tell, and a writer of prose who concentrates on the individual sentence as his unit will never write very concise or developing paragraphs. Chesterton tends to repeat himself with variations; the surprises become monotonous, the reader feels a drastic desire to compress. Yet at his best he is serious and perceptive; we continue to read him for the moments when the Chesterton-machine stops working, and the Chesterton-creature speaks.

Chesterton was at least a much better critic than his friend Belloc, who was too much of an egoist really to enjoy losing himself in other men's books. In all his writings, Belloc had, even more than Chesterton, the habit of imposing a pattern on his material rather than waiting to see what pattern emerged from it. Thus in his book on Milton, he is determined to see Milton as the solitary great English example of the 'classical' tradition: where Milton in truth is a great, extravagant poet of the baroque age, and *Paradise Lost* is as much a typical late-renaissance piece of controlled exuberance, and as little strictly 'classical' as St Paul's Cathedral; and where Milton might perhaps be described as 'classical', in the sober design and diction of *Paradise Regained*, Belloc does not really like him.

In considering the critical revolution against the Edwardians, the revolution of the decade of the First World War, we ought to bear in mind the temperament and background of the young rebels. The two most important of them, Eliot and Pound, were American, with the American inclusive view of European culture. Pound had come to Europe to escape the Philistinism of the Middle West and Eliot to complete a typical mandarin education, of the New England sort, at Oxford, the Sorbonne, and in Germany. Both had a range of interests very unusual among English writers of that time. Eliot had been regarded by Bertrand Russell, when Russell taught him at Harvard, as his most brilliant pupil; Pound had been a teacher of Romance languages at a minor American university and had been dismissed for being 'too much of a "Latin Quarter" type'. To both of them, the hearty and shallow approach of the typical Edwardian man of letters seemed boring, and the general literary atmosphere of England before the Great War stuffily provincial. Eliot has admitted that the poetry that was being written in the United States and England in his youth simply wearied him; to find anything interesting, he had to go back to the 1890s and to the French Symbolist tradition. Pound was an admirer of Swinburne and Hardy and Henry James, which is to say that his roots were in the 1880s; his attitude was rather that of a belated pre-Raphaelite, or of an admirer of the aesthetic movement before it had become consciously decadent. Both of them differed from the Georgian poets in being consciously metropolitan. Uprooted in a strange setting, and full of general impulsiveness, Pound was recurrently whipping into being new literary or artistic 'movements', and writing programmes, for instance, for Imagism. In the two Englishmen who had most to do with the critical revolution, Percy Wyndham Lewis and T. E. Hulme, the most notable characteristic, to an outside

observer, would probably seem to be a certain violent im-
pàtience. A great deal has been written about Hulme as the
rediscoverer, for the literary world, of original sin and the
notion of man as a finite creature; he attacked romantic
poetry, which he described as 'spilled religion', and foresaw
a revival of a classical poetry which would be 'hard' and
'dry'. His reading was largely in German art criticism and
philosophy, he lectured on Bergson, surely a very romantic
philosopher, and translated Sorel on violence. He was a
militarist, who had been sent down from his university for
brawling, and who during the Great War, in which he fought
bravely and was killed, fiercely attacked Bertrand Russell's
pacifism. It is hard not to see a pre-Fascist element in him,
and also in the title of Wyndham Lewis's Vorticist periodical
Blast. Pound, Eliot, Hulme, and Wyndham Lewis had, in
fact, no 'philosophy' in common but they did have in common a furious contempt for the dull contemporary scene.

As a critic, Eliot is more important than Hulme, Pound,
or Wyndham Lewis; and, in a quieter way, his criticism was
to effect as profound a revolution as his poetry. It is to him
that must be attributed the general reaction among English
undergraduates for some years (I allude to undergraduates
because, when they go down, they became 'carriers' of shifts
of taste to a wider public) against the romantic movement,
against the great Victorian poets, and in favour of 'difficult'
poetry generally, whether it is that of Donne or Hopkins
(not that Eliot ever very much admired Hopkins). To Eliot
also must be attributed the current critical questioning of
the reputation of Milton (a questioning which has led in the
end to a strong and widespread reassertion of Milton's
major status). His excellent essays on Dryden and on the
poetry of Dr Johnson perhaps account for our new sympathy with, and understanding of, the eighteenth century.
In a narrower field, the current critical view of the Elizabethan dramatists other than Shakespeare – of Marlowe,
Jonson, Middleton, and Tourneur – is largely Eliot's view,
expanded and qualified. He has written the best short English introduction to Dante, and good essays on two writers

whom Englishmen find it hard to get morally to grips with, Pascal and Baudelaire. But he has also (and this in the long run may be even more important) thrown out, in the course of such close and sensitive examinations, or in dealing with general topics like the relation of the individual talent to tradition, a number of suggestive or disturbing ideas – ideas often compressed into a single phrase – that have fertilized the thinking of other critics. Empson has wittily described him as a penetrating and inescapable influence, rather like an east wind.

Some of the seminal ideas are connected with the notions of tradition and originality. For Eliot a stress on the notion of tradition had two basic tactical uses; as an alternative to the romantic stress on 'inspiration' and on poetry as the expression of the poet's 'inner being'; and also to clarify the point that in his own poetry, Eliot is not merely making, as his more obtuse early critics tended to think, a 'clean break with the past'. He wanted to deflect attention from the poet's personality (the scandalous Byron, the dying Keats, the drowning Shelley) to the poem itself; he wanted to suggest that the poem itself, if it is a good one, fits into, extends, and alters a pattern of other existing poems. In an excellent preface to a selection of Pound's shorter poems, Eliot pointed out that a *merely* traditional poet would be an imitator, doing over again what had been done better already, while an *utterly* original poet, who derived literally nothing from his forerunners, would not be able to communicate anything at all. Thus, 'the tradition' is a large and changing order which works of literature make among themselves. We might also think of it as an order in space rather than time, spread out like a map; for there is a sense in which all great works of literature are eternally contemporary with each other, in our appreciation of them *now*. Thus, if we know more than the ancients, Eliot has said, it is because 'they are what we know'; and the importance of the emotions expressed in poetry has relation to an ideal order (the order of emotions properly expressible in poetry), not to the poet's own life.

Eliot's prose should be read, however, not only for such seminal ideas, or for its acute examinations of particular writers, but for the general attitude of mind that underlies it. As a censor of the age, Eliot has inherited, with a very different theology, some of the preoccupations of Arnold. And if he is a better pure critic than Arnold, he is also perhaps a deeper though not such a ranging censor of general manners. Pamphlets and small books of Eliot's like *After Strange Gods, Thoughts After Lambeth, The Idea of a Christian Society*, and *Notes Towards the Definition of Culture* lack the vivacious urgency that makes Arnold's *Culture and Anarchy*, for all its faults (flimsiness of construction, padding by repetition, condescension and flippancy of tone, a too genial self-regard), a central social document of its own period and one still disturbingly relevant to ours. But Eliot comes to grips with his subject with a precision which Arnold, in his elegant airiness, lacks. Eliot, going deeper than Arnold, relates two apparently unconnected senses of the word 'culture' – culture as mental cultivation, and culture as the general pattern of a society's traditional habits, what anthropologists call its folkways or *mores*. Eating boiled cabbage mashed and cut into strips, to take a rather unattractive illustration of Eliot's own, is part of English 'culture' just as dating or drugstores are part of American 'culture'.

Eliot's interest in the traditional rhythms of life, fed by and feeding higher values, the habits and *mores* of the local organic community as a cultural source greatly influenced two modern writers, Raymond Williams and Richard Hoggart. Eliot speaks as a Tory and an Anglo-Catholic, as one who holds the respectable viewpoint of an older conventionally-educated minority, rooted in traditional life, who have studied and lived in organic communities. It is indeed impressive that these two modern radicals should have such respect for Eliot's social thinking. But all three show the same dangers of the social approach to the theme of culture. In *The Uses of Literacy* Hoggart writes about the differences between good and bad *popular* literature but he does not envisage the common people reading what he,

Eliot, and Williams would call good literature *as such.* They are all anti-individualists and if they consider at all the possibility of the individual remaking himself by mainly mental cultivation, it is with more pity for his losses, in becoming estranged from his roots, from the social background he came from, and failing to adjust to another, than delight in his gains.

I have brought in Williams and Hoggart here because of their acknowledged debt to Eliot; but they seem to me more important as social thinkers about culture than strictly as literary critics. Neither of them would, I imagine, very much admire the criticism of Eliot's friend and mentor, Ezra Pound. Writers of the school of Dr Leavis (another strong influence on both Williams and Hoggart) would accuse Pound of an 'abstract' interest in literary handling, as apart from literary substance – technique, from their point of view, being interesting only in relation to the moral worth of content.

Pound seems to consider the art or craft of writing quite without reference to moral ordering of experience. He thinks of writing as a skill which anyone with certain basic aptitudes can learn. And for Leavis the moral content of Pound's own later writing – the opinions on economics, politics, and so on – tends also to be abstract, to exist at the level of wilful prejudice, of a cranky and sometimes violent 'viewiness', rather than at that of a deeper ordering of the self. Pound's critical manner also, especially when compared with Eliot's, seems gauche, abrupt, schoolboyish. Yet it is probably difficult for any skilful poet, writing about poetry, not to write to some degree as a technical specialist. If he wanted to be a moralist, to discuss human conduct in general terms, such a man would not aim at the implicit and concrete morality of poetry itself; *Hugh Selwyn Mauberley*, so to say, is Pound's *Culture and Anarchy* or his *Notes Towards the Definition of Culture*. And technical questions were certainly something Pound had a right to be dogmatic about. A fine traditional poet like Laurence Binyon was not ashamed to go to Pound for detailed advice about his translation of Dante; it was

Pound's will, not Eliot's, that imposed its present shape on *The Waste Land*. Pound in a sense 'discovered' Joyce and Eliot, and gave them practical help that no one else was in a position to give. He is a very vulnerable critic in many ways, full of gaps and stridencies, and he could never have conquered the academic world with his criticism as, slowly, from his first volume of criticism *The Sacred Wood* onwards, Eliot did. But one can think of plenty of critics who have none of Pound's faults of tone and taste and emphasis, and also none of his virtues. He is not a 'sound' critic in the academic sense; but he is something more important, a man who has helped great literature to struggle into notice, and even into existence.

A critic who should be ranged alongside Pound, as anti-academic but extremely stimulating, is D. H. Lawrence. Leavis claims that Lawrence is the greatest of modern critics. He must be basing this claim, I think, on Lawrence's general reflections on the novel, for instance, rather than on his remarks on particular authors, which largely consist either of hastily written reviews (often on novels of ephemeral interest) or passing, and often extremely impatient, remarks in letters. With all respect, I cannot see that it needed genius to see that John Galsworthy was not a novelist of the first rank, and yet this (certainly a fine piece of polemical prose) is often cited as evidence of Lawrence's critical mastery. Nor did it need genius to discover a sinister element in the *material* handled by Joyce and Proust, but it needed a considerable obstinacy to be blind to the major, and transforming, art of their handling of the material. Lawrence's critical world was largely one of 'goodies' and 'baddies': sometimes his social prickliness displays itself (as when he denounces Turgenev, of all people, for vulgarity, I suppose because that sad, liberal, delicately and sensitively strong aristocrat made Lawrence feel vulgar himself). But one book, *Classic American Literature*, is a masterpiece. And what is extremely interesting is that the standard by which this wild and wayward man, this impatient romantic, judges American literature is a classical one: 'Nothing too much.' He attacks the great American writers of the nineteenth century for what he considers one-sided excess. 'Oh,' he says of Poe's decadent romantic eroticism, so obscenely 'spiritual', 'the indecency of all this intimate talk!' He notes Whitman's greatness but also the sinister side of his cult of immersion in the mass: 'It all slides into death. ... Death, the last merging, that was the goal of manhood.' He notes how even the transcendental idealism of New England, which represented at least a dilution of what had been a living Puritan tradition, which sprang (unlike Poe's attitudes or Whitman's) from a remembered 'way of life', has its morbidities: Hawthorne's characters in *The Blithedale Romance*, anxious self-perfectionists one and all, seem to be 'going slightly rotten'. And he puts his finger on a central and terrifying paradox in the American tradition when he contrasts the smugness of Franklin's moralizing:

Imitate Jesus Christ and Socrates,

with the very different smugness of his political realism:

And, indeed, if it be the design of Providence to extirpate these savages in order to make room for the cultivators of the earth it seems that rum may be the appointed means.

In classic American literature, nevertheless, Lawrence recognizes life-building forces under a dangerous surface. Whitman's lust for death as the great sea is wrong, since life, not death, for Lawrence is 'a recognition of souls, all down the open road' – 'the great riches, the great souls'. Lawrence's vocabulary in his criticism as in his novels too often – 'souls', 'the open road' – smacks of the battered literary ornament, the wayside pulpit: but what is being said is always being felt with intensity and sometimes, like very many of the judgements in *Classic American Literature*, is profound and sane.

Lawrence did not consciously 'react' against the new critical orthodoxy of Hulme, Pound, and Eliot, the 'new traditionalism' or the 'new classicism': he had no real interest in any of these writers, his own thought was enough for him.

But his one-time friend and all-time admirer, John Middleton Murry, carried on for years in his magazine the *Adelphi* a public debate on behalf of the 'inner voice' and 'romanticism' against the authoritarianism and 'classicism' of Eliot. Some of Murry's early essays are splendid: that on *Coriolanus*, for instance, is still the best short treatment in English of that play (ironically enough Eliot's favourite Shakespearian tragedy). But Murry was on the whole a bad judge of immediately contemporary literature, particularly poetry, and dismissed for instance Yeats's great volume of 1919, *The Wild Swans at Coole*, as the work of a used-up aesthete. Unfortunately, though very highly gifted as a pure critic, he came to see himself as a sage, and the results were unfortunate. Thus his followers were presented from time to time with a version of Christianity which left both the divinity of Christ and the actual existence of God, in any traditional sense, out; and with a version of Communism which met the moral objections to that creed by abolishing the class struggle and the necessity for revolutionary change. Serious and thoughtful, making a great appeal to the emancipated Nonconformist conscience, these new creeds were rather like the chassis of an expensive motor-car from which the engine had been quietly removed; they were comfortable, but they would not get you anywhere. Murry's relations with the Lawrences were complicated; culminating, after years of estrangement from D. H. Lawrence (who had written a brutally insulting letter to Murry's dying wife), in Murry's hastening to France, on hearing the news of Lawrence's death, and making love to the widow. Murry was a pacifist in the Second World War and showed sympathy for the ideas of Sir Oswald Mosley shortly after it. I thought it typical of Murry, in these years after the Second World War, that, wanting in some article to select a figure to typify the traditions of English liberty, he chose Cromwell, who abolished parliament, reigned as a despot, supported the closing of the theatres, the censorship of the Press, and the prohibition of the celebration of the feasts of the Church, and who is remembered, in Ireland at least, as a bloodthirsty tyrant. To the last, when he wrote pure criticism or literary biography, like his book on Swift, Murry wrote excellently; indeed, whatever he was writing about, and however wrongheaded and muddled he seemed, he never wrote bad prose; but one might almost cite him as an example for critics of the dangers of too much 'thinking', or at least of too much thinking at large. He suggests also that the delicate balance which a good critic sustains, when doing pure criticism, may be so difficult to sustain that the critic is perhaps a person peculiarly liable to unbalance when he writes in a loose way upon large subjects. By all accounts he was a most amiable man, handsome, amorous, a lover of wine and company, but driven by inner uncertainty and melancholy and restlessness to projects that failed and relationships that became tormenting. The critic's temperament is, unlike the creative artist's, not a self-sufficient one; and Murry, a very fine critic indeed at his best, should perhaps be thought of as the martyr of a vocation that perpetually drove him vainly to seek escape from it.

It would be silly, however, to say that ideological commitment is *always* fatal to critical intelligence or suggestiveness. One would have expected the 1930s to have produced some good critical writing based on a Marxist vision of society; one young Marxist writer had at least a splendid reach and intention. Christopher St John Sprigg (Christopher Caudwell) was a suburban middle-class Londoner, born in Putney, educated at the Benedictine School at Ealing, which he left at sixteen, and was till twenty a reporter on the *Yorkshire Observer*. He then came back to London and joined a firm of aeronautical publishers, and before he was twenty-five had published twelve books, seven text-books on aeronautics and five detective stories. He also wrote short stories and poems and published one not very successful serious novel. In 1934, when he was about twenty-seven, he came across some Marxist classics, joined the Poplar branch of the Communist Party, visited Paris, immersing himself in the politics of the Popular Front, and began to write a number of critical and philosophical books, *Illusion and Reality*,

Studies in a Dying Culture, The Crisis of Physics, Further Studies in a Dying Culture, all of which were published after his death. In the Spanish Civil War, he at first drove an ambulance through France to Spain, then joined the International Brigade, and was killed covering a small retreat with his machine-gun at Jarama in February 1937. His Marxist thinking, writing, and acting thus covered three crowded years.

There had been previous heroic treatments of Marxism, like Sorel's *Reflections on Violence*, which saw the class-war as a combat that must be perpetually engaged, even if perpetually lost. Caudwell's treatment of Marxism was heroic, but rationally optimistic. He interpreted Communism not as in any sense aiming to subject the individual to society but rather as seeking to break down barriers that in bourgeois society constrict and thwart the individual urge towards heroic action and self-realization. Optimistically again, he saw history as a set of revolutionary movements recurrently breaking down such barriers, though, by a subtle dialectic, tending to set them up again in a different shape. Thus a feudal system gave men more freedom than a clan or tribal system did, and a bourgeois system more than a feudal system did, but through internal contradictions these new systems simultaneously set up new kinds of barriers against freedom. This is orthodox Marxist theory, but Caudwell had the gift of both outlining it in an easily graspable way, and of illustrating it concretely and vividly. His prose was remarkably free of orthodox jargon. He differed also from many Socialist writers in being less interested in social progress as relieving the masses from oppression than in its effect in giving individuals a greater scope for a full life. Writing about Shakespeare, he says:

Even the meanest creature, the empty, discredited braggart Parolles, realizes this unbounded self-realization to be the law of his stage existence and in some sort of justification of his character

Simply to be the thing I am
Shall make me live.

In this intemperate self-expression, by which they seem to expand and fill the whole world with their internal phantasmagoria, lies the significance of Shakespeare's heroes. That even death does not end their self-realization, that they are most essentially themselves in death – Lear, Hamlet, Cleopatra, and Macbeth – in this too is the secret of their death and the solution of their tragedy.

Shakespeare, for Caudwell, was the poet of the ruthlessness of the Renaissance bourgeois era, the era of primary accumulation. He was a poet at one with a society progressing, however brutally; and Caudwell related the growing specialization, as in the Augustans; retreat or withdrawal, as in the Romantics; and alienation, as in modern poets like Eliot or the Surrealists, to a progressive crystallization of the contradictions in bourgeois society. He sees social arrangements not as a way of placating individual energies, but as a way of giving them fuller scope; he admired the heroic energy of T. E. Lawrence, but regretted that Lawrence, in Arabia, had to seek a 'liberty shared by a few men, savage and ignorant', and 'disdainful of the rest of humanity'. He saw D. H. Lawrence as being perfectly right in his rebellion against the crampedness of a bourgeois society but wrong in seeking an escape from that in the even more cramped surviving remnants of primitive society. His insistence was that every new stage in human organization in history had been, comparatively, a liberation, however much it cost. D. H. Lawrence's error was to think that man is 'free not through but *in spite of* his social relations'. But he has a fine Lawrentian sentence of his own: 'Social relations must be changed so that love returns to the earth and man is not only wiser but more full of emotion.'

The critic who is called in a wide sense a liberal (and in America, at least, this can mean a semi-Marxist) tends often to be afraid of emotion, and a little afraid, both in literature and in life, of the epical, the tragical, the intensely lyrical, the wish in the individual for full self-realization. Progressive politics and social ideas often seem dreary because they sound like the attitudes of a probation officer or social welfare worker, seeking only to repress the destructive impulses in individuals, even at the cost of repressing the creative impulses also; terrified of exceptional gifts or talents, of ambition, of passion, of all strong drives and emotions. The social ideal of progressive thinkers often sounds like a universal tepid conformism and placid acceptance of mediocre satisfactions. And it is difficult not to detect a certain terror of individual excellence even in writings of very well-informed and well-meaning thinkers of the Left today, like Raymond Williams.* There was nothing of this in Caudwell. He was no doubt in some ways naïve, but to read him is to become aware of a certain meanness in many contemporary critics, an unwillingness of the young critic to commit himself, not necessarily at all to Marxism or Communism, but to some large, noble, and generous enthusiasm for what human life at its best could be.

* I should document this: Williams once wrote a *New Statesman* 'Books in General' article about new volumes of poetry. Its upshot seemed to be: 'How socially good that so many people try to write verse: what a relief that none of it is important!'

24

Critics from Cambridge

WITH an expert training in psychology, and a special interest in languages as an explorable system of communication, it was a Cambridge don, I. A. Richards, who, early in the 1920s, became interested in what light a scientific approach could throw on the nature of poetry. Two questions specially interested him: firstly, what is the relationship of the kinds of statement poetry makes to the kinds of statement that a scientific student of language believes to be true or possibly true? Secondly, what exactly is the difference, not in terms of the poem itself, but in terms of what happens to us when we read it, between a 'good' poem and a 'bad' one? His answer to the second question was more speculative than his answer to the first. It rested on the idea of the human psyche as a fairly loose self-balancing system of impulses which seeks to satisfy as many of these impulses as possible, while still keeping itself alert to readjust its balance to new stimuli.

An 'impulse', in Richards's semi-technical language, consists of the response to a stimulus which finally transforms itself into overt action, unless it can be fed back into the total system of impulses. Somebody being rude to me is a stimulus, my wanting to hit him is an impulse, my not hitting him but becoming for a time rather curt and irritable with other people is a wider assimilation of the impulse. If I reflect that he did not mean to be rude, or that I had unconsciously provoked him or that anger is in any case usually unprofitable, if I try to see things from his point of view, in each of these cases I am more and more steadily swinging my disturbed balance-system back into harmony. Yet the recurrent impulse to hit, whatever happens to it in the end, is necessary for a creature that has to defend itself.

The process of civilization consists in teaching us in general to assimilate our impulses as widely as possible, to have the balance of our system in mind, but if impulses of aggression, appetite, and concupiscence were fed back completely, the human race would come to an end. For Richards, a 'satisfactory' balance of 'impulses' is one which allows play to as many as possible, thus producing a sense of well-being, while at the same time leaving the psyche in a free and flexible state, ready to respond to new situations. An 'unsatisfactory' balance is one which owing to a jamming of the machinery at some points – to 'local fixations' – leads in the long run to a failure to adjust, except along a few deeply grooved channels, and to a sense of ill-being. If Richards were a theologian, the tendency of the human psyche to jam up when confronted with new situations would be his equivalent of original sin. His implied theology has this in common with Christianity or Buddhism, that what the psyche aims at is suitable states of itself, in proper relation to what is more widely presented to it. He is, in fact, by temperament a profoundly religious man and he has described to me his early masterpiece, *Principles of Literary Criticism,* as a sermon disguised in the fashionable scientific language of its time.

A good poem for Richards is one which helps to induce a satisfactory balance, or which evokes a satisfactory 'attitude' – an attitude that is not necessarily an attitude *to* anything, or connected with any beliefs about the outer world. I have found these ideas of his most useful in my own attempts to be a critic, but I think also that, very early on, I adopted this idea of free swing in the self – it is rather like Matthew Arnold's idea of 'the free play of mind' – as a semi-religious discipline, without realizing that I was doing so. From the point of view of practical criticism, it is obviously a vulnerable idea. I may have an almost infinite number of impulses – I may be exposed to a thousand tiny stimuli and make or check tens of thousands of responses to them – every moment of my life. Good poems *may* in fact – it sounds very plausible – produce a satisfactory balance of impulses in the proper reader. But there seems to be no way of assuring oneself that one is a proper reader. If a poem pleases us we may be yielding to lazy stock responses or even to vicious habits (the taste for Verlaine might be like a taste for liqueurs, and that for Macaulay or the cruder Kipling, like a taste for raw spirits). If, on the other hand, a poem puzzles or depresses us, it *may* be that, because of some local fixation, we are failing to apprehend it properly. But when we are genuinely in doubt about a poem, we check our responses, at least, by examining the *poem* more carefully; not the poem by examining our *responses*. It is true, of course, as Richards would point out, that we cannot examine the poem *in itself*, but only this instance of ourselves reading it. It remains true, however, that when we are puzzled, an attention to syntax, to metre, to the sense and bearing of particular words that worry us in a poem, and perhaps to other poems of a comparable sort, is always more useful than attention to our own state. Our own state always contains so much that is not relevant.

But what is a poem *about*? Or what is the relation between the use of language in poetry and its use as a means, primarily, of conveying information? Richards noticed that many mathematicians, for instance, find it impossible to read poetry because the kind of statements poetry makes for them have no sense; he himself feels sure that poetry does not make sense – does not refer to real states of affairs – in the way scientific prose does. Nevertheless, we can read poetry profitably not so much for what it says to us – not so much for some abstract meaning it leaves behind, some 'message' – as for what it does to us. The language of poetry is emotive; it aims not at describing states of affairs and working out theories about them or suggesting practical ways of dealing with them, but at evoking desirable attitudes. Poetry, for Dr Richards, is thus in some degree a substitute for religion – not for the dogmas but for the practice of religion – in producing satisfactory states of mind; but without linking these up, as most religions do, with misleading notions about the nature of the universe. Richards is thus making a distinction between a scientific view of the world, which is knowledge, and various theological, mythological, or metaphysical or mystical views which may be very valuable as ideas around which human feelings have richly accreted themselves or as metaphors expressing obscure truths about our feelings, but which are not knowledge but belief (and unfounded belief, Richards thinks, or at this stage thought). Richards's practice as a critic has, in fact, been strangely at odds with his more general theories. In what is still his most useful book for the young reader, *Practical Criticism*, he does not stress either the complexities of inner balance or the emotive nature of poetic language so much as the necessity, if we are to read a poem properly, of a close and disinterested attention. For poetry, even if its ultimate effect is some kind of emotional release, some kind of psychic therapy, requires an effort of attention – an effort comparable, at its lower level, to the effort required in concentrated prayer to exclude distraction – as intense as any we know. Let me expose this idea in a way which is my own rather than Richards's. It is wrong to be too eager to get beyond the 'prose sense' of a poem, even if that at first feels dull and fantastic, just as it is wrong to be too eager to get beyond the strain, the feeling of making a formal or empty offering, the sense almost of dereliction, which often accompany prayer, to the sense of spiritual comfort, of consolation, which may sometimes succeed prayer. In both cases, the rewards are in a sense by-products, or are occasional and gratuitous, and what is really valuable is the effort, the strain, the attention, and the habits it forms. A critic, reading a good new poem, probably feels far less delight and excitement than a young untrained reader new to poetry, but at the same time forms a far juster estimate of the poem's worth; and the effort of attention, which was at first a burden, becomes, as habit strengthens it, a pleasure and even a consolation itself. But both in praying and in reading poems, at all stages, the great danger is that of cheating, of providing the emotional rewards or the spiritual comfort (or a simulacrum of them) ourselves.

It is this aspect of Richards's teaching, the necessity of

close attention to what the poem 'says', that has most attracted the attention of his most brilliant student, William Empson. Empson's first critical book (begun as a thesis under Richards's supervision), *Seven Types of Ambiguity*, was an attempt to analyse the kind of statements we find in poems as closely and even captiously as the historian and critic of thought, for instance, might examine statements by Pascal or Hulme. Such examinations of sentences and paragraphs in great thinkers generally probe for inconsistencies of which the thinkers themselves were unaware. Empson, similarly, was looking for a basic ambivalence in poetic thinking that would display itself unconsciously in the detail of language. He claimed that Wordsworth torn between a humanistic theory of natural pantheism, that the life of nature is a projection of our own deep emotions, and the necessity of not saying anything that would conflict too sharply with Christian orthodoxy managed unconsciously, by a tactfully muffled use of language, to mask these divisions from himself and his readers:

> ... a sense sublime
> Of something far more deeply interfused,
> Whose dwelling is the light of setting suns,
> And the round ocean, and the living air,
> And the blue sky, and *in* the mind of man,
> All thinking things, all objects of all thought,
> And rolls through all things.

The key word in that passage is the tiny word, which I have italicized, 'in': the key question is whether we take the phrase, insulated by commas, 'and in the mind of man', with what precedes or with what follows it. Empson examines the passage like a lawyer examining a brief. Wordsworth may be contrasting the spirit that *seems* to be immanent in outer nature with the spirit that *is* immanent in man and leads him to project his life into outer nature. But if the 'something far more deeply interfused' dwells indifferently in outer nature and the human mind, 'under this less fortunate arrangement' – though it does assure Wordsworth that his feelings about nature are not a hallucination – 'a God who

is himself nature subjects us at once to determinism and predestination'. This is highly ingenious, but having read more
thoroughly in Wordsworth now than I had when I wrote the
first version of this book, I have found no passage of verse
or prose which suggests that he was in the least interested
in, or worried about, determinism or predestination: it is
one of Empson's faults as a critic to suppose that any author
he is dealing with must share some of his own preoccupations. There were critics of Empson who considered this
kind of approach to great poetry mean and fussy; but in a
sense Empson shows his respect for great poets by taking
what they say seriously and expecting it to cohere.

Yet a much more coherent point of view than Wordsworth's, the orthodox Christian joint of view of the seventeenth century, need not exclude these equivocal effects.
Empson quotes from George Herbert's poem about the
crucifixion, *The Sacrifice* (the dying Christ on the cross is
speaking):

> But now I die: Now, all is finished,
> My woe, man's weal; and now I bow my head:
> Only let others say, when I am dead,
> Never was grief like mine.

The intended sense is almost certainly: 'Let others admit,
once I am dead (and accepted as their Redeemer), that there
never was such grief as mine is now.' But because of the
ambiguity of indirect speech in English we can also take it:
'Let others as myself say, once I am dead (and once I have
pronounced judgement on their sins), "Never was grief like
mine".' Christ is our judge as well as our Redeemer. Thus
the possible secondary meaning is relevant: 'Let those whom
even the Redemption shall not redeem, whom I came to save
but whom I shall now have to judge, admit that no fate
could be more terrible than theirs!' This Empson sees as the
central paradox of Christianity, the paradox of the 'vengeful
God of Love'. Another very striking stanza, which Empson
quotes quite without detailed comment, has again, whether
consciously or not, the same implications:

Between two thieves I spend my utmost breath,
As he that for some robberie suffereth.
Alas! what have I stolen from you? Death:
    Was ever grief like mine?

'Death' with that punctuation (I notice that in Auden's and Pearson's *Poets of the English Language* after 'Death' there is not a colon but a less dramatic full stop) sounds not so much like an answer to a question as like an imprecation. There is bitterness in it. Christ, by dying, has robbed us of death. *Therefore* we are angry with him, we treat him as a robber. For if the death which he has robbed us of shut us out from the hope of bliss it also freed us from the fear of torment. And there is a weariness of life, a sense of life less as a gift than as a burden, with which Christian religion finds it hard to deal, though this weariness (the central core of feeling in Empson's own poetry) is at the basis of the great Far Eastern religions, Hinduism and Buddhism. If a rich young man had approached the Buddha, he might have asked: 'What shall I do that I may inherit eternal death?' Freud's notion of the death-wish had, in Empson's youth, made westerners aware of this eastern sense of the need to escape from the Great Wheel; this had been expressed earlier, indeed, in Kipling's *Kim*. Empson, by what at a first glance might seem a frivolous or trivial attention to verbal niceties, can, as in this example, display the basic ambiguities of what might seem a massively coherent attitude, like that of the orthodox Christian. A poet like George Herbert has his own kind of special poetic honesty and cannot help showing us, as the writer of a prose dogmatic treatise or an edifying sermon might not, the reverse of the medal. Empson, however, has never been very strong in the historical sense; seventeenth-century theologians were obsessed, in fact, with the paradoxical relationships between God's justice and His Mercy, between Grace and Free-will, and it may well be that the equivocal meanings which Empson finds in Herbert were quite deliberately intended.

Empson's second volume, *Some Versions of Pastoral*, dealt with this kind of equivocal effect on a larger scale, as it displays itself in drama or poetry. The American title of this volume, *English Pastoral Poetry*, is singularly misleading, for pastoral poetry in the strict sense (Spenser's *Shepherd's Calendar*, or Milton's *Lycidas*, or Shelley's *Adonais*, or Arnold's *Thyrsis*) is one of the subjects on which this extremely wide-ranging volume does not touch. The notion of the pastoral mode is used by Empson in a wide and elastic sense to cover every attempt in literature to deal with complex issues through ideal simplification: and the mode also involves a certain wistful hankering in those who use it for simplicity, primal energy, or innocence. But the pastoral mode, in this wide sense, may be also used for cover criticism of established values. Thus Falstaff is a pastoral figure who suggests doubts about the heroic values of the action that goes on around him – both about the dashing, shortsighted, attractive heroism of Hotspur and the calculating patriotic machiavellianism of Prince Hal. Milton, asserting that the various classical paradises, which he evokes in long similes with wistful vividness, were *less* beautiful than the Garden of Eden (and lies, not Bible truth, anyway) expressed the secret hankering of the well-educated Puritan after Renaissance paganism. Gay, in *The Beggar's Opera* (which, in fact, he *called* a 'Newgate Pastoral'), uses the comic pastoral mode not only for fairly open criticism of contemporary politics (he stands, against Walpole, for the surly honesty of the permanent Tory opposition), but also to express something which the Augustan cult of decorum could not express directly – and the feeling that though a hero may merely be a great rogue, still a rogue may be genuinely a small hero; and that though both the hero's and the highwayman's use of energy are socially improper, still in their energy itself there is something we sneakingly admire. Lewis Carroll's Alice, who lays herself open to Freudian interpretation (an early enthusiasm of Empson's, which he has latterly tended to drop), represents a typically Victorian attempt to combine an intense covert interest in sex with a cult of innocence; and the 'nonsense' of the Alice books may be, much of it, rather sharp hidden satire on Victorian political and university life. Through the pastoral framework Lewis Carroll is able to embody, and to criticize, the unconscious fantasies and self-deceptions that made Victorian compromise work.

It is obvious that 'pastoral' here, like 'ambiguity' in the first book, is a conveniently elastic notion; but it is no real criticism of some concepts that they can stretch. (If the word 'culture', for instance, was as unstretchable as the word 'civilization', Arnold, Eliot, Hoggart, and Williams would have had to find another pair of braces to hold up their cultural books.) In Empson's third book, *The Structure of Complex Words*, the concepts are more rigid and more mechanically elaborated; and though a useful book, it is not so entertaining as the two earlier books, and not so good, for the beginner critic or reviewer, to steal from. Empson here takes issue with Richards's theory, which we have already considered, that the use of words in poetry is primarily emotive. He thinks (and in this he is at one with the American critic, Yvor Winters, though owing no direct debt to him) that if words move us, it is, broadly speaking, because the things they refer to move us: the word 'child' can seem moving in a poem because most people like children. More technically, the contrasting emotive values of words like 'childish' (a negative emotive value) and 'childlike' (in many cases, a positive emotive value) could be explained by a consideration not only of their dictionary sense but also of their social uses. We want people to grow up and become responsible adults: 'childish' is used, say, by an official superior about an inferior, by a husband about a wife, or a wife about a husband, who has been behaving in a silly way, to chide irresponsibility. But there are many things we love about children, and there is a directness and simplicity in their behaviour, and a clear sense of what is good and bad, right and wrong, which we would like no adult to lose completely: so we might say that Gandhi, for instance, had a 'childlike' simplicity or that Blake had a 'childlike' purity of vision. There may be a touch of humour or condescension in this use, we are at once claiming a practical superiority – *we* are sensible and grown-up – and admitting, we hope gracefully, a spiritual inferiority. This is not an example Empson uses, but it provides a fairly clear example of what he means by a complex word. *The Structure of Complex Words* was Empson's last book embodying technical innovations in criticism, or paying close attention to the niceties of verbal detail. He has since written a number of large and sweeping essays on Fielding, on Joyce, on various plays by Shakespeare, on Donne's interest in the possibility of a plurality of worlds; they ride, often, rather loosely to the text, but are full of stimulating insights and speculations. His last book, *Milton's God*, partly used Milton as a stick to beat Christianity with, but was hampered as anti-Christian polemic by Milton's untypicalness; it showed, however, a wonderful feeling for the quality, the effect, of *Paradise Lost*, and the polemical intention gave Empson the energy to do a lot of excellent old-fashioned descriptive and appreciative literary criticism. If I derived my idea of a critical attitude from Richards, I derived my idea of a critical detailed practice – how to tackle a text – from Empson. Gratitude to both may, possibly, make me overstate their virtues and understate their vulnerabilities. But to young readers, at least, I can still think of no first books on how to read as useful as Richards's *Practical Criticism* or as awakening as *Seven Types of Ambiguity* and *Some Versions of Pastoral*. There is, indeed, a real danger (some of the American 'New Critics' exemplify it) of people taking up some of Empson's methods and applying them quite mechanically. This is never his own danger; the whole man, and his whole response, is always present in Empson's criticism, though the whole man may often, in a strange way, balance apparent rigour of method with an impulsive and mischievous rashness, starting and pursuing will o' the wisps as well as hares. But there is a pleasure in watching Empson's mind in full canter that has little to do with which pack he thinks he is following or whether he is in at the kill.

In universities, in grammar schools, and with a wide audience of earnest, self-improving readers, Dr F. R. Leavis has probably a far higher reputation than either Richards or Empson, partly, no doubt, because he has never been boldly speculative outside the realms of strict literary criticism, as Richards has, and has never had a touch of Empson's mischievous delight in using all the ingenuities of analysis to complicate, rather than simplify, one's appreciation of a text. He has a much narrower range of general interests than these two, a range confined, broadly speaking, to imaginative literature, the criticism of imaginative literature, the use of both of these in education, and the moral centrality, as he sees it, of a serious literary education in a world of commercial values and mass standards in which we can no longer rely on the close-knit, traditional community to pass on the best values. Modern metropolitan culture, as represented by the Bloomsbury group, by the literary weeklies, by the British Council, by the B.B.C., seems to Dr Leavis hopelessly frivolous and corrupt. He sees the preservation of culture as the job of a minority. Only a minority, he feels, at any time have real intelligence or are capable of real sensibility; but Dr Leavis has a strong sense of social responsibility, and feels that a larger number of people are capable at least of cultivating decent habits and impulses and of being taught, for instance, to be cautious about advertisements and propaganda. They might be taught, also, to recognize the more obvious kinds of literary faking. A number of critics, like Raymond Williams and Richard Hoggart, who have a great reverence for Leavis and have learned much from him, feel, however, that the concept of 'minority culture' is morally, socially, and politically deplorable, and that both popular tastes, and some kinds of popular writing, deserve more respect than Dr Leavis has accorded them. A more purely literary critic than these two, John Speirs, who studied English literature at Cambridge under Leavis, is much more interested than Leavis in literature like Scottish ballads and some medieval poetry, and like the poems of Burns, which seems in some sense to spring directly from the people (though Leavis himself is always impressed by a quality which he calls 'rootedness' – implying rootedness in the nature of the English language, and in traditional English social attitudes – in poetry).

The modern writers on whom Leavis and the contributors to the very influential periodical *Scrutiny* (of which he was one of the editors) concentrated, tended there to be set against this gloomy though not necessarily desperate historical perspective. Thus, for such critics, D. H. Lawrence perceived a general decay of metropolitan culture, a starving in our time of the deep roots of life, but he did not (in a phrase of his that Leavis quotes) 'do dirt' on life itself: James Joyce in *Ulysses* seemed to. If *The Waste Land* seemed to express almost complete despair, yet its pessimism was not as slackly and complacently negative as that of Joyce. The *Scrutiny* crew could, in fact, be sympathetically receptive to the work of even very minor writers who seemed to them to express their own reverence for life: L. H. Myers was applauded because of his hatred for Bloomsburian cleverness and triviality; the rural themes of T. F. Powys (in spite of Powys's obsession with death, lust, and cruelty) and even of Adrian Bell, a pleasant but very slight chronicler of farming and village life, suggested that here and there in England the tradition of 'organic community' was still alive. But the work of dangerously smart or fashionable writers like the Sitwells or Mrs Woolf or Aldous Huxley, or of the poets of the 1930s onwards from Auden to Dylan Thomas, was on the whole (with some exceptions for Auden's early power and promise, for Bottrall, and, with many more reservations, for Empson) not welcomed. Whether by concentrating on politics, like Auden in much of his early work, or by remaining content with a confused romantic subjectivism, like Thomas, the poets of the 1930s – and even more the popular novelists of the 1930s, like Evelyn Waugh and Graham Greene and Elizabeth Bowen, apparently involved deeply in urban worlds, smart or comic or sinister – must have seemed to the *Scrutiny* critics to be ignoring, as Lawrence and Eliot and Pound have not, the profounder theme of cultural disintegration and the need for getting back to the deep sources of life.

Thus *Scrutiny* in its heyday represented an influential but isolated point of view: 'modernist' in relation to the older academicism (it was Leavis and his friends who forced university teachers of English to treat Eliot and Lawrence seriously); but conservative in relation to many other manifestations of 'modernism' (such as Joyce, for instance). *Scrutiny* should have exacted respect, however, even from those who most disagreed with it, by its refusal to act on three principles which are widely diffused throughout the rest of literary journalism; the 'group' principle, the 'personal' principle, and the 'deference' principle. The 'group' principle consists, for instance, in taking T. S. Eliot's work seriously, knowing that Eliot takes the work of Charles Williams seriously, and feeling that one is therefore bound to take Williams seriously oneself. The 'personal' principle derives from the fact that in London most reviewers know each other, and know the authors they are reviewing, perhaps quite intimately; they are tempted, therefore, in reviewing each other's work sometimes to see more in it than is there (reinforcing, as it were, somewhat meagre purely literary impressions with rich and warm personal ones), and sometimes, when their verdict is unfavourable, to pull their punches (personal spite, of course, can have its innings too). The 'deference' principle is that, when on the whole one admires an author's work very much, one should treat the book of his under notice, even if one feels that it does not represent his highest achievement, with tender forbearance. Leavis's great admiration for some of the earlier poems of Pound and for much of Eliot's work has not prevented him from being very severe about the *Cocktail Party*: and an early hearty admiration for Eliot's critical prose (Eliot's attitudes to poetry are a formative influence behind Leavis's own *Revaluation*) has now been cut back, or pruned down, to a slightly grudging admiration for two or three seminal early essays. It might be said, indeed, of Leavis that he cannot have two great trees in his garden at once: as Lawrence burgeoned, Eliot had to wilt. But the *principle* of non-deference is admirable; and after the *Lady Chatterley* trial

Leavis applied it splendidly to his central hero, in a sparkling short article in which he pointed out, in arguments of crushing conclusiveness and simplicity, that the central and obvious thing about *Lady Chatterley's Lover* is that the class animus and the didactic intention make the book, however honourable and sincere the motives behind it may have been, a bad novel.

Like Matthew Arnold, Dr Leavis takes a great pleasure in finding fastidious reasons for rejecting what has been too carelessly admired. He is as reluctant as Arnold to reduce his ideas to a system, and much more cautious than Arnold about large generalizations. He once said: 'I wish I knew enough about metaphysics to know how to keep it out of literary criticism.'* His standards are not yardsticks, to be applied mechanically from without; his 'method', in so far as he can be said to have anything so crude, is to read with concentration and to try to express precisely, even at the cost of cumbrousness, what he has felt and thought. The only book of which I feel this is not wholly true is what seems to me Leavis's weakest book, *D. H. Lawrence: Novelist*. His almost religious reverence for Lawrence seems to me, here, to have had a softening effect on his prose; he seems too full of unction, over-anxious, as not elsewhere, to *persuade* the reader, and perhaps to persuade himself. Generally (again, I have some reservations about *D. H. Lawrence: Novelist*), what Leavis says can always be referred to, and often rises out of, the particular illustrative passages he quotes. He is not interested in form in abstraction from content, in a writer's general intention apart from its detailed presentation, or in that presentation itself apart from the 'quality of life' presented. (Art is necessary to the kind of writer Leavis approves of, but art by itself is not enough; hence his coldness about Flaubert, his disgust with Joyce.) The 'quality of life' is what Leavis is primarily interested in, and in literature as serving that, but he is a moralist who refuses to generalize.

* Not in a book: answering a question after a lecture, at which I had been taking the chair for him.

Crudely generalizing for him, a reader might say what Leavis is looking for is the enacted image of life in its rootedness and fine blossoming, and behind the image he is also looking not for system, not for the dead abstractions of intellect, but for the intelligence which is the specifically human manifestation of life, the quality, to take it at its lowest, by which the race has survived. He is also looking for reverence, seriousness, purpose, a breaking down through literature of cold dividing barriers, though the separateness and difference of each individual living creature is to be reverenced, too. Though Leavis is an agnostic, whose father was a Victorian rationalist, he is also (as some of favourite critical terms of praise – rootedness, seriousness, integrity – make clear) a profoundly religious man. 'Life', in his vocabulary, plays a role not dissimilar to 'grace' in the vocabulary of Pascal: it does not mean just being alive, even just being alive in a state of reasonable health and efficiency, it means being reverently alive, with an immediacy of response, quick and alert, to other life. Leavis's famous case against Milton, for instance, is based primarily on a sense that Milton lacks, not reverence certainly, but quickness, alertness, immediacy, that Milton's perceptions are conventional and 'literary' – 'the smooth enamelled green' – and that Milton's thinking about life, for all his claims to 'justify the ways of God to man', is not sufficiently intelligent; he finds in Milton what may be called a grand obtuseness. In the same way he looks through a lyrical poem of Shelley's, rather as he might look through an undergraduate essay, alert for vague undirected enthusiasms and sloppy uses of language. On the other hand, a writer like Swift, for all his vivacity of detail and powers of ruthless organization, gets bad marks too: because, however energetic, he seems to express, to Dr Leavis, only destructive and negative values. Similarly, Dr Leavis can forgive the heaviness and clumsiness of much of George Eliot's writing, or the melodramatic literary showmanship that puts up a barrier between some readers and Conrad, because of his sense of the liveliness of the material presented and the author's moral and imaginative grasp.

It might almost be said that Leavis's final standards are those of 'moral taste'. Not, it should be emphasized, of aesthetic taste. Aesthetic critics will, for instance, praise the 'beautiful style' of George Moore, while admitting that they find much of his matter boring; but if there is something wrong with the tenor, there must be something wrong with the vehicle too.

More subtly, aesthetic critics will praise the complex organization of a late novel by Henry James, like *The Ambassadors*. Dr Leavis, though a great admirer of James, finds this novel a bore. James, he feels, has got so lost in problems of formal patterning that the story and characters he started with have lost their crude substance; have become pretexts for merely verbal elaboration. Thus our sense in the end about Dr Leavis is (if we can reconcile ourselves to his cutting edge and rasping surface, to a tart flavour that can verge on becoming sour, to a personality that has its proper authority but also its own kind of assumingness, or of almost self-importance) that here is a mind always inquiring, never resting slackly on its assumptions, probing most remorselessly what it is most drawn to admire; though a mind also (like most of our minds as we grow older) given somewhat to the reiteration of its favoured positions, of the judgements about which it feels secure. It is a mind, at least, never satisfied with tactful approximations; prickly and combative because of what seems to it the insincerity of more stolid wits; a mind, also, with a touch of mischief in it, taking a faintly malicious pleasure – but also, and probably more profoundly, a public-spirited one – in undermining lazy self-esteem.

What, on the whole, however, has been the effect of the tradition with which Dr Leavis's name is so specially connected, on younger critics and on younger imaginative writers? Among university critics of English literature, Dr Leavis can count some disciples who are in their own right men of great distinction, like John Speirs, L. C. Knights, and D. A. Traversi: these three have carried a moral and imaginative approach to literature, closely resembling his, into fields which he himself has not explored, like medieval poetry and the general working of Shakespeare's imagination. There are other disciples, of whom David Holbrook is one who springs immediately to mind, but not as an utterly isolated example, who parrot all the Leavisian catchwords – 'integrity', 'maturity', and so on – and assume the Leavisian pose of authority, without seeming to have earned the right, by any closeness of argument, sharpness of perception, or *finesse* in analysis, to do so. In some of Leavis's weaker disciples, too, there is a rather obvious and disagreeable class animus, a flaunting of a rather vaguely conceived 'puritanism': Leavis himself, in *Revaluation*, is never in any doubt that the main tradition of lyrical poetry in the seventeenth century is cavalier not puritan, and he does not, like some of his disciples, make the mistake of confusing heaviness with seriousness. Dr Leavis has a wide influence on university teachers and on schoolmasters, and perhaps rather generally his dimmer disciples have attempted to flatten out, to methodize, to systematize his insights in a way that he himself would be the last to approve of. Conformism is the great disease of intellectuals as of other social groups; very few of us have the courage to make up our own minds on literary questions, to risk being out of step with some body of opinion we approve of or *need the approval of*. It is sad that Dr Leavis, the least conformist of critics, should have built up, unconsciously, a band of echoers and diluters around him.

More broadly, the wider Cambridge critical tradition, of which Dr Leavis is only a part, though a very central part, has perhaps had a cramping and discouraging influence on potential imaginative writers exposed to its impact in youth. One should here also consider what is called the 'New Criticism' in America, though this owes much more to Richards and Empson than to Leavis, whose attitudes are much too English to bear transplanting easily. In America, poets like Randall Jarrell have complained that they feel themselves flattened out by a new orthodoxy; anything creative they do, they feel, is 'placed' and 'placed' with a 'limiting judgement' in advance; and yet in point of fact, as Jarrell complains, it is on the whole more difficult to write even a 'good minor poem' or a 'good naturalistic short story' than to write a ponderous critical essay. (In a sense this is obviously true: what is also true is that there have been fewer 'great' critics than 'great' poets, that the critical gift in its plenitude – as in Johnson, Coleridge, or Arnold, seems to be bestowed, in our English culture, not more than once or twice in a century.) In England, it was at least at one time true that the Cambridge tradition did tend to have a constipating and intimidating effect on young potential novelists or poets who came under its influence. A young man's first efforts in verse or fiction are bound to be crude and immature; if he ever learns to write well it will be because, at one time, he has been allowed and even encouraged to write imperfectly but abundantly. We learn by trying, by failing, by almost succeeding but not quite, and then trying again. The company of other young men with the same raw ambitions is likely to be more useful to the young imaginative writer than the pervading sense of an ideal he cannot attain; and there is a real danger of his attempting, before he has acquired mature experience, to lay a pattern of sophistication and complexity on his writing from, as it were, above. This would be a fair criticism to some of the earlier work of Cambridge poets like Bottrall, Empson, or Madge: do they have to be so clever, oblique, and allusive all the time? Of a later generation of Cambridge poets, David Holbrook, Peter Redgrove, Philip Hobsbaum, Christopher Levenson, for instance, it might be a just criticism to say that, in evading the dangers of an imposed surface complexity, they have run the risk of appearing heavy and lumpish and prosy. 'Maturity' can be thought of as involving the abrogation of the primary duty of any writer, whatever his other duties are: the duty of pleasing.

There is, however, a deeper question to be asked. Apart from young creators, may it not be good for young readers sometimes to have passionate and immature admirations? It is good, no doubt, for a young man to be sobered up who has become intoxicated with Shelley; but is it beneficial for any young man, in whose life poetry is going to matter, never to have gone through the Shelley stage? It was Iago, after all, who said, 'I am nothing if not critical': and Donald Carne-Ross, in an amusing if unfair polemical article, once compared – as John Bayley in *The Characters of Love* has more recently done – Dr Leavis's view of Othello's character to Iago's own. There is certainly a danger that the *Scrutiny* attitude may breed a habitual suspicion of all kinds of rhetoric, like Othello's or like Milton's (or like Shelley's or like Yeats's) that make an overt claim to nobility. Thus *Scrutiny*, as Carne-Ross noted, has always been a little grudging and cautious in its recognition of Yeats; yet Yeats is the most consciously noble of modern poets. And *Scrutiny*'s heroes of thought of the last century, Mill, Stephen, Sidgwick, worthy souls though they all are, are all a little on the good grey side: one wonders sometimes what Dr Leavis would make of a man who wrote so much more beautifully than any of these, and whose mind was in some directions so much more subtle and penetrating, Newman. ... Yet when all these reservations have been made, most young writers and critics in England today, and certainly almost all teachers of literature, would admit that they owe to the Cambridge tradition a solid debt of gratitude.

25

The Prospects Today

REALLY important works of criticism are published
frequently than novels, plays, or volumes of verse th
seem, at least, to claim lasting importance. The te
and more since I wrote the first version of this bo
not seen the emergence of any new major critic or
revolutionary critical approach. What is a new soc
and probably a healthy one, is that there is today
closer relationship between the reviewing of new b
the London weeklies and monthly literary journals
teaching of English in the universities. A number
most interesting younger critics, like Frank Kerm
Alverez, or John Wain, have alternated between t
or research and reviewing, or switched, like Wain, f
career of a university teacher to that of a freelance
letters or, like Kermode, energetically and copious
bined both tasks. One result is that any new idea th
up in university common-rooms is likely to reach th
public without the old time-lag; another result is th
university teachers, at least, are more energetically
in 'keeping up with' contemporary literature than th
to be. But there is a danger, perhaps, of new idea
aired before they have sufficiently matured, and of
versity critic, in his eager 'keeping up with' the nev
that sense of coolness, detachment, and perspective
is a traditional academic virtue. One other trend
notable over the last ten years is one away from strict
criticism towards criticism of the culture out of whic
ture arises, or fails to arise; this has been most
exemplified in the work of Richard Hoggart and R
Williams, about which I have already said somethin
been exemplified also in a number of interesting revi

articles by younger writers (Gabriel Pearson and Philip
Hobsbaum are two who spring to mind) in *New Left Review*
and elsewhere. These critics feel that even when, over at
least a broad segment of society, the older economic priva-
tions have been abolished, there will still remain cultural
privation. In the last ten years, there has been a growth in
first-generation grammar school attenders, and in first-generation university students. These, whatever their natural
intelligence, are often handicapped by coming from homes
where there are few books and the discussion of literature,
or even of general ideas, is rare. Such students feel a painful
emotional tension between their eagerness for learning and
their loyalty to old roots from which learning will cut them
off; and there remains, of course, an even larger class who
do not attend grammar schools, and who will not go to
universities, and feel themselves relegated to a category of
inferiors, of *natural* inferiors. (And it is more galling to feel
oneself a natural inferior than to feel that unjust or inevitable social arrangements have deprived one of one's full
human rights.) Culture should not be a gift from the natural
superiors to the natural inferiors, or to such of them as are
capable of receiving it, but it should be something springing
from the whole life of the community, particularly perhaps
from the life of the working classes. This attitude explains
the tone of ardour in much of Raymond Williams's and
Richard Hoggart's writing, the new interest of scholars like
Margaret Dalziel in popular fiction of the nineteenth century, which scholars of an older generation would have
hardly considered as literature at all, and the enthusiasm
that gathers behind a movement like Arnold Wesker's
Centre 42. One very much respects the feeling that lies behind such activities and such writings; at the same time, it
must be admitted that the demand for a rootedly working-
class literature has been more conspicuous over the past ten
years than the supply of it, and that when a piece of writing
that is in some sense 'working class', like some of Pinter's
plays and some of Sillitoe's stories, achieves real distinction,
it removes itself from the social category of the working-

class art to the more broadly human category of art as such. And art, as such, invites detached appreciation, invites criticism in the strict sense, rather than social enthusiasm or condemnation. It has also seemed to me that much writing about working-class culture has been vitiated by an assumption that the middle classes are *all* great lovers of good novels and plays and poems. It is my own experience that a genuine enthusiasm for poetry is very unusual in all the social classes with which I am acquainted, but that where it exists it draws people rapidly together and makes class barriers seem unimportant. It may be that in all classes, or even in a classless society, should one eventually emerge, the number of people who genuinely care about literature and the arts will always be a minority, though a growing minority. This is not necessarily so tragic a prospect as it may seem to those who create art or literature or who earn a living by trying to teach others to share their own appreciation of art or literature. There are, after all, other sources of human happiness, and of human consolation. There are other ways of being aware of what matters than the literary way. But it would certainly be a great pity if literary culture were thought of as a sinister mark of class privilege, or were used to build up a spirit of exclusiveness; and those who fight against this danger deserve every moral encouragement. To be human, to appeal to wide and deep human sympathies, is the mark of all fine literature, whether it springs from a society that takes its tone from an aristocracy or a middle class or a proletariat. I think it very probable that English art and literature will take its tone in future more and more from a populace; I do not mean by that what Marxists mean by a proletariat, I mean what Eliot means when he says we are moving into a lower-middle-class culture. The fortunes of new writers will be made in future less, as it were, by great London hostesses, of the type that Henry James dined with, than by earnest adult-education tutors in the provinces. In the novel, for instance, the high, dry comedy of social manoeuvring and pretences, such as Anthony Powell or Evelyn Waugh excel in, will become less and less popular,

while John Braine's accounts of social climbing from the
decent working-class to the comforts of provincial suburbs
will become more popular. The reading class likes to see its
own full life reflected in books. But the question of what
sort of class literature in general takes its tone from will
remain a quite separate question from how good, as a work
of art, any particular piece of literature is. Powell and
Waugh are, for instance, quite obviously better *artists* than
Braine. And since so much, though not by any means all,
of the best English literature has reflected an upper-middle-
class or at least a professional culture, there is likely to be
for a long time much good writing that fails to reflect, or
fails to approve of, the tone of the populace.

We tend to forget, also, that literature is only *one* of the
arts, that literary appreciation is in itself by no means the
whole of culture. I have the impression, for instance, that
university students, and I am thinking of the more intelligent and hard-working of them, read less today for mere
curiosity and pleasure than I did in my youth. On the other
hand, tape-recorders and long-playing gramophone records
give them a far better appreciation of music than I had; and
modern techniques of reproduction enable them also to look
at pictures with a more appreciative eye than I possessed.
What they gather also, from, for instance, an excellent anthology of close criticism like John Wain's *Interpretations*,
is an early sense of the techniques of close reading, of reading in depth; if their reading is not wide, if their sense of
the history of literature is full of gaps, in compensation they
can often analyse a difficult passage of prose or verse straight
off, with a confidence which I certainly did not possess at
their age. These provincial university students, who are
growing in numbers every year, will be the critical part of
the reading public of the future; they will also (and, indeed,
in a poet like Brian Higgins or a novelist like Malcolm
Bradbury, they have already begun to do so) provide some
of the interesting poets and novelists of the future. Increasingly, perhaps, literature in England may cease to be a
fashionable and metropolitan career, and the approval of a

smart and sophisticated public may come to matter less, even at the level of 'vulgar success', to the young writer.

I do not think that the immediately contemporary literary period is a great one; it is certainly not, except for the great surviving elders, a major period in criticism. But if ours is a day of medium-sized men, it is also a day of widely-diffused critical candour and scrupulousness, and, in literature generally, of talents which are not of the first order but are often farmed well. There is a lot of sham and vulgarly smart writing, but I think people are less deeply taken in by it than they were by similar writing in the 1920s and 1930s – the consumer of books, as of other commodities, is less of a passive victim of advertising and propaganda. There is much in the contemporary world to numb or stupefy, indeed to terrify us. Literature remains one of the great humanizing influences, and a career in literature can still be one of the most honourable careers. In criticism, over the last ten years or so, though there have been no new Eliots, Richardses, Empsons, or Leavises, still, a critic like A. Alvarez has brought the general shape of modern poetry into clear and yet not over-simple perspective; a critic like Frank Kermode, with fine historical scholarship, has made us aware of the inextricable continuity of what we call the 'modern' movement in literature with the late developments of what we call the romantic movement; a scholarly critic like Ian Watt, in *The Rise of the Novel*, has given us a clearer notion than we had before of what a novel is; and something is slowly emerging that might be called an agreed technique for criticizing novels, just as, over the previous thirty years or so, there had been emerging, thanks to the pioneer efforts of Eliot, Richards, Leavis, and Empson, an agreed technique for criticizing poems. On particular topics, Donald Davie has directed sharp attention to the diction and syntax of poetry; John Holloway has gone back to Aristotle and reminded us of the primary importance in plays and novels of plot or story, the progressive imitation of an action. What we lack is a young critic in whom scholarship and detailed insights are combined with some broad general sense – his own sense, not a derived sense – of the meaning for the sensitive heart and alert mind today of our world.

These remarks suggest that the most interesting recent criticism in England has had an academic flavour, and perhaps a slightly provincially academic flavour. But one should mention one book of a very different sort, W. H. Auden's collected critical pieces, *The Dyer's Hand*. This is the notebook of a working poet, an appreciator of more arts than literature, an intuitive psychologist, and a pouncing and paradoxical Christian moralist. It is full of sweeping generalizations and sometimes slightly undergraduatish 'bright ideas', as well as of new perceptions about familiar works of a most startling sort. Falstaff, for instance, is seen as a distorted image of Christian joy and charity in a cold world of power politics; Iago as a practical joker destroying others out of a hatred of his own inner nothingness; the disturbing comic novels of Nathanael West are seen not as farce or satire but as explorations of a special kind of Hell. The strength of Auden's criticism is that it seems not to push to one side but to include firmly in its scope the general sense of terror and bewilderment of our age, and yet, through that central awareness, to seek joy. He writes at once like a disabused man of the world and like an evangelist. He makes jokes, not placatingly, but to illuminate. He is no model for other critics; but he has a kind of largeness which academic critics might well humbly note and admire.

One wonders, at the end of writing an informal history of this sort, what history is. Somebody said it was an agreed fiction. But perspectives change, conventions crumble. Something, no doubt, is building somewhere, but how much else is being bull-dozed, how many landmarks have vanished even since one last turned one's head? Can any fiction, today, be even an agreed fiction? And if so, for how long? One can only hope that, in some areas near the centre, such a map as this may be for some time useful, however rapidly the shapes at the edges change.

Acknowledgements

I am indebted to the following authors and publishers for permission to quote from works in copyright: Mr Edward Blunden (Edward Blunden's *Collected Poems 1914–1930*); Messrs Jonathan Cape (William Plomer's *Collected Poems*); Messrs Cassell (Robert Graves's *Collected Poems*) and Mr Robert Graves; Messrs Chatto and Windus (William Empson's *Poems* and *Collected Poems*, and *The Poems of Wilfred Owen*); Messrs J. M. Dent (*Collected Poems of Dylan Thomas*); Messrs Duckworth (Hilaire Belloc's *Sonnets and Verses*); Editions Poetry, London (Kathleen Raine's *Stone and Flower*, Keith Douglas's *Collected Poems*, and David Gascoyne's *Poems*); Messrs Faber and Faber (W. H. Auden's *Collected Shorter Poems*, Roy Campbell's *Collected Poems*, Lawrence Durrell's *Collected Poems*, T. S. Eliot's *Collected Poems*, *The Cocktail Party*, and *Family Reunion*, William Empson's *Gathering Storm*, W. S. Graham's *The White Threshold*, Louis MacNeice's *Collected Poems*, Edwin Muir's *Collected Poems*, Stephen Spender's *Poems*, and translations of passages by Éluard, Soupault, Picasso, and Chirico from *Surrealism*, edited by Sir Herbert Read); Messrs Faber and Faber and the Committee for Ezra Pound (Ezra Pound's *Personae* and *The Pisan Cantos*); Messrs William Heinemann and Mrs Frieda Lawrence (D. H. Lawrence's *Collected Short Stories*); Messrs Macmillan, Messrs Methuen, and Mrs George Bainbridge (Kipling's *Collected Poems*); Messrs Macmillan and Mrs Yeats (W. B. Yeats *Collected Poems*); Messrs Macmillan and the Trustees of the Hardy Estate (Hardy's *Collected Poems*); Messrs Macmillan and Mrs Sturge Moore (T. Sturge Moore's *Poems*); Messrs Macmillan (Edith Sitwell's *Green Song*); Messrs John Murray (John Betjeman's *Selected Poems*); Messrs Methuen (G. K. Chesterton's *Collected Poems*, John Heath Stubbs's *A Charm Against the Toothache*); Oxford University Press (*The Poetical Work of Robert Bridges* and Christopher Fry's *The Lady's Not for Burning*); The Pound Press (a prose passage in the magazine *Nine* by Iain Fletcher); Messrs Sidgwick and Jackson (Ronald Bottrall's *Collected Poems*); The Hogarth Press (Terence Tiller's *Unarm, Eros*); Miss Elizabeth Jennings (Elizabeth Jennings's *Poems*). In spite of all efforts we have been unable to trace the publishers of the poems by Bernard Spencer.

G. S. FRASER

Suggestions for Further Reading

General Background

Erich Auerbach: *Mimesis* (New York, 1949: London, 1954).

C. M. Bowra: *The Creative Experiment* (London, 1949).

Kenneth Burke: *The Philosophy of Literary Form* (New York, 1949).

Attitudes Towards History (Los Altos, California, 1959).

Christopher Caudwell: *Further Studies in a Dying Culture* (London, 1949).

J. M. Cohen: *Poetry of This Age, 1908–1958* (London, 1960).

Donald Davie: *The Heyday of Sir Walter Scott* (London, 1961).

T. S. Eliot: *Selected Essays* (London, 1932: rev. ed., 1951).

After Strange Gods (London, 1934).

Clark Emery: *Ideas into Action: A Study of Pound's Cantos* (Miami, 1958).

Iain Fletcher: *Walter Pater* (London, 1959).

Wallace Fowlie: *The Age of Surrealism* (London, 1953).

Robert Graves: *The Common Asphodel* (London, 1949).

The White Goddess (London, 1948: revised edition, 1952).

Graham Hough: *The Last Romantics* (London, 1949).

Arnold Kettle: *An Introduction to the English Novel. Volume II: Henry James to the Present Day* (London, 1953).

D. H. Lawrence: *Phoenix*, ed. E. D. McDonald (London, 1936).

Selected Literary Criticism, ed. A. Beal (London, 1955).

F. R. Leavis: *For Continuity* (London, 1933).

New Bearings in English Poetry (London, 1932: Peregrine Books, 1963).

The Great Tradition (London, 1948: Peregrine Books, 1962).

Wyndham Lewis: *Time and Western Man* (London, 1927).

Men Without Art (London, 1934).

Winifred Nowottny: *The Language Poets Use* (London, 1962).

Ezra Pound: *Literary Essays of Ezra Pound*, edited with an introduction by T. S. Eliot (London, 1954).

Philip Rahv: *Image and Idea* (London, 1957).

I. A. Richards: *Principles of Literary Criticism* (London, 1924: revised edition, 1926).

Practical Criticism (London, 1929).

Robin Skelton: *The Poetic Pattern* (London, 1956).

Stephen Spender: *The Destructive Element* (London, 1935).

Denys Thompson: *Reading and Discrimination* (London, 1934: revised edition, 1954).

Ian Watt: *The Rise of the Novel: Studies in Defoe, Richardson, and Fielding* (London, 1960: Peregrine Books, 1963).

Basil Willey: *Nineteenth-Century Studies* (London, 1949).
  More Nineteenth-Century Studies: A Group of Honest Doubters (London, 1956).

Edmund Wilson: *Axel's Castle* (New York, 1932).
  The Triple Thinkers (London, 1952: Pelican Books, 1962).

Virginia Woolf: *The Common Reader: Second Series* (London, 1932).

W. B. Yeats: *A Vision* (private edition, 1925: revised edition, London, 1937: corrected edition, 1962).
  Essays and Introductions (London, 1961).

The Novel

Walter Allen: *The English Novel: A Short Critical History* (London, 1954: Pelican Books, 1958).

Joseph Warren Beach: *The Twentieth Century Novel* (New York, 1932).

Marius Bewley: *The Complex Fate* (London, 1953).
  The Eccentric Design (London, 1959).

David Daiches: *The Novel and the Modern World* (revised edition, Cambridge, 1960).

Leon Edel: *The Psychological Novel 1900–1950* (London, 1955).

E. M. Forster: *Aspects of the Novel* (London, 1927: Pelican Books, 1962).

Stuart Gilbert: *James Joyce's Ulysses: A Study* (revised edition, London, 1952: Peregrine Books, 1963).

A. J. Guerard: *Conrad the Novelist* (London, 1959).

D. Hewitt: *Conrad: A Reassessment* (London, 1952).

R. Humphrey: *The Stream of Consciousness in the Modern Novel* (London, 1954).

Henry James: *Notebooks*, ed. F. O. Matthiessen and Kenneth B. Murdoch (New York, 1947).
  The House of Fiction, ed. Leon Edel (London, 1957).

F. R. Leavis: *The Great Tradition* (London, 1948: Peregrine Books, 1962).

D. H. Lawrence: Novelist (London, 1955).

Rose Macaulay: *The Writings of E. M. Forster* (London, 1938).

M. B. Mesnet: *Graham Greene and the Heart of the Matter* (London, 1954).

Edwin Muir: *The Structure of the Novel* (London, 1932).

William Van O'Connor (ed.): *Forms of Modern Fiction* (Minnesota, 1948).

Lionel Trilling: *E. M. Forster* (Norfolk, Conn., 1943: London, 1944).

John Wain: *Preliminary Essays* (London, 1957). (For essay on Arnold Bennett.)

Morton D. Zabel: *Craft and Character in Fiction* (London, 1957).

The Drama

William Archer: *The Old Drama and the New* (London, 1923).

Max Beerbohm: *Around Theatres: Reviews 1898–1910* (revised edition, London, 1953).

Eric Bentley: *Shaw: A Reconsideration* (New York, 1947).

   The Playwright as Thinker: A Study of Drama in Modern Times (New York, 1946).

   The Modern Theatre (London, 1948).

Maurice Bourgeois: *Synge and the Irish Theatre* (London, 1913).

G. K. Chesterton: *George Bernard Shaw* (rev. ed., London, 1935).

Denis Donoghue: *The Third Voice: Modern British and American Verse Drama* (Princeton and London, 1959).

T. S. Eliot: *Poetry and Drama* (London, 1959).

Una Ellis-Fermor: *The Irish Dramatic Movement* (London, 1954).

Martin Esslin: *Brecht: A Choice of Evils* (London, 1959).

   The Theatre of the Absurd (New York, 1961).

Ronald Gray: *Brecht* (Edinburgh, 1962).

F. Lumley: *Trends in Twentieth Century Drama* (London, 1956).

B. Macnamara: *Abbey Plays 1899–1948* (Dublin, 1949).

Norman Marshall: *The Other Theatre* (London, 1947).

R. H. Mottram: *John Galsworthy* (London, 1953).

Hermann Ould: *John Galsworthy* (London, 1934).

Ronald Peacock: *The Poet in the Theatre* (London, 1949).

D. Reynolds: *Modern English Drama* (London, 1949).

Lennox Robinson: *Ireland's Abbey Theatre 1899–1951* (London, 1951).

Suggestions for Further Reading

J. Setterquist: *Ibsen and the Beginnings of Anglo-Irish Drama* (Upsala, 1951).

George Bernard Shaw: *Plays and Players*, a World's Classics selection ed. A. C. Ward (London, 1952).

John Russell Taylor: *Anger and After* (London, 1962: Pelican Books, 1963).

Peter Ure: *Yeats the Playwright* (London, 1963).

John Willett: *The Theatre of Bertolt Brecht* (London, 1959).

Raymond Williams: *Drama from Ibsen to Eliot* (London, 1952: Peregrine Books, 1964).

W. B. Yeats: *Autobiographies* (London, 1955).
 Essays and Introductions (London, 1962).

Poetry

A. Alvarez: *The Shaping Spirit* (London, 1958).

R. P. Blackmur: *Language as Gesture* (London, 1954).

C. M. Bowra: *The Heritage of Symbolism* (London, 1943).
 The Creative Experiment (London, 1949).

Cleanth Brooks: *Modern Poetry and the Tradition* (Chapel Hill, 1939: London, 1948).

Douglas Brown: *Thomas Hardy* (London, 1954).

Vincent Buckley: *Poetry and Morality* (London, 1959).

David Daiches: *Poetry and the Modern World* (Chicago, 1940).

Richard Ellman: *Yeats, the Man and the Masks* (New York, 1948: London, 1949).
 The Identity of Yeats (New York, 1954).

G. S. Fraser: *Vision and Rhetoric* (London, 1959).
 Ezra Pound (Edinburgh, 1960).

Helen Gardner: *The Art of T. S. Eliot* (London, 1949).

Robert Graves: *The Common Asphodel* (London, 1949).

Robert Graves and Laura Riding: *A Survey of Modernist Poetry* (London, 1927).

Richard Hoggart: *Auden: An Introductory Essay* (London, 1951).

David Holbrook: *Llareggub Revisited: Dylan Thomas and the State of Modern Poetry* (London, 1962).

Randall Jarrell: *Poetry and the Age* (London, 1955).

T. H. Jones: *Dylan Thomas* (Edinburgh, 1963).

Frank Kermode: *Romantic Image* (London, 1957).

F. R. Leavis: *New Bearings in English Poetry* (revised edition, London, 1950: Peregrine Books, 1963).

Louis MacNeice: *Modern Poetry* (Oxford, 1938).

Josephine Miles: *Eras and Modes of English Poetry* (Berkeley and Los Angeles, 1957).

Winifred Nowottny: *The Language Poets Use* (London, 1962).

Herbert Read: *Form in Modern Poetry* (London, 1932).

D. S. Savage: *The Personal Principle* (London, 1936).

Francis Scarfe: *Auden and After: The Liberation of Poetry, 1930–41* (London, 1942).

Grover Smith: *T. S. Eliot's Poetry and Plays: A Study in Sources and Meaning* (revised edition, Chicago, 1946).

Martin Seymour Smith: *Robert Graves* (London, 1955).

Leonard Unger: *The Man in the Name* (Minneapolis, 1956).

George Williamson: *A Reader's Guide to T. S. Eliot* (New York, 1953: London, 1955).

Edmund Wilson: *Axel's Castle* (New York, 1931).

Yvor Winters: *On Modern Poets* (London, 1955).

Critics and Criticism

Matthew Arnold: *Essays in Criticism* (London, 1865).
  Culture and Anarchy (London, 1869).
  Essays in Criticism II (London, 1888).

Walter Bagehot: *Literary Studies* (London, 1879).

G. K. Chesterton: *Robert Browning* (London, 1902).
  Charles Dickens (London, 1906).

T. S. Eliot: *The Sacred Wood* (London, 1920).
  The Use of Poetry and the Use of Criticism (London, 1933).
  Notes Towards the Definition of Culture (London, 1948).

William Empson: *Seven Types of Ambiguity* (London, 1930: Peregrine Books, 1961).
  Some Versions of Pastoral (London, 1935).
  The Structure of Complex Words (London, 1951).

Henry James: *Hawthorne* (London, 1879).
  Partial Portraits (London, 1888).
  Notes on Novelists (London, 1914).
  The Art of the Novel, ed. R. P. Blackmur (New York, 1934).
  The House of Fiction, ed. Leon Edel (London, 1957).

D. H. Lawrence: *Studies in Classic American Literature* (London, 1923).
  Selected Literary Criticism, ed. A. Beal (London, 1955).

F. R. Leavis: *For Continuity* (London, 1933).
  Education and the University (London, 1943).

Suggestions for Further Reading

Wyndham Lewis: *Time and Western Man* (London, 1927).
Men Without Art (London, 1934).

John Middleton Murry: *Countries of the Mind* (London, 1922).
Keats and Shakespeare (London, 1925).

Ezra Pound: *ABC of Reading* (London, 1934).
Selected Literary Essays, ed. T. S. Eliot (London, 1954).

I. A. Richards: *Principles of Literary Criticism* (London, 1924: revised edition, 1926).
Practical Criticism: A Study of Literary Judgment (London, revised edition, 1935).
Speculative Instruments (London, 1955).

George Saintsbury: *A Short History of English Literature* (London, 1898).
A History of Criticism and Literary Taste in Europe (3 volumes, London, 1900 to 1904).

John Wain (ed.): *Interpretations: Essays on Twelve English Poems* (London, 1955).
Preliminary Essays (London, 1957).

George Watson: *The Literary Critics* (Pelican Books, 1962).

Yvor Winters: *The Function of Criticism* (New York, 1957: London, 1962).

Index

415

416

Index

Index

Index

Index

Index

Index

Index

Index

Index